Joe Martin
Brett Tomson

SAMS
Teach Yourself
ASP.NET

in 24 Hours

SAMS

201 West 103rd St., Indianapolis, Indiana, 46290 USA

Sams Teach Yourself ASP.NET in 24 Hours

Copyright ©2002 by Sams Publishing

International Standard Book Number: 0672321262

Library of Congress Catalog Number: 00-111069

Printed in the United States of America

First Printing: August 2001

02 01 00 99   4 3 2 1

Trademarks

Warning and Disclaimer

ASSOCIATE PUBLISHER
Linda Engelman

ACQUISITIONS EDITOR
Karen Wachs

DEVELOPMENT EDITOR
Elizabeth Gehrman

TECHNICAL EDITORS
Kourosh Ardestani
Wendy Chun

MANAGING EDITOR
Charlotte Clapp

PROJECT EDITOR
George E. Nedeff

COPY EDITOR
Bart Reed

INDEXER
Erika Millen

PROOFREADER
Harvey Stanbrough
Juli Cook

TEAM COORDINATOR
Chris Feather

MEDIA DEVELOPER
Dan Scherf

INTERIOR DESIGNER
Gary Adair

COVER DESIGNER
Aren Howell

PAGE LAYOUT
Cheryl Lynch

Contents at a Glance

Contents

About the Authors

JOE MARTIN has been developing client-server, client, and Web-based applications for more than a decade. He is currently working as a senior software engineer for NetIQ Corporation, a leading provider of e-business infrastructure management and intelligence solutions, from back-end servers, networks, and directories to front-end Web servers and applications. His expertise covers a large number of Microsoft development technologies, including Visual Basic, C++, ASP, IIS, MTS, Access, and SQL Server.

You can reach Joe at `JMartin-24Hours@nc.rr.com`.

BRETT TOMSON is a partner and developer with OSIRIS interactive, a digital media services company specializing in custom Web application development, Web hosting, multimedia, graphic design, training, and consulting. His portfolio includes Web applications designed and developed for companies ranging from small businesses to multinational corporations. Brett has an extensive background building applications with ASP, JavaScript, Dynamic HTML, COM+, Microsoft SQL Server, and Oracle.

You can reach Brett at `brett.tomson@osirisinteractive.com`.

About the Contributors

KOUROSH ARDESTANI is an e-Business Consultant in the Microsoft Technologies branch of IBM Global Services. He specializes in building Internet solutions based on the Windows DNA and Microsoft .NET platforms, and has been working with ASP.NET and other .NET technologies since the first release of the ASP.NET runtime (when it was still called NGWS runtime). Kourosh has a B.Sc. in Information and Computer Science, plus an MCSE, an MCSD, an MCDBA, and several other prominent IT certifications. He can be reached at `Kourosh@us.ibm.com.`

ERIC WOOD has been working with ASP, Visual Basic, and SQL Server for four years as a developer and senior project manager building enterprise scale-intranet applications for a Fortune 500 company. He graduated with a degree in Business Systems from Taylor University and currently telecommutes from Muncie, Indiana where he lives with his wife April and their two sons, Jordan and Christian. He can be reached at `ericwood_24hrs@yahoo.com.`

AJOY KRISHNAMOORTHY is a consultant with more than five years of experience working in Microsoft technologies such as ASP, VB, IIS, MTS, and most recently .NET. He writes regularly for leading online publications. He received an M.S. in Systems and Information from the Birla Institute of Technology and Science (BITS), at Pilani, India and is currently working on his M.B.A. at Fisher College of Business, Ohio State University. His interests include writing, hanging out with friends, and travel. He is originally from Chennai, India and currently lives in Columbus, Ohio with his wife Vidhya. He and his wife are excitedly awaiting their first child in October. He can be reached at `ajoyk@ajoys.net.`

About the Technical Reviewers

WENDY HARO-CHUN, MCSD, holds a BA in Computer Science and an MBA with an emphasis on international business. She is assistant vice president of research and development for Sungard Insurance Systems. Her areas of technological expertise include .NET, C#, ASP, DHTML, JavaScript, XML, COM, Visual Basic 6, ADO, and Microsoft SQL Server. Wendy has also served as technical editor and reviewer on numerous computer technology books. She lives in Miami with her husband Dave and her two beagles, Buster and Belle.

KOUROSH ARDESTANI is an e-Business Consultant in the Microsoft Technologies practice of IBM Global Services. He specializes in building Internet solutions based on the Windows DNA and Microsoft .NET platforms and has been working with ASP.NET and other .NET technologies since the very first release of the ASP.NET runtime (when it was still called NGWS runtime). Kourosh has a B.Sc. in Information and Computer Science, plus MCSE, MCSD, MCDBA, and several other prominent IT certifications. He can be reached at Kourosh@us.ibm.com.

Dedication

Joe Martin:

This book is dedicated to my wife, Lisa, and daughter, Christian.
Thank you for being so supportive and understanding.

Brett Tomson:

This book is dedicated to my wife, Meghan, and my daughter, Abigail,
for making me go outside and play.

Acknowledgments

Joe Martin:

I really can't thank Karen Wachs enough for being so patient and optimistic even though I think I gave her more excuses for missed deadlines than actual finished chapters! She kept me motivated; as a first-time author, I found that this is quite a task. Elizabeth Gehrman was also a joy to work with and a great asset to the team. Her experience and dedication have made the chapters more consistent and easier to read, as I know a lot of times my thoughts outpaced my typing. Kourosh Ardestani and Wendy Chun did an excellent job of making sure that the material was as technically accurate as possible.

I also need to acknowledge some good friends of mine who really helped me turn a life-long dream into a reality. Gary Quint was an excellent teacher and sounding board as he helped me learn about the features of ASP and Web application development. I owe Johnny Papa a huge hug (well, maybe a handshake will do!) for helping me find the opportunity to write a book and convince me that I could really do it. And a huge amount of thanks go to John Steigerwald, my boss, for allowing me to do what I needed to do to get this book written, without any hesitation. I won't forget it.

Finally I want to thank my wife, Lisa, and daughter, Christian, for helping me stay focused on accomplishing this goal and realize just what really does matter.

Brett Tomson:

They say Rome wasn't built in a day, and neither was this book. In fact, just about as many people were involved with this book as were involved in the construction of the Coliseum. I am truly indebted to all for their hard work in bringing this project to completion.

I want to thank Karen Wachs, who took the reins of the wild beast that this book was and tamed it. Karen, thank you for your patience, your understanding, and for not using the cattle prod on me to get those chapters in on time. Special thanks to Kourosh Ardestani and Wendy Chun, who made sure I sounded like I knew what I was talking about. Thanks to Kourosh Ardestani (again), Eric Wood, and Ajoy Krishnamoorthy for stepping in and contributing when things looked bleak. Thanks to Elizabeth Gehrman for making sure the text was clear, concise, and lucid; George Nedeff for keeping the process moving; and Bart Reed for making everything fit on the page.

I would like to thank Bruce Suitt, Jason Stanley, Todd Robert, and my family for their support and help during the writing of this book.

Finally and most important, I would like to thank my wife, Meghan, and my daughter, Abigail, for their love, support, and, above all, patience during this entire process. You never let me waver from my goal, no matter how hard I tried.

Tell Us What You Think!

As the reader of this book, *you* are our most important critic and commentator. We value your opinion and want to know what we're doing right, what we could do better, what areas you'd like to see us publish in, and any other words of wisdom you're willing to pass our way.

As an Associate Publisher for Sams Publishing, I welcome your comments. You can fax, e-mail, or write me directly to let me know what you did or didn't like about this book— as well as what we can do to make our books stronger.

Please note that I cannot help you with technical problems related to the topic of this book, and that due to the high volume of mail I receive, I might not be able to reply to every message.

When you write, please be sure to include this book's title and author as well as your name and phone or fax number. I will carefully review your comments and share them with the author and editors who worked on the book.

Fax: 317-581-4770
E-mail: feedback@samspublishing.com
Mail: Linda Engelman
        Sams Publishing
        201 West 103rd Street
        Indianapolis, IN 46290 USA

Introduction

Chances are you are eager to dive into learning about Microsoft's latest Web development environment. To make sure that this is the right book for you, and to understand what you can hope to learn by reading it, please take a few moments to acquaint yourself with the contents of this book and its approach.

Who Should Read This Book

This book is intended for a beginner- to intermediate-level audience. We assume that the reader has a fundamental knowledge of the way the Web works, some experience with server-side programming, and preferably at least passing experience with current or past versions of ASP. We do not assume that readers have experience with object-oriented languages; however, we provide you with a tutorial to Visual Basic.NET to get you up to speed with one of the most popular vehicles for writing ASP.NET pages.

This book strives to introduce readers to ASP.NET through individual lessons contained in each hour. These lessons begin with a thorough overview of the framework and technologies involved, and gradually build into more difficult lessons requiring a deeper knowledge base. Though each hour is self-contained, each hour builds on previous lessons to ensure that each topic is not only taught and explained, but used. The culmination in Hour 24 will be the presentation of a sample application that draws upon the functionality and techniques explored throughout the preceding hours.

What This Book Will Do For You

Although this is not a reference book, you'll learn virtually everything a Web programmer needs to know to be functional and productive with the ASP.NET environment.

This book presents both the background and the theory that a new ASP.NET Web programmer needs to begin intelligently programming ASP.NET pages. In addition to the background discussions, this book is practical and provides numerous step-by-step tasks that you can work through to grasp the new functionality.

Can This Book Really Teach ASP.NET in 24 Hours?

Because ASP.NET is such a robust tool, it would be a challenge to truly learn everything you'd need or want to know about the programming environment in a day. This book, however, will provide you with a 24-hour crash course that will allow you to get up and running with confidence.

You can master each hour in one hour or less. Although some lessons are longer than others, the material is balanced. The longer lessons contain several tasks, and the shorter lessons contain background material and/or reference information. The balance of the material is provided by tasks, backgrounds, and insightful explanations and tips that will keep you on your toes in your introduction to ASP.NET.

What You Need

This book assumes that you have Windows 2000 installed on your computer. Although ASP.NET works on both Windows 2000 Professional and Server Editions, this book provides most of its examples using Windows 2000 Server. We also assume that you have Visual Studio.NET installed, although again, you do not actually need to write your ASP.NET pages within the Visual Studio IDE.

Conventions Used in This Book

This 24-hour course uses several common conventions to help teach the programming topics included in this book. Here is a summary of the typographical conventions:

- Commands and computer output appear in a special monospaced font.
- Words you type appear in a **bold monospaced** font.
- If a task requires you to choose from a menu, the book separates menu commands with a comma. Therefore, this book uses File, Save As to indicate that you should open the File menu and choose the Save As command.

In addition to typographical conventions, you will notice other features common to the chapters, including Quiz and Exercise sections to test your knowledge of the concepts discussed in each hour, as well as notes, tips, and to dos.

PART I

Setting the Stage for ASP.NET

Hour

HOUR 1

Getting Started with ASP.NET

ASP.NET is a new Internet programming technology from Microsoft that applies a more streamlined, object-oriented approach to building dynamic Web applications. With existing Active Server Pages technology, server-side code is intermingled and interspersed with client-side HTML. This often results in large, complex pages of code, where following the logic of the program can be difficult at best, especially if you are new to programming.

In this hour, you will learn more about what ASP.NET has to offer. To be more specific, you will learn

- What ASP.NET is
- What the system requirements are to implement an ASP.NET application
- How to install the ASP.NET Framework on your system
- What tools can be used to create ASP.NET applications
- How to create an ASP.NET page
- How to view the output of your ASP.NET pages

What Is ASP.NET?

In the early days of Internet Web site design and development, technologies were limiting. Static HTML pages served up the necessary information that a person wished to convey to his audience. Because technologies were more limiting back then, it was easier to get away with a site that was not as interactive as it needed to be. Nowadays, however, it is important to learn how to build dynamic, interactive Web sites, especially with the increasing use of multimedia elements such as Flash and Shockwave and the development of e-commerce and e-business sites that require database integration.

To meet this need, Microsoft created a Web-development platform called *Active Server Pages*, or *ASP*. ASP was widely used and accepted throughout the industry because most developers could utilize their existing Visual Basic or VBScript skill sets when developing Web applications.

Despite this widespread acceptance, using Active Server Pages was limiting in some respects. For example, validation of form data sometimes required extensive coding on both the client browser and the server. Also, some aspects of Active Server Pages were not scalable in an enterprise environment and didn't function robustly in high-volume sites (although there were ways around these problems). In addition, combining server-side code on the same page as HTML and JavaScript often resulted in Web pages that were a convoluted mixture of server-side logic code and fancy HTML code designed for the user interface, which among other problems made code maintenance a real issue.

To overcome these problems and many others, Microsoft has introduced ASP.NET—its next-generation Web development environment. If you have experience in programming applications, you will find that the ASP.NET Framework is very similar to building client/server applications. Even if you've never written a line of code in your life, you will find that ASP.NET is a relatively easy programming language to learn.

Is ASP.NET Browser Specific?

ASP.NET is a browser-independent programming model. ASP.NET will run on the latest versions of Internet Explorer and Netscape Navigator, as well as on other widely used browsers, such as Opera. Also, ASP.NET applications will gracefully downgrade to older versions of Internet Explorer and Netscape Navigator. This means that the vast majority of users on the Internet will be able to use your Web applications without you needing to write browser-specific code. This feature takes a great burden off the shoulders of current Web developers, although it is still important to be aware that not all browsers accept Dynamic HTML (DHTML) in the same way. For instance, Netscape Navigator versions

1

4.0 through 4.75 do not allow text properties, like color and font on the page to be changed unless the page is reloaded in the browser. Internet Explorer versions 4.0 and higher, on the other hand, do allow text properties to be changed on the page. These inconsistencies, and many others, still need to be considered when writing client-side code.

What Programming Languages Can Be Used with ASP.NET?

The .NET Framework specifies that applications can be written in any programming language that supports the Common Language Runtime (CLR). The Common Language Runtime translates any CLR-compliant application to Microsoft Intermediate Language (IL). This intermediate-level code is then compiled for the platform where it will be executed. This simple process allows you to create an application in one language that can be used on any operating system using CLR. Furthermore, you can take an application that is written in one programming language and use it in an application that is written in a completely different programming language. No longer do you have to learn a completely different programming language whenever a new technology is released.

For the latest version of the .NET Framework, Microsoft is releasing four different languages that can be used to write CLR-specific code. These languages are Visual Basic.NET (also known as *VB.NET*), C# (pronounced *c-sharp*), C++.NET, and JScript.NET. Third-party languages are also being developed, such as Perl, Smalltalk, and Cobol, with more languages expected to join the list as the technology becomes more prevalent. Here's a brief description of each of these Microsoft languages:

- Visual Basic.NET: VB.NET is a relatively easy programming language to learn. It is considered a high-level programming language, which means that its syntax is close to human languages and not similar to machine languages, such as Assembly. Of the programming languages mentioned in this section, VB.NET is probably one of the easiest languages to learn. For this reason, all the code examples in this book will be written in VB.NET.

- C#.NET: C# is a simple, modern, object-oriented, type-safe programming language derived from C and C++. C# aims to combine the high productivity of Visual Basic and the raw power of C++. This language is geared toward more accomplished developers who are used to the somewhat-cryptic structure of C++. Beginning developers are advised to start with Visual Basic and then move on to C#.

- Visual C++.NET: Visual C++.NET is the next iteration of Microsoft's existing Visual C++ programming language, which is a powerful, object-oriented programming language. Typically, this language is used to create very complex and sophisticated applications.

- JScript.NET: JScript is a powerful scripting language targeted specifically at the Internet. It is also the first scripting language to fully conform to ECMAScript— the Web's only standard scripting language. This language is similar in syntax to C# and C++, although it is a little easier to implement.

What Is Needed to Run ASP.NET?

In order to run ASP.NET pages, you will need to configure a computer with the .NET Framework installed. As of this writing, the .NET Framework is supported on Windows NT 4.0, Windows 2000, and Windows XP. However, Windows NT 4.0 with Service Pack (SP) 6a or Windows 2000 with SP 2 is strongly recommended. You will also need to install Internet Explorer 5.5 and Microsoft Data Access Components (MDAC) 2.6 as pre-requisites to the .NET Framework. In addition, if you are not running Windows 2000, you must install Internet Information Server (IIS), known as Personal Web Server (PWS) in Win9X and Me. IIS 5.0 could be easily added to Windows 2000 Professional via Add/Remove Windows Components in the Control Panel. Make sure the IIS service has been started.

Configuring Internet Information Server 5.0

In order to configure IIS 5.0 for ASP.NET, you have to start by creating a virtual directory; to do this, follow these steps (note that we will use IIS 5.0 on Windows 2000 to host all the examples in this book):

1. Click the Start button and choose Programs, Administrative Tools, Internet Services Manager.

2. Click the Web server name. On the right side of the screen, Default Web Site should have a status of "Running." If this is not the case, highlight Default Web Site by clicking it and then click the Play icon on the toolbar at the top.

3. Clicking the plus sign (+) next to the Web server name will display a list of the available Web sites on this server, as shown in Figure 1.1.

4. Clicking the plus sign (+) next to Default Web Site will display a list of the virtual directories for this Web site, as shown in Figure 1.2. Virtual directories are simply logical directories that can contain physical directories.

5. Right-click Default Web Site and then select New, Virtual Directory (a virtual directory is a link to another physical directory that resides outside of the Web site tree).

FIGURE 1.1

A list of virtual directories is displayed below Default Web Site.

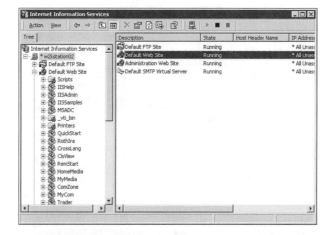

FIGURE 1.2

Creating a virtual directory for the default Web site.

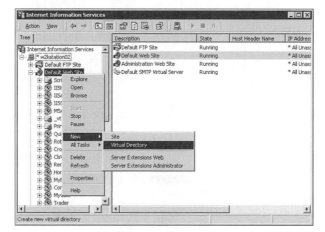

6. Figure 1.3 shows the screen that appears. From this screen, enter the alias that you wish to use to gain access to this directory (for example, ASP_Net_Examples) and then click Next.

7. In the next screen, shown in Figure 1.4, browse to the location where you want your virtual directory to be and click Next. If no directory has been created for your ASP.NET pages, create one now, calling it `C:\Inetpub\wwwroot\ASP_Net_Examples`, for example.

8. In the next screen, shown in Figure 1.5, select the appropriate access permissions for this directory and click Next. The default access permissions are Read and Run Script. These permissions are acceptable for all ASP.NET applications that will be hosted on this server.

FIGURE 1.3

The Virtual Directory Alias screen.

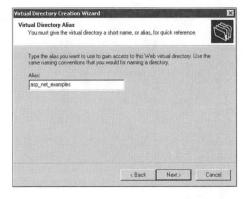

FIGURE 1.4

The Web Site Content Directory screen.

FIGURE 1.5

The Access Permissions screen.

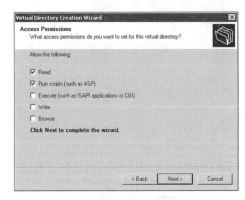

9. In the final screen, shown in Figure 1.6, click the Finish button, and the virtual directory will be completed.

FIGURE **1.6**

Congratulations! You have finished creating a virtual directory.

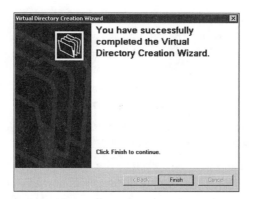

The new virtual directory will now appear as a node under the Default Web Site tree. Hour 2, "Presenting Internet Information Services," will provide a more detailed overview of the features and benefits of Internet Information Services (IIS) on Windows 2000.

Installing the .NET Framework SDK

In order to work with ASP.NET, you will first need to install the .NET Framework SDK on your Web server.

Make certain that your Web server has all the .NET Framework prerequisites installed. You must have Internet Explorer 5.5 as well as MDAC 2.6, although MDAC 2.7 is recommended, installed prior to installing the .NET SDK. Follow these instructions to install the .NET Framework SDK on your Web server:

1. To install Internet Explorer, go to `http://www.microsoft.com/windows/ie/download/ie55sp1.htm` and run the IE setup program.

2. Once the setup program is loaded and you have accepted the terms of the license agreement, Internet Explorer 5.5 will be installed on the computer. Reboot when the installation wizard prompts you.

3. Download MDAC 2.6 from `http://www.microsoft.com/data/download_260SDK.htm` and install it on your Web server. MDAC 2.6 is necessary on the Web server for retrieving data from a database system such as SQL Server 2000. Follow the installation instructions on the page and continue to the next step when the MDAC installation is completed.

▼   4. You can download a copy of the .NET Framework SDK if you don't already have a
         copy. Be warned though: The .NET SDK is a 127MB download. You can either
         download it in one huge file or break it up into 13 smaller downloads, depending on
         your bandwidth. The URL to retrieve the .NET Framework SDK is
         `http://msdn.microsoft.com/downloads/default.asp?url=/downloads/`
         `sample.asp?url=/msdn-files/027/000/976/msdncompositedoc.xml&frame=true`.

     5. Once you've expanded the .NET Framework SDK download, double-click the
         `setup.exe` icon to begin installing the .NET Framework SDK.

     6. A message will appear asking whether you want to install the .NET Framework
         SDK. When you click Yes, the installation program will extract all the .NET instal-
         lation files necessary to complete the setup process. The .NET Framework SDK
         extraction process will take a few minutes to complete.

     7. Scroll through the screens, pausing to accept the terms and conditions in the licens-
         ing agreement, until you reach the Install Options screen presented in Figure 1.7.
         Make sure the Software Development Kit box is checked; then click the Next button.

FIGURE 1.7

The .NET Framework
SDK Install Options
screen.

     8. Choose the destination folder for the .NET Framework SDK and click the Next
         button. By default, the SDK installs to the directory `C:\Program Files\`
         `Microsoft.Net\FrameworkSDK\`.

     9. The installation routine will begin installing the .NET components onto the Web
         server at this time (see Figure 1.8). Wait for the installation to complete and then
▼   reboot, when prompted, for the changes to take effect.

FIGURE 1.8

The .NET Framework SDK installing on the server.

Once the .NET Framework SDK has been installed, you can begin developing ASP.NET applications. In the next hour, you will learn how to create your first ASP.NET page, along with which tools work best in the creation of these types of applications.

If you install or plan to install the VS.NET development environment then you can skip the preceding instructions. The VS.NET installation will install the necessary prerequisites and .NET framework.

Summary

In this hour's lesson, you were introduced to ASP.NET—part of Microsoft's new .NET Framework strategy for distributed application development. You were also introduced to Internet Information Services on Windows 2000. Finally, you were shown the requirements necessary to host ASP.NET pages and how to install the .NET Framework SDK on your Web server.

Q&A

Q. Where can I get more information on the .NET Framework SDK?

A. The first source of information is the *.NET Framework Reference Guide* that's installed with the SDK. To access it, click the Start button and then click Programs, Microsoft .NET Framework SDK, Reference Guide. You can also access information from Microsoft's Web site at http://msdn.microsoft.com/net or http://www.microsoft.com/net. A third source of information is from newsgroups. Microsoft has set up several newsgroups for discussions of the .NET Framework SDK. The following newsgroups will be of interest to ASP.NET developers: `microsoft.public.dotnet.framework.aspnet`, `microsoft.public.dotnet.framework.aspnet.mobile`, and `microsoft.public.dotnet.framework.aspnet.webservices`. Finally, there are numerous sites devoted to ASP and ASP.NET programming. Some of the ones to visit include `www.asp.net`, `www.gotdotnet.com`, `www.aspfree.com`, `www.4guysfromrolla.com`, and `www.asptoday.com`.

Q. **Will I be able to run my existing ASP pages along with ASP.NET pages on the same server?**

A. Absolutely! ASP.NET has been designed to coexist in complete harmony with ASP pages on the same server. In fact, you can have half of your Web site done in regular ASP and the other half in ASP.NET. This certainly helps the application migration path from ASP to ASP.NET.

Workshop

The quiz questions and exercises are provided for your further understanding of the material presented.

Quiz

1. On which operating systems can you install the .NET Framework SDK?

2. What operating systems can host ASP.NET pages?

3. Do ASP.NET pages use interpreted code, where an interpreter reads each line of code in the page for processing, or compiled code, where the page code is compiled into executable code for the Web server?

Exercises

1. Explore the files in the directory of your default Web site. Notice the creation of a new folder called "aspx." This folder holds the latest version of the ASP.NET validation code for ASP.NET pages. Do not modify anything in this page without first making a backup copy. Continue navigating your Web server using the Internet Services Manager Console.

Answers for Hour 1

Quiz

1. On which operating systems can you install the .NET Framework SDK?

   Windows XP, Windows 2000, Windows NT 4.0 with
   Service Pack 6a.

2. What operating systems can host ASP.NET pages?

   Windows XP, Windows 2000 and Windows NT 4.0.

3. Do ASP.NET pages use interpreted code, where an interpreter reads each line of
   code in the page for processing, or compiled code, where the page code is compiled into executable code for the Web server?

   All ASP.Net pages are compiled into executable code.

HOUR 2

Presenting Internet Information Services

In order to host ASP.NET applications, you will need Internet Information Server 5.0. What platforms can run IIS 5.0? You can develop ASP.NET applications on just about any Windows platform, but what editors should you use? We will answer these and other questions this hour. The following topics will be discussed:

- Web servers that you can use to host ASP.NET applications
- What's required to develop ASP.NET applications
- How to set up a new Web site
- Why use ASP.NET over other technologies

Choosing Your Hosting Environment

Creating and hosting ASP.NET applications is not as simple as it was with ASP applications, but the features now available with ASP.NET make it well worth it.

Who's Out? Who's In?

In the past, ASP applications could be developed and tested on Windows 95/98/Me
and Windows NT 4.0 Workstation/Server. In order to host ASP pages on Windows
95/98/Me, you were required to install and configure Microsoft Personal Web Server
(PWS). On Windows NT 4.0 Workstation, NT Option Pack 4 had to be installed.
Unfortunately, the choices are a little slimmer for hosting ASP.NET applications. In
order to host ASP.NET applications you must either have Windows NT 4.0 with Service
Pack 6a or Windows 2000.

IIS on Windows 2000

Windows 2000 is the preferred operating system for hosting ASP.NET applications, and
is the operating system we use to host our samples in this book.

FIGURE 2.1

*Internet Information
Services inside the
Microsoft Management
Console.*

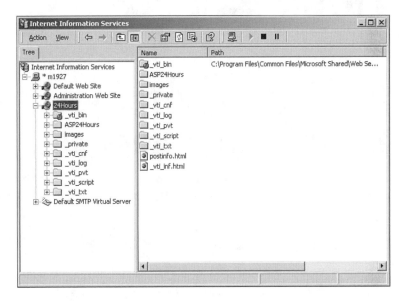

Microsoft has standardized the management and configuration of server applications
through the Microsoft Management Console (MMC), which provides a consistent user
interface for performing administrative tasks on servers. The Internet Services Manager
Console, shown in Figure 2.1, is an example of an administration module that runs inside
of the MMC. One of these tasks, creating a new virtual directory for our first application,
will be performed a little later in this hour. Internet Information Services 5.0 (IIS)
extends the features and performance provided in past versions of IIS. There are several
features and applications provided with IIS:

- Digest Authentication is a new authentication protocol available along with Anonymous, HTTP Basic and integrated Windows authentication (this used to be called Windows NT Challenge/Response). An authentication protocol is a set of steps that a client and a server application go through to establish whether the current user using the client application should gain access to the server application and its resources.

- Secure Sockets Layer (SSL) and Transport Layer Security may be used to provide encrypted communications between clients and servers.

- Security Wizards simplify the tasks of assigning Web site access privileges and managing Web Server Certificates used to encrypt information sent across a network during secure communications. Certificates contain user information and encryption keys that are used when connections are made between a client and server over a network.

- Index Server provides full-text indexing and searching capabilities for Web sites

- An SMTP service is provided for sending e-mail. The SMTP service is an application that implements the industry standard Simple Mail Transfer Protocol for sending and receiving mail across the internet.

- Finally! An easy way to restart IIS without having to reboot your machine! Figure 2.2 presents the restart IIS menu option.

Figure 2.2

New Restart IIS menu option in Internet Services Manager.

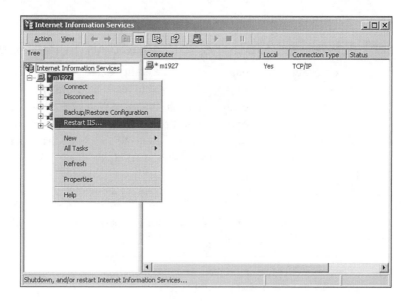

Choosing Your Development Environment

As mentioned in Hour 1, to run, or host, ASP.NET applications you need Windows 2000 or higher, or Windows NT4 with SP6. However, to *develop* ASP.NET applications, you can use Windows 98/Me or higher.

Just What Do I Need?

As you learned in Hour 1, the Microsoft .NET Framework SDK installs updated system files and applications necessary to host ASP.NET Applications, and only needs to be installed on the Web Server where the applications will reside. Any text editor can be used to code ASP.NET applications, but we strongly recommend installing Visual Studio.NET, as that is what we will be using throughout this book.

Creating Your First Web Site

Enough talk. Let's make a Web site! When IIS is installed on a computer, a single Web site is created with the name Default Web Site. This site is initially configured to be where all Web content is published from your computer. For example, if the name of your computer is COMPUTER1, then a client could browse your Web server by typing `http://COMPUTER1/{some Web page}` into their browser. Any directories that exist, either physical or virtual, under the Default Web Site will be available for clients to browse.

Advanced Options for Windows Server Computers

Windows Server computers provide the ability to create additional Web sites in addition to the Default Web Site. This allows you to leave the Default Web Site as the location of production-ready applications and use alternate Web sites as the location of your applications that are in development or test phases. The following steps are not necessary if you don't mind having all of your development Web applications under the Default Web Site that's created as part of the installation of IIS. Each of the following steps is covered in more detail in this hour:

- Adding an IP address to the network adapter
- Optionally adding a DNS entry for this new IP address or add an entry to hosts file
- Creating a new Web site
- Setting default documents
- Creating a virtual directory
- Optionally setting additional security permissions

These steps are also not possible if your Web server is using DHCP to set the IP address of its network adapter.

Add an IP Address to the Network Adapter

When a computer is running Windows 2000, only one IP address is ordinarily assigned to its network adapter. If the network adapter is configured to use DHCP, then the IP address as well as other settings will be automatically assigned when the computer is started. Additional IP addresses may be assigned to a network adapter card, and then mapped to Web sites, as we will explain later in this section. To perform these tasks you will need to have administrator privileges on the Web server machine, as well as unused IP addresses for your network and their related subnet masks.

To Do: Add IP Address to Network Adapter in Windows 2000

1. Open the Control Panel and double-click the Network and Dial-up Connection application.

2. Double-click the Local Area Connection.

If there is more than one network adapter in the computer, then there will be more than one Local Area Connection, as is shown in Figure 2.3. Make sure you select the correct one.

FIGURE 2.3
Network and Dial-up Connections showing more than one network adapter.

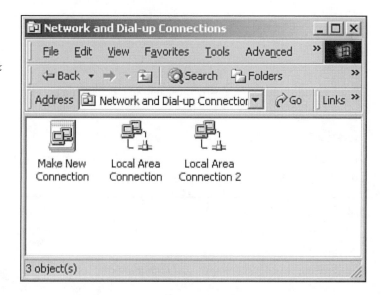

▼   3. Select the Internet Protocol (TCP/IP) item in the list and press the Properties
        button.

    4. Press the Advanced button. This will bring up the Advanced TCP/IP Settings dia-
        log box. Additional IP addresses may be added by pressing the Add button and
        then supplying an IP address and a subnet mask. Figure 2.4 shows the Advanced
        TCP/IP Dialog box. You will need to create at least one IP address if one does not
        already exist.

FIGURE 2.4

*Additional IP
addresses may be
added to a network
adapter in the
Advanced TPCP/IP
Settings dialog box.*

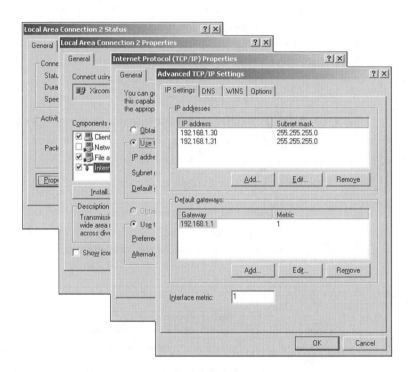

▲   5. Close all dialog boxes by pressing the OK button and restart the computer if
        prompted to do so.

Optionally Create an IP Address Alias

In order to make browsing our development Web site easier, you need to create an alias
for the IP address you just created. There are two ways to do this: 1) make an entry in
the DNS records for the DNS server on your network, or 2) make an entry in the hosts
file for this new IP address. A network administrator typically performs the former so I
will not go into detail on this item. The latter is a much simpler process:

- Use Notepad to open the following file: `[SystemDrive]:\WINNT\system32\` `drivers\etc\hosts`

- Add a new line with the IP address first, followed by a tab, then a name, or alias, for this IP address. In my example, the alias is `www.24Hours.com`, so the new line looks like the one shown in Figure 2.5.

FIGURE 2.5

Aliases for IP addresses may be entered into the local hosts file.

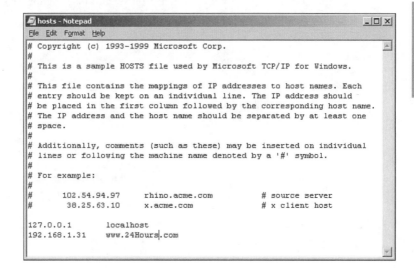

```
hosts - Notepad                                                    _|□|x|
File  Edit  Format  Help
# Copyright (c) 1993-1999 Microsoft Corp.
#
# This is a sample HOSTS file used by Microsoft TCP/IP for Windows.
#
# This file contains the mappings of IP addresses to host names. Each
# entry should be kept on an individual line. The IP address should
# be placed in the first column followed by the corresponding host name.
# The IP address and the host name should be separated by at least one
# space.
#
# Additionally, comments (such as these) may be inserted on individual
# lines or following the machine name denoted by a '#' symbol.
#
# For example:
#
#      102.54.94.97     rhino.acme.com          # source server
#       38.25.63.10     x.acme.com              # x client host

127.0.0.1       localhost
192.168.1.31    www.24Hours.com
```

- Save the file and close Notepad.
- You will now be able to reference this new IP address using the alias `www.24Hours.com`.

Using the New Web Site Wizard

As we discussed above, you want to differentiate your development content from the default Web site on the Web server. You can accomplish this by creating a new Web site and associating it with the new IP address you assigned to the network adapter.

You need to create a directory on your computer that will be used to store the code for your ASP.NET applications, such as `C:\24Hours\`. You can create this directory using the Windows Explorer.

To Do: Create the 24 Hours Web Site

1. Open the MMC by selecting Internet Services Manager (ISM) in the Administrative Tools program group.

2. The ISM opens in an MMC window displaying the local machine name in the list of servers.

▼   3. Double-click on the machine name to view the list of sites currently set up on this
        server. You should see the Default Web Site minimally, but may also see a Default
        FTP site, and an Administration Web Site and a Default SMTP Virtual Server site
        as well.

    4. To create your new Web site, right-click on the machine name and select New, Web
        Site to bring up the Web Site Creation Wizard (see Figure 2.6).

FIGURE 2.6

Using the ISM to
create a Web site.

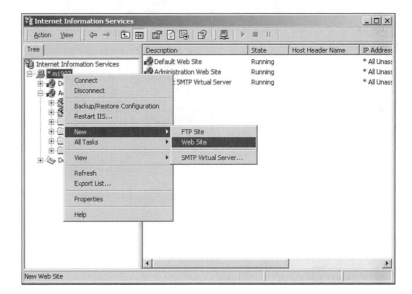

    5. The Web Site Creation Wizard guides you through the process of creating a new
        Web site. Enter **24Hours** for the Web Site Description field in the first step of the
        process.

    6. In the second step, select the new IP address that you created earlier from the drop-
        down list of available IP addresses. Leave the TCP port set to 80, which is the stan-
        dard port for Web servers.

    7. For the third step, specify the directory that you created earlier, C:\24Hours, as the
        home directory for this Web site.

    8. The last step deals with access permissions for his new Web site. The following
        options are available:

        • Read

        • Run Scripts (such as ASP)

▼   • Execute (such as ISAPI applications or CGI)

▼
- Write

- Browse

The first two options are selected by default. These two allow HTML and ASP access, respectively. If you want to be able to see a directory listing of the files available in this Web site, you may check the Browse option.

9. Complete the Web site creation process by left-clicking the Next and Finish buttons.

10. You should be able to test this Web site in a browser at this point to verify that it is working properly. To do this, open a Web browser and connect to the site using the IP address (http://192.168.1.1), the DNS name (http://COMPUTER1) or the alias (http://www.24Hours.com). If the site is running (and you enabled directory browsing) you should see an empty directory listing, as shown in Figure 2.7.

FIGURE 2.7

Using Internet Explorer to view the newly created Web site.

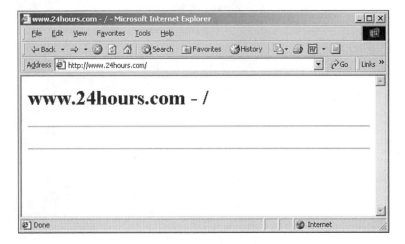

▲

That's all there is to creating a generic Web site.

Setting Default Documents

The default document is the document that is displayed when a browser request does not specify a document name. You can configure which documents are considered default documents and in what priority. To view or modify the default documents for a Web site, right-click on the Web site in the ISM and select Properties; then select the Documents tab (see figure 2.8). When a browser request is made without specifying a document name (for example, http://www.24Hours.com as opposed to http://www.24Hours.com/somepage.html), IIS will search these files and will serve the first document in the list that it finds. If no default document is found in the site directory, and if Directory Browsing is not enabled, IIS will return an error. Otherwise, IIS will display a directory listing of the folders and files in the site path that was specified in the browser request. Directory Browsing is acceptable when your site is still under development, but you should disable it when you are moving into production.

Figure 2.8

Configuring Default documents for the 24Hours site.

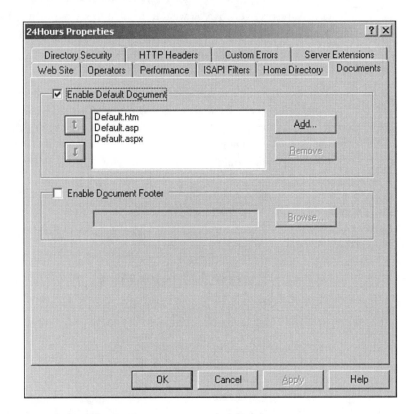

Creating a Virtual Directory

The home directory of your Web site is specified when you create the site. The default path for the Default Web Site is `[system drive]:\inetpub\wwwroot`. You can add physical directories to this directory using Windows Explorer, and they can be referenced from a browser by including the directory name in the URL address. If you have directory browsing enabled, these directories will show up when you browse the home directory of the site as shown in figure 2.9.

Another type of directory that can be added to a Web site is a virtual directory. A virtual directory is a link to another physical directory that resides somewhere other than under the home directory for the Web site or even on a different server. One common practice is to create a virtual directory that maps to the location where your ISAPI and CGI applications reside. Since these applications are executable programs, they need to reside in a directory that has the Execute permission turned on.

Figure 2.9

Listing Directories when Directory Browsing is enabled.

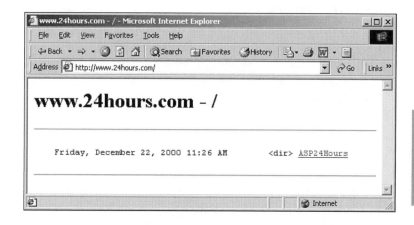

To Do: Create a Virtual Directory with Execute Permissions

1. Start the ISM and select the 24Hours site.

2. Start the Virtual Directory Creation Wizard by right-clicking on the site and then selecting New, Virtual Directory.

3. Type a descriptive name into the Alias field of the first step of the wizard. This alias will appear as a subdirectory under the home directory of the site.

4. Specify the physical location for this virtual directory in the next step of the wizard.

5. If you specify a location outside of local directories, you will need to provide a valid user name and password for the remote directory.

6. The last step of the wizard allows you to specify access permissions. Select the Execute check box to enable CGI and ISAPI applications and scripts to run.

7. Left-click the Next and Finish buttons to complete the creation process.

First Web Page

Now that you have a Web site, you need to create your first Web page. Using Notepad, create a file named default.asp. If you are working on a Windows Server machine and created the development Web site following the steps above, you can save the file in the C:\24Hours folder. Otherwise, save the file in the C:\InetPub\wwwroot folder. Listing 2.1 shows the contents for this sample ASP page. Don't worry too much about the contents of this file yet.

Listing 2.1   DEFAULT.ASP—First ASP Web Page

```
1  <%@ Language=VBScript %>
2  <HTML>
3  <TITLE>"Hello World!!!"</TITLE>
4  <HEAD>
```

LISTING 2.1   continued

```
 5  </HEAD>
 6  <BODY>
 7  <script language="javascript">

 8  function goBack(){
 9      window.history.back(1);
10  }

11  </script>
12  <FORM name="frmHello" action="default.asp" method="POST">
13      <table>
14      <%      if request("txtName") = "" then %>
15          <tr>
16              <td>
17                  Enter your name
18              </td>
19              <td>
20                  <input type="text" name="txtName">
21              </td>
22          </tr>
23          <tr>
24              <td colspan="2" align="right">
25                  <input type="submit" value="Submit">
26              </td>
27          </tr>
28      <% else %>
29          <tr>
30              <td>
31                  Hello, <% response.write request("txtName") %>.  How are you
➥doing today?
32              </td>
33          </tr>
34          <tr>
35              <td>
36                  <input type="button" name="btnBack" value="Back"
➥onClick="goBack();">
37              </td>
38          </tr>
39      <% end if %>
40      </table>

41  </FORM>
42  </BODY>
43  </HTML>
```

Now view this page in your browser. You should see something like what is shown in Figure 2.10.

When you type your name into the text box and press Submit, you should see something like what is shown in Figure 2.11. Notice that we are still looking at the same file in the browser. This example shows dynamic Web content in action using ASP.

FIGURE 2.10
Viewing default.asp *in Internet Explorer.*

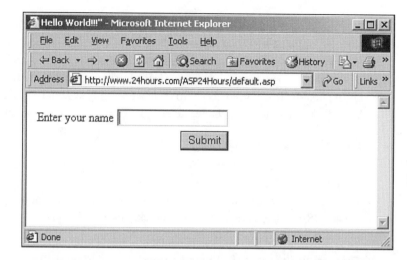

FIGURE 2.11
Your page after typing in a name and pressing Submit.

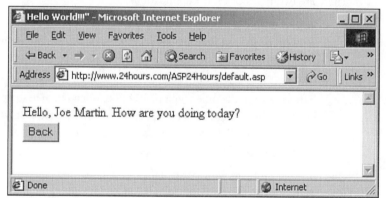

Why Use ASP.NET Over Other Technologies

Why should you use ASP.NET for creating dynamic Web applications? ASP.NET is not the only option for creating dynamic content on IIS 5.0. There are four main technologies used to publish dynamic content on IIS: CGI applications, ISAPI filters and extensions, ASP and now ASP.NET.

CGI Applications

CGI, or Common Gateway Interface, applications are usually written in Perl or C, but may be written in any language that can be compiled into an executable application or executed by a scripting engine. One reason for using CGI is that it gives the programmer access to the operating system and resources on the computer. Another reason is speed, especially if the CGI application is compiled into an executable program.

CGI support is available in IIS, but CGI is not a desirable method for providing dynamic Web site content for several reasons. These applications are difficult to debug. Another issue is performance. Each request for a CGI application spawns a new process. This can take a lot of resources and time. This problem is magnified greatly when there are multiple client requests. If you need access to certain operating system resources from within your Web site but want to avoid the resource and processing issues, you could use the ISAPI.

ISAPI Applications

ISAPI applications are implemented as DLLs (dynamic link libraries), and are developed using languages such as C and Delphi. These DLLs are loaded into the same process spaces as the Web server, thus bypassing the need to create a new process for each request. ISAPI applications are more quickly executed than CGIs, because they are in the same process as the Web Server.

There are two types of ISAPI applications:

- Filters, which get loaded into the Web server's process space during server startup and remain loaded until the server is shut down, are driven by Web server events and is typically used to monitor requests, perform custom authentication algorithms, perform just-in-time data translation, and many other Web server events.

- Extensions are the other type of ISAPI application. These applications get loaded into the Web server's process space when the first request from a client is made for this ISAPI DL. Extensions typically process form data from requests, perform business rules and work with data in databases.

One potential problem with ISAPI DLLs is that one misbehaving application could wreak havoc on the entire Web server because everything is in the same process space. However, ISAPI applications provide the fastest and most powerful method for creating Web applications.

ASP Applications

ASP applications are based on server-side scripting using VBScript or JScript as the language. These applications can access databases easily using Active Data Objects (ADO). The developer also has the ability to extend ASP with third-party- or in-house-developed ActiveX components. ASP has been widely accepted in the industry as a technology that allows developers to create rich and functional dynamic Web sites without consuming large amounts of server resources or processing time.

ASP.NET Applications

ASP.NET represents the latest evolution in Web development technologies. The biggest change from ASP to ASP.NET is that the application code is now compiled code that is executed, instead of interpreted as pages were requested, on the server.

Because ASP.NET is based on the Common Language Runtime, the components and power of the complete .NET platform are made available to Web-application developers. A large number of richly featured, helpful components are readily available to the developer to be incorporated into his or her Web application. The ASP.NET framework allows for the clean separation of presentation code from the application logic, which makes an application much easier to follow as well as maintain.

Summary

This hour started with a summary of which operating systems can be used to host and develop ASP.NET applications. The discussion ended with a summary of technologies that are available and explains why ASP.NET is the best of these. ASP.NET applications must be hosted on either Windows 4.0 server or Windows 2000, though they may be developed on any Windows platform after Windows 95. It is strongly recommended that you develop your applications with Visual Studio.NET, but it is not required.

You also learned how to create additional Web sites in the Internet Services Manager application, including how to set up default documents and virtual directories.

Once these setup tasks were completed, you were presented with a summary of the technologies available for developing Web applications with dynamic content within IIS. The possibilities are CGI, ISAPI, ASP and ASP.NET, with ASP.NET being the easiest and most powerful application development tool.

Q&A

Q. I am currently using Windows 98 with PWS. Will I be able to host ASP.NET applications?

A. No. In order to host ASP.NET applications you must have Windows NT 4.0 with service pack 6a or Windows 2000 or Windows XP.

Q. I don't have any network adapters on my computer. Is there anything I can do to still be able to develop and host ASP.NET applications?

A. You will need to install the Microsoft Loopback Adapter and configure it with at least one valid IP address. You can learn about this using the Windows Help.

Q. Can I still program in ASP, or do I have to completely convert to ASP.NET?

A. Yes. ASP and ASP.NET can coexist. The <% %> code render blocks can still be used to program VBScript intermingled with HTML.

Workshop

The quiz questions are provided for your further understanding.

Quiz

1. What application is used to configure IIS?

2. What platforms can host ASP.NET applications?

3. What platforms can be used to develop ASP.NET applications?

4. What can you do to retrieve a listing of available files on a Web site if no document is specified in the request and no default document is found?

5. What access permission needs to be applied in order to execute ASP.NET applications?

6. What is a common use for Virtual Directories?

7. Name four server-side technologies that can be used for developing dynamic Web content.

Answers for Hour 2

Quiz

1. What application is used to configure IIS?

   The Internet Services Manager Console.

2. What platforms can host ASP.NET applications?

   Windows 2000 and Windows NT 4.0 with service pack 6 and Windows XP.

3. What platforms can be used to develop ASP.NET applications?

   Anything. If you are going to use Visual Studio.NET, you will be limited to Microsoft Windows® 2000, Microsoft Windows XP and Microsoft Windows NT®.

4. What can you do to retrieve a listing of available files on a Web site if no document is specified in the request and no default document is found?

   Enable directory browsing for the Web virtual directory.

5. What access permission needs to be applied in order to execute ASP.NET applications?

   Read.

6. What is a common use for Virtual Directories?

   To isolate executable applications such as CGI and ISAPI applications to a specific location.

7. Name four server-side technologies that can be used for developing dynamic Web content.

   CGI, ISAPI, ASP, ASP.NET

HOUR 3

Introduction to Visual Basic.NET

In the previous hour, you learned why you should use ASP.NET over existing Active Server Pages as well as the system requirements needed to run it. Before you begin to do any development with ASP.NET, it is essential that you understand one of the languages supported by ASP.NET. For the examples in this book, we will discuss ASP.NET as it works with Visual Basic.NET. If you are already familiar with VB.NET, go ahead and skip to the next hour.

In this hour, you will begin to become more familiar with using VB.NET and will learn about the following items:

- Variable data types and scope
- Arrays
- Conditional statements and looping logic
- Procedures
- Classes

Visual Basic.NET

If you are familiar with Visual Basic's syntax and operation, you will notice that there are several major differences between the existing iteration of Visual Basic and VB.NET. This hour will provide you with a crash course in VB.NET. It is beyond the scope of this book to provide a thorough explanation of all the aspects of VB.NET, but you will be provided with the background necessary to program in ASP.NET with VB.NET.

> The examples in the rest of the book will draw more or less upon the topics discussed in this hour. Any example discussed later that cannot be related to this hour will have an accompanying explanation.

Variables

Variables are containers that hold values that can change over the course of an application; very little, if any, programming can be done without them. In ASP.NET, variables exist on several layers.

The first layer is the Application layer. Here, all variables are available to all users across every page in the application. Typically, a relatively small piece of data that is subject to frequent use, such as database connection information, is stored in this layer.

The second layer is the Session layer. Here, all variables are available to a specific user across the entire application, or as long as the user's session is current.

The third and final layer is the Page layer. Here, all variables declared on the page are available throughout that page. Variables declared on one ASP.NET page are not accessible from another page.

Furthermore, when using code-behinds (discussed in a later hour) on your ASP.NET pages, you have access to Public-, Private-, Procedure-, and Block-level scoped variables in your class modules. Publicly scoped variables are available throughout the classes they were created in as well as to other class modules. Publicly scoped variables are preceded with the `Public` keyword. Privately scoped variables are only available to functions and routines within the classes in which they were declared. Privately declared variables are preceded with the `Private` keyword. Procedure-level variables are only available in the functions or routines where they were initially created. Block-level variables are only available within the blocks of code that created them. Procedure- and Block-level variables are preceded with the `Dim` keyword. Table 3.1 illustrates the different levels of variable scope within your VB.NET code.

TABLE 3.1   Variable Scope Levels in VB.NET

Scope	Example
Public	```' Include at module level (not inside any procedure).``` ```Public strMsg As String```

Private	```' Add the following code at module level```
	```(not in any procedure).```
	```Private strMsg As String```
	```' ...```
	```Sub InitializePrivateVariable()```
	``` strMsg = "This variable cannot be used outside this module."```
	```End Sub```
	```' ...```
	```Sub UsePrivateVariable()```
	``` Response.Write(strMsg)```
	```End Sub```

Procedure	```Sub LocalVariable()```
	``` Dim strMsg As String```
	``` strMsg = "This variable cannot be used outside this proce-```
	```dure."```
	``` Response.Write(strMsg)```
	```End Sub```
	```' ...```
	```Sub OutsideScope()```
	``` Response.Write(strMsg) ' strMsg is not visible```
	``` outside LocalVariable().```
	```End Sub```

Block	```If N < 1291 Then```
	``` Dim Cube As Integer```
	``` Cube = N ^ 3 'the Cube variable is only visible in```
	```the within the If block```
	```End If```

One other thing to keep in mind is that you must always declare the data type of your variable. Table 3.2 contains a list of data types supported in VB.NET.

TABLE 3.2   Variable Data Types Supported in VB.NET

Data Type	Description	Value Range
Boolean	True or False	True and False.
Byte	Container for binary data	0–255.

TABLE 3.2 continued

Data Type	Description	Value Range
Char	Container for one Unicode character	0–65535.
Date	Date and Time information	January 1, 1 C.E. to December 31, 9999, and 0:00:00 to 23:59:59.
Decimal	Numeric information	+/-79,228,162,514,264,337,593,543,950,335 with no decimal point; +/-7.9228162514264337593543950335 with 28 places to the right of the decimal. The smallest nonzero number is +/-0.0000000000000000000000000001.
Double	Numeric data	-1.79769313486231E308 to -4.94065645841247E-324 for negative values; 4.94065645841247E-324 to 1.79769313486232E308 for positive values.
Integer	Numeric data	-2,147,483,648 to 2,147,483,647.
Long	Numeric data	-9,223,372,036,854,775,808 to 9,223,372,036,854,775,807.
Object	Default container variable	Any type can be stored in a variable of type Object.
Short	Numeric data	-32,768 to 32,767.
Single	Numeric data	-3.402823E38 to -1.401298E-45 for negative values; 1.401298E-45 to 3.402823E38 for positive values.
String	Character data	0 to approximately 2 billion Unicode characters.

In previous versions of Visual Basic and in VBScript, all variables were, by default, of the Variant data type. Variant doesn't exist in VB.NET and has been replaced with the Object data type.

When converting between data types, it is recommended that you explicitly convert the variable to its new data type by casting it. For example, to convert an Integer variable to a string variable, you would cast the Integer variable and can use the following syntax:

```
Response.Write("Your age is " & CStr(age))
```

Arrays

Arrays are logical groupings of data that can be accessed by a common name and a unique index value that differentiates between the values. Arrays can between one and 60 dimensions, although anything over three dimensions is oftentimes unwieldy and confusing. Each dimension of an array has an upper bound and a lower bound. The lower bound of an array dimension is always 0, and the upper bound of the dimension is set by the application when the array is created. The upper bound of an array could change as more elements are added to it.

Declaring Arrays

Arrays are declared in your VB.NET code through the use of one of the variable-declaration statements: `Dim`, `Static`, `Public`, or `Private`. When declaring the variable as an array, you need to include a pair of parentheses after the variable. The parentheses indicate that the variable is an array instead of a regular variable.

For example, the statement

```
Dim myArray() as String
```

declares a one-dimensional array that will hold strings.

To initialize an array with an upper boundary, you add the boundary value between the parentheses. Keep in mind that because an array is "zero based," it will always have one more element than the number specified in the boundary. For example,

```
Dim myArray(10) as String
```

will create an array of 11 elements. Therefore, if your intention is to create an array with only 10 elements, you would need to use the following syntax:

```
Dim myArray(9) as String
```

To create a multidimensional array, you separate the bounds with commas. The following example illustrates the code needed to create a two-dimensional array:

```
Dim myArray(5,8) as String
```

This array has six elements in the first dimension and nine in the second.

The preceding arrays were declared in such a way as to prevent them from storing values other than strings. To get an array to store different data types, you will need to declare the array as an Object type. Once that is done, you can store any type of data in its elements.

An array can also be resized in VB.NET. To do so, you execute a ReDim statement on the array along with the new upper bound. For example,

```
Dim myArray(10) as Object
...
ReDim myArray(20)
```

declares the myArray variable as a one-dimensional array with 11 elements in that dimension. The myArray array is then resized to have 21 elements in the next code statement. When the ReDim statement is used to resize an array, all the data stored in the elements of the array is lost. In order to prevent data loss, you can use the Preserve keyword with the ReDim statement:

```
Dim myArray(10) as Object
...
ReDim Preserve myArray(20)
```

This code will create a one-dimensional array with 11 elements in it. The array is then resized to hold 21 elements, but this time, all the existing values in the array are saved.

When resizing multidimensional arrays, you can resize only the last dimension of the array. Any attempt to resize any of the other dimensions will result in a runtime error during execution.

Using Arrays

To store a value in an array, you will need to use the following syntax:

```
arrayName(index) = value
```

For example, to initialize the elements of an array to a value of 100, you would use the following code:

```
Dim PercentArray(99) as Integer
Dim I as Integer
For I = 0 To 99
    PercentArray(I) = 100
Next I
...
```

Setting the values of a multidimensional array is very similar to setting the value of a one-dimensional array. Simply specify the index of each dimension that is to be modified and assign the value to it. Here's an example:

```
Dim X, Y as Integer
Dim MultiArray(5, 5) as Integer
For X = 0 To 5
    For Y = 0 To 5
        MultiArray(X, Y) = 0
    Next Y
Next X
```

This code will create a two-dimensional array and loop through each of the dimensions of the array and set the initial value of 0 into each element.

You can also use a function to determine the upper bound of an array. This function is called UBound, and it takes two arguments (or *parameters*), one of which is optional. The first argument is the name of the array to check. The second, optional argument is the dimension to check. By default, the UBound function checks the first dimension. For example, to check the upper bound of PercentArray from the previous code listing, you would use the following statement:

```
Dim intUpper as Integer
intUpper = UBound(PercentArray)
```

This code will assign the upper bound of PercentArray to the intUpper variable. When executed, the intUpper variable will hold the value 99. To get the upper bound of the second dimension of the multidimensional array, MultiArray, you would use the following code:

```
Dim intUpper as Integer
intUpper = UBound(MultiArray, 2)
```

When executed, intUpper will have the value 5, which is the upper bound of the second dimension of MultiArray.

Conditional Statements

A *conditional statement* is a statement that executes a given set of commands if a certain condition is met. In the VB.NET world, there are four possible conditional statements: Choose, If...Then...Else, Select Case, and Switch. Probably the most often used conditional statement is the If...Then...Else statement.

The If...Then...Else Statement

The most basic syntax for the If statement is as follows:

```
If [logical condition] Then [action]
```

This syntax is used if there is only one course of action when the logical condition is met (or true).

For a more complex structure than the basic If syntax, you can use the following:

```
If [logical condition] then
    [statements]
[ElseIf [logical condition] -n Then
    [ElseIf statements]]
[Else
    [Else statements]]
End If
```

The following example of the `If` statement illustrates its proper use:

```
Dim Number as Integer
Dim Digits as Small

Number = 72

If Number < 10 Then
    Digits = 1
ElseIf Number < 100 Then
    Digits = 2
Else
    Digits = 3
End If
```

When the preceding example is evaluated, the `Digits` variable would equal 2 upon completion of the statement. To review, when the code begins, two variables are declared. The first variable holds the actual number that being tested, 72. The second variable begins with no value but is later assigned a value based on the value of the variable being tested. The first statement in the conditional expression checks to see whether the value of the `Number` variable is less than 10. Because the value of the `Number` variable is set to 72, the expression resolves to `False` and moves on to the second conditional statement. Checking the value against the second condition evaluates to `True`, and the statement immediately following the conditional statement is executed. Once `Digits` is set to 2, the `If` statement ends.

The `Select Case` Statement

`Select Case` statements are similar in function to `If` statements, except that they execute one of several groups of statements depending on the value of an expression. The following syntax illustrates the generic use of the `Select Case` statement:

```
Select Case testexpression
[Case expressionlist-n
  [statements-n]] ...
[Case Else
  [else statements]]
End Select
```

The `Select Case` statement is best used when you want to take a different action based on different values of the same variable or expression.

Borrowing the scenario from the previous example will yield something like the following code snippet:

```
Dim Number as Integer
Dim Digits as Small

Number = 72
```

```
Select Case Number
    Case < 10
        Digits = 1
    Case < 100
        Digits = 2
    Case Else
        Digits = 3
End Select
```

When this code is executed, the resulting value of Digits will again be 2.

Loops

VB.NET offers many loop structures for repeating code statements based on the value of an expression. Do While loops allow you to repeat code as long as a given condition is true. A Do Until loop allows you to repeat code as long as the condition being evaluated is not true. The For Next loop allows you to loop through statements a specified number of times using a counter variable. Finally, a For Each Next loop allows you to loop through objects in a collection or array.

The For...Next Loop

When you want to iterate through a series of statements a specified number of times, you want to use a For loop.

The following is the syntax for this type of loop (keep in mind that intCounter and intSum are both variables of type Integer and both start with 0):

```
For counter = start To end [Step increment]
  [statements]
[Exit For]
  [statements]
Next [counter]
```

Applied to an example, this syntax would yield the following:

```
Dim intSum as Integer
For intCounter = 0 to 10
    intSum = intSum + intCounter
Next
Response.Write(intSum)
```

When executed, the For loop runs the addition statement and prints out the result at the end of the listing. The result would be 45.

The Do... Loop

The Do loop repeats a block of statements as long as a condition is true or until a condition becomes true. Here's the syntax:

```
Do [{While | Until} condition]
  [statements]
  [Exit Do]
  [statements]
Loop
```

Or, you can use this syntax:

```
Do
  [statements]
  [Exit Do]
  [statements]
Loop [{While | Until} condition]
```

When [While | Until] is located after the Do loop, the statements located within the loop may not run if the condition doesn't evaluate properly. If, however, you want the loop to run at least once, using the alternate syntax for your loop will result in the inner loop statements being executed at least once.

For example, the previous example yields the following code:

```
Do Until intCounter = 10
    intSum = intSum + intCounter
    intCounter = intCounter + 1
Loop
Response.Write(intSum)

Do While intCounter <= 10
    intSum = intSum + intCounter
    intCounter = intCounter + 1
Loop
Response.Write(intSum)

Do
 intSum = intSum + intCounter
 intCounter = intCounter + 1
Loop While intCounter <= 10
Response.Write(intSum)

Do
 intSum = intSum + intCounter
 intCounter = intCounter + 1
Loop Until intCounter = 10
Response.Write(intSum)
```

All the previous examples yield a result of 45 when executed.

Procedures

In VB.NET, procedures are the lifeblood that keeps everything working. There are two types of procedures: subs and functions. Both are collections of statements that can be called upon by other procedures and events on demand. The only difference between the two procedure types is that functions have a return value when called, whereas subs do not. Both procedure types accept arguments.

If arguments are defined for a sub or function, you should explicitly state whether the argument is being passed by reference (ByRef) or by value (ByVal). In VB.NET, the default for all arguments is ByVal, unless explicitly stated otherwise, whereas in the previous versions of Visual Basic, all arguments are passed in by default as ByRef. Therefore, it is best to explicitly declare how the argument is being passed instead of trying to remember what the default value is.

Here's an example of a sub:

```
Private Sub PrintName(ByVal UserName as String)
Response.Write("Hello " & UserName)
End Sub
```

This example, when called, will print "Hello" and the UserName argument that is passed into it on the Web page.

The only other difference between the two procedure types involves when they are called. The preceding sub would be called by one of the following two methods:

```
PrintName("John Doe")
```

or

```
Call PrintName("John Doe")
```

Here's an example of a function:

```
Private Function PrintName(ByVal UserName as String) as String
PrintName = "Hello" & UserName
End Function
```

When calling a function, you would use the following syntax:

```
strHello = PrintName("John Doe")
```

When the PrintName function is executed, strHello is set to the return value of "Hello John Doe".

Classes

A *class module* is a custom object created by the developer that can be instantiated across the application or, if self-contained in a DLL file, across multiple applications. In ASP.NET, each page is an instance of the Page class, which is located in the System namespace. Namespaces will be discussed in the next hour.

When a class module is created, custom properties, events, and methods are generated for use in your application. For example, you can create a property in a class by declaring a public variable outside of the procedures in the class. The more correct method of creating properties is to use the following syntax within your class module:

```
Public Property ThisProperty As String
Get
    ThisProperty = InternalValue
End Get

Set
    InternalValue = ThisProperty
End Set
```

In previous versions of Visual Basic, the `Property Let`, `Property Get`, and `Property Set` statements were necessary for manipulating custom class properties. This is no longer the case. From now on, the simple `Get` and `Set` statements are all that is necessary to utilize custom properties in a class module. Subs and functions are also important parts of class modules, although not much has changed with them.

Summary

In this hour, you were introduced to VB.NET, one of a plethora of programming languages that can be used with Microsoft's new .NET platform. You were also introduced to the data types and levels of scope in VB.NET as well as to conditional and looping logic using statements such as `If...Then...Else` and loops such as `For Next`. Arrays were defined and described in this hour, as were procedures and class modules.

Q&A

Q. Is that all there is to VB.NET?

A. No! There is much more to VB.NET that has not been covered. But this isn't a book about VB.NET; it's a book about ASP.NET. Pick up a book specializing in VB.NET or visit MSDN online at www.msdn.microsoft.com to learn more about the language.

Q. Is VB.NET an object-oriented language?

A. Yes. VB.NET now has support for the three features that make it truly object oriented: inheritance, recursive procedures, and polymorphism.

Workshop

The quiz questions and exercises are provided for your further understanding of the material. See Appendix A, "Answers," for the answers.

Quiz

1. What is the default data type of a variable in ASP.NET?

2. How do you create an array with two dimensions that will hold any data type? Make the first dimension hold nine elements and the second dimension hold two elements.

3. True or false? 1.5746 is a valid Integer value.

4. What is the difference between a sub and a function?

Exercise

1. If you have MSDN for Visual Studio.NET installed on your system, browse through the VB.NET documentation and familiarize yourself with the differences between Visual Basic 6 and VB.NET.

Answers for Hour 3

Quiz

1. What is the default data type of a variable in ASP.NET?

   The Object data type.

2. How do you create an array with two dimensions that will hold any data type? Make the first dimension hold nine elements and the second dimension hold two elements.

   ```
   Dim myArray(8, 1) as Object
   ```

3. True or false? 1.5746 is a valid Integer value.

   False.

4. What is the difference between a sub and a function?

   A function returns a value, whereas a sub does not.

HOUR 4

Working with ASP.NET

In the first hour, you learned why you should use ASP.NET over existing Web technologies. The second hour discussed Internet Information Services (IIS) and basic configuration for ASP.NET applications. The third hour introduced you to Visual Basic.NET (VB.NET), which will be the programming language used throughout this book. Now, before beginning any development with ASP.NET, you need to understand what comprises this technology and how it behaves.

In this hour, you will become more familiar with how ASP.NET operates. In particular, you learn about the following topics:

- The file architecture of ASP.NET
- Namespaces and how they will be used in your applications
- Programming languages in ASP.NET
- The various development tools that can be used with ASP.NET

ASP.NET File Architecture

Many files are used in the construction and operation of ASP.NET applications. Table 4.1 lists the files that comprise an ASP.NET application and defines their respective roles in the application.

TABLE 4.1   ASP.NET Application Files

File Extension	Description
.asax	This file type contains event syntax for coding against the ASP.NET application-level events. It can be found in the root directory of an ASP.NET application. ASP.NET applications are discussed in further detail in Hour 9, "ASP.NET Web Applications."
.ascx	This file type indicates an ASP.NET user-defined control. ASP.NET pages are typically composed of server controls—text boxes, list boxes, buttons, and so on—that form the basic elements of a Web page. As in traditional Visual Basic programming, ASP.NET allows for the creation of user-defined controls. These controls typically consist of a combination of server controls and programming to accomplish a specific task or a set of specific tasks. User controls are discussed in further detail in Hour 7, "Web Forms Server Controls."
.asmx	This file type is used by host Web services that are exposed to .NET applications, either remotely or locally. A *Web service* is a programmable entity that provides a particular element of functionality to an application. Web services and their associated files will be the focus of Hour 22, "Configuration, Localization, and Deployment."
.aspx	This is the core file type you will be working with. It is within this file structure that you will create and program your Web pages. ASPX pages are discussed in further detail in the next hour.
.axd	This file type is associated with ASP.NET application tracing, which allows the ASP.NET Framework to collect information about HTTP requests for an application. This is discussed in more detail in Hour 15, "Using Databases."
.vsdisco	This is an XML file that exposes links to other resources that describe a Web service. The VSDISCO file is used to discover Web services that are publicly available.
.htm	This is a standard HTML file containing static elements and content.
.xml	This is an XML document for use by the ASP.NET application. The XML file can be used for a variety of purposes, including holding application information as well as datasets returned from a database.
.vb	This is a code file that contains Visual Basic code that is, in turn, inherited by an ASPX or ASCX file. This type of file is also called a *code-behind* and is discussed in greater detail in future hours.

TABLE 4.1 continued

File Extension	Description
.config	This file type denotes a *configuration file*, which is a file used to set the various attributes of the application. These attributes include debug settings, security authentication, tracing functionality, session maintenance, and globalization. Configuration files are discussed in Hour 23, "Optimizing and Profiling ASP.NET Applications."

Namespaces

An important point to note when using the new .NET Framework is that namespaces are included in the construction of your applications. A *namespace* is a logical naming scheme for grouping related classes. It helps prevent classes that use the same identifier for methods and properties from interfering with one another.

For example, the .NET Framework uses a hierarchical naming scheme for grouping types into logical categories of related functionality, such as ASP.NET application framework and remoting functionality. Design tools use namespaces to make it easier for developers to browse and reference types in their code.

Suppose, for example, you are writing the following code:

```
Public Class NewClass
   [Procedures and Functions]
End Class

Public Class NewClass
   [Procedures and Functions]
End Class
```

This code would result in an error because the compiler has no way of differentiating the classes from one another. To overcome this problem, a namespace can be used that allows the two classes to coexist on the page. The following code snippet shows the delineation of the two classes into unique namespaces:

```
Namespace One
  Public Class NewClass
     [Procedures and Functions]
  End Class
End Namespace

Namespace Two
     Public Class NewClass
     [Procedures and Functions]
  End Class
End Namespace
```

4

In this code, there is no conflict between the two classes named `NewClass` because each has been placed into a separate namespace. The first class can be implemented by using the syntax `One.NewClass`, whereas the second class can be implemented by using the syntax `Two.NewClass`.

You can apply a hierarchal structure to your namespaces. Grouping together similar objects under subheadings in a common namespace makes it easier to identify the purpose of the namespace, and it also makes your code much more object oriented.

To illustrate the namespace, picture a book and its constituent parts. The root namespace would be the book itself and would be called `book` in this example. This namespace contains everything that makes up the book. The book's constituent parts are defined by child namespaces. That is, to refer to the chapters of a book and all their properties, you would use the syntax `book.chapter`; this is an example of a child namespace. Chapters can be further defined by their content. For example, in addition to chapters, there is typically a table of contents in a book as well as, perhaps, an appendix and an index. These examples can be expressed with the following syntax: `book.chapter.tableofcontents` for the Table of Contents chapter of the book, `book.chapter.chapter1content` for the content chapters of the book, and `book.chapter.index` and `book.chapter.appendix`, respectively, for the index and appendix of the book. One can go even further by breaking down the chapters into `paragraph`, `sentence`, `word`, and `letter` namespaces. See Figure 4.1 for the `book` namespace hierarchical structure.

FIGURE 4.1

Book namespace and its respective child namespaces.

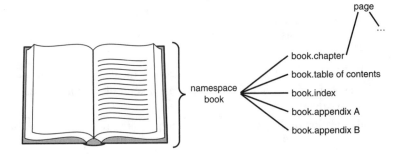

Namespaces will play an important role in developing ASP.NET applications. Fortunately, you will not need to develop your own namespace classification system for all the objects that can be used by ASP.NET pages. This problem has been taken care of for you by Microsoft. Two root namespaces, and their children namespaces, can be imported into your ASP.NET pages. The first is called `System`, and the second is called `Microsoft`. These namespaces are discussed in further detail in the following subsections.

The System Namespace

The System namespace is the core namespace for developing ASP.NET and all other .NET Framework–based applications. Everything that can be done in your application is handled through the System namespace. For example, array handling, mathematical operations, and data type conversion are handled through the System namespace and its children namespaces. There are nine default namespaces—the System namespace and eight of its children—added to every ASP.Net page:

- System
- System.ComponentModel.Design
- System.Data
- System.Drawing
- System.Web.SessionState
- System.Web
- System.Web.UI
- System.Web.UI.WebControls
- System.Web.UI.HTMLControls

Eight namespaces (excluding the System namespace) are automatically imported with every ASP.NET page when developing with Visual Studio.NET (VS.NET). These namespaces are defined in Table 4.2.

4

TABLE 4.2   .NET Namespaces

Namespace	Description
System.ComponentModel.Design	Contains classes that can be used to design custom support for components at design time and access the services provided by the .NET Framework designer architecture.
System.Data	Provides access to the classes and interfaces that comprise the ADO.NET architecture for universal data access.
System.Drawing	Contains classes and interfaces that provide basic graphics functionality. The System.Drawing namespace also provides more advanced functionality through the System.Drawing.Drawing2D, System.Drawing.Imaging, and System.Drawing.Text namespaces.
System.Web	Supplies classes and interfaces that enable browser/server communication. This namespace includes the HTTPRequest class (which provides extensive information about the current HTTP request), the HTTPResponse class (which manages

TABLE 4.2   continued

Namespace	Description
	HTTP output to the client), and the HTTPServerUtility object (which provides access to server-side utilities and processes). System.Web also includes classes for cookie manipulation, file transfer, exception information, and output cache control.
System.Web.SessionState	Provides classes and methods for session state management.
System.Web.UI	Supplies classes and interfaces for the user interface of the ASP.NET application that enable the application to communicate with the different facets of the page. The core class of this namespace is the Page class, which contains all the properties, methods, and constructors for the page. The following Active Server Page intrinsic objects are properties in the Page class: Server, Request, Response, Application, and Session.
System.Web.WebControls	Provides the extended ASP.NET controls, such as the Calendar control.
System.Web.UI.HTMLControls	Supplies classes for standard HTML elements, including forms, input controls (such as check boxes and hidden text fields), anchors, tables, text areas, and others. HTML controls look and feel exactly like standard HTML with the inclusion of a runat="server" attribute/value pair in the opening tag of the HTML element.
System.Web.UI.WebControls	Supplies classes for server controls that are similar to HTML controls but offer more flexibility and more complex functionality.

Other important System namespaces are listed in Table 4.3.

TABLE 4.3   .NET System Namespaces

Namespace	Description
System.IO	Contains interfaces and classes that allow synchronous and asynchronous reading from and writing to data streams and files.
System.Data.OleDb	Provides access to classes and interfaces for accessing a data source through ADO.
System.Data.SqlClient	Provides access to classes and interfaces for accessing Microsoft SQL Server–specific data through ADO.

TABLE 4.3 continued

Namespace	Description
System.Web.Security	Provides access to classes and interfaces for security in your ASP.NET application. Within this namespace is access to cryptography, permissions, and policy settings for the application.
System.Web.Services	Provides access to classes and interfaces for building and using Web services.
System.XML	Provides access to classes and interfaces for processing XML documents.

The `Microsoft` Namespace

In addition to the System namespaces found in the .NET framework, Microsoft has included several namespaces that provide functionality for the programming language you are going to use in your application. The following two namespaces are used frequently:

- `Microsoft.VisualBasic`: The `Microsoft.VisualBasic` namespace contains the Visual Basic.NET runtime. This runtime is used with the Visual Basic.NET language. The namespace also contains classes that support compilation and code generation using the Visual Basic language.

- `Microsoft.JScript`: The `Microsoft.JScript` namespace contains classes that support compilation and code generation using the JScript language.

- `Microsoft.CSharp`: The `Microsoft.CSharp` namespace contains classes that support compilation and code generation using the C# language.

- `Microsoft.Win32`: Provides classes and interfaces for working with Registry hives and keys.

Although many namespaces are already provided, you can also create your own namespaces for use in your ASP.NET application. A namespace is generated for every class created by the developer.

Using Namespaces on Your ASP.NET Pages

There are two ways to add a namespace to your ASP.NET application. Both use the @Import page directive for ASP.NET pages and the `Import` keyword to add the namespace directly to your Visual Basic code page. The first way is to add the namespace directly to your ASPX page. The following code snippet demonstrates the syntax necessary to add the System.Web.UI.WebControls namespace to your ASP.NET page:

4

```
<% @Import namespace="System.Web.UI.WebControls"%>
```

The second way to add a namespace is through your code-behind page, where most of the code resides. (Code-behinds are discussed in greater detail in Hour 5, "ASP.NET Page Syntax," and Hour 6, "Creating a User Interface with ASP.NET Web Forms.") To add a namespace to your code-behind, use the following syntax at the top of your code page:

```
Imports System.Web.UI.WebControls
```

If you want to add multiple namespaces to your ASP.NET page or Visual Basic code-behind page, you will need to add each one separately. For example, to add the System.Web.UI.HTMLControls namespace to the pages with the existing namespaces, go to the next line right after the last import statement and add **Imports System.Web. UI.HTMLControls**. Note that as soon as you type Imports System, VS.NET will pop up a list of namespaces to choose from, and you can simply click the desired namespace. The advantage of the pop-up list is that you don't have to have all the .NET namespaces memorized—you can simply select from the list. This feature is better known as *Intellisense*.

For ASP.NET pages, use this:

```
<% @Import namespace="System.Web.UI.WebControls"%>
<% @Import namespace="System.Web.UI.HTMLControls"%>
<% @Import namespace="namespace name"%>
...
```

For Visual Basic code-behind pages, use this:

```
Imports System.Web.UI.WebControls
Imports System.Web.UI.HTMLControls
Imports namespace
...
```

Programming Languages in ASP.NET

When you're actually developing code for your ASP.NET application, keep in mind that you have several programming languages from which to choose. Most Active Server Pages developers are familiar with VBScript. Unfortunately, ASP.NET does not support VBScript within the .NET Framework. The only languages that are currently supported are VB.NET, C#, and Visual C++.NET, and JScript.NET.

C# is the default language for developing ASP.NET pages. However, because most people using this technology have experience with VBScript, and VBScript is similar to Visual Basic, all examples will be displayed in VB.NET.

On each ASPX page you create, you will need to declare the programming language in which your code will be written. This declaration is done with a page directive, similar to the script language directive on existing Active Server Pages.

To declare a programming language (in this case, VB.NET), use the following syntax.

```
<% @Page Language="vb" %>
```

Here's the declaration for C#:

```
<% @Page Language="C#" %>
```

You cannot change your programming language across script blocks on your page. All code for the page *must* be written in the programming language declared in the page directive at the top of the page.

Development Tools

Because ASP.NET code isn't actually compiled until the designated ASPX page is accessed for the very first time, you can write your code in your favorite text editor. Although a text editor such as Notepad is okay to work with, there are several other tools with which you can write ASP.NET application code. The best is Visual Studio.NET from Microsoft, which provides a lot more functionality than a text editor.

VS.NET provides Intellisense to help you, as the developer, when you are writing your code. It also provides a data-viewing environment for connecting to your data source as well as other features, such as debugging and color coding your code to help correct common errors such as misspellings and improper syntax.

 For the remainder of this book, all code examples will be written in Visual Studio.NET. If you do not have a copy of the latest beta version, you can download it at http://msdn.microsoft.com/vstudio/.

Summary

In this hour, you learned what namespaces are and how they are used as well as the significance of some of the important namespaces. Namespaces are the very heart of the .NET Framework. They provide the key functionality of ASP.NET and are a major aspect of developing ASP.NET applications. You also learned about the files used in the creation of an ASP.NET application—primarily the ASPX file, which stores your HTML and ASP.NET code; the ASCX file, a user-defined control that can be used in multiple locations in your application and even in other applications; and the VB file, a code-behind file that keeps your VB.NET code separate from your HTML code for easier administration of your site.

Q&A

Q. What languages are currently supported in the development of ASP.NET pages?

A. Currently, Microsoft supports the use of VB.NET, C#, JScript.NET, and C++.NET in the development of ASP.NET applications.

Q. What is a namespace?

A. A *namespace* is a logical naming scheme for grouping related types of objects together.

Workshop

The quiz questions and exercises are provided for your further understanding of the material.

Quiz

1. In what namespace is the `Page` class located?

2. How do you utilize a namespace in an ASP.NET page? In a code-behind?

3. What information is stored in an ASPX file?

Exercise

1. Take some time to browse through the .NET reference guide to familiarize yourself with the various namespaces that can be imported into your application. If you have MSDN for VS.NET installed on your system, browse through the VB.NET documentation and familiarize yourself with the differences between Visual Basic 6 and VB.NET.

Answers for Hour 4

Quiz

1. In what namespace is the Page class located?

   The Page class is in the `System.Web.UI` namespace.

2. How do you utilize a namespace in an ASP.NET page? In a code-behind?

   In an ASP.NET page, `<%@import namespace%>`. In a code-behind, `imports namespace`.

3. What information is stored in an ASPX file?

   Typically, an ASPX file stores all of the code necessary to generate your Web page.

4

PART II

Putting Together the ASP.NET Page

Hour

HOUR 5

ASP.NET Page Syntax

ASP.NET "page" files are text files that contain code to be executed at the Web server to produce dynamic content. This code consists of markup syntax that is processed by the ASP.NET DLL file `aspnet_isapi.dll`, which runs on the Web server. Page files typically have an extension of `.aspx` or `.ascx`, which you learned in the previous hour. However, the Internet Services Manager allows you to configure other file extensions to be mapped to the DLL so that they may be processed as ASP.NET pages as well. This hour will introduce you to the syntax of ASP.NET pages. You will learn the following:

- How to create a Visual Basic Web application with Visual Studio
- Definitions and examples of the 10 ASP.NET syntax elements

Jumping into Visual Studio

The markup syntax for ASP.NET is made up of various elements; the top 10 elements are listed here:

- Page directives
- Code-declaration blocks
- Code-render blocks
- Server-side comments
- HTML-control syntax
- Custom server-control syntax
- Server-control event-binding syntax
- Data-binding expressions
- Server-side object tag syntax
- Server-side Include directive syntax

Page content that does not fit into any of these categories is considered literal text. This text can include string literals and HTML code.

 This hour assumes you have installed Visual Studio 7.0 (a.k.a. Visual Studio.NET or VS.NET).

To define and demonstrate the use of these directives, we will create a sample Visual Basic Web Application project using VS.NET. This may seem scary, but don't worry about all the details just yet. The best way to learn about new technology is to use it!

Start VS.NET and select File, New, Project from the menu bar. The type of project we are going to create is an ASP.NET Web Application. Select Visual Basic Projects in the Project Types pane on the left side of the New Project dialog box. Then select ASP.NET Web Application from the Templates pane on the right side of the dialog box, as shown in Figure 5.1. You can enter a name for the application, which will be how we reference this application through Internet Explorer (I chose Hour5 for this example). You will also need to specify the Web Server where this application will be hosted. Your local web server will be selected by default. Once you press the OK button, Visual Studio starts adding the base files, or the files that are necessary to compile and run your Web Application.

Once all the base files are added to the project, the WebForm1.aspx file will be loaded into the main window of the Integrated Development Environment (IDE) for editing.

FIGURE 5.1

Creating a new Visual Basic Web Application project with VS.NET.

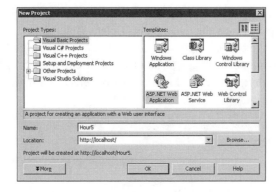

FIGURE 5.1

Creating a new Visual Basic Web Application project with VS.NET.

Visual Basic, Visual C++, Visual C#, and Microsoft Developer Network (MSDN) make up the Visual Studio IDE.

Our first page is going to consist of two text boxes for the user to enter an e-mail address and password as well as a button for submitting the form. We are going to use the HTML and Web Forms controls from the toolbox on the left of the development window inside Visual Studio. Double-click the Table item from the HTML tab of controls, as shown in Figure 5.2. This will create a three-row, three-cell table on the form.

FIGURE 5.2

Selecting the HTML Table control.

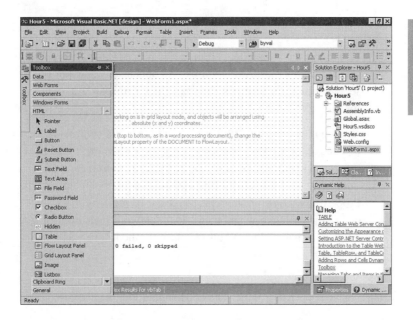

5

Now select the last cell on the first row of this table and right-click to reveal a list of actions you can perform on the table. Select Delete, Columns to create a two-column table. Now select the bottom, rightmost cell and remove it by right-clicking and selecting Delete, Cells. Notice how you can manipulate the size of a table by simply right-clicking and selecting to delete or insert columns, rows, or cells (see Figure 5.3).

FIGURE 5.3

Deleting a cell from an HTML table.

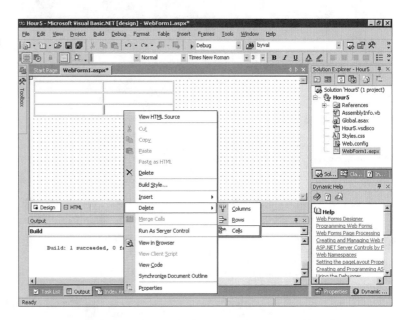

Now make the remaining cell in the bottom row span two columns by right-clicking and selecting Properties. A dialog box will appear, as shown in Figure 5.4, in which you can set the number of columns that the cell should span. Also, set the horizontal alignment for this cell to Center.

You are now ready to add some text and text box controls to the form. Select the top-left cell and enter **E-Mail Address**. Select the cell below it and enter **Password**. Now select the top-right cell and then select the TextBox item from the Web Forms tab of the Toolbox and double-click. This will place a text box control in the cell. Use the Properties window on the right to set the ID property to txtEMail. Select the right-most cell of the middle row and then add a Password Field control from the HTML tab of the Toolbox. Finally, place a button control in the last row and set its ID property to btnLogin and its Text property to Login.

You can view the source code for this Web page as HTML by right-clicking and selecting View HTML Source. The code should look something like this:

FIGURE 5.4

The property page for a cell in an HTML table.

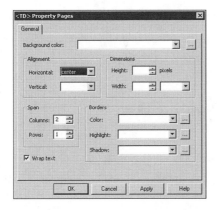

```
1  <%@ Page Language="vb" AutoEventWireup="false"
2  Codebehind="WebForm1.aspx.vb"
3  Inherits="Hour5.WebForm1"%>
4  <!DOCTYPE HTML PUBLIC "-//W3C//DTD HTML 4.0 Transitional//EN">
5  <HTML>
6    <HEAD>
7    <title></title>
8    <meta name="GENERATOR" content="Microsoft Visual Studio.NET 7.0">
9    <meta name="CODE_LANGUAGE" content="Visual Basic 7.0">
10   <meta name="vs_defaultClientScript" content="JavaScript">
11   <meta name="vs_targetSchema"
12       content="http://schemas.microsoft.com/intellisense/ie5">
13   </HEAD>
14   <body MS_POSITIONING="GridLayout">
15    <form id="Form1" method="post" runat="server">
16      <TABLE
17                style="Z-INDEX: 101; LEFT: 8px; POSITION: absolute; TOP: 8px"
18                cellSpacing="1"
19                cellPadding="1"
20                width="300"
21                border="1">
22      <TR>
23        <TD>
24            E-Mail Address
25        </TD>
26        <TD>
27            <asp:TextBox id="txtEMail" runat="server"></asp:TextBox>
28        </TD>
29      </TR>
30      <TR>
31        <TD>
32            Password
33        </TD>
34        <TD>
```

5

```
35                        <asp:TextBox id="txtPassword"
36                                      runat="server"
37                                      TextMode="Password">
38                                  </asp:TextBox>
39              </TD>
40          </TR>
41          <TR>
42              <TD align="middle" colSpan="2">
43                  <asp:Button id="btnLogin"
44                                  runat="server"
45                                  Text="Login">
46                              </asp:Button>
47              </TD>
48          </TR>
49          </TABLE>
50      </form>
51  </body>
52  </HTML>
```

Now build this application by selecting Build, Build from the menu bar. The Output window at the bottom of the IDE will indicate when the process has completed. Now view the application in a browser by selecting Debug, Start from the menu (see Figure 5.5).

FIGURE 5.5

WebForm1.aspx *with text, label, and button controls.*

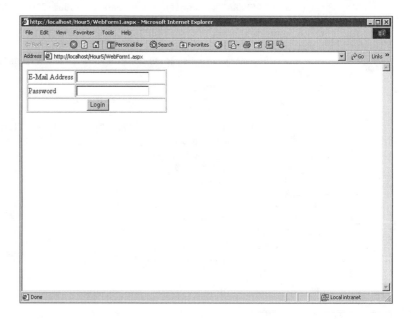

Now that our sample Web application is complete, it's time for you to learn a little more about the 10 syntax elements introduced at the beginning of this hour.

ASP.NET Syntax Elements

This section provides a brief overview of each of the various elements of ASP.NET markup syntax.

Page Directives

Page directives define page-specific attributes used by the ASP.NET page parser and compiler. Here are the supported page directives:

- @ Page
- @ Control
- @ Import
- @ Register
- @ Assembly
- @ OutputCache

@ Page

The @ Page directive is used to configure attributes related to the page when it is processed and compiled. Because you can have only one @ Page directive per ASPX page, you must specify multiple attribute=value pairs as a space-separated list. It is important to not include any space around the equals sign. For example, the previous sample ASPX page has the following @ Page directive:

```
<%@ Page Language="vb"
        Trace="false"
        Codebehind="WebForm1.aspx.vb"
        Inherits="Hour5.WebForm1"%>
```

Notice the attributes Language, AutoEventWireup, Codebehind, and Inherits with their corresponding values.

The @ Page directive has a number of attributes, but we'll cover only a few of the more common ones here. A complete listing of the available attributes is provided in the Microsoft Developer Network (MSDN) for VS.NET. The MSDN for VS.NET is included with the VS.NET product. It can also be accessed via the Internet at http://msdn.microsoft.com/default.asp.

Language

The Language attribute is used to specify what language to use when compiling inline rendering (<% %> and <%= %>) and what code declaration blocks are in the page. The list of available languages can include any .NET-supported language (for example, VB, C#, JScript.NET, and so on).

5

Codebehind

The Codebehind attribute is used to specify the source file for the code-behind class to compile. Code-behinds offer a way to separate the application code from user-interface content, which allows for better code readability and easier maintenance.

Inherits

The Inherits attribute is used to specify the code-behind class for the current page to inherit. The class name is defined in the source file associated with the Codebehind attribute.

Trace

The Trace attribute is used to generate tables of detailed information that will be displayed below the content of your page each time it is accessed. To enable tracing output, set the attribute value to True. The default value is False.

@ Control

The @ Control directive is used to specify attributes related to user controls. The concept of user controls will be introduced in Hour 6, "Creating a User Interface with ASP.NET Web Forms." This directive can only be included in ASCX files.

@ Import

The @ Import directive is used to import a namespace into the current page. This allows the classes and interfaces defined in the namespace to be available to the page. The imported namespace can be part of the .NET Framework class library or a user-defined namespace. If you add the following code to the top of your WebForm1.aspx page and change the From and To e-mail addresses to valid ones, the recipient will receive an e-mail each time the page is loaded:

```
<%@ Import NameSpace="System.Web.Mail.SmtpMail" %>
<%
    Dim objSMTP As New System.Web.Mail.SmtpMail()
    Dim ret as object
    objSMTP.Send("FromSomebody@someplace.com", _
      "ToNobody@nowhere.com", "Test SMTP Mail", "This is a test!")
%>
```

@ Register

The @ Register directive is used in conjunction with custom server-control syntax to associate aliases with namespaces and class names.

@ Assembly

The @ Assembly directive is similar to the @ Import directive. This directive links an assembly, or DLL, to the current page, which allows all the classes and interfaces exposed in the assembly to be accessible to the current page.

@ OutputCache

The @ OutputCache directive configures the output-caching rules for a page. This is a way to increase Web server application performance by caching response content. Output caching allows subsequent requests for a page to be satisfied from the cache so that the code that creates the page does not have to be run again. For example, the code

```
<%@ OutputCache Duration="30" %>
```

causes page content to be cached for 30 seconds.

Code-Declaration Blocks

Code-declaration blocks are used to define variables and methods that are compiled into the page and executed at the Web server when the page is accessed. These blocks are defined using <script> tags with a runat attribute set to "server". The language can be defined for the code block using the language attribute. If this attribute is not defined, the inner code language will be the language defined for the page, as configured with the @ Page directive:

```
<script runat="server" [language="C#"]>
    Script code...
</script>
```

The src attribute specifies the path and filename of a script file to load. This allows the use of an external script file. When this attribute is used, any other code in the declaration block is ignored. Here's an example:

```
<script runat="server" [language="C#"] src="scriptfile" />
```

The following example shows how to use a code-declaration block to define an event handler for the Login button on our sample application. When a user enters a valid e-mail address and clicks the Login button, an e-mail will be sent to that user from himself. The changes to our sample application are shown in bold.

```
1<%@ Import NameSpace="System.Web.Mail.SMTPMail" %>
2<%@ Page Language="vb"
3    AutoEventWireup="false"
4    Codebehind="WebForm1.aspx.vb"
5    Inherits="Hour5.WebForm1"%>
```

5

```
6  <!DOCTYPE HTML PUBLIC "-//W3C//DTD HTML 4.0 Transitional//EN">
7  <HTML>
8    <HEAD>
9      <title></title>
10     <meta name="GENERATOR" content="Microsoft Visual Studio.NET 7.0">
11     <meta name="CODE_LANGUAGE" content="Visual Basic 7.0">
12     <meta name="vs_defaultClientScript" content="JavaScript">
13     <meta name="vs_targetSchema"
14     content="http://schemas.microsoft.com/intellisense/ie5">
15   </HEAD>
16   <body MS_POSITIONING="GridLayout">
17     <script runat="server">
18       Public Sub btnLogin_Click(ByVal sender As Object, _
19         ByVal e As System.EventArgs)
20       Dim objSMTP As New System.Web.Mail.SmtpMail()
21       objSMTP.Send(txtEMail.text, txtEMail.text, _
22         "Test SMTP Mail", "This is a test!")
23       End Sub
24     </script>
25     <form id="Form1" method="post" runat="server">
26       <TABLE style="Z-INDEX: 101; LEFT: 8px; POSITION: absolute; TOP: 8px"
27         cellSpacing="1"
28         cellPadding="1"
29         width="300"
30         border="1">
31       <TR>
32         <TD>
33             E-Mail Address
34         </TD>
35         <TD>
36             <asp:TextBox id="txtEMail" runat="server"></asp:TextBox>
37         </TD>
38       </TR>
39       <TR>
40         <TD>
41             Password
42         </TD>
43         <TD>
44             <asp:TextBox id="txtPassword"
45               runat="server"
46               TextMode="Password">
47           </asp:TextBox>
48         </TD>
49       </TR>
50       <TR>
51         <TD align="middle" colSpan="2">
52             <asp:Button id="btnLogin"
53               runat="server"
54               Text="Login">
55           </asp:Button>
56         </TD>
```

```
57              <TD>
58              </TD>
59            </TR>
60          </TABLE>
61        </form>
62      </body>
63 </HTML>
```

Code-Render Blocks

Code-render blocks are used to declare statements of code that execute when the page is rendered. The language for these statements is the language defined for the page. The sample code used for the preceding @ Import directive demonstrates the use of code-render blocks, as shown here:

```
1 <%@ Import NameSpace="System.Web. Mail.SmtpMail" %>
2 <%
3    Dim objSMTP As New System.Web.Mail.SmtpMail()
4    Dim ret as object
5    objSMTP.Send("FromSomebody@someplace.com", _
6        "ToNobody@nowhere.com", __
7        "Test SMTP Mail", "This is a test!")
8%>
```

Server-Side Comments

Server-side comments allow for the inclusion of code comments in the body of an ASPX file. Any content (code or text) between the opening and closing tags of the server-side comment elements will not be processed on the server or rendered to the resulting page. Server-side comments, like traditional language-specific comments, are mainly used for documentation and testing. The syntax of server-side comments provides a simple and effective way to insert multiple documentation comments or exclude multiple lines of code by commenting out the code lines. Commenting out code is the process of enclosing the selected code lines within server-side comment tags; this prevents the enclosed code lines from being processed on the server. The following example shows how to use server-side comments to prevent an e-mail from being sent. The btnLogin_Click method is still executed at the server, but the code lines have been commented out, thereby leaving the subroutine of btnLogin_Click with commented lines, but no code to execute:

```
1 <script runat="server" >
2    Public Sub btnLogin_Click(ByVal sender As Object, _
3      ByVal e As System.EventArgs)
4 <%--
5        Dim objSMTP As New System.Web.Mail.SmtpMail()
6        objSMTP.Send(txtEMail.text, txtEMail.text, _
7            "Test SMTP Mail", "This is a test!")
```

```
8  --%>
9     End Sub
10  </script>
```

HTML-Control Syntax

Normally, HTML-control syntax is treated as literal text, rendering the controls program-matically unavailable at the server. ASP.NET provides a way to enable these controls to be available at the server for programming by including a `runat="server"` attribute/value pair in the declaration of the HTML control. These controls must be contained in a form that also has `runat="server"` specified. In the following example, I have modified our sample application again by adding a couple of HTML controls with associated code to be executed at the server. These changes are highlighted in bold.

```
1  <%@ Page Language="vb"
2        AutoEventWireup="false"
3        Codebehind="WebForm1.aspx.vb"
4        Inherits="Hour5.WebForm1"%>
5  <%@ Import NameSpace="System.Web.Mail.SMTPMail" %>
6  <!DOCTYPE HTML PUBLIC "-//W3C//DTD HTML 4.0 Transitional//EN">
7  <HTML>
8   <HEAD>
9          <title></title>
10         <meta content="Microsoft Visual Studio.NET 7.0" name="GENERATOR">
11         <meta content="Visual Basic 7.0" name="CODE_LANGUAGE">
12         <meta content="JavaScript" name="vs_defaultClientScript">
13         <meta content="http://schemas.microsoft.com/intellisense/ie5"
14       name="vs_targetSchema">
15   </HEAD>
16  <body MS_POSITIONING="GridLayout">
17          <script runat="server">
18            Public Sub btnLogin_Click(ByVal sender As Object, _
19                  ByVal e As System.EventArgs)
20            Dim objSMTP As New System.Web.Mail.SmtpMail()
21            objSMTP.Send(txtEMail.text, _
22                txtEMail.text, "Test SMTP Mail", "This is a test!")
23          End Sub
24          Public Sub Button2_Click(ByVal sender As Object, _
25                ByVal e As System.EventArgs)
26            Dim objSMTP As New System.Web.Mail.SmtpMail()
27            objSMTP.Send(txtEMail.text, txtEMail.text, _
28              "Test SMTP Mail", txtMessage.Value)
29          End Sub
30          </script>
31     <form id="Form1" method="post" runat="server">
32       <TABLE style="Z-INDEX: 101; LEFT: 8px; POSITION: absolute; TOP: 8px"
33     cellSpacing="1" cellPadding="1" width="300" border="1">
34          <TR>
35            <TD>
36              E-Mail Address
```

```
37              </TD>
38              <TD>
39                 <asp:textbox id="txtEMail" runat="server"></asp:textbox>
40              </TD>
41           </TR>
42           <TR>
43             <TD>
44                Password
45             </TD>
46             <TD>
47                <asp:textbox id="txtPassword"
48                     runat="server"
49                     TextMode="Password">
50               </asp:textbox>
51             </TD>
52           </TR>
53           <TR>
54            <TD align="middle" colSpan="2">
55                <asp:button id="btnLogin"
56                     runat="server"
57                     Text="Login">
58                 </asp:button>
59            </TD>
60            <TD>
61            </TD>
62           </TR>
63           <tr>
64             <td>
65                Message Text
66             </td>
67             <td>
68                <input type="text"
69                     id="txtMessage"
70                     name="txtMessage"
71                     size="50"
72                     runat="server">
73             </td>
74           </tr>
75           <tr>
76             <td align="middle" colSpan="2">
77                 <input type="button"
78                     id="Button2"
79                     runat="server"
80                     value="Server Side HTML Button"
81                     OnServerClick="Button2_Click"
82                     name="Button2">
83             </td>
84           </tr>
85         </TABLE>
86      </form>
87  </body>
88 </HTML>
```

5

An event is a message sent by an object to signal the occurrence of an action (such as a mouse click, a button click, and so on).

Note the use of `OnServerClick` instead of `OnClick` as an event handler. `OnClick` still works, but it expects the method code for the event handler to be a traditional client-side procedure implemented in either JavaScript or VBScript. `OnServerValidate` and `OnServerChange` are two other special event handlers available for server-side programming of HTML controls.

Custom Server-Control Syntax

VS.NET comes with a rich set of Web controls you can use in developing your ASP.NET application. To use these controls in your ASP.NET page, you use element tags that reference the namespaces for these controls and then the control types. From our sample application, the following line shows how to create an instance of a `TextBox` Web control:

```
<td>
    <asp:TextBox id=txtPassword runat="server" TextMode="Password">
    </asp:TextBox>
</td>
```

The syntax for creating the control follows this format:

```
<NamespaceAlias:ControlName id="Control ID" runat="server" >
</NamespaceAlias:ControlName>
```

In our example, the namespace alias for Web controls is "ASP", and this alias is automatically registered for us. Later on, you will learn about creating your own custom server controls, and you will use the `@ Register` directive, discussed earlier in this hour, to create an alias for your namespace. In order to reference any control's properties and methods as well as to react to its events, you need to specify a unique ID value.

The following example, shown in Figure 5.6, shows how we can change our sample application to use a Label Web control and how to set its appearance properties:

```
<tr>
    <!--<td>E-Mail Address</td>-->
    <td>
        <asp:label runat="Server" font-bold="True"
            font-names="Verdana" font-size="18" text="E-Mail Address">
        </asp:label>
    </td>
    <td>
```

```
        <asp:TextBox id=txtEMail runat="server"
            width="400"></asp:TextBox>
    </td>
</tr>
```

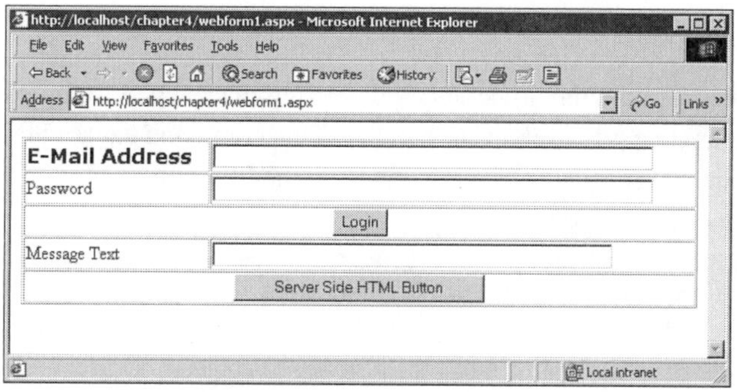

FIGURE 5.6

A Label *Web control
that's used in place of
literal text.*

Server-Control Event-Binding Syntax

One of the benefits of using server controls is being able to link, or *bind*, application
code to an event that occurs at the client machine. In our sample application, we created
instances of several server controls, including a button. When the button is clicked, a
message is sent from the client machine to the server, where we react by sending an e-
mail. When we used VS.NET to create our application, it placed the code for the event
handling in a separate file, WebForm1.aspx.vb, because we created a Visual Basic Web
Application project. This separate file is called a *code-behind*, as mentioned in earlier
hours, and it demonstrates the separation of code for the appearance of our user interface
from the application code. This also makes it easier to see the separation between the
client-side user activity and the server-side event handling to which it corresponds.

Data-Binding Expression Syntax

Data-binding expressions provide a means of linking property values of server controls
to values from data sources. The data source can be any property on the current page.
This includes values from other server controls, property values from the page object, or
any public variables you may have defined on the page, such as arrays or SQL datasets.
To implement data binding, you include a reference to the value you want bound
between the <%# and %> characters. The following changes to our sample application show
an example of data binding:

```
<asp:TextBox id="txtActivity" runat="server"
                TextMode="MultiLine"
        font-names="Verdana" font-size="12" columns="30" rows="5"
```

```
                    width="513" height="165"
                    text='<%# txtEMail.text & _
                    " was sent the following message at " & _
                    Now() & ": " & _
                    chr(10) & txtMessage.Text%>'
                    >
</asp:TextBox>
```

To force all bindings to be updated, we can place a call to the `Page.DataBind()` method in the `btnLogin_Click` event handler. This command causes all bindings on the page to be updated. This call is demonstrated in the following code:

```
<script runat="server" >
    Public Sub btnLogin_Click(ByVal sender As Object, __
        ByVal e As System.EventArgs)
        Dim objSMTP As New System.Web.Mail.SmtpMail()

        objSMTP.Send(txtEMail.text, txtEMail.text, _
            "Test SMTP Mail", txtMessage.text)
        Page.DataBind()
    End Sub

</script>
```

Another way would be to call `txtActivity.DataBind()` to update the data for the `txtActivity` control only.

Server-Side Object Tag Syntax

Object tags are used to create instances of COM or .NET objects that will be used as part of your page-processing code. The following is an example of creating an instance of the file system object, which is part of the Scripting Runtime (notice the `Scripting.FileSystemObject` reference on the first line):

```
<object id="objFS" progid="Scripting.FileSystemObject" runat="server">
</object>

<script runat="server" >
    Public Sub SomeSub()
        Dim objFile as object
        objFile = objFS.CreateTextFile("C:\Temp\Hour5.txt", True)
        objFile.WriteLine("This is Hour5 Speaking!!!")
        objFile.Close
    End Sub
</script>
```

As you can see from this example, the object is created as a global object, which means any code on the page will be able to reference the object's properties and methods.

Server-Side Include Directive Syntax

Server-side Include directives provide a means for including common code and code for client-side execution, such as JavaScript functions, HTML, and ASP.NET server code. The contents of the included file are inserted before any processing of the page occurs. The syntax for including files is as follows:

```
<!-- #include PathType = Filename -->
```

Here, *PathType* can either be File or Virtual (no quotes). If *PathType* is File, the filename needs to specify a relative path from the current document to the file you want to include. If *PathType* is Virtual, the filename needs to specify a full path to a virtual directory and file on your Web server. Some basic uses for server-side Include directives are for common headers and footers and common utility functions that all your pages may need.

Summary

This hour began with an introduction to VS.NET and the creation of a Visual Basic Web Application project, which familiarized you with the development environment and showed you some of the benefits of using VS.NET for developing your applications. Some of these benefits include Intellisense, which was mentioned in Hour 3, "Introduction to Visual Basic.NET," and being able to select a visual component on your page and set its properties via its property page. These are only a couple of the many features of VS.NET, which you will learn about more as you continue through this book.

Q&A

Q. Do I have to use Visual Studio to create my ASP.NET applications?

A. No. You can use any text editor you choose. When using a text editor, you will need to compile your applications manually if any code-behinds are implemented.

Q. Are all 10 of the ASP.NET syntax elements required in every ASP.NET page?

A. No. Some elements will be more common than others, such as code-declaration blocks and HTML-control syntax.

Workshop

The quiz questions and exercises are provided for your further understanding.

5

Quiz

1. True or false? The only way to create controls on an ASP page is to use the IDE toolbox to add the controls.

2. True or false? Visual Studio's IDE only works with Visual Basic.

3. Why are server-side comments within code necessary or helpful?

Exercise

1. Create an ASP.NET page that takes as input a user name and password and provides a button for logging in. Examine the values that the user enters and display a message in a text box indicating whether the values he or she entered are accepted. The criteria for a successful login should be your name and a password that you make up. (Hint: To compare string values in VB, you can use the equals operator.)

Answers for Hour 5

Quiz

1. True or false? The only way to create controls on an ASP page is to use the IDE toolbox to add the controls.

   False. You can use the following syntax to add controls to your ASP page:

   ```
   <NamespaceAlias:ControlName id="Control ID" runat="server" >
   </NamespaceAlias:ControlName>
   ```

2. True or false? Visual Studio's IDE only works with Visual Basic.

   False. C# and C++ are also accessible via the IDE.

3. Why are server-side comments within code necessary or helpful?

   Comments can be used in the documentation of code within ASPX files. Comments are also helpful in testing applications, in that they provide a way to exclude code from being executed on the server.

HOUR **6**

Creating a User Interface with ASP.NET Web Forms

In the previous hour, you learned the proper syntax necessary for working with ASP.NET pages. Now it's time to focus on the meatier elements of ASP.NET programming: ASP.NET Web forms. In this hour, you will be introduced to the following topics:

- Web forms and how to use them in your ASP.NET application
- What happens when a page is processed
- How to create a Web application using Visual Studio.NET (VS.NET)
- How to add Web forms to your Web application

An Introduction to Web Forms

In ASP.NET, Web forms are used to create programmable Web pages. They allow you, the developer, to separate user-interface HTML development from the server-side code that comprises the dynamic portion of a Web page. Here are some additional points you should know about Web forms:

- Web forms allow for browser independence by automatically rendering the correct code for whichever browser is used to access the page. You can also set up your Web forms to target specific browsers to take advantage of rich features that are not present in other browsers.

- Web forms can be programmed in any of the .NET-accepted programming languages, including VB.NET, C#, C++.NET, and JScript.NET.

- Web forms provide all the benefits of the .NET Framework, including managed code, type safety, and inheritance.

- Web forms use server-based controls that help separate user interface development from code development.

- Web forms allow for easy retention of user-entered data while the user is navigating around your Web site.

- Web forms provide a consistent object model for Web application development.

Web Forms Code Model

Web forms are divided into two parts. The first part is the visual component; the second is the code. The code works in conjunction with the HTML that is generated to create the Web page in order to create fully dynamic Web pages. Figure 6.1 illustrates the two components of a Web form.

FIGURE 6.1

The two components of a Web form—the visual component and the code.

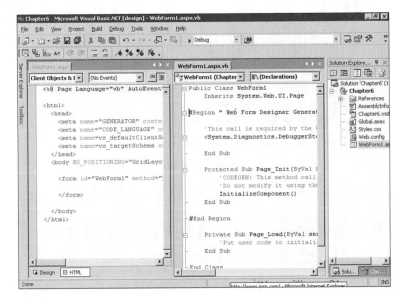

The visual component of a Web form consists of HTML and the Web form server controls, which come in two flavors: HTML controls and Web controls. HTML controls look and feel exactly like standard HTML form elements, with the addition of `runat="server"` within the other tag attributes. Web controls are more abstract objects that, when processed, create standard HTML syntax. Web controls are especially helpful because they provide you with an object interface that includes properties, methods, and events. All these features can be incorporated into the code portion of your Web forms. A more in-depth discussion of server controls can be found in Hour 7, "Web Forms Server Controls."

Now, let's take a look at the code that's necessary to generate an ASPX file. The following example illustrates the development of a user-profile form for a typical Web site. On the page, we are going to capture user information, including the user's name and address. Listing 6.1 is an example of the code that creates the visual component of this Web form. When looking over the code, notice the combination of server controls and standard HTML tags.

LISTING 6.1 *UserProfile.aspx* Source Code

```
1: <%@ Page Language="vb" CodeBehind="UserProfile.asx.vb"
➥Inherits="UserProfileExample.UserProfile"%>
2: <html><head>
3: <title>User Profile Example</title>
4:    <LINK rel="stylesheet" type="text/css"
➥href="http://OSIRIS_HOME/UserProfileExample/Styles.css">
5: </head>
6:    <body bgcolor="#ffffcc">
7:       <form id="frmUserProfile" method="post" runat="server">
8:          <table id="tblUserProfile" border="0" align="center" cellspacing="1"
➥cellpadding="1">
9:          <tr>
10:             <td colspan="2"><asp:Label id=lblHeader runat="server"
➥Width="115" Height="19" Font-Bold="True">
–User Profile</asp:Label></td>
11:          </tr>
12:          <tr>
13:             <td valign="middle"><asp:Label id=lblFirstName runat="server"
➥Width="115"
 Height="19" font-size="small"
➥Font-Bold="True">First Name:</asp:Label></td>
14:             <td valign="middle"><asp:TextBox id=txtFirstName runat="server"
➥Width="266" Height="24"></asp:TextBox></td>
15:          </tr>
16:          <tr>
17:             <td valign="middle"><asp:Label id=lblLastName runat="server"
➥Width="118" Height="19" Font-Bold="True">Last Name:</asp:Label></td>
```

6

LISTING 6.1 continued

```
18:              <td valign="middle"><asp:TextBox id=txtLastName runat="server"
➥Width="266" Height="24"></asp:TextBox></td>
19:          </tr>
20:          <tr>
21:              <td valign="middle"><asp:Label id=lblAddress1 runat="server"
➥Width="118" Height="19" Font-Bold="True">Address 1:</asp:Label></td>
22:              <td valign="middle"><asp:TextBox id=txtAddress1 runat="server"
➥Width="266" Height="24"></asp:TextBox></td>
23:          </tr>
24:          <tr>
25:              <td valign="middle"><asp:Label id=lblAddress2 runat="server"
➥Width="118" Height="19" Font-Bold="True">Address 2:</asp:Label></td>
26:              <td valign="middle"><asp:TextBox id=txtAddress2 runat="server"
➥Width="266" Height="24"></asp:TextBox></td>
27:          </tr>
28:          <tr>
29:              <td valign="middle"><asp:Label id=lblCity runat="server"
➥Width="118" Height="19" Font-Bold="True">City:</asp:Label></td>
30:              <td valign="middle"><asp:TextBox id=txtCity runat="server"
➥Width="266" Height="24"></asp:TextBox></td>
30:          </tr>
31:          <tr>
32:              <td valign="middle"><asp:Label id=lblState runat="server"
➥Width="118" Height="19"
Font-Bold="True">State:</asp:Label></td>
33:              <td valign="middle"><asp:TextBox id=txtState runat="server"
➥Width="28" Height="26"maxlength="2"></asp:TextBox></td>
34:          </tr>
35:          <tr>
36:              <td valign="middle"><asp:Label id=lblPostalCode runat="server"
➥Width="118" Height="19" Font-Bold="True">Postal Code:</asp:Label></td>
37:              <td valign="middle"><asp:TextBox id=txtPostalCode runat=
➥"server"
➥Width="78" Height="26" maxlength="10"></asp:TextBox></td>
38:          </tr>
39:          <tr><td colspan="2"> </td></tr>
40:          <tr>
41:              <td align="center" colspan="2">
42:                  <asp:button id="btnSave" onclick="btnSave_Click"
➥runat="Server" text="Save"></asp:button>  
43:                  <input type="reset" id="btnReset" runat="server"
➥value="Reset">
44:              </td>
45:          </tr>
46:      </table>
47:      </form>
48:  </body></html>
```

Line 1 contains the directives for the page. As you learned in the previous hour, page directives tell the parser how to compile the page. Here, the `language="vb"` directive tells the page that all the code on the page will be written in Visual Basic.NET (VB.NET). The `CodeBehind="userprofile.aspx.vb"` attribute tells the page where to find the code-behind (defined later), and the `inherits="UserProfileExample.UserProfile"` attribute tells the page what class in the code-behind the page is going to inherit and extend.

Lines 2–9 contain standard HTML tags, with the addition of the `runat="server"` attribute on the `<FORM>` tag. Line 10 shows something new: The `<asp:label>` tag is an example of a Web form server control. Notice that attributes can be set on the control, similar to the way attributes are set on a standard HTML control.

Lines 11–41 contain a combination of HTML interspersed with Web form server controls.

In line 42, the `<asp:button>` server control is introduced. This server control has an additional attribute called `onclick`. This attribute associates or binds a piece of code to an event. In this case, the `onclick` event of `asp:button` is bound to a piece of code in the code-behind called `btnSave_Click`. Whenever the `asp:button` server control is clicked, the bound code executes.

Line 43 is an example of an HTML server control. Notice that the syntax exactly matches the syntax for a regular HTML control, with the addition of the `runat="server"` attribute setting. Now, let's take a look at the code created for the code component of the Web form.

The code component of the Web form allows for programmatic interaction with the visual component as well as interaction with client-side events initiated by the user. The code component, as mentioned in earlier hours, is also known as a *code-behind*. Listing 6.2 is an example of what you will see when you look at the code component of your Web form.

In its simplest form, a code-behind is a file that contains code. The code is bound to system events and other events generated by the visual elements of a Web form, as shown in line 42 of Listing 6.1, where the `onclick` event is bound to `btnSave_Click` (`onclick="btnSave_Click"`). This is a drastic change from ASP, where the code for both the code component and the visual component were in the same file. Code-behinds can be written with any .NET-compliant language, but the most common languages are VB.NET and C#.

6

LISTING 6.2   *UserProfile.aspx.vb* Source Code

```
 1: Imports System
 2: Imports System.ComponentModel.Design
 3: Imports System.Data
 4: Imports System.Drawing
 5: Imports System.Web
 6: Imports System.Web.SessionState
 7: Imports System.Web.UI
 8: Imports System.Web.UI.WebControls
 9: Imports System.Web.UI.HtmlControls
10: Imports Microsoft.VisualBasic
11:
12: Public Class UserProfile
13:     Inherits System.Web.UI.Page
14:     Protected WithEvents btnSave As System.Web.UI.WebControls.Button
15:     Protected WithEvents btnReset As
➥System.Web.UI.HtmlControls.HtmlInputButton
16:     Protected WithEvents txtPostalCode As System.Web.UI.WebControls.TextBox
17:     Protected WithEvents lblPostalCode As System.Web.UI.WebControls.Label
18:     Protected WithEvents txtState As System.Web.UI.WebControls.TextBox
19:     Protected WithEvents lblState As System.Web.UI.WebControls.Label
20:     Protected WithEvents txtCity As System.Web.UI.WebControls.TextBox
21:     Protected WithEvents lblCity As System.Web.UI.WebControls.Label
22:     Protected WithEvents txtAddress2 As System.Web.UI.WebControls.TextBox
23:     Protected WithEvents lblAddress2 As System.Web.UI.WebControls.Label
24:     Protected WithEvents txtAddress1 As System.Web.UI.WebControls.TextBox
25:     Protected WithEvents lblAddress1 As System.Web.UI.WebControls.Label
26:     Protected WithEvents txtLastName As System.Web.UI.WebControls.TextBox
27:     Protected WithEvents lblLastName As System.Web.UI.WebControls.Label
28:     Protected WithEvents txtFirstName As System.Web.UI.WebControls.TextBox
29:     Protected WithEvents lblFirstName As System.Web.UI.WebControls.Label
30:     Protected WithEvents lblHeader As System.Web.UI.WebControls.Label
31:
32: #Region " Web Forms Designer Generated Code "
33:
34:     Dim WithEvents WebForm1 As System.Web.UI.Page
35:
36:     Sub New()
37:         UserProfile = Me
38:     End Sub
39:
40:     'CODEGEN: This procedure is required by the Web Form Designer
41:     'Do not modify it using the code editor.
42:     Private Sub InitializeComponent()
43:
44:     End Sub
45:
46: #End Region
47:
```

LISTING 6.2   continued

```
48:     Protected Sub UserProfile_Load(ByVal Sender As System.Object,
➥ByVal e As System.EventArgs)
49:         If Not IsPostback Then    ' Evals true first time browser hits
➥the page
50:
51:         End If
52:     End Sub
53:
54:     Protected Sub UserProfile_Init(ByVal Sender As System.Object,
➥ByVal e As System.EventArgs)
55:         'CODEGEN: This method call is required by the Web Form Designer
56:         'Do not modify it using the code editor.
57:         InitializeComponent()
58:     End Sub
59:
60:     Public Sub btnSave_Click(ByVal Sender As System.Object,
➥ByVal e As System.EventArgs)
61:
62:         'Do something with the data
63:
64:     End Sub
65: End Class
```

As you can see, a significant amount of code is created for each visual component. Lines 1–10 initialize the page by importing all the namespaces it will need. Line 12 creates the class for this code-behind, and line 13 inherits the Page class for this class to extend.

> A shortcut for inheriting the Page class is to use the following syntax when declaring the public class for the code-behind:
>
> Public Class UserProfile : Inherits System.Web.UI.Page

6

Lines 14–30 declare the variables that correspond to the Web form server controls and HTML server controls on the visual component of the Web form. The WithEvents keyword tells the compiler that these are objects that respond to events on the visual component of the page.

Lines 32–46 are generated automatically by VS.NET. This code is necessary for the Web form designer, which you will be introduced to later in this hour.

Lines 48–64 are methods that correspond to events initiated by the page and elements on the visual component. The Load and Initialize events are discussed in more detail in the next section, "Web Forms Page Processing." The last method was created to handle the onclick event for the button btnSave. When the button is clicked, an onclick event is raised. The custom method `btnSave_Click` captures and executes this event, and the data sent from the browser is then processed on the server.

Now that we've looked at what's going on behind the scenes with Web forms, let's see the source code generated by ASP.NET when the page is accessed by a browser. Listing 6.3 displays the source code of the Web form, and Figure 6.2 shows what the page looks like when viewed with Internet Explorer 5.5.

FIGURE 6.2

`UserProfile.aspx` *in Internet Explorer 5.5.*

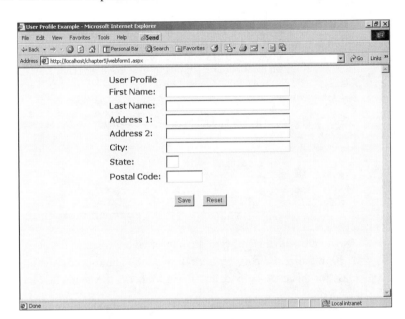

LISTING 6.3 *UserProfile.aspx* Source Code from Internet Explorer 5.5

```
1: <html><head>
2: <title>User Profile Example</title>
3:    <LINK rel="stylesheet" type="text/css"
➥href="http://OSIRIS_HOME/UserProfileExample/Styles.css">
</head>
4:    <body bgcolor="#ffffcc">
5:       <form name="frmUserProfile" method="post" action="userprofile.aspx"
➥id="frmUserProfile">
6: <input type="hidden" name="__VIEWSTATE"
➥value="YTB6LTUzNDczMzg4Ml9fX3g=83f0ed73" />
7:       <table id="tblUserProfile" border="0" align="center" cellspacing="1"
➥cellpadding="1">
8:          <tr>
9:             <td colspan="2"><span id="lblHeader" style="font-weight:bold;
➥height:19px;width:115px;">
User Profile</span></td>
```

LISTING 6.3 continued

```
10:        </tr>
11:        <tr>
12:            <td valign="middle"><span id="lblFirstName" style="font-size:
➥Small;
font-weight:bold;height:19px;width:115px;">First Name:</span></td>
13:            <td valign="middle"><input name="txtFirstName" type="text"
➥value="asdfasf as"
id="txtFirstName" style="height:24px;width:266px;" /></td>
14:        </tr>
15:        <tr>
16:            <td valign="middle"><span id="lblLastName"
➥style="font-weight:bold;height:19px;width:118px;">Last Name:</span>
➥</td>
17:            <td valign="middle"><input name="txtLastName" type="text"
➥value="asdf 34 34t "
id="txtLastName" style="height:24px;width:266px;" /></td>
18:        </tr>
19:        <tr>
20:            <td valign="middle"><span id="lblAddress1"
➥style="font-weight:bold;height:19px;width:118px;">Address 1:</span>
➥</td>
21:            <td valign="middle"><input name="txtAddress1" type="text"
➥id="txtAddress1" style="height:24px;width:266px;" /></td>
22:        </tr>
23:        <tr>
24:            <td valign="middle"><span id="lblAddress2"
➥style="font-weight:bold;height:19px;width:118px;">Address 2:</span>
➥</td>
25:            <td valign="middle"><input name="txtAddress2" type="text"
➥value="asdgf 2 " id="txtAddress2" style="height:24px;width:266px;
➥" /></td>
26:        </tr>
27:        <tr>
28:            <td valign="middle"><span id="lblCity"
➥style="font-weight:bold;height:19px;width:118px;">City:</span></td>
29:            <td valign="middle"><input name="txtCity" type="text"
➥value="2 r23223r" id="txtCity"
style="height:24px;width:266px;" /></td>
30:        </tr>
31:        <tr>
32:            <td valign="middle"><span id="lblState"
➥style="font-weight:bold;height:19px;width:118px;">State:</span></td>
33:            <td valign="middle"><input name="txtState" type="text"
➥value="23" maxlength="2"
id="txtState" style="height:26px;width:28px;" /></td>
34:        </tr>
35:        <tr>
36:            <td valign="middle"><span id="lblPostalCode"
➥style="font-weight:bold;height:19px;width:118px;">Postal Code:
➥</span></td>
```

6

LISTING **6.3**   continued

```
37:               <td valign="middle"><input name="txtPostalCode" type="text"
➥maxlength="10" id="txtPostalCode" style="height:26px;width:78px;
➥" /></td>
38:        </tr>
39:        <tr><td colspan="2"> </td></tr>
40:        <tr>
41:            <td align="center" colspan="2">
42:                <input type="submit" name="btnSave" value="Save"
➥id="btnSave" />  
43:                <input name="btnReset" id="btnReset" type="reset"
➥value="Reset" />
44:            </td>
45:        </tr>
46:    </table>
47:    </form>
48:  </body></html>
```

Listing 6.3 and Figure 6.2 show how everything comes together to create a Web page that contains common HTML. The only difference you will notice from other HTML files is the inclusion of a type="hidden" input tag in line 6. There is nothing unusual about input tags, but this particular input tag is used to save state between multiple roundtrips to the server. This means that when a roundtrip is made to the server and back to the browser, the information input by the user is not lost. In ASP, saving state was no simple task and resulted in some very creative solutions; in ASP.NET, you don't have to concern yourself with passing data back and forth when building your application.

Web Forms Page Processing

So that you better understand how Web forms work, we are going to focus on what happens when the Web server processes them. The important thing to remember is that ASP.NET applications are very much like other Web applications in that information is passed to and from the Web server via HTTP. Also remember that a Web page exists in the stateless environment of the Internet; that is, the server only knows about the call it is currently processing and does not remember anything about previous or future calls. When you call a Web page, the server responds to your request and then promptly forgets about you; it didn't know anything about you prior to the request, and it doesn't know or care if you will ever return. A stateless environment is not a product of ASP.NET but rather of HTTP and its lack of a persistent connection. Before getting into what happens when a Web form is processed, let's take a look at the lifecycle of a Web form in a Web application.

Web Form Lifecycle

When a user requests a Web page from a Web server, several things happen. First, the page is created by the server and streamed down to the client browser. Next, the user interacts with the page by submitting the form back to the server for processing. The Web server may automatically return a Web page to the user in the same state it was in before it left. This may be a lot to swallow at once, so let's break it down:

- The user requests a Web page for the first time. The Web server compiles the Web form and streams the content to the browser.

- The user then interacts with the Web page, causing it to be submitted to the Web server, by clicking a button or hyperlink.

- If the user clicks a button, the form is submitted to the server, where the button's `onclick` event is fired, some processing occurs, and the page is sent back to the user with potential modifications as a result of the processing. This is known as a *roundtrip*, where the form is posted, or *submitted*, back to the server for processing and then returned to the user.

- During this whole process, any data on the page is automatically preserved by the Web server and returned back to the user when a roundtrip is completed. This topic is further explored in the next section, "State Management."

> Not all form elements cause a postback to the Web server. Because this involves a roundtrip to the Web server and back, it is not feasible for all events to be sent back to the server for processing. For example, it would not be feasible for the `onmouseover` event, which has a high rate of fire, to always post back to the Web server. This would have an adverse effect on response time for the application.
>
> Note that the `onmouseover` event is commonly used for graphic rollovers (that is, when you move your mouse pointer over a graphic, the picture changes to some other graphic).

6

Now let's review the stages a Web form goes through during processing. When a page is processed, it goes through a series of stages in which the page processor calls a specific method. These methods are defined in Table 6.1.

TABLE 6.1 Typical Processing Stages for Web Forms

Stage	Description
Configuration	This stage checks to see whether this is the first time the page has been accessed. If it's not, this stage restores the values preserved by the Web server and then fires the Page_Load event.
Event Handling	If the page was called in response to a form event, the Event Handling stage fires off the event and then checks to see whether any other events need to be triggered.
Cleanup	When the page has finished rendering, the Cleanup stage discards any resource-intensive objects, such as database connections, and discards the page from the server.

Now that you have a basic understanding of what happens when a page is processed, let's take a look at how state management is achieved in ASP.NET.

State Management

State management is the process of preserving and managing values and data in a traditionally stateless environment, such as the Internet. Every time a page is rendered on a Web server and sent to the client, the page is then discarded along with all the information important to that page. Web programmers have created ways to overcome this obstacle and retain data across multiple trips to and from the Web server. One such method involves posting form data, returning that data parsed from the query string of the URL, posting the data back to itself, and then retrieving the values from the Request object.

In ASP.NET, the values, properties, and variables of a form are automatically maintained and preserved by the Web server across roundtrips and across other pages. There are several methods of retaining state information in your Web application. These methods are discussed in more detail in Hour 9, "ASP.NET Web Applications."

Web Forms Event Model

Events on Web form pages are captured by the browser and transmitted to the Web server for processing. All processing of Web form server controls is executed on the Web server. The data entered by the user can be processed in a number of ways, such as performing edits, sending an e-mail, and saving the data in a database. Because the Web server handles events for Web form server controls, many events are not supported. For example, the onmouseover event is not supported because it would cause a high rate of postbacks to the Web server, which in turn would have an adverse effect on performance. HTML server controls, on the other hand, have a default server-side event, such as the click event or the change event, but they also have events that are controlled via client-side script. This provides you with more flexibility when developing applications with server controls.

Some server controls allow for child controls that have events within them. Instead of each child control raising its own event, the event will bubble up to the parent control. The parent control then raises an event called ItemCommand, which informs the server which child control raised the original event.

If you paid attention in Listing 6.2, you probably noticed a pattern in the events of the code-behind. Take the following event declaration, for example:

```
Public Sub btnSave_Click(ByVal Sender As System.Object, ByVal e As
System.EventArgs)
```

This function is used to handle the click event of the Save button on the UserProfile.aspx Web form. The sub contains two arguments that are required by all server-side events for both Web form and HTML server controls. The first argument, ByVal Sender as System.Object, is an object that represents the object that raised the event. For example, if the button was clicked on UserProfile.aspx, then Sender would be an object that represents the button on the ASPX page. The second argument, ByVal e as System.EventArgs, is an object that contains event-specific information for that control. Some controls don't use the EventArgs object as the second argument to the event. An example of this type of control is the ImageButton server control. This control has a second argument called ImageClickEventArgs, which contains, among other things, coordinates where the user clicked on the image.

Using Web Forms with Visual Studio.NET

Now comes the good part. Building your first ASP.NET application and adding Web forms to it. For this part of the hour, we are going to create a Web application that needs a user-profile page. The first step is to create the Web application. Then we will add the Web form to the application. This form will be used in Hour 7, "Web Forms Server Controls."

Creating a Web Application

The first step in creating a Web application is to open VS.NET. Then follow these steps to create a Web application:

6

1. After you have opened Visual Studio.NET, click the Create New Project link in the center of VS Home Page or click the New Project icon on the toolbar.

2. When the Create New Project dialog box appears, click Visual Basic Projects under Project Types and click Web Application under Templates. Then enter **UserProfileExample** in the Project Name text box. Your screen should look like the one shown in Figure 6.3. Click OK to continue.

FIGURE 6.3
The New Project dialog box.

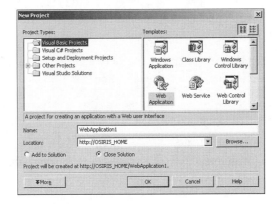

3. VS.NET will set out to create your Web application. This process can take a few moments. Once the project creation is complete, you will be presented with a blank Web form called WebForm1.aspx, and we are ready to add a new Web form to the project.

Adding Web Forms to a Web Application

Now that your project has been created, let's add a Web form to it. Follow these steps to add a Web form to your project:

1. Right-click the project name and select Add, Add Web Form. Figure 6.4 illustrates the menu selection to add a Web form.

2. When the Add New Item dialog box appears, enter **UserProfile.aspx** in the Name field. Click the Open button to continue.

3. The UserProfile.aspx file will then be added to your project, and it will be displayed in the development window.

FIGURE 6.4

Adding a Web form to your Web application.

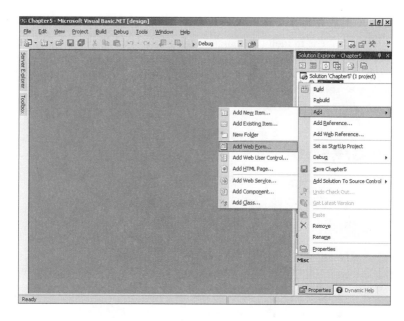

FIGURE 6.4

Adding a Web form to your Web application.

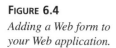

The next step in the process is to add server controls to the Web form. This step will be continued in Hour 7.

Summary

In this hour, you have been introduced to Web forms, an ASP.NET technology that allows you, the developer, to create dynamic, code-driven Web pages with ease. You learned that a Web form is divided into two parts: the visual component and the code-behind. The two parts become a whole when processed and display as normal HTML to the Web browser. You also learned what happens when a page is processed as well as what events are supported by Web forms. Finally, you created your first ASP.NET Web application and added a Web form to it. In Hour 7, you will work with the server controls to create a rich Web page that collects user-profile information.

Q&A

Q. What two types of events are most commonly supported by server-side event programming?

A. The click event and the change event are the two most commonly supported server-side events.

Q. What is the function of the hidden input tag on a rendered Web form page?

A. The hidden tag contains an ID value that allows the Web server to maintain state on the page. This allows data stored in controls to remain in those controls when the page is posted to the server and back to the client.

Workshop

The quiz questions and exercises are provided for your further understanding of the material.

Quiz

1. What two attributes are common among server controls?
2. What two files are associated with a Web form and what is their purpose?
3. What class is inherited by all Web form code-behinds?
4. What are the three processing stages of a Web form?

Answers for Hour 6

Quiz

1. What two attributes are common among server controls?

   `id` and `runat`.

2. What two files are associated with a Web form and what is their purpose?

   aspx for visual presentation and vb for the code that provides page functionality.

3. What class is inherited by all Web form code-behinds?

   `System.Web.UI.Page`.

4. What are the three processing stages of a Web form?

   Configuration, Event Handling, Cleanup.

HOUR 7

Web Forms Server Controls

ASP.NET applications contain Web forms that are processed on the Web server and streamed down to the client's browser. These Web forms usually contain controls for displaying and gathering information, as well as for reacting to user actions.

In this hour, we will discuss the following:

- The four types of server controls
- Some of the most common controls, as both HTML and ASP.NET server controls

What Are Server Controls?

Before ASP.NET, pages were considered programmable. When a Web page was processed at the server, you could use VBScript to customize its appearance based on the user's identity or other user input. ASP.NET takes that a step further. The Web page is now a Web form containing *server controls*.

Server controls are components that can be programmed at the server and provide an object model that can be referenced in the code of the Web form. When a client browser references the Web form, the server controls generate the specific HTML elements and attributes as text and stream the text down to the browser.

Four types of controls can be used on Web forms:

- HTML server controls
- ASP.NET server controls
- Validation controls
- User controls

You can use more than one type of control on the same Web form.

HTML Server Controls

HTML server controls are really just programmable versions of HTML elements. They are programmable both on the server and in the client's browser. On the server, the attributes of the HTML elements are implemented as properties; all values for the attributes are strings. Within the client's browser (for example, Internet Explorer), the control can be referenced in client-side scripts because it will appear as a standard HTML element in the browser.

ASP.NET Server Controls

ASP.NET server controls have more features than the HTML server controls, and do not correspond directly to HTML elements. ASP.NET server controls can detect the client's browser type in order to generate appropriate HTML for down-level (HTML 3.2 and earlier) browsers.

ASP.NET server controls provide a richer object model where the properties and methods for objects are strongly typed, meaning that you can use variable types other than just strings.

Validation Controls

Validation controls are special types of controls that are used to test a user's input against specific criteria. They can be used with either ASP.NET or HTML server controls.

User Controls

User controls are controls that are created as Web forms and embedded in other Web forms. They allow you to create reusable components and develop complex user-input controls.

Using HTML Server Controls

HTML server controls are not new; they are standard HTML elements with special server-processing attributes added. Listing 7.1 is an example of standard HTML elements on a standard HTML form.

LISTING 7.1   Example of Standard HTML Elements on a Form

```
 1: <html>
 2: <body>
 3: <form name="WebForm1" method="post">
 4:  <table align="center">
 5:   <tr>
 6:    <td>
 7:     Name:
 8:    </td>
 9:    <td>
10:     <input type="text" name="txtName">
11:    </td>
12:   </tr>
13:   <tr>
14:    <td>
15:     Password:
16:    </td>
17:    <td>
18:     <input type="password" name="txtName">
19:    </td>
20:   </tr>
21:   <tr>
22:    <td colspan="2">
23:      
24:    </td>
25:   </tr>
26:   <tr>
27:    <td colspan="2" align="center">
28:     <input type="submit" name="btnSubmit" value="Submit">
29:    </td>
30:   </tr>
31:  </table>
32: </form>
33: </body>
34: </html>
```

Figure 7.1 shows the result as it appears in a browser.

7

FIGURE 7.1

Standard HTML elements on a form.

To use HTML server controls, you need to add the `runat="server"` and `id="[somevalue]"` attributes to the HTML element you want to be able to program on the server, and to include the `runat="server"` attribute in the form in which the HTML element is defined. The filename must end with the `.aspx` extension. When this is done, your HTML pages will be transformed into Web forms. Listing 7.2 shows the changes that need to be made to convert the HTML controls in Listing 7.1 to HTML server controls.

LISTING 7.2 Example Showing HTML Elements Converted to HTML Server Controls

```
1: <html>
2: <script language="VB" runat="server">
3: Sub btnSubmit_Click(Source as Object, E as EventArgs)
4:
5: End Sub
6: </script>
7: <body>
8: <form name="WebForm1" method="post" runat="server" id="WebForm1">
9:  <table align="center" runat="server" id="tblUser">
10:   <tr>
11:   <td>
12:    Name:
13:   </td>
14:   <td>
15:    <input type="text" name="txtName" runat="server" id="txtName">
16:   </td>
```

LISTING 7.2   continued

```
17:    </tr>
18:    <tr>
19:     <td>
20:      Password:
21:     </td>
22:     <td>
23:      <input type="password"
24:      name="txtPassword"
25:       runat="server"
26:       id="txtPassword">
27:     </td>
28:    </tr>
29:    <tr>
30:     <td colspan="2">
31:       
32:     </td>
33:    </tr>
34:    <tr>
35:     <td colspan="2" align="center">
36:      <input type="submit"
37:       name="btnSubmit"
38:       value="Submit"
39:       runat="server"
40:       id="btnSubmit"
41:       OnServerClick="btnSubmit_Click">
42:     </td>
43:    </tr>
44:   </table>
45: </form>
46: </body>
47: </html>
```

Figure 7.2 shows the results.

Listing 7.2 shows the syntax requirements for converting standard HTML elements into server controls. These basic changes apply to all HTML elements.

One immediate benefit to converting to server controls is the automatic state management of ASP.NET Web forms. Any values that your HTML controls contain when the form is submitted will be managed automatically. If your form is posted back to itself, the controls will automatically have the values they had when the form was submitted to the server.

Programming Event Handlers for HTML Server Controls

As mentioned earlier, HTML server controls can be programmed at the server. Programming event handlers for server controls is a common example of this.

7

FIGURE 7.2
*HTML elements con-
verted to HTML server
controls.*

 We introduced earlier, in Hour 5, the idea of separating user-interface code from application logic by using the CodeBehind directive to indicate that the application logic is in a separate code file. For the sake of simplifying the HTML server control examples, we will write the application logic in the same file as the user interface. We will show examples of the CodeBehind directive in the "Using ASP.NET Server Controls" section of this hour.

To add an event handler to our previous example, we need to add a script block with, guess what, the runat="server" attribute. We then add the code to respond to the events that the controls on the form generate. Listing 7.3 shows the implementation of the event handler for the Submit button on the form.

LISTING 7.3   Example of Client-Side and Server-Side Event Handlers and Dynamic HTML Server-Control Creation

```
1: <html>
2: <head>
3: <script language="VB" runat="server">
4:  Sub btnSubmit_Click(Source as Object, E as EventArgs)
5:   Dim objRow as HTMLTableRow
6:   Dim objCell as HTMLTableCell
7:
8:   objRow = new HTMLTableRow
9:   objCell = new HTMLTableCell
```

LISTING 7.3   continued

```
10:    objCell.ColSpan=2
11:    objCell.Align="Center"
12:    if (txtName.Value="anonymous") and (txtPassword.Value="password") then
13:     objRow.BgColor = "Green"
14:     objCell.InnerText = "Login Successful!"
15:    else
16:     objRow.BgColor = "Red"
17:     objCell.InnerText = "Login Failed!"
18:    end if
19:    objRow.Cells.Add(objCell)
20:    tblUser.Rows.Add(objRow)
21:   End Sub
22: </script>
23: <script language="JavaScript">
24:   var doSubmit=true;
25:   function clientSubmit(){
26:    return(doSubmit);
27:   }
28:   function Client_Click(){
29:    doSubmit = confirm("Are you sure you want to submit this form?");
30:   }
31: </script>
32: <body>
33: <form name="WebForm1"
34:  method="post"
35:  runat="server"
36:  id="WebForm1"
37:  OnSubmit="return clientSubmit();"
38:  >
39:  <table align="center"  runat="server" id="tblUser">
40:   <tr>
41:    <td>
42:     Name:
43:    </td>
44:    <td>
45:     <input type="text" name="txtName" runat="server" id="txtName">
46:    </td>
47:   </tr>
48:   <tr>
49:    <td>
50:     Password:
51:    </td>
52:    <td>
53:     <input type="password"
54:       name="txtPassword"
55:       runat="server"
56:       id="txtPassword">
57:    </td>
58:   </tr>
```

7

LISTING 7.3 continued

```
59:    <tr>
60:    <td colspan="2">
61:      
62:    </td>
63:    </tr>
64:    <tr>
65:    <td colspan="2" align="center">
66:     <input type="submit"
67:      name="btnSubmit"
68:      value="Submit"
69:      runat="server"
70:      id="btnSubmit"
71:      OnClick="Client_Click()"
72:      OnServerClick="btnSubmit_Click">
73:    </td>
74:    </tr>
75:   </table>
76:  </form>
77:  </body>
78:  </html>
```

Listing 7.3 shows examples of both client- and server-side event handlers, and demonstrates how to dynamically add controls to a Web form. The `btnSubmit` control has two new attributes: `OnClick="Client_Click()"` and `OnServerClick="btnSubmit_Click"`. The first tells the browser to handle a client-side click event by executing the client-side event handler `"Client_Click()"`, which is implemented in a JavaScript script block in lines 23 through 31 of Listing 7.3. Figure 7.3 shows the `OnClick` event handler.

The second new attribute tells the server to handle the click event by executing the server-side event handler `"btnSubmit_Click"`, which is implemented in Visual Basic in lines 3 through 22 in Listing 7.3. The form also has a client-side event handler called `clientSubmit()`, which is implemented in JavaScript in lines 25 through 27.

Two other server-side events can be implemented in your code: `OnServerChange` (for `<input type=text|hidden|checkbox ...>`, `<select>...</select>`, and `<textarea>...</textarea>` elements), and `OnServerValidate` for validation controls.

Let's walk through the code shown in Listing 7.3. When the Web form is displayed, you are presented with name (line 45) and password text-input (line 53) controls and a Submit button (lines 63–69). When you click the Submit button, a dialog box pops up asking whether or not you want to submit the form; it is displayed as a result of the `OnClick` client-side event handler, declared on line 68. If you select OK, the form is submitted. If you select Cancel, the form is not submitted: The form's `OnSubmit` client-side event handler cancels the submit action if the Boolean variable that received the result of the confirmation dialog box is false (see lines 24–30). This is an example of both client and server programming of an HTML server control. When the form is submitted to the server, when you select Yes from the confirmation dialog box, the server-side event handler `btnSubmit_Click` is executed (see lines 4–23).

FIGURE 7.3

Client-side `OnClick` event handler.

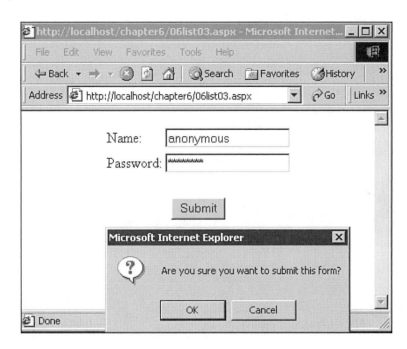

This block of code demonstrates dynamically creating HTML server controls by using instances of an `HTMLTableRow` and an `HTMLTableCell` control (lines 5–9). It then sets some attributes for these controls, such as alignment and number of columns to span(lines 10–11). Then, it determines what color to use for the background of the new row based on the values passed for the Name and Password on the Web form. The text for the new cell is assigned using the `InnerText` property of the `HTMLTableCell` control (lines 12–18). The `InnerText` and `InnerHTML` properties are available for any HTML element that is required to have a closing tag. This includes the following HTML elements with their HTML server-control counterparts:

```
<table></table>        HTMLTable
<tr></tr>              HTMLTableRow
```

7

`<td></td>`	HTMLTableCell
`<button></button>`	HTMLButton
`<form></form>`	HTMLForm
`<a></a>`	HTMLAnchor
`<select></select>`	HTMLSelect
`<textarea></textarea>`	HTMLTextArea

The `HTMLGenericControl` is a special HTML server control that handles HTML elements that do not correspond directly to HTML server controls, such as the `<span>`, `<font>`, `<body>`, and `<div>` elements. This control also implements the `InnerText` and `InnerHTML` properties.

The last step we perform is adding the newly created and formatted row to the rows collection of the table control, `tblUser`. Figures 7.4 and 7.5 show the dynamically created table row and table cell controls in a client browser.

FIGURE 7.4

Adding `HTMLTableRow` *and* `HTMLTableCell` *controls dynamically.*

FIGURE 7.5
*Incorrect name and
password entered.*

You can also add new controls to the form's `Controls` collection. For example, the following code creates a new button with some JavaScript to display a message box when it is clicked. The JavaScript code is added as an attribute of the new button control in line 3 of Listing 7.4.

LISTING 7.4   Adding a Control to the Form's `Controls` Collection

```
1: Dim objButton As New Button()
2: objButton.Text = "Dynamic Button"
3: objButton.Attributes.Add("OnClick", "alert(" & "'" & "I am Dynamic" & "')")
4: objButton.Visible = True
5: WebForm1.Controls.Add(objButton)
```

The `Attributes` collection allows you to specify individual HTML attributes for any given HTML element. These attributes are passed through to the browser for processing. In Listing 7.4, we added the attribute `"OnClick"` to a dynamically created button and assigned its value to some JavaScript to generate a message box when the button is clicked.

7

Using ASP.NET Server Controls

ASP.NET server controls can be added directly to .aspx files. These controls are declared with the `<asp:servercontrol>` tag, which references the asp namespace, where *servercontrol* is the name of the specific control you are instantiating. All ASP.NET server controls must be properly closed with an ending `</asp:servercontrol>` tag.

ASP.NET server controls are similar to HTML server controls in that they also require the `runat="server"` and `id=someuniquevalue` attributes.

Using Visual Studio.NET

To see the use of ASP.NET server controls, open Visual Studio.NET and create a new Visual Basic Web application. Visual Studio will add a starting Web form named WebForm1 to your new application for you. It will also create a code-behind file named `WebForm1.aspx.vb`, and will configure your Web form to use this file.

The default view for the Web form is Design, as shown in Figure 7.6. Change to HTML view by clicking the HTML tab at the bottom of the design window. Figure 7.7 shows the HTML view.

FIGURE 7.6

New VB Web application in Visual Studio.NET: Default form view is Design.

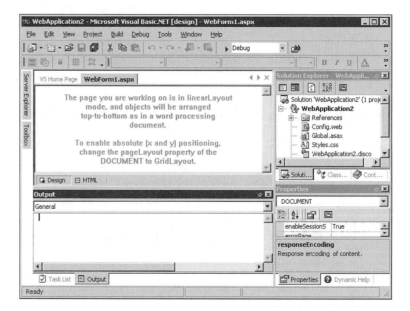

Notice the Codebehind directive at the top of the page that tells ASP.NET where to go to find the application logic that processes your user-interface Web form. Now we can start adding ASP.NET server controls to our Web form. First, we want to declare a table with four rows and two columns. We are going to use an ASP.NET server table control because we will eventually add code to dynamically add a row and button to this table. Listing 7.5 shows the code to create the ASP.NET table.

FIGURE 7.7

Visual Studio HTML form view.

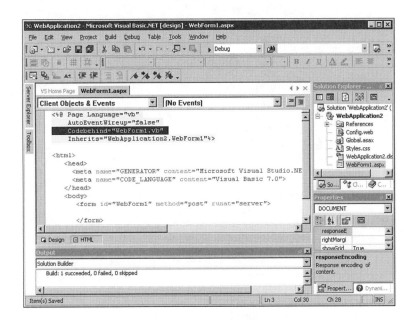

LISTING 7.5 Adding an ASP.NET Table Control to a Web Form

```
 1: <%@ Page Language="vb"
 2: AutoEventWireup="false"
 3: Codebehind="WebForm1.aspx.vb"
 4: Inherits="WebApplication2.WebForm1"%>
 5: <html>
 6: <head>
 7: <meta name="GENERATOR" content="Microsoft Visual Studio.NET 7.0">
 8: <meta name="CODE_LANGUAGE" content="Visual Basic 7.0">
 9: </head>
10: <body>
11:  <form id="WebForm1" method="post" runat="server">
12:   <asp:table runat=Server
13:    id=tblUser
14:    borderstyle=Double
15:    horizontalalign=center>
16:   <asp:tableRow>
```

7

LISTING 7.5 continued

```
17:    <asp:tablecell>
18:     Name
19:    </asp:tablecell>
20:    <asp:tablecell>
21:     <asp:textbox runat=Server
22:      id=txtName>
23:     </asp:textbox>
24:    </asp:tablecell>
25:   </asp:tablerow>
26:   <asp:tableRow>
27:    <asp:tablecell>
28:     Password
29:    </asp:tablecell>
30:    <asp:tablecell>
31:     <asp:textbox runat=Server
32:      id=txtPassword
33:      textmode=Password>
34:     </asp:textbox>
35:    </asp:tablecell>
36:   </asp:tablerow>
37:   <asp:tableRow>
38:    <asp:tablecell columnspan=2>
39:    </asp:tablecell>
40:   </asp:tablerow>
41:   <asp:tableRow>
42:    <asp:tablecell columnspan=2 horizontalalign=Center>
43:     <asp:button runat=Server
44:      id=btnSubmit
45:      text="Submit">
46:     </asp:button>
47:    </asp:tablecell>
48:   </asp:tablerow>
49:   </asp:table>
50:  </form>
51: </body>
52: </html>
```

The code in Listing 7.5 also includes the declarations of a TextBox control for the name, a text password control for the password, and a button to submit the form to the server for processing. If you compile this code and then view it in a browser, the output should appear as shown in Figure 7.8.

FIGURE 7.8

Simple Web application demonstrating ASP.NET server controls.

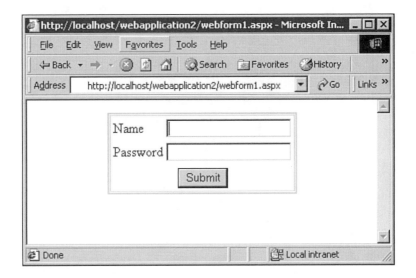

If you enter text in some TextBox controls, and then click the Submit button, you'll notice that the values remain after the form has been rendered again in the browser. This form posts to itself, and because we are using server controls, state management is handled for us, meaning that the values are preserved and reassigned when the page is sent back to the browser. This is true only for server controls that are declared at compile time. If you generate any server controls dynamically, you will have to manage their state manually.

Programming Event Handlers for ASP.NET Server Controls

Now let's add an event handler for the Submit button to evaluate the text values entered and create a new row for the table and display a message. To edit the code-behind file, select View, Code from the menu. Then select the btnSubmit class from the Class drop-down list control in the upper-left corner of the code window, and the Click method from the Method drop-down list control in the upper-right corner of the design window. Figure 7.9 shows the results.

The code for the event handler should look like that shown in Listing 7.6.

7

FIGURE 7.9

Adding an event handler for the Click *event of the Submit button.*

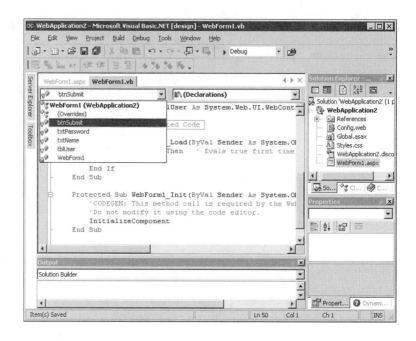

FIGURE 7.9

Adding an event handler for the Click *event of the Submit button.*

LISTING 7.6   Adding a Server-Side Event Handler

```
1: Public Sub btnSubmit_Click(ByVal sender As Object, ByVal e As
➥System.EventArgs) Handles btnSubmit.Click
2:   Dim objRow As TableRow
3:   Dim objCell As TableCell
4:   objRow = New TableRow()
5:   objCell = New TableCell()
6:   objCell.ColumnSpan = 2
7:   objCell.HorizontalAlign = WebControls.HorizontalAlign.Center
8:   If (txtName.Text = "anonymous") And (txtPassword.Text = "password") Then
9:     objRow.BackColor = Color.Green
10:    objCell.Text = "Login Successful!"
11:  Else
12:    objRow.BackColor = Color.Red
13:    objCell.Text = "Login Failed!"
14:  End If
15:  objRow.Cells.Add(objCell)
16:  tblUser.Rows.Add(objRow)
17: End Sub
```

This code is similar to the event handler we developed in the "Using HTML Server Controls" section earlier. But instead of using HTMLTableRow and HTMLTableCell, we are using TableRow and TableCell objects, because we originally declared our table as an

ASP.NET `Table` control. If you try to use the HTML versions of objects with controls that are originally declared as ASP.NET controls, you will get a compile error.

> As noted earlier, you *can* mix the types of controls on a Web form, but you need to be consistent with object and control types when you are programming against your controls on a Web form.

The property names are different for the ASP.NET versions of the objects. The `Text`, `BackColor`, and `HorizontalAlign` properties are examples of properties that are common to some ASP.NET server controls.

When you are working with a Web form that has a code-behind file, such as our example, you need to compile the project before you can see the application in a browser. To compile a VB Web application in Visual Studio, select Build, Build from the menu. Figure 7.10 shows a successful result in the browser. If there are any errors, they will be displayed in an Output window (see Figure 7.11). When the application has compiled successfully, test it in a browser.

FIGURE 7.10

VB Web application showing server-side event handler.

To demonstrate other ASP.NET server controls, we will modify the login page to redirect to a new page if the login is successful. This new page will be a user-profile page designed to gather information about the user, such as name, address, e-mail address, street address, and so on.

7

FIGURE 7.11

Incorrect name and password submitted.

The first step is to modify the event handler for the Submit button. The changes shown in Listing 7.7 implement the redirection.

LISTING 7.7   Modifying an Event Handler to Redirect to Another Page

```
 1: Public Sub btnSubmit_Click(ByVal sender As Object, ByVal e As
➥System.EventArgs) Handles btnSubmit.Click
 2:   Dim objRow As TableRow
 3:   Dim objCell As TableCell
 4:   objRow = New TableRow()
 5:   objCell = New TableCell()
 6:   objCell.ColumnSpan = 2
 7:   objCell.HorizontalAlign = WebControls.HorizontalAlign.Center
 8:   If (txtName.Text = "anonymous") And (txtPassword.Text = "password") Then
 9:   '    objRow.BackColor = Color.Green
10:   '    objCell.Text = "Login Successful!"
11:     Response.Redirect("UserProfile.aspx")
12:   Else
13:     objRow.BackColor = Color.Red
14:     objCell.Text = "Login Failed!"
15:     objRow.Cells.Add(objCell)
16:     tblUser.Rows.Add(objRow)
17:   End If
18:   '  objRow.Cells.Add(objCell)
19:   '  tblUser.Rows.Add(objRow)
20: End Sub
```

Now we need to create a new Web form for our user profile. Select Project, Add Web Form from the menu in Visual Studio. Specify UserProfile.aspx as the name of the new form. Then switch to the HTML view and add the code shown in Listing 7.8.

LISTING 7.8 Code for User Profile Web Form

```
 1: <%@ Page Language="vb"
 2: AutoEventWireup="false"
 3: Codebehind="UserProfile.aspx.vb"
 4: Inherits="WebApplication2.UserProfile"%>
 5: <html>
 6: <head>
 7:  <TITLE>User Profile</TITLE>
 8:  <LINK href="http://localhost/WebApplication2/Styles.css"
 9:   type="text/css"
10:   rel=stylesheet>
11:  <meta content="HTML 4.0" name=vs_targetSchema>
12:  <meta content="Microsoft Visual Studio.NET 7.0" name=GENERATOR>
13:  <meta content="Visual Basic 7.0" name=CODE_LANGUAGE></head>
14: <body text=#e00ae0>
15: <form id=UserProfile method=post runat="server">
16:  <table borderColor=maroon
17:   width=500 align=center border=1>
18:   <tr bgColor=maroon>
19:    <td colSpan=2>
20:     <table cellSpacing=0 cellPadding=3 border=0>
21:      <tr bgColor=maroon>
22:       <td class=formheader>
23:        <font color=#ffffff>
24:         User Profile
25:       </font>
26:      </td>
27:     </tr>
28:    </table>
29:   </td>
30:  </tr>
31:   <tr>
32:    <td>
33:     <table border=0>
34:      <tr>
35:       <td class=label width=200>
36:        *E-Mail Address
37:       </td>
38:       <td>
39:        <asp:textbox id=txtEmail
40:         runat="server"
41:         text=""
42:         cssclass="smalltext"
```

LISTING 7.8   continued

```
43:             width="<%#TextBoxWidth%>"
44:             maxlength="50">
45:           </asp:textbox>
46:         </td>
47:       </tr>
48:       <tr>
49:         <td class=label>
50:          *Name
51:         </td>
52:         <td>
53:           <asp:textbox id=txtFirstName
54:             runat="server"
55:             text=""
56:             cssclass="smalltext"
57:            width="<%#TextBoxWidth%>"
58:             maxlength="30">
59:           </asp:textbox>
60:         </td>
61:       </tr>
62:       <tr>
63:         <td class=label>
64:          Birth Year
65:         </td>
66:         <td>
67:           <asp:textbox id=txtBirthYear
68:             runat="server"
69:             text="1950"
70:             cssclass="smalltext"
71:            width="50"
72:             maxlength="4"
73:             ontextchanged="txtBirthYear_TextChanged"
74:             autopostback="True">
75:           </asp:textbox>
76:         </td>
77:       </tr>
78:       <tr>
79:         <td class=label>
80:          *Birth Date
81:         </td>
82:         <td>
83:         <asp:calendar id=calBirthDate
84:          runat="Server"
85:          cssclass="smalltext"
86:          titlestyle-cssclass="label"
87:          selectorstyle-cssclass="smalltext"
88:          selecteddaystyle-cssclass="smalltext"
89:          daystyle-cssclass="smalltext"
90:          dayheaderstyle-cssclass="label"
91:          TodayDayStyle-CssClass="smalltext"
```

LISTING 7.8 continued

```
 92:            forecolor="Maroon">
 93:            </asp:calendar>
 94:        </td>
 95:      </tr>
 96:      <tr>
 97:       <td colSpan=2>
 98:          <hr width="85%">
 99:        </td>
100:        </tr>
101:        <tr>
102:         <td class=label>
103:          *Address
104:         </td>
105:         <td>
106:          <asp:textbox id=txtAddress1
107:            runat="server"
108:            text=""
109:            cssclass="smalltext"
110:           width="<%#TextBoxWidth%>"
111:           maxlength="30">
112:          </asp:textbox>
113:        </td>
114:      </tr>
115:      <tr>
116:       <td class=label>
117:        *City
118:       </td>
119:       <td class=smalltext>
120:        <asp:textbox id=txtCity
121:          runat="server"
122:          text=""
123:          cssclass="smalltext"
124:         width="<%#TextBoxWidth%>"
125:         maxlength="50">
126:        </asp:textbox>
127:       </td>
128:      </tr>
129:      <tr>
130:       <td class=label>
131:        *State
132:       </td>
133:       <td>
134:        <asp:dropdownlist id=selState
135:          runat="server"
136:          cssclass="smalltext">
137:         <asp:listitem
138:         text="-Select a State-"
139:         value=""
140:         selected="True">
```

LISTING 7.8 continued

```
141:          </asp:listitem>
142:          <asp:listitem text="Alabama" value="AL"></asp:listitem>
143:          <asp:listitem text="Alaska" value="AK"></asp:listitem>
144:          <asp:listitem text="Arizona" value="AZ"></asp:listitem>
145:          <asp:listitem text="Arkansas" value="AR"></asp:listitem>
146:          <asp:listitem text="California" value="CA"></asp:listitem>
147:          <asp:listitem text="Colorado" value="CO"></asp:listitem>
148:          <asp:listitem text="Connecticut" value="CT"></asp:listitem>
149:          <asp:listitem text="Delaware" value="DE"></asp:listitem>
150:          <asp:listitem text="Florida" value="FL"></asp:listitem>
151:          <asp:listitem text="Georgia" value="GA"></asp:listitem>
152:          <asp:listitem text="Hawaii" value="HI"></asp:listitem>
153:          <asp:listitem text="Idaho" value="ID"></asp:listitem>
154:          <asp:listitem text="Illinois" value="IL"></asp:listitem>
155:          <asp:listitem text="Indiana" value="IN"></asp:listitem>
156:          <asp:listitem text="Iowa" value="IA"></asp:listitem>
157:          <asp:listitem text="Kansas" value="KS"></asp:listitem>
158:          <asp:listitem text="Kentucky" value="KY"></asp:listitem>
159:          <asp:listitem text="Louisiana" value="LA"></asp:listitem>
160:          <asp:listitem text="Maine" value="ME"></asp:listitem>
161:          <asp:listitem text="Maryland" value="MD"></asp:listitem>
162:          <asp:listitem text="Massachusetts" value="MA"></asp:listitem>
163:          <asp:listitem text="Michigan" value="MI"></asp:listitem>
164           <asp:listitem text="Minnesota" value="MN"></asp:listitem>
165:          <asp:listitem text="Mississippi" value="MS"></asp:listitem>
166:          <asp:listitem text="Missouri" value="MO"></asp:listitem>
167:          <asp:listitem text="Montana" value="MT"></asp:listitem>
168:          <asp:listitem text="Nebraska" value="NE"></asp:listitem>
169:          <asp:listitem text="Nevada" value="NV"></asp:listitem>
170:          <asp:listitem text="New Hampshire" value="NH"></asp:listitem>
171:          <asp:listitem text="New Jersey" value="NJ"></asp:listitem>
172:          <asp:listitem text="New Mexico" value="NM"></asp:listitem>
173:          <asp:listitem text="New York" value="NY"></asp:listitem>
174:          <asp:listitem text="North Carolina" value="NC"></asp:listitem>
175:          <asp:listitem text="North Dakota" value="ND"></asp:listitem>
176:          <asp:listitem text="Ohio" value="OH"></asp:listitem>
177:          <asp:listitem text="Oklahoma" value="OK"></asp:listitem>
178:          <asp:listitem text="Oregon" value="OR"></asp:listitem>
179:          <asp:listitem text="Pennsylvania" value="PA"></asp:listitem>
180:          <asp:listitem text="Rhode Island" value="RI"></asp:listitem>
181:          <asp:listitem text="South Carolina" value="SC"></asp:listitem>
182:          <asp:listitem text="South Dakota" value="SD"></asp:listitem>
183:          <asp:listitem text="Tennessee" value="TN"></asp:listitem>
184:          <asp:listitem text="Texas" value="TX"></asp:listitem>
185:          <asp:listitem text="Utah" value="UT"></asp:listitem>
186:          <asp:listitem text="Vermont" value="VT"></asp:listitem>
187:          <asp:listitem text="Virginia" value="VA"></asp:listitem>
188:          <asp:listitem text="Washington" value="WA"></asp:listitem>
189:          <asp:listitem text="Washington DC" value="DC"></asp:listitem>
```

LISTING 7.8 continued

```
190:           <asp:listitem text="West Virginia" value="WV"></asp:listitem>
191:           <asp:listitem text="Wisconsin" value="WI"></asp:listitem>
192:           <asp:listitem text="Wyoming" value="WY"></asp:listitem>
193:         </asp:dropdownlist>
194:       </td>
195:     </tr>
196:       <tr>
197:       <td class=label>
198:        *Postal Code
199:       </td>
200:       <td class=smalltext>
201:        <asp:textbox id=txtPostalCode
202:         runat="server"
203:         text=""
204:         cssclass="smalltext"
205:         width="<%#TextBoxWidth%>"
206:         maxlength="30">
207:        </asp:textbox>
208:       </td>
209:     </tr>
210:       <tr>
211:       <td colSpan=2>
212:        <hr width="85%">
213:       </td>
214:     </tr>
215:       <tr>
216:       <td class=label align=middle colSpan=2>
217:        <asp:checkbox id=chkEmails
218:         runat="Server"
219:         text="Receive email notifications about future offerings?"
220:         cssclass="label">
221:        </asp:checkbox>
222:       </td>
223:     </tr>
224:       <tr>
225:       <td class=label>
226:        How did you hear about us?
227:       </td>
228:       <td>
229:      <asp:radiobutton id=RadioButton1
230:       runat="server"
231:       checked=True
232:       CssClass="smalltext"
233:       Text="TV"
234:       GroupName="rbSource"
235:       Height="20">
236:      </asp:RadioButton><br>
237:      <asp:radiobutton id=RadioButton2
238:       runat="server"
```

7

LISTING 7.8   continued

```
239:          CssClass="smalltext"
240:          Text="Radio"
241:          GroupName="rbSource"
242:          Height="20">
243:        </asp:RadioButton><br>
244:        <asp:radiobutton id=RadioButton3
245:         runat="server"
246:         CssClass="smalltext"
247:         Text="Newspaper"
248:         GroupName="rbSource"
249:         Height="20">
250:        </asp:RadioButton>
251:      </td>
252:     </tr>
253:      <tr>
254:       <td class=label vAlign=top>
255:        Comments
256:       </td>
257:       <td>
258:        <asp:textbox id=txtComments
259:          runat="Server"
260:          columns="35"
261:          rows="3"
262:         textmode="MultiLine">
263:        </asp:textbox>
264:       </td>
265:      </tr>
266:     <tr>
267:      <td colspan="2">
268:       <hr color="maroon">
269:      </td>
270:     </tr>
271:     <tr>
272:      <td colspan="2" align="middle">
273:       <asp:button runat=Server
274:        id="btnSubmit"
275:        text="Save">
276:       </asp:button>
277:      </td>
278:     </tr>
279:     </table>
280:    </td>
281:   </tr>
282:  </table>
283: </form>
284: </body>
285: </html>
```

Cascading Style Sheets

The first new item worth noting in Listing 7.8 is the use of a cascading style sheet. A default style sheet is created for you when you make a Web application using Visual Studio. We added a couple of styles to this default style sheet and then referred to it at the top of the Web form (lines 8–10). The results are shown in Figure 7.12.

FIGURE 7.12

Two styles added to default style sheet Styles.css.

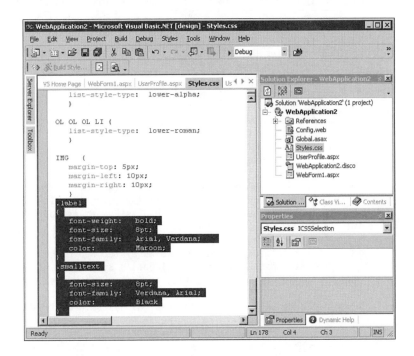

We used the styles from the style sheet for HTML element declarations as well as for ASP.NET server control declarations. Style sheets provide a way to group attributes in a global definition file so that you don't have to type the same attributes over and over again for all your element and control declarations.

Because we are using server controls, we need to have a single server form control on the page. Line 15 gives the form declaration, assigns a unique ID, and provides the required runat="server" attribute.

Data-Binding TextBox Controls

Lines 39 through 45 contain a declaration for an ASP.NET TextBox control. Note the interesting item on line 43: width="<%#TextBoxWidth%>". This is an example of data

7

binding, which is discussed in Hour 5. In this example we are using data binding to assign a width to the TextBox controls on the Web form. The <%#TextBoxWidth%> text is evaluated during the Web form's load event and replaced with the value of the TextBoxWidth variable.

LISTING 7.9   Code-Behind VB Module for User Profile Web Form

```
1: Imports System
2: Imports System.ComponentModel.Design
3: Imports System.Data
4: Imports System.Drawing
5: Imports System.Web
6: Imports System.Web.SessionState
7: Imports System.Web.UI
8: Imports System.Web.UI.WebControls
9: Imports System.Web.UI.HtmlControls
10: Imports Microsoft.VisualBasic
11: Public Class UserProfile
12:   Inherits System.Web.UI.Page
13:   Protected WithEvents btnSubmit As System.Web.UI.WebControls.Button
14:   Protected WithEvents txtComments As System.Web.UI.WebControls.TextBox
15:   Protected WithEvents RadioButton3 As System.Web.UI.WebControls.RadioButton
16:   Protected WithEvents RadioButton2 As System.Web.UI.WebControls.RadioButton
17:   Protected WithEvents RadioButton1 As System.Web.UI.WebControls.RadioButton
18:   Protected WithEvents chkEmails As System.Web.UI.WebControls.CheckBox
19:   Protected WithEvents txtPostalCode As System.Web.UI.WebControls.TextBox
20:   Protected WithEvents selState As System.Web.UI.WebControls.DropDownList
21:   Protected WithEvents txtCity As System.Web.UI.WebControls.TextBox
22:   Protected WithEvents txtAddress1 As System.Web.UI.WebControls.TextBox
23:   Protected WithEvents calBirthDate As System.Web.UI.WebControls.Calendar
24:   Protected WithEvents txtBirthYear As System.Web.UI.WebControls.TextBox
25:   Protected WithEvents txtName As System.Web.UI.WebControls.TextBox
26:   Protected WithEvents txtEmail As System.Web.UI.WebControls.TextBox
27:   Protected WithEvents tblUser As System.Web.UI.HtmlControls.HtmlTable
28:   Protected WithEvents txtDayPhone As System.Web.UI.WebControls.TextBox
29:   Public TextBoxWidth As New System.Web.UI.WebControls.Unit()
30:
31: #Region " Web Forms Designer Generated Code "
32:   Dim WithEvents UserProfile As System.Web.UI.Page
33:   Sub New()
34:     UserProfile = Me
35:   End Sub
36:   'CODEGEN: This procedure is required by the Web Form Designer
37:   'Do not modify it using the code editor.
38:   Private Sub InitializeComponent()
39:
40:   End Sub
41:
42: #End Region
```

LISTING 7.9 continued

```
43: Protected Sub UserProfile_Load(ByVal Sender As System.Object, _
44:   ByVal e As System.EventArgs)
45:   If Not IsPostback Then    ' Evals true first time browser hits the page
46:    calBirthDate.VisibleDate = DateSerial(1950, 1, 1)
47:   End If
48:   'Set up default text box width
49:   TextBoxWidth = System.Web.UI.WebControls.Unit.Pixel(300)
50:
51:   'Perform databinding to set default widths
52:   UserProfile.Page.DataBind()
53:
54: End Sub
55:
56: Protected Sub UserProfile_Init(ByVal Sender As System.Object, _
57:   ByVal e As System.EventArgs)
58:   'CODEGEN: This method call is equired by the Web Form Designer
59:   'Do not modify it using the code editor.
60:   InitializeComponent()
61: End Sub
62:
63: Public Sub txtBirthYear_TextChanged(ByVal sender As Object, _
64:   ByVal e As System.EventArgs) Handles txtBirthYear.TextChanged
65:   calBirthDate.VisibleDate = DateSerial(Cint(txtbirthyear.Text()), _
66:    1, calBirthDate.SelectedDate.Day)
67:   calBirthDate.SelectedDate = DateSerial(Cint(txtbirthyear.Text()), _
68:    1, calBirthDate.SelectedDate.Day)
69: End Sub
70:
71: Public Sub calBirthDate_VisibleMonthChanged(ByVal sender As Object, _
72:   ByVal e As System.Web.UI.WebControls.MonthChangedEventArgs) _
73:   Handles calBirthDate.VisibleMonthChanged
74:   calBirthDate.SelectedDate = DateSerial(calBirthDate.VisibleDate.Year, _
75:    calBirthDate.VisibleDate.Month, calBirthDate.SelectedDate.Day)
76: End Sub
77: End Class
```

Lines 43 through 54 in Listing 7.9 show the data-binding code. We assign the value of 300 pixels as the width to the public variable TextBoxWidth (line 49) and then call the DataBind method on the page (line 52). This in turn calls the DataBind method on all controls contained in the page.

The AutoPostBack Property

The TextBox control supports a property called AutoPostBack that, when set to True, causes the form in which this control exists to be posted to the server whenever a change

7

in its value is detected. Several other controls support this property as well, including Checkbox, RadioButton, DropDownList, and ListBox. We also assigned a server-side event handler (lines 63 through 69) for the TextChanged event for this TextBox control. It uses the text value from the txtBirthYear control to reset the VisibleDate property of the Calendar control.

The ASP.NET Calendar Control

The ASP.NET Calendar control is useful for retrieving dates on Web forms. The HTML rendered in the browser consists of a table with rows, cells, and client-side JavaScript functions that post the form back to the server. We declared a Calendar control and set some style properties in lines 83 through 93 of Listing 8.9.

The ASP.NET DropDownList Control

The ASP.NET DropDownList control is similar to the HTML <SELECT...></SELECT> element. The items in it are declared using the <asp:ListItem...></asp:ListItem> tags.

The ASP.NET CheckBox Control

The ASP.NET CheckBox can be used to retrieve or display a true or false value. To determine whether a checkbox control has been checked or unchecked, you evaluate the Checked property of the control. An example of the CheckBox control can be found in lines 217 through 221.

The ASP.NET RadioButton Control

The ASP.NET RadioButton control is used to provide a way for the user to select only one of a group of values. RadioButton controls are associated in a group by the GroupName property. Only one RadioButton control can be selected out of a group of controls that have the same GroupName. To determine which RadioButton control out of a group has been selected, you evaluate the Checked property of each control in the group.

The ASP.NET Multiline TextBox Control

The last control demonstrated in this Web form (lines 258 through 263) is the multiline TextBox control. When rendered, this control resembles the <TextArea...></TextArea> HTML element. The ASP.NET declaration uses the TextBox control with the TextMode property set to MultiLine. The TextMode property can also be set to SingleLine or PassWord.

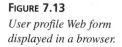

FIGURE 7.13

User profile Web form displayed in a browser.

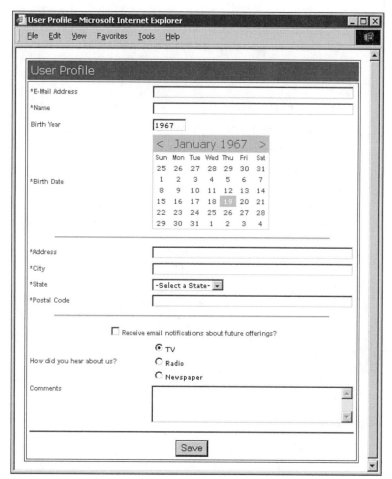

Summary

This hour begins with a description of the four types of controls that can be used in Web forms. You then learn how to use HTML server controls and how to program both client and server-side event handlers for these controls. You also learn how to dynamically create HTML server controls.

You then examine how to use ASP.NET server controls in Web forms, developing server-side event handlers for some of them and learning how to compile a Visual Basic Web Application using Visual Studio.

7

Q&A

Q. Can I use standard HTML elements, HTML server controls, and ASP.NET server controls on the same form?

A. Yes.

Q. Can I have more than one form declaration on a Web form page?

A. Unfortunately you can't, unlike prior versions of ASP.

Q. Can I have client-side event handlers and server-side event handlers for ASP.Net server controls?

A. Yes. To do this you will need to declare the event handlers for the specific events you want to handle. The following example declares one client-side and one server-side event handler for the `Click` event of an HTML submit button:

```
1:                    <input type="submit"
2:                        name="btnSubmit"
3:                        value="Submit"
4:                        runat="server"
5:                        id="btnSubmit"
6:                        OnClick="Client_Click()"
7:            OnServerClick="btnSubmit_Click">
```

Workshop

The quiz questions are provided for your further understanding of the material.

Quiz

1. What are the four types of controls that can be used in Web forms?

2. How do you convert a standard HTML element into an HTML server control?

3. How do you set the style properties for an ASP.NET server control to use the style from a cascading style sheet?

Exercise

We introduced several of the ASP.NET server controls in this hour. Quite a few more controls are available, such as the `ListBox`, `Image`, `DataList`, and `DataGrid` controls. The description and use of these controls can be found in the online help for Visual Studio.NET. Try to use some of these additional controls in the user profile Web form that we developed during this hour.

Answers for Hour 7

Quiz

1. What are the four types of controls that can be used in Web forms?

   The four types of controls that can be used in Web forms are: standard HTML elements, ASP.NET server controls, validation controls, and user controls.

2. How do you convert a standard HTML element into an HTML server control?

   To convert a standard HTML element into an HTML server control, add the `"runat=server"` attribute to the form that contains the HTML element and to the declaration of the element itself.

3. How do you set the style properties for an ASP.NET server control to use the style from a cascading style sheet?

   To set the style properties for an ASP.NET server control to use the style from a cascading style sheet, you specify the name of the class for the `cssClass` attribute of the ASP.Net server control.

7

Hour **8**

Web Forms Validation

Now that we've slogged through server controls and Web form controls, let's move on to bigger and better things: validation controls. As every Web programmer will tell you, writing client- and server-side validation code can be some of the slickest and sexiest stuff you'll ever do on a Web page. Okay, maybe that's not really true. All right, it's not true. Nevertheless, writing validation code is indeed an indispensable part of Web development that must be dealt with effectively. The good news is that ASP.NET vastly improves upon a developer's productivity in writing validation code.

In this hour, you will be introduced to the validation controls that are included in ASP.NET. You will also learn the following:

- What the different types of validation controls are
- When to use what type of validation control
- How to use the different validation controls properly
- Incorporating validation controls with client-side validation

Introduction to Web Forms Validation

When you're developing Web-based applications, it is important to make sure the data being entered by the user is being entered properly. This is done through validation, which checks a value against a specific condition and raises an error if the condition is not met. In ASP.NET pages, validation is ensured through the use of server-side validation controls, which check the value of an input control for several types of error conditions and display a description of the problem if the condition is met.

Using Validation Controls

In ASP.NET, you can add validation controls to almost all input controls on the page that are either HTML server controls or Web form server controls. More than one type of validation control can be assigned to a particular input control, enabling validation with various criteria. When the ASP.NET page with the validation controls is executed, the values of the input controls affected by the validation controls are processed against the corresponding logic, as stated in the validation controls. Upon the evaluation of all the logic, the properties of the validation controls are set to True or False, depending on the outcome of the evaluation. Once all the validation controls have been processed, the page itself sets a property based on the values of the validation properties on the controls. If any of the controls failed their validation, the page property automatically sets the validation property to False. When you're coding your validation logic, the page property will be an important property that you will need to check to ensure that all your validation logic has been successfully met. After the page property is checked and a failed validation reading is received, the page is typically returned to the user and any error messages assigned to the failed validation controls are displayed.

Normally, an input control on a page receives a validation control for each type of error condition you are looking to check. For example, if you want to make sure that a field has a value in it and that the value is less than 10 but greater than 5, you would use one validation control that checks to make sure a value was entered and another that checks the value against a range of acceptable values.

Types of Validation Controls

ASP.NET has six types of validation controls: RequiredFieldValidator, RegularExpressionValidator, CompareValidator, RangeValidator, CustomValidator, and ValidationSummary. All these controls share a common set of properties and methods, most of which are inherited from the BaseValidator class and the WebControl class found in the System.UI.WebControls namespace, and the Control class found in the System.Web.UI namespace. An exception to this rule is the Text property, which is inherited from the Label class.

Common validation control properties are outlined in Table 8.1.

TABLE 8.1 Common Validation Control Properties

Property	Description
AccessKey	Specifies a shortcut key for setting focus on the Web control. For example, Ctrl+F can set focus on the First Name field on a user profile data-entry form. Access keys work only on Internet Explorer versions 4.0 and higher.
BackColor	Specifies the background color of the error message displayed by the validation control.
BorderColor	Specifies the border color of the error message displayed by the validation control.
BorderStyle	Specifies the border style of the error message displayed by the validation control.
BorderWidth	Specifies the border width of the error message displayed by the validation control.
ControlStyle	Returns the current style of the Web control. This property is primarily used by control developers.
ControlToValidate	Specifies the HTML or Web form control to validate.
CssClass	Specifies the Cascading Style Sheet class associated with the validation control.
Display	Specifies the display behavior of the validation control. The three settings are Dynamic, Static, and None.
Enabled	Specifies whether the validation for the control is enabled.
EnabledClientScript	Specifies whether client-side validation is enabled.
ErrorMessage	Specifies the text for the error message.
Font	Returns the font information of the Web control.
ForeColor	Specifies the text color of the validation error message.
Height	Specifies the height of the validation control.
ID	Specifies the identifier, or *name*, of the validation control. If this property is not specified on a control, either declaratively or programmatically, you cannot write event handlers and the like for the control.
IsValid	Specifies whether the referenced control has passed validation.
Style	Specifies style attributes that define the appearance of the validation control.
TabIndex	Specifies the tab index of the Web control.
Text	Specifies the text content of the validation control.
ToolTip	Specifies the tooltip for the Web control to be displayed when the mouse cursor hovers over the control. This feature is available only in Internet Explorer 4.0 and higher.
Visible	Specifies whether the validation control should be displayed on the page.
Width	Specifies the width of the validation control.

8

This is by no means an exhaustive list of the properties associated with validation controls. For the comprehensive list of properties associated with validation controls, check out the .NET Framework reference that is included with the .NET SDK installation.

The most important properties in Table 8.1 are `ControlToValidate`, `ErrorMessage`, `ForeColor`, and `IsValid`. These are the primary properties you will be working with when using validation controls. Other important properties to pay attention to are the `Visible`, `Enabled`, and `Display` properties.

The `Visible` property determines not only whether the validation control is displayed but also whether it is set to `True` or `False`. If it's set to `False`, the control is not processed for rendering. Therefore, setting the `Visible` property to `False` disables the validation control from performing its task.

The `Enabled` property is similar to the `Visible` property in that when it is set to `False`, the control's validation routine will not function. However, on browsers that support client-side validation, the validation routine is transferred to the browser, but in a disabled state. Here, it can be enabled through a client-side script. The client-side script function to call to enable a validator is `ValidatorEnable()`.

The `Display` property affects whether the validation control is displayed on the page. Even if the `Display` property is set to `None`, the validator will still perform its validation function. This property is typically used in conjunction with a ValidationSummary control. The error message defined by the validation control is passed to the ValidationSummary control for display.

There are three ways to display your validation error messages with validation controls. The three methods used are `Dynamic`, `Static`, and `None` (which does not imply the absence of validation altogether):

- `Dynamic`: This method for displaying validation messages is performed right alongside the designated validation control on the page. In this instance, the validation control takes up space on the page only when the error message is actually displayed.

    This type of display allows multiple validation controls to be placed in the same place on the page. The only drawback to this method of display is that the page layout may alter drastically when the error message is displayed. To correct this problem, simply size the HTML control that holds the validation control to the largest text size. That way, when the error message is displayed, it will not move any of the page elements out of the way to make room for itself.

- `Static`: This is the second method for displaying validation error messages. The `Static` display method works similarly to the `Dynamic` display method, except that the validation control takes up the section of the page where it is placed. In this manner, when the error message is displayed, none of the elements in the page will be altered because the validation control is already a part of the page. The drawback to this method of error message delivery is that multiple validation controls for the same control must be placed at different locations on the page.

- `None`: This is the third and final display method. Simply stated, this method will not display any error messages on the page unless it used in conjunction with a validation summary control. In that case, it captures all of the error messages from all the validation controls on the page and displays them all as a summary in one location on the page.

Common validation control methods are outlined in Table 8.2.

TABLE 8.2 Common Validation Control Methods

Property	Description
`CheckControlValidatorProperty`	Determines whether the specified control has a validation property
`GetValidationProperty`	Returns the validation property of a control if it exists
`RegisterValidationCommonScript`	Registers code on the page for client-side validation on browsers that support client-side scripting languages
`Validate`	Evaluates validity and updates the `IsValid` property on the validation control

Again, this is not a comprehensive list of the methods associated with validation controls. The most important method in Table 8.2 is the `Validate` method; you will call this method often to ensure that the data in your controls is valid.

Now that you have been introduced to the shared properties and methods among ASP.NET validation controls, let's take a closer-look at each control and its properties, events, and methods.

RequiredFieldValidator

The RequiredFieldValidator control checks to make sure the user entered or selected a value in the input control. Once assigned to an input control, this validation control ensures that a value is entered into that input control's field. Along with the common validation control properties, RequiredFieldValidator has a property unique to itself: the InitialValue property. It specifies an initial value to compare to the control being validated. If the value in the control being validated is equal to the value in the InitialValue property, validation fails for the control.

The syntax for using this control is as follows:

```
<asp:RequiredFieldValidator id="RequiredFieldValidator1" runat="server"
  ControlToValidate="txtLastName"
  ErrorMessage="Last name is a required field"
  ForeColor="Red"
  CssClass="rqfldStyle"
  Visible="true"
  Display="Dynamic">
</asp:RequiredFieldValidator>
```

This example creates a RequiredFieldValidator control called RequiredFieldValidator1, which validates the txtLastName control. If there is no value in the control when the page is submitted, the "Last name is a required field" error message will appear. When the error message displays, it will appear as red text on the page.

RegularExpressionValidator

The RegularExpressionValidator control checks that an entry matches a pattern defined by a regular expression. A *regular expression* is a pattern of text that consists of ordinary characters and special characters, known as *metacharacters*. The pattern serves as a template by describing one or more strings to match when searching a body of text.

This type of validation allows you to check for predictable sequences of characters, such as those in social security numbers, e-mail addresses, telephone numbers, postal codes, and so on. There is one unique property associated with RegularExpressionValidator controls: ValidationExpression. It specifies the regular expression that defines the validation criteria.

Table 8.3 lists some of the more useful regular expressions you will use on your ASP.NET pages.

TABLE 8.3   Useful Regular Expressions

Regular Expression	Description
`[a-zA-Z]`	Checks to make sure that the value being validated contains only alphabetic characters.
`[0-9]{5}-[0-9]{4}|[0-9]{5}`	Checks the ZIP Code field to make sure that only numeric data was entered or that the ZIP Code + 4 value was entered correctly.
`[0-9]{3}|[0-9]{4}` or `[0-9]{3}-[0-9]{3}-[0-9]{4}`	Checks to make sure that the phone number was entered correctly.
`[a-zA-Z0-9\.\_]+@[a-zA-Z.]` `+\.[a-zA-Z]{3}`	Ensures that an e-mail address was entered correctly. This expression will work only on e-mail addresses that end in `.com`, `.gov`, `.edu`, `.net`, or `.org`.

A full discourse on the proper syntax of regular expressions is beyond the scope of this book. To gain a better understanding of how to use regular expressions, you should consult MSDN (`www.msdn.microsoft.com`) or another online developer resource.

The syntax for using the RegularExpressionValidator control is as follows:

```
<asp:RegularExpressionValidator id=" RegularExpressionValidator1" runat="server"
  ControlToValidate="txtZipCode"
  ErrorMessage=" Please enter a valid zip code."
  ForeColor="Red"
  ValidationExpression="\d{5}(-\d{4})?">
</asp:RegularExpressionValidator>
```

This example can be used in conjunction with the example for the RequiredFieldValidator control. When a value is entered, it is compared to the `ValidationExpression` property of the RegularExpressionValidator control. In this case, if any alphabetical characters are entered, the validation will fail and the error message "Please enter a valid zip code." will be displayed.

CompareValidator

The CompareValidator control compares the value of one control to a value in another control. This type of control is especially useful for a password-confirmation field. Several unique properties are associated with the CompareValidator control, including `ControlToCompare`, `ValueToCompare`, `Type`, and `Operator`.

The `ControlToCompare` property specifies which control is going to be compared to the `ControlToValidate` property. By default, it-performs a string comparison, but it can also perform comparisons of dates and numbers.

The ValueToCompare property specifies the value to which the control is to be compared. This value can be a currency value, a date, a numeric value, or a string. If both the ValueToCompare property and the ControlToCompare property are set, the ControlToCompare value will take precedence.

The Type property specifies the data type comparison validation that will be performed. The valid members of this property include Currency, Date, Double, Integer, and String.

The Operator property specifies the type of comparison to perform: DataTypeCheck, Equal, GreaterThan, GreaterThanEqual, LessThan, LessThanEqual, or NotEqual. Here are some specifics:

- The DataTypeCheck operator specifies that the value is going to be compared only to a particular data type. The following data types are valid for this type of comparison: Currency, Date, Double, Integer, and String.

- The Equal comparison is the default comparison operator for the CompareValidator control. It compares two values to make sure that they are equal to one another.

- The remaining comparison operators—GreaterThan, GreaterThanEqual, LessThan, LessThanEqual, and NotEqual—evaluate to one control being greater than, greater than or equal to, less than, less than or equal to, or not equal to the control be compared.

The syntax for the CompareValidator control is as follows:

```
<asp:CompareValidator id="CompareValidator1" runat="server"
  ControlToValidate="txtPassword"
  ErrorMessage="Passwords do not match."
  ForeColor="Red"
  CssClass="rqfldStyle"
  ControlToCompare="txtRePassword">
</asp:CompareValidator>
```

This example compares the txtRePassword value to the txtPassword value. If the two values do not match, the validation fails and the error message "Passwords do not match." is displayed.

The syntax for using CompareValidator to validate a control against a specific value is as follows:

```
<asp:CompareValidator id="CompareValidator2" runat="server"
  ControlToValidate="txtPassword"
  ErrorMessage="The value entered is not correct."
  ForeColor="Red"
  ValueToCompare="myPassword"
  Type="String">
</asp:CompareValidator>
```

The syntax for using CompareValidator to validate a control against a particular data type is as follows:

```
<asp:CompareValidator id="CompareValidator3" runat="server"
  ControlToValidate="txtAtomicWeight"
  ErrorMessage="That is NOT the atomic weight of Cesium."
  ForeColor="Red"
  ControlToCompare="txtAtomicWeight2"
  Type="Double">
</asp:CompareValidator>
```

When CompareValidator is performing its validation routine, if the control being validated contains no value, validation will succeed. To prevent this from occurring, you must use a RequiredFieldValidator control on the control being validated. Also, validation will succeed even if the value in the ControlToCompare property is not the same data type as the one specified in the Type property. This occurs because only the value in the ControlToValidate property is converted to the data type specified in the Type property. If the value cannot be converted to the data type in the Type property, an error is raised and the validation processing stops. Finally, setting the Operator property to DataTypeCheck compares the value in the control being validated only to the data type specified in the Type property. No comparison of the ControlToCompare or the ValueToCompare properties is performed.

RangeValidator

The RangeValidator control compares the value of an input control to a range of values. The range of values can be two numbers, two alphabetic characters, or two dates. Several properties are important to the RangeValidator control: MinimumValue, MaximumValue, and Type.

The MinimumValue and MaximumValue properties specify the minimum and maximum values, respectively, of the validation range and are used in conjunction with one another.

The Type property defines the data type of the value being validated in the RangeValidator control. The valid data types for this control are Currency, Date, Double, Integer, and String (the default is String).

The syntax for using the RangeValidator control to check for a predetermined range of values is as follows:

```
<asp:RangeValidator id="RangeValidator1" runat="server"
  ErrorMessage="The value entered does not fall between 1 and 10."
  ForeColor="Red"
  ControlToValidate="txtPickANumber"
  Type="Integer"
  MinimumValue="1"
  MaximumValue="10">
</asp:RangeValidator>
```

CustomValidator

The CustomValidator control allows you to create your own custom validation logic for your ASP.NET controls. This type of control is typically used to validate values against a database, or to validate a control based on a validation routine that is not already provided.

Typically, a validation function is written for both the server and the client. The server-side validation function can be written in any of the .NET-compliant languages mentioned in Hour 1, "Getting Started with ASP.NET," but the client-side validation function must be written in a browser-compliant language such as JavaScript, JScript, or VBScript. At the moment, only Internet Explorer supports client-side VBScript, so you will most likely write your functions in JavaScript or JScript so that they are more compatible with browsers other than Internet Explorer.

One property and one method need to be defined for the CustomValidator control. The property is `ClientValidationFunction`. It defines the name of the client-side function that needs to be called to perform the custom validation task. Client-validation functions can expect two parameters to be passed into them, although declaring these parameters is not required for your function to work properly. The first parameter is the reference to the control being validated; the second is the value that is being validated. If you are going to rely totally on server-side validation, you will not need to define this parameter.

The method that must be defined for the CustomValidator control is the `OnServerValidate` method. It specifies which server-side function to call to perform the validation routine. Typically, this function works in conjunction with the client-side validation function to properly validate controls in browsers that either do not support client-side scripting or have it disabled.

The syntax for the CustomValidator control is as follows:

```
<asp:CustomValidator id="CustomValidator1" runat="server"
  ErrorMessage="This user name is already taken."
  ForeColor="Red"
  ControlToCValidate="txtUserName"
  OnServerValidate="CheckUserName">
</asp:CustomValidator>
```

This example calls the server-side function `CheckUserName` and passes it the value in the control being compared. This function will check the username requested by the user and will return the Boolean value `False` if it is already in use by another user.

The CustomValidator control is necessary for checking controls that otherwise cannot be validated. These might include check box lists, standalone radio buttons, and groups of controls that need to be validated together.

When using the CustomValidator control, remember that the validation routine will succeed if there is no value in the control being validated.

Another important consideration involves browsers that do not support client-side scripting (or have this feature disabled). In this case, any client-side code you write needs to be enclosed in HTML comment tags so as not to raise an error just by being defined.

ValidationSummary

The ValidationSummary control gathers up the error messages defined by each validation control on the page and displays them all in one area. This control works in unison with the other validation controls on the page, and it does not prevent them from displaying their own messages to the user. For example, you can have an asterisk displayed next to the label for your control, along with a more descriptive error message displayed at the top of the screen.

DisplayMode, ForeColor, HeaderText, ShowMessageBox, and ShowSummary are the properties associated with the ValidationSummary control.

The DisplayMode property defines how the error messages will be displayed on the screen. The three display settings are BulletList, List, and SingleParagraph. The default setting, BulletList, displays each error message in its own bulleted line. The List option displays each error message on its own line, and the SingleParagraph option displays all the error messages together in one paragraph (in this type of display, the error messages are separated by double spaces).

The ForeColor property sets the text color of the control. The default color is red.

The HeaderText property defines the text to be displayed above the summary list of error messages. You can include HTML tags in the HeaderText property because the header text is not HTML encoded.

The ShowMessageBox property is a True/False property that determines whether summary message data is displayed in a pop-up message box via a JavaScript alert call. The default value for this property is False.

The ShowSummary property is a True/False property that determines whether the summary text is displayed inline with the other elements on the page. The default value for this property is True.

The syntax for using a ValidationSummary control is as follows:

```
<asp:ValidationSummary id="ValidationSummary1" runat="server"
  DisplayMode="BulletList"
  HeaderText="The following errors have occurred:"
  ForeColor="Red"
  ShowMessageBox="false"
  ShowSummary="true">
</asp:CustomValidator>
```

Putting It All Together

COMPANION
Website
Now that we've examined the various validation controls in more detail, let's take a look at an ASPX page that uses them. Listing 8.1 creates a page that lets a user create an account for our application by inputting some personal information and then selecting a username and password.

LISTING 8.1   User Profile—*userprofile.aspx*

```
1: <%@ Page Language="vb" AutoEventWireup="false"
➥CodeBehind="userprofile.aspx.vb" Inherits="Chapter8.userprofile"%>
2:   <html>
3:     <head>
4:       <title>User Profile</title>
5:       <LINK rel="stylesheet" type="text/css"
➥href="http://OSIRIS_HOME/UserProfile/Styles.css">
6:     </head>
7:     <body marginheight="0" marginwidth="0" leftmargin="0" topmargin="0">
8:       <form id="frmRegister" method="POST" runat="server">
9:         <table border="0" cellpadding="0" cellspacing="0" width="100%">
10:         <tr>
11:           <td align="center"><asp:validationsummary displaymode="BulletList"
➥headertext="The following errors were found:" forecolor="red"
➥id="valUserProfile" showsummary="True" font-size="10pt"
➥runat="Server"></asp:validationsummary> </td>
12:         </tr>
13:         <tr>
14:         <td align="middle">
15:           <table border="0" cellpadding="2" cellspacing="1" width="600">
16:           <tr>
17:             <td valign="top">
18:               <asp:label id=label1 font-size="8pt" font-bold="true"
➥runat="Server">User Profile</asp:label>
19:             </td>
20:           </tr>
21:           <tr>
22:             <td valign="top" align="right">
23:               <table border="0" cellpadding="4" cellspacing="2" width="100%">
24:               <tr>
25:                 <td colspan="4" align="left"><asp:label id=Label2 font-
➥size="8pt" font-bold="true" runat="Server">Personal Information
➥</asp:label></td>
26:               </tr>
27:               <tr>
28:                 <td align="right">
29:                   <asp:requiredfieldvalidator id="reqFirstName"
➥controltovalidate="FirstName" text="*" font-size="8pt" font-bold="True"
➥errormessage="You must enter a first name." runat="Server">
➥</asp:requiredfieldvalidator>
```

LISTING 8.1 continued

```
30:                <asp:regularexpressionvalidator id="regFirstname"
➡controltovalidate="firstname" text="*" font-size="8pt" font-bold="True"
➡errormessage="Only alphabetical characters may used for first names."
➡runat="Server" forecolor="red" validationexpression="[a-z]">
➡</asp:regularexpressionvalidator>
31:                <asp:label id=Label4 font-size="8pt" font-bold="false"
➡runat="Server"> First Name</asp:label>
32:                </td>
33:                <td><asp:textbox id="FirstName" width="200" maxlength="25"
➡runat="Server"></asp:textbox></td>
34:                <td align="right">
35:                <asp:requiredfieldvalidator id="reqLastName"
➡controltovalidate="LastName" text="*" font-size="8pt" font-bold="True"
➡errormessage="You must enter a last name." runat="Server">
➡</asp:requiredfieldvalidator>
36:                <asp:regularexpressionvalidator id="regLastName"
➡controltovalidate="LastName" text="*" font-size="8pt" font-bold="True"
➡errormessage="Only alphabetical characters may used for last names."
➡runat="Server" forecolor="red" validationexpression="[a-zA-Z]">
➡</asp:regularexpressionvalidator>
37:                <asp:label id=Label5 font-size="8pt" font-bold="false"
➡runat="Server"> Last Name</asp:label>
38:                </td>
39:                <td><asp:textbox id="LastName" width="200" maxlength="25"
➡runat="Server"></asp:textbox></td>
40:            </tr>
41:            <tr><td align="middle" colspan="4"> </td></tr>
42:            <tr>
43:                <td colspan="4" align="left"><asp:label id=Label3 font-
➡size="8pt" font-bold="true" runat="Server">Login Information</asp:label></td>
44:            </tr>
45:            <tr>
46:                <td align="right">
47:                <asp:requiredfieldvalidator id="reqUserName"
➡controltovalidate="UserName" text="*" font-size="8pt" font-bold="True"
➡errormessage="You must enter a user name." runat="Server">
➡</asp:requiredfieldvalidator>
48:                <asp:regularexpressionvalidator id="regUserName"
➡controltovalidate="UserName" text="*" font-size="8pt" font-bold="True"
➡errormessage="The User Name must be between 6-16 characters."
➡runat="Server" forecolor="red" validationexpression="[[^\s]{6,16}]">
➡</asp:regularexpressionvalidator>
49:                <asp:customvalidator id="custUserName"
➡controltovalidate="UserName" text="*" font-bold="True" font-size="8pt"
OnServerValidate="ValidateUserName"
➡runat="Server" errormessage="The user name selected is already in use.
➡Please select another."></asp:customvalidator>
50:                <asp:label id=Label14 font-size="8pt" font-bold="false"
➡runat="Server"> User Name</asp:label>
51:                </td>
52:                <td><asp:textbox id="UserName" width="200" maxlength="16"
```

8

LISTING 8.1 continued

```
➥runat="Server"></asp:textbox></td>
53:              <td align="right">
54:              <asp:requiredfieldvalidator id="reqPassword"
➥controltovalidate="Password" text="*" font-size="8pt" font-bold="True"
➥errormessage="You must enter a password." runat="Server">
➥</asp:requiredfieldvalidator>
55:              <asp:label id=Label15 font-size="8pt" font-bold="false"
➥runat="Server"> Password</asp:label>
56:              </td>
57:              <td><asp:textbox textmode="Password" id="Password" width="200"
➥maxlength="16" runat="Server"></asp:textbox></td>
58:          </tr>
59:          <tr>
60:              <td colspan="2" align="right"> </td>
61:              <td align="right">
62:              <asp:requiredfieldvalidator id="reqRePassword"
➥controltovalidate="RePassword" text="*" font-size="8pt" font-bold="True"
➥errormessage="You must re-enter a password." runat="Server">
➥</asp:requiredfieldvalidator>
63:              <asp:comparevalidator id="compRePassword"
➥controltovalidate="RePassword" text="*" font-size="8pt" font-bold="True"
➥errormessage="Passwords do not match." controltocompare="Password"
➥runat="Server"></asp:comparevalidator>
64:              <asp:label id=Label16 font-size="8pt" font-bold="false"
➥runat="Server"> Confirm Password</asp:label>
65:              </td>
66:              <td><asp:textbox textmode="Password" id="RePassword" width="200"
➥maxlength="16" runat="Server"></asp:textbox></td>
67:          </tr>
68:          <tr>
69:              <td align="middle" colspan="4"> </td>
70:          </tr>
71:          <tr>
72:              <td colspan="4" align="middle"><asp:button id="Submit"
➥text="Submit"runat="Server"></asp:button></td>
73:          </tr>
74:          </table>
75:          </td>
76:        </tr>
77:      </table>
78:        </td>
79:      </tr>
80:    </table>
81:    </form>
82:  </body>
83:  </html>
```

This code runs using the external file `userprofile.vb`, found below in Listing 8.2.

LISTING 8.2 User Profile—*userprofile.aspx.vb*

```
 1:  Public Class userprofile
 2:      Inherits System.Web.UI.Page
 3:      Protected WithEvents lblTo As System.Web.UI.WebControls.Label
 4:      Protected WithEvents txtTo As System.Web.UI.WebControls.TextBox
 5:      Protected WithEvents lblFrom As System.Web.UI.WebControls.Label
 6:      Protected WithEvents txtFrom As System.Web.UI.WebControls.TextBox
 7:      Protected WithEvents Label1 As System.Web.UI.WebControls.Label
 8:      Protected WithEvents txtSubject As System.Web.UI.WebControls.TextBox
 9:      Protected WithEvents lblMessage As System.Web.UI.WebControls.Label
10:      Protected WithEvents txtMessage As System.Web.UI.WebControls.TextBox
11:      Protected WithEvents lblHTMLEncode As System.Web.UI.WebControls.Label
12:      Protected WithEvents chkHTMLEncode As System.Web.UI.WebControls.CheckBox
13:      Protected WithEvents btnSendEmail As System.Web.UI.WebControls.Button
14:  #Region " Web Form Designer Generated Code "
15:
16:      'This call is required by the Web Form Designer.
17:      <System.Diagnostics.DebuggerStepThrough()> Private Sub
➥InitializeComponent()
18:
19:      End Sub
20:
21:      Protected Sub Page_Init(ByVal Sender As System.Object, ByVal e As
➥System.EventArgs) Handles MyBase.Init
22:          'CODEGEN: This method call is required by the Web Form Designer
23:          'Do not modify it using the code editor.
24:          InitializeComponent()
25:      End Sub
26:
27:  #End Region
28:
29:      Private Sub Page_Load(ByVal sender As System.Object, ByVal e As
➥System.EventArgs) Handles MyBase.Load
30:          'Put user code to initialize the page here
21:      End Sub
32:
33:      Public Sub ValidateUserName(ByVal source As Object, ByVal args As
➥System.Web.UI.WebControls.ServerValidateEventArgs)
34:          ' Validate unique user name...
35:      End Sub
36:  End Class
```

Figures 8.1 and 8.2 illustrate this code in action. Figure 8.1 shows the page before any data has been entered; Figure 8.2 shows the page after validation has been completed. Notice the summary display of error messages related to the data on the page.

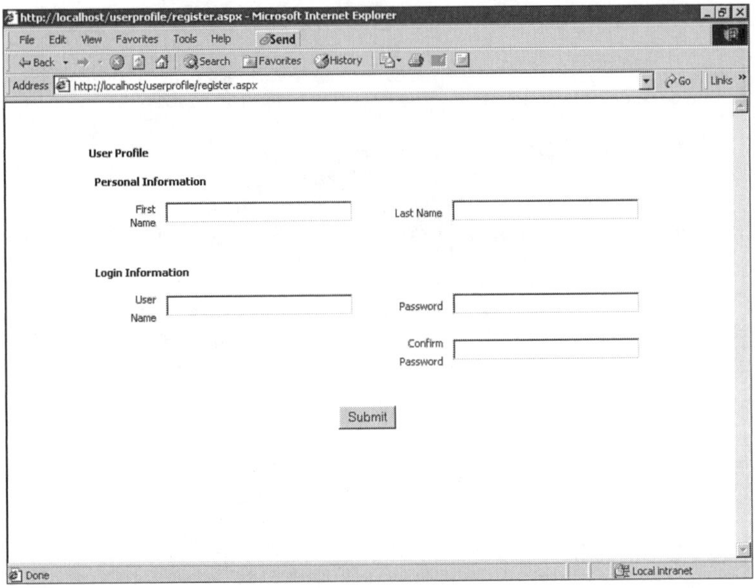

FIGURE **8.1**

The user profile page before data entry.

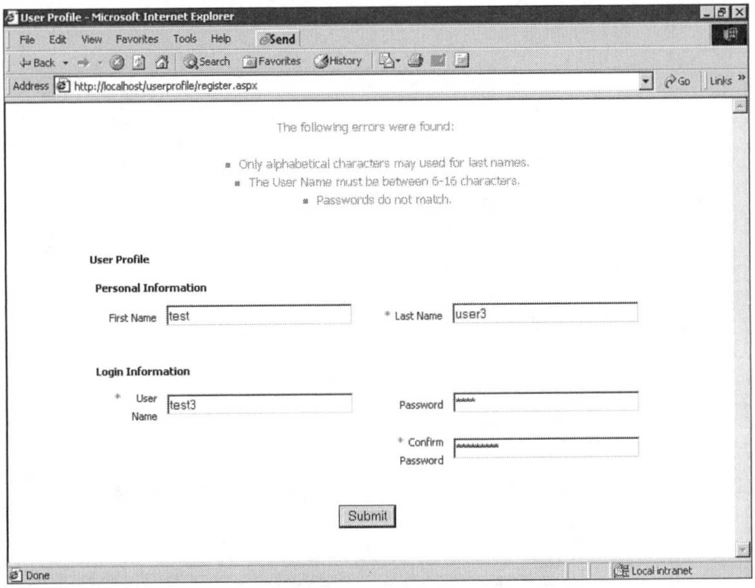

FIGURE **8.2**

The user profile page after data entry.

Summary

In this hour, you were introduced to the Web form validation controls `RequiredFieldValidator`, `CompareValidator`, `RegularExpressionValidator`, `RangeValidator`, `CustomValidator`, and `ValidationSummary`. These controls will help speed along the development of your Web-based application, because they remove much of the validation programming from your application-development cycle while still capturing valid and accurate data for your application.

Q&A

Q. Is it possible to use more than one validation control on a Web form control?

A. Yes. It is possible, and it is recommended that you use as many validation controls on your server controls as possible. This practice will help eliminate unwanted and invalid data that could potentially corrupt the data you are trying to capture.

Q. How can I validate groups of check boxes?

A. The best way to validate a group of related check boxes is to use a `CustomValidator` control and write a custom client-side and server-side routine to make sure that the check box data captured is valid. Always remember that even if you have client-side validation, you must also have server-side validation to prevent malicious users from circumventing your client-side code and posting improper and potentially harmful data.

Workshop

The quiz questions and exercises are provided for your further understanding.

Quiz

1. What is the name of the control that makes sure a value was entered into a control being validated?

2. What are the unique properties of the `RangeValidator` control?

3. What happens when a validation control's `Enabled` property is set to `False`?

Exercise

Write your own input screen to capture credit card information. You will want to capture the person's name, the credit card type (Visa, MasterCard, and so on), the credit card number, and the credit card expiration date. Add the appropriate validation controls necessary to ensure that the data entered is valid. Try to use all the validation controls if you can.

Answers for Hour 8

Quiz

1. What is the name of the control that makes sure a value was entered into a control being validated?

   RequiredFieldValidator.

2. What are the unique properties of the `RangeValidator` control?

   `MinimumValue`, `MaximumValue`, and `Type`.

3. What happens when a validation control's `Enabled` property is set to `False`?

   The control's validation routine will not function. However, on browsers that support client-side validation, the validation routine is transferred to the browser, but in a disabled state. Here, it can be enabled through a client-side script. The function to call to enable a validator is `ValidatorEnable()`.

PART III

ASP.NET Application Considerations

Hour

HOUR 9

ASP.NET Web Applications

This hour deals with ASP.NET applications. You will learn what ASP.NET applications are, how they can be configured, and how to manage their state information.

You will learn about the following topics in this hour:

- ASP.NET applications
- Application lifecycle events
- The `Global.asax`, `Global.asax.vb` and `Web.config` files
- Application and session state management

What Are ASP.NET Web Applications?

ASP.NET applications can be defined as all pages and executable code that exist and are processed within a given virtual directory on a Web server. When you start a new VB ASP.NET Web Application project using Visual Studio, a virtual directory is created automatically with the name you specify for the project (see Figure 9.1).

FIGURE 9.1

*Creating a VB
ASP.NET Web
Application project.*

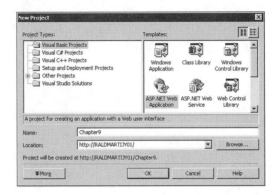

You can modify the settings of a Web application using the Internet Services Manager (see Figure 9.2).

FIGURE 9.2

*Viewing an IIS Web
application's proper-
ties using the Internet
Services Manager.*

You can also create a Web application using the Internet Services Manager, as we discussed in Hour 2, "Presenting Internet Information Services."

Any files and subdirectories that exist under the main virtual root directory are considered to be part of one Web application. The only exception to this would be the existence of another virtual directory underneath the main virtual root, which can belong to the same Web application or can be an independent application of its own.

Lifecycle of a Web Application

A Web application remains dormant until the first time a client accesses a page or resource that exists in the virtual directory. When the first request is received, a pool of application objects is created and the `Application_OnStart` event is raised on the first object created. Each application object created is referred to as a *session*. The `Session_OnStart` event is then raised on each `Session` object. The `Session` object has a timeout value that can be set in the `Web.config` file for the application. Listing 9.1 shows the session-state tag and attributes from the applications `Web.config` file. This file is an XML file containing configuration parameters for the application.

LISTING 9.1 Session State Settings in a `Web.config` File

```
1:  <sessionstate
2:          mode="InProc"
3:            stateConnectionString="tcpip=127.0.0.1:42424"
4:            sqlConnectionString="data source=127.0.0.1;user id=sa;password=
5:            cookieless="false"
6:            timeout="20"
7:      />
```

If the `Session` object remains idle (no additional requests occur from the browser that started the session) for the number of minutes specified by the `timeout` value, the `Session_OnEnd` event is fired for the session and the `Session` object is destroyed. Once the last `Session` object is destroyed, the `Application_End` event is raised.

The `Global.asax` File

All the aforementioned events may be programmed against in your ASP.NET application. When you create a Web application using Visual Studio, a special file is created for you in the root of your virtual directory: `Global.asax`. This file is considered the ASP.NET application file and contains the code for any lifecycle event handlers.

In the case of a VB Web Application project, this file initially contains an application directive declaring a code-behind file as `Global.asax.vb`. Listing 9.2 shows the `Global.asax.vb` file, which is where the default event handlers are located.

LISTING 9.2 Default `Global.asax.vb` File Created by Visual Studio

```
1:   Imports System.Web
2:   Imports System.Web.SessionState
3:
4:   Public Class Global
5:     Inherits System.Web.HttpApplication
6:
7:     #Region " Component Designer Generated Code "
8:
9:     Public Sub New()
10:      MyBase.New()
```

LISTING 9.2   continued

```
11:
12:       'This call is required by the Component Designer.
13:       InitializeComponent()
14:
15:       'Add any initialization after the InitializeComponent() call
16:
17:     End Sub
18:
19:     'Required by the Component Designer
20:     Private components As System.ComponentModel.Container
21:
22:       'NOTE: The following procedure is required by the Component Designer
23:       'It can be modified using the Component Designer.
24:       'Do not modify it using the code editor.
25:       <System.Diagnostics.DebuggerStepThrough()>
➥ Private Sub InitializeComponent()
26:         components = New System.ComponentModel.Container()
27:       End Sub
28:
29:     #End Region
30:
31:     Sub Application_BeginRequest(ByVal sender As Object,
➥ ByVal e As EventArgs)
32:       ' Fires at the beginning of each request
33:     End Sub
34:
35:         Sub Application_AuthenticateRequest(ByVal sender As Object,
➥ ByVal e As EventArgs)
36:             ' Fires upon attempting to authenticate the use
37:         End Sub
38:
39:         Sub Application_Error(ByVal sender As Object, ByVal e As
➥ EventArgs)
40:             ' Fires when an error occurs
41:         End Sub
42:
43:         End Class
```

Listing 9.3 presents code found in the Global.asax.vb file that demonstrates the life-cycle of the application and session objects.

LISTING 9.3   Application Lifecycle Event Code Example

```
1:     Imports System.Web
2:     Imports System.Web.SessionState
3:
4:     Public Class Global
5:         Inherits System.Web.HttpApplication
6:
```

LISTING 9.3   continued

```
 7:    #Region " Component Designer Generated Code "
 8:
 9:        Public Sub New()
10:            MyBase.New()
11:
12:            'This call is required by the Component Designer.
13:            InitializeComponent()
14:
15:            'Add any initialization after the InitializeComponent() call
16:
17:        End Sub
18:
19:        'Required by the Component Designer
20:        Private components As System.ComponentModel.Container
21:
22:        'NOTE: The following procedure is required by the Component Designer
23:        'It can be modified using the Component Designer.
24:        'Do not modify it using the code editor.
25:        <System.Diagnostics.DebuggerStepThrough()>
➥ Private Sub InitializeComponent()
26:            components = New System.ComponentModel.Container()
27:        End Sub
28:
29:    #End Region
30:
31:        Sub Application_BeginRequest
➥ (ByVal sender As Object, ByVal e As EventArgs)
32:            ' Fires at the beginning of each request
33:            Response.Write(Date.Now.ToLongTimeString +
➥" - Application_BeginRequest" + "<BR>")
34:        End Sub
35:
36:        Sub Application_AuthenticateRequest
➥ (ByVal sender As Object, ByVal e As EventArgs)
37:            ' Fires upon attempting to authenticate the use
38:        End Sub
39:
40:        Sub Application_Error(ByVal sender As Object, ByVal e As EventArgs)
41:            ' Fires when an error occurs
42:        End Sub
43:
44:        Sub Application_OnStart(ByVal Sender As Object, ByVal e As EventArgs)
45:            Application("AppStart") = Date.Now.ToLongTimeString
46:        End Sub
47:
48:        Sub Session_OnStart(ByVal Sender As Object, ByVal e As EventArgs)
49:            Response.Write(Application("AppStart").ToString +
➥" - Application_Start" + "<BR>")
```

LISTING 9.3   continued

```
50:        Response.Write(Date.Now.ToLongTimeString + " - Session_Start" + "<BR>")
51:     End Sub
52:
53:     Sub Application_EndRequest
➥ (ByVal Sender As Object, ByVal e As EventArgs)
54:        Response.Write(Date.Now.ToLongTimeString +
➥" - Application_EndRequest" + "<BR>")
55:     End Sub
56:
57:     Sub Session_OnEnd(ByVal Sender As Object, ByVal e As EventArgs)
58:        Response.Write(Date.Now.ToLongTimeString +
➥" - Session_End" + "<BR>")
59:     End Sub
60:
61:     Sub Application_OnEnd(ByVal Sender As Object, ByVal e As EventArgs)
62:        Response.Write(Date.Now.ToLongTimeString +
➥" - Application_End" + "<BR>")
63:     End Sub
64:
65:  End Class
```

For this example, we need to edit the Web.config file as well and set the session timeout value to 1 minute. This will allow us to see what happens when the session and application shut down, as shown in Figure 9.3.

FIGURE 9.3

ASP.NET application lifecycle event handlers (first page access).

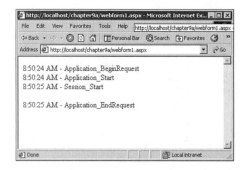

When the first page of this application is referenced, the application is started (note that we didn't show the code for any specific page because these event handlers will execute for any page in the application). The output shows that the Begin_Request event is fired first, followed by the Session_OnStart and Application_EndRequest events. However, we don't see any indication of the Session_OnEnd and Application_OnEnd events. Why not? Because the session hasn't ended yet, and neither has the application. If you wait for the timeout period to pass and then refresh the page in your browser, the

Session_OnStart event will fire again. This is our only indication that the Session_OnEnd event fired. Because the Response object that our code is referencing in these event handlers is no longer valid and has already been sent to the client browser, we don't see any output from these event handlers.

If you refresh the page in your browser before the timeout period has expired, you will see output only from the Application_BeginRequest and Application_EndRequest event handlers (see Figure 9.4).

FIGURE 9.4

ASP.NET application lifecycle event handlers (second page access).

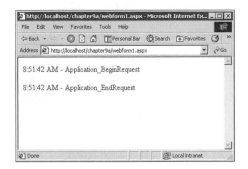

State Management

State management refers to storing or using information received from the client to alter the behavior of an application. This can be as simple as remembering a user's name or as complex as managing caches of data from a database to share among multiple sessions.

In Listing 9.3, we get the current time and store it in the application collection with the following line of code:

```
Application("AppStart") = Date.Now.ToLongTimeString
```

Name-value pairs may be added directly to the application collection in this manner. These values are global to all instances of the application. This is an example of application state management.

Application State Data

There are two basic types of state data: application and session. Application state data may be added directly to the application collection, as demonstrated previously. You can store any type of data in the application, even complex data structures such as datasets. However, it is recommended that large objects, such as datasets with lots of data, not be persisted in an Application variable due to performance issues. The application collection is an instance of the HTTPApplication state object and has many properties and methods. Some of these are outlined in the following list. You can also refer to the MSDN help section for a complete listing of all properties and methods of the HTTPApplication state object.

Here are the methods and properties available on the HttpApplicationState collection:

- Add: Adds a new object to the HttpApplicationState collection.
- AllKeys: Gets the access keys in the HttpApplicationState collection.
- Clear: Removes all objects from an HttpApplicationState collection.
- Count: Overridden. Gets/returns the number of objects in the HttpApplicationState collection.
- Get: Returns an HttpApplicationState object by name or index.
- GetKey: Returns an HttpApplicationState object name by index.
- Item: Overloaded. Gets access to an object in an HttpApplicationState collection. This property is overloaded to allows access to an object by name or numerical index.
- Lock: Locks access to an HttpApplicationState variable to facilitate access synchronization.
- UnLock: Unlocks access to an HttpApplicationState variable to ease access synchronization.

If you do not call the Unlock method, ASP.NET will unlock the application collection when the request ends, times out, or encounters an unhandled error.

Session State Data

Session state data may be added to the session collection, just as it may be added to the application collection. With the advent of the .NET Framework, a separate process now manages session data. This allows session data to remain intact if IIS shuts down or if the application is hosted on a Web farm or bank of IIS servers.

By default, the session data is managed by a Windows service process—although it may also be stored in a SQL Server database, in which case a connection string is needed to connect to the appropriate database resource.

Session Tracking

An application can be configured to use either cookies or query strings to track sessions. To configure an application *not* to use cookies to track sessions, you need to modify the SessionState section of the Web.Config file. The session collection contains many methods and attributes. The five main attributes used to configure session state management in ASP.NET are listed here:

- Mode: Specifies the persistence mode used to store session state. There are four modes to choose from: Off, Inproc, StateServer, and SQLServer.

- Timeout: Specifies the number of minutes of idle time before the session shuts down.

- ConnectionString: Required only if Mode is set to StateServer. ConnectionString specifies the port as well as the name or address of the server where session state is stored.

- SQLConnectionString: Required when Mode is set to SQLServer. It specifies the connection string needed to connect to a database server.

- Cookieless: A Boolean value that indicates whether the application should use cookies or munged URLs to track sessions.

State Management Examples

The code examples shown in Listings 9.4 through 9.8 demonstrate the use of application and state management within an application. For these examples, the timeout value for the session needs to be set to 1 minute.

LISTING 9.4   *Global.asax.vb*

```
1:    Imports System
2:    Imports System.ComponentModel
3:    Imports System.Web
4:    Imports System.Web.SessionState
5:
6:    Public Class Global
7:        Inherits System.Web.HttpApplication
8:
9:    #Region " Component Designer Generated Code "
10:
11:       Public Sub New()
12:           MyBase.New()
13:
14:           'This call is required by the Component Designer.
15:           InitializeComponent()
16:
```

LISTING 9.4   continued

```
17:             'Add any initialization after the InitializeComponent() call
18:
19:      End Sub
20:
21:      'Required by the Component Designer
22:      Private components As System.ComponentModel.Container
23:
24:      'NOTE: The following procedure is required by the Component Designer
25:      'It can be modified using the Component Designer.
26:      'Do not modify it using the code editor.
27:      <System.Diagnostics.DebuggerStepThrough()> _
28:      Private Sub InitializeComponent()
29:        components = New System.ComponentModel.Container()
30:      End Sub
31:
32:  #End Region
33:
34:    Sub Application_OnStart(ByVal Sender As Object, _
35:      ByVal e As EventArgs)
36:      Application("Application Start Time") = Now.ToLongTimeString
37:      Application("SessionCount") = 0
38:      Application("RequestCount") = 0
39:    End Sub
40:
41:    Sub Session_OnStart(ByVal Sender As Object, _
42:      ByVal e As EventArgs)
43:      Dim lngCount As Long
44:
45:      Application.Lock()
46:      lngCount = CLng(Application.Get("SessionCount").ToString) + 1
47:      Application("SessionCount") = lngCount
48:      Application(Replace(System.Guid.NewGuid.ToString, "-", "")) = _
49:        "Session " + Session.SessionID + _
50:        " Started " + Now.ToLongTimeString
51:      Application.UnLock()
52:    End Sub
53:
54:    Sub Application_BeginRequest(ByVal Sender As Object, _
55:      ByVal e As EventArgs)
56:      Application.Lock()
57:      Application("RequestCount") = _
58:        CLng(Application("RequestCount").ToString) + 1
59:      Application.UnLock()
60:    End Sub
61:
62:    Sub Application_EndRequest(ByVal Sender As Object, _
63:      ByVal e As EventArgs)
64:
```

LISTING 9.4   continued

```
65:    End Sub
66:
67:    Sub Session_OnEnd(ByVal Sender As Object, ByVal e As EventArgs)
68:       Dim lngCount As Long
69:
70:       Application.Lock()
71:       lngCount = CLng(Application("SessionCount").ToString) - 1
72:       Application("SessionCount") = lngCount
73:       Application(Replace(System.Guid.NewGuid.ToString, "-", "")) = _
74:         "Session " + Session.SessionID + _
75:          " Ended " + Now.ToLongTimeString
76:       Application.UnLock()
77:    End Sub
78:
79:    Sub Application_OnEnd(ByVal Sender As Object, _
80:       ByVal e As EventArgs)
81:
82:    End Sub
83:
84: End Class
```

9

LISTING 9.5   *WebForm1.aspx*

```
1:    <%@ Page Language="vb" AutoEventWireup="false"
2:       Codebehind="WebForm1.aspx.vb"
3:       Inherits="Chapter9.WebForm1"%>
4:
5:    <html>
6:      <head>
7:        <meta name="GENERATOR" content="Microsoft Visual Studio.NET 7.0">
8:        <meta name="CODE_LANGUAGE" content="Visual Basic 7.0">
9:      </head>
10:     <body>
11:
12:       <form id="WebForm1" method="post" runat="server">
13:       <table>
14:        <tr>
15:          <td valign=top>
16:            Session ID
17:          </td>
18:          <td>
19:            <% response.write(Session.SessionID) %>
20:          </td>
21:        </tr>
22:        <tr>
23:          <td valign=top>
24:            Application Contents
```

LISTING 9.5   continued

```
25:            </td>
26:            <td>
27:              <asp:listbox id=lstSessions runat=server rows=15>
28:
29:              </asp:listbox>
30:            </td>
31:          </tr>
32:          <tr>
33:            <td valign=top>
34:              Session Timeout
35:            </td>
36:            <td>
37:              <% response.write(Session.TimeOut) %>
38:            </td>
39:          </tr>
40:        </table>
41:        </form>
42:
43:      </body>
44:  </html>
```

LISTING 9.6   *WebForm1.aspx.vb*

```
1:    Public Class WebForm1
2:       Inherits System.Web.UI.Page
3:       Protected WithEvents lstSessions As System.Web.UI.WebControls.ListBox
4:
5:    #Region " Web Form Designer Generated Code "
6:
7:       'This call is required by the Web Form Designer.
8:       <System.Diagnostics.DebuggerStepThroughAttribute()> _
9:        Private Sub InitializeComponent()
10:
11:       End Sub
12:
13:     Protected Sub Page_Init(ByVal Sender As Object, _
14:       ByVal e As System.EventArgs) Handles MyBase.Init
15:       'CODEGEN: This method call is required by the Web Form Designer
16:       'Do not modify it using the code editor.
17:       InitializeComponent()
18:     End Sub
19:
20:    #End Region
21:
22:     Private Sub Page_Load(ByVal sender As Object, _
23:       ByVal e As EventArgs) Handles MyBase.Load
24:       Dim txtCount As New System.Web.UI.WebControls.TextBox()
```

LISTING 9.6 continued

```
25:
26:        Dim obj As IEnumerator
27:
28:        lstSessions.Items.Clear()
29:        Application.Lock()
30:        obj = Application.AllKeys.GetEnumerator
31:        Do While obj.MoveNext
32:          lstSessions.Items.Add(obj.Current.ToString + ": " _
33:            + Application(obj.Current.ToString).ToString)
34:        Loop
35:        obj = Nothing
36:        Application.UnLock()
37:    End Sub
38:
39: End Class
```

LISTING 9.7 *WebForm2.aspx*

```
1:   <%@ Page Language="vb"
2:       AutoEventWireup="false"
3:       Codebehind="WebForm2.aspx.vb"
4:       Inherits="Chapter9.WebForm2"%>
5:
6:   <HTML>
7:     <HEAD>
8:       <meta name="GENERATOR" content="Microsoft Visual Studio.NET 7.0">
9:       <meta name="CODE_LANGUAGE" content="Visual Basic 7.0">
10:      <META HTTP-EQUIV="Refresh" CONTENT="5">
11:    </HEAD>
12:    <body>
13:
14:      <form id="WebForm2" method="post" runat="server">
15:      <table>
16:        <tr>
17:          <td valign=top>
18:            Session ID
19:          </td>
20:          <td>
21:            <% response.write(Session.SessionID) %>
22:          </td>
23:        </tr>
24:        <tr>
25:          <td valign=top>
26:            Current Time
27:          </td>
28:          <td>
29:            <%
```

LISTING 9.7 continued

```
30:                    response.write(Now.ToLongDateString)
31:                    response.write(" ")
32:                    response.write(Now.ToLongTimeString)
33:                %>
34:              </td>
35:            </tr>
36:            <tr>
37:              <td valign=top>
38:                Application Contents
39:              </td>
40:              <td>
41:                <asp:listbox id=lstSessions runat=server rows=15>
42:
43:                </asp:listbox>
44:              </td>
45:            </tr>
46:          </table>
47:        </form>
48:
49:      </body>
50:    </HTML>
```

LISTING 9.8 *WebForm2.aspx.vb*

```
1:    Public Class WebForm2
2:        Inherits System.Web.UI.Page
3:        Protected WithEvents lstSessions As System.Web.UI.WebControls.ListBox
4:
5:    #Region " Web Forms Designer Generated Code "
6:
7:        'CODEGEN: This procedure is required by the Web Form Designer
8:        'Do not modify it using the code editor.
9:        Private Sub InitializeComponent()
10:
11:    End Sub
12:
13:    #End Region
14:
15:      Private Sub Page_Init(ByVal sender As Object, _
16:        ByVal e As EventArgs) Handles MyBase.Init
17:
18:        Dim obj As IEnumerator
19:
20:        Application.Lock()
21:        obj = Application.AllKeys.GetEnumerator
22:        Do While obj.MoveNext
```

LISTING 9.8 continued

```
23:        lstSessions.Items.Add(obj.Current.ToString + ": " _
24:          + Application(obj.Current.ToString).ToString)
25:        Loop
26:        Application.UnLock()
27:        obj = Nothing
28:      End Sub
29:    End Class
```

To start this application, first view the WebForm1.aspx page in a browser window. Next, open a new browser window and then open the WebForm1.aspx page again (don't use the menu option in your browser because the new browser will share the same session as the first browser). Now open the WebForm2.aspx page in a third new browser window. The WebForm2.aspx page has a header value that causes this page to be refreshed every 5 seconds:

```
<META HTTP-EQUIV="Refresh" CONTENT="5">
```

When the window first opens, the Application Contents list box should indicate that three sessions have started. As this page refreshes, the request count increases. If you refresh one of the other browser windows, you'll notice that the request count increases. If you let the WebForm1.aspx browser windows remain idle for a full 60 seconds, the WebForm2.aspx page will reflect the shutdown of the sessions in the other two browser windows as well as in the first.

Figures 9.5 through 9.8 demonstrate the preceding examples.

FIGURE 9.5

The first
WebForm1.aspx
browser.

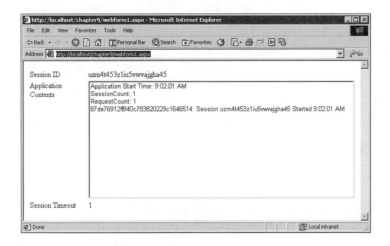

Figure 9.5 illustrates the first session being created as WebForm1.aspx is launched. Notice that the session count equals 1 and a unique session ID has been assigned to this session.

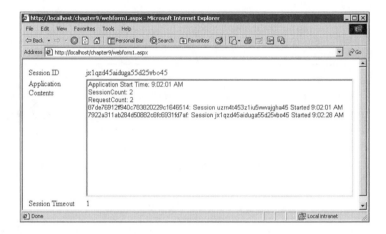

Figure 9.6 illustrates a second session of WebForm1 being created. Notice that the application session count now equals 2. Also, a new unique session ID has been assigned to this second instance of the WebForm1.aspx file.

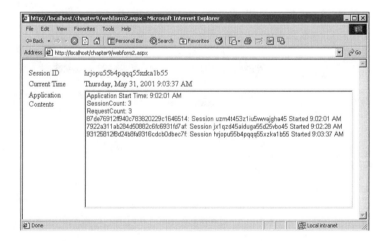

Figure 9.7 illustrates the first instance of the WebForm2.aspx file. This is the first instance created of the WebForm2.aspx file, but it's the third session created for the application. Notice in the Application Contents box that the session count is now equal to 3. This

Application Contents box also displays each current session's unique identifier (session ID) with the start time of when the session was created. These IDs and start times can be cross-referenced with the previous figures.

FIGURE 9.8

WebForm2.aspx browser output after the initial two sessions have ended due to timing out.

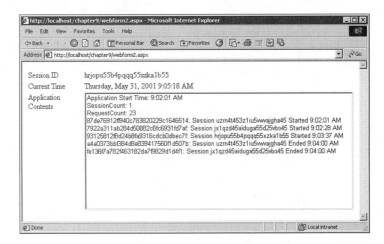

Figure 9.8 illustrates the timing out of the two `WebForm1.aspx` sessions. As mentioned earlier, if we let the browsers stay idle for the timeout period (set to 1 minute in this example), the browsers will time out and their sessions will end. Figure 9.8 illustrates in the Application Contents box that the session count is now 1. This last active session is the `WebForm2.aspx` session. Also notice that the session IDs of the active session and the closed sessions, with their corresponding start times, are listed in the Application Contents box. This box also displays the newly closed session IDs and end times of the initial WebForm1 sessions.

The following list contains code snippets seen in the previous listings. These bullets illustrate code integral in our previous State Management example.

- Creates a new globally unique identifier (GUID)

```
Application(replace(System.Guid.NewGuid.ToString, "-", "")) = "Session " +
Session.SessionID + " Started " + Now.ToLongTimeString
```

- Data type conversion

```
        lngCount = CLng(Application.Get("SessionCount").ToString) + 1
```

- Locking and unlocking the `Application` object

```
        Application.Lock()
        Application("RequestCount") = _
```

```
CLng(Application("RequestCount").ToString) + 1
Application.UnLock()
```

- Retrieving session properties

```
<% response.write(Session.SessionID) %>
<% response.write(Session.TimeOut) %>
```

- Looping through the items in the application collection

```
Dim obj As IEnumerator
obj = Application.AllKeys.GetEnumerator
Do While obj.MoveNext
lstSessions.Items.Add(obj.Current.ToString + ": " +
Application(obj.Current.ToString).ToString)
Loop
obj = Nothing
```

Summary

This hour you learned about ASP.NET applications' common lifecycle event handlers and how to configure application parameters such as `timeout`. You also learned about state management and how to use the Application and Session dictionaries to store global application variables as well as session global variables. Also, the `Application` object has locking capabilities that allow you to synchronize global application data values across all instances of your application, but these should be used only when necessary and with caution because they can cause major issues with the overall stability of your application.

Q&A

Q. Where do I set the session `timeout` settings?

A. In the `sessionstate` section found in the `Web.config` file.

Q. When would I configure state data as application data instead of session data?

A. When the data being set is not unique to an individual user/session. Application data is available globally to all active sessions.

Q. What are the two ways to track session data?

A. By using cookies and query strings.

Q. If session timeouts are never instituted on a Web application, what happens to the session data when the user logs off?

A. The session data would remain on the server, using up resources. The application would not know when it was safe to end the session and clean up any session variables.

Workshop

Quiz

1. When is an `Application_End` event called?

2. True or false? There are three types of state data: application, session, and browser.

3. What is the purpose of the `Global.aspx` file?

Exercise

Create a Web application with two Web forms. The first Web form should ask the user to enter his or her name. The second Web form will confirm the user's name. Place a Submit button on the first Web form to launch the second Web form. Using session state variables you set in WebForm1, display the username in WebForm2.

Answers for Hour 9

Quiz

1. When is an `Application_End` event called?

   When the last session object has been destroyed.

2. True or false? There are three types of state data: application, session, and browser.

   False. There are two types of state data: application and session.

3. What is the purpose of the `Global.aspx` file?

   The `Global.aspx` file contains the code for any lifecycle event handles (`Application_Start`, `Application_End`, `Session_Start`, `Session_End`, and so on).

Hour **10**

Security

One of the most critical aspects of any type of Web development is securing your application. This is especially true if you are going to be handling sensitive data that must be encrypted or if you need to authenticate your users and provide access to portions of your site based on their defined roles. ASP.NET and Internet Information Server provide several features that aid in securing your application.

In this hour, you will be introduced to the security mechanisms and considerations for ASP.NET applications running on IIS. You will also learn about

- ASP.NET architecture and data flow
- The various types of authentication available in IIS and ASP.NET
- Securing your Web server

Security Overview

An important part of any Web application is the need to identify who your user is and apply security settings for that user. In order to fully implement security in your application, you must understand how ASP.NET handles security as well as how ASP.NET interacts with IIS.

ASP.NET Data Flow

You can implement security in ASP.NET applications in two ways. The first method relies on IIS and Windows security permissions. This type of security is called *imperson-ation*, because once IIS has authenticated the user, a token is passed to the ASP.NET application for use. Because you are relying on the Windows environment to process security credentials, it is important to use the NTFS file system so that permissions can be set on your resources.

For this method, the following sequence of events occurs:

1. The user attempts to access a page on the Web server.

2. IIS authenticates the client using anonymous access or basic, digest, or integrated Windows authentication.

3. If the client authenticates properly; then IIS transfers the initial resource request to the ASP.NET application in the form of a token.

4. The ASP.NET application impersonates the client using the token passed to it and uses the NTFS permissions assigned to the server resources for granting access.

5. If access is granted through NTFS permissions, the ASP.NET application returns the requested resource to the user through IIS.

The second method for handling security requests is called *ASP.NET authentication*, and it relies on built-in ASP.NET security. In this form of security, an application uses a cookie created by ASP.NET that typically stores username and password information. The ASP.NET application then takes that information and makes its own determination of the authenticity of this information. For this type of authentication to work best, you turn on anonymous access in your IIS box. Otherwise, IIS will attempt to authenticate the user through its own means before sending the request over to your ASP.NET appli-cation to be authenticated again. Anonymous access, the default IIS authentication method, is discussed in more detail in the section titled "Windows Authentication Through IIS."

For ASP.NET authentication, server-resource requests go through the following series of events:

1. The user attempts to access a page on the Web server.

2. IIS takes this request and either authenticates it, itself, or, if anonymous access is turned on, passes the request over to the ASP.NET application.

3. If the authentication cookie is present on the client's computer, the information in that cookie is compared to security-configuration information stored with the ASP.NET application. If the credentials are authenticated, the request is processed and ASP.NET sends the page to the user.

If the authentication cookie is not present on the client machine, the user is redirected to the login page defined by the ASP.NET application's configuration settings. Here, the user must enter his or her username and password and submit them for authentication.

4. The ASP.NET application then validates the user, typically through a user-validation function, and transmits the security cookie to the user's computer. If user validation fails, an "Access Denied" message appears on the screen.

5. If the user is authenticated through the ASP.NET application, the process cycles back to step 3 to see whether access to the requested resource or page is permitted. If it is not, an "Access Denied" message appears on the screen.

ASP.NET Security Architecture

10

The ASP.NET security architecture consists of two. The first component is its integration with IIS. The second component is located in the root directory of your ASP.NET application, in a file called Web.config. This file stores different configuration settings, including security settings, for your application.

Windows and IIS Security

The first step to securing your application begins with the Web server that is hosting your site. In most cases, that Web server is Internet Information Server 5.0, which is automatically installed with Windows 2000 Server and can be manually added to Windows 2000 Professional. IIS gives you several methods of securing your Web site. These options are located under the Directory Security tab of the Properties window for your site. To access the Directory Security tab, follow these instructions:

To Do

1. Click Start, Programs, Administrative Tools. Then select Internet Services Manager.

2. Once the IIS console appears, expand the plus sign to the left of the computer name. Right-click Default Web Site and select the Properties option.

3. In the Default Web Site Properties window, click the Directory Security tab.

On this screen, you can set the authentication mechanism for your site, specify the IP address and domain name restrictions, and manage secure communications. You can also modify these settings for each virtual directory on the Web server hosting your site (with the exception of the secure communication) as well as for every other Web site installed on the server.

IP Address and Domain Name Restrictions

In IIS, you can grant or deny certain IP addresses and domain names access to your Web site. Figure 10.1 shows the IP Address and Domain Name Restrictions screen.

FIGURE 10.1

The IP Address and Domain Name Restrictions screen.

By default, IIS grants access to all IP addresses and domain names that visit your site, unless you specify a particular IP address or domain name you wish to exclude. Alternately, you can set IIS to deny access to all IP addresses and domain names except for the ones you have specified. This method is much more restrictive and is recommended only if you have information on your site that should be made available to just a small number of users.

Windows Authentication Through IIS

Another security mechanism built in to IIS is its capability to authenticate0 users. Figure 10.2 illustrates the administrative screen used to set authentication options.

FIGURE 10.2

The Authentication Methods screen.

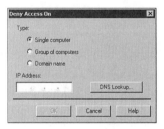

The first level is *anonymous access*. If the Anonymous Access box is checked, all users are authenticated to the site using the built-in Windows account IUSR_*computername*, where *computername* is the name of your Web server. One nice feature of IIS is that it can create a unique password for this account, which means users with server administration privileges won't need to generate a suitable password for your Internet user account or keep up with the necessary password changes that occur on well-maintained networks.

The second level of authentication is *basic*. This type of authentication prompts the user for logon credentials in the form of a username and password. This is a good way to secure your Web site's content; however, this method's major drawback is that the username and password are transmitted as clear text—that is, without any encryption—to the Web server for authentication. This means that anyone with a packet sniffer, software that monitors and divulges the content of TCP/IP packets and the ability to read the packets can gain access to your site.

To overcome this drawback, you must create a secure connection to your Web server using Secure Sockets Layer (port 443), also known as *SSL*. When you see "`https://`" at the beginning of a URL, you know that the Web site is using SSL. SSL uses a public-key system to encrypt all data that is passed between the user's computer and the Web server. It also authenticates the user's computer to ensure that no one else has stolen his or her online identity. A full discussion of SSL is beyond the scope of this book, although it will be covered in more detail later in this hour. The important point to remember now is that it is critical to fully utilizing basic authentication on your Web site.

The third level of authentication on IIS 5.0 is *digestauthentication*. This method is similar to basic authentication, except that the password is not transmitted to the Web server as clear text. Instead, it is encrypted in the form of a hash value before getting sent back to the server.

A hash value, or *message digest*, contains binary data that is generated using a *hashing algorithm*. All hash values have four common properties, regardless of the type of algorithm used:

- All hash values are between 128 and 160 bits long, even if the message being encrypted is several kilobytes, or even gigabytes, in length.

- All messages that are hashed will create a completely different hash value, even if the messages being hashed differ by only one bit.

- Each and every time an algorithm is applied to a message, it will always produce the same hash value.

- All hashing algorithms are performed "one-way." It is impossible to recover the original message, even if you have a copy of the algorithm used in the hashing process.

Several steps occur during digest authentication:

1. The Web server sends the browser certain information to be used in the authentication process.

2. The Web browser adds this information, along with some other information that is beyond the scope of this book, to its username and password along with some other information and performs a hash on it.

3. The resulting hash is sent back to the Web server.

4. The Web server adds the information it sent to the browser to a clear-text copy of the password stored on the Web server and performs the same hash on it.

5. The Web server compares the hash value transmitted to it by the browser to the hash value it calculated on the server.

6. If the hash values are identical, access is granted. Otherwise, an error is returned to the browser and the user must try to authenticate again.

The additional information that is sent to the client is added to the username and password to prevent unauthorized users from capturing the hash and trying to impersonate an actual client. This information is used by the Web server to aid in identifying the client, the client's computer, and the domain to which the client belongs. A timestamp is also sent to the browser to prevent clients from accessing the site after their privileges have been revoked.

Digest authentication is a new feature to HTTP 1.1 and is not supported by all browsers. At the moment, Internet Explorer 5 is the only browser to support digest authentication. Noncompliant browsers receive an error message from the Web server if they attempt to access a resource that uses digest authentication. One benefit of using digest authentication, though, is that it can be used over a firewall or proxy server.

In order to use digest authentication, your Web server must work in conjunction with a Windows 2000 domain controller. Furthermore, Web servers must have a clear-text copy of the password in order for digest authentication to operate properly. The lack of encryption of these passwords means that it is extremely important to secure the Web server from both physical and network-based attacks. Finally, a Windows user account must be set up for each user who wishes to access your resource. These accounts can be either local accounts residing on the Web server or global ones residing on the domain controller.

The fourth and final level of authentication is *integrated Windows*. Integrated Windows authentication never actually transmits any username or password information to the Web server. Instead, the browser proves to the Web server that it knows the username and password by using the current user role.

This form of authentication is available only to Internet Explorer servers, version 2.0 and higher. The benefit of using this type of authentication is that in most instances users will not need to actually log on to the Web site, because they are already authenticated to the domain controller on the network. Therefore, anyone accessing your Web site through this type of authentication must have a user account on the domain controller. Unfortunately, this form of authentication does not work through a proxy server or firewall. The best use of it is usually on intranet sites, where all users are on the same domain and using Internet Explorer.

`Web.config` Security

If you want our ASP.NET application to validate your users, you must use the `Web.config` file. Stored as an XML file in the root directory, `Web.config` describes various configuration settings. There is a node in this file called `<security>` that contains security configuration information for your ASP.NET application. The following code shows some of the attributes of the `<security>` node of a `Web.config` file:

```
<authentication mode="[Windows/Cookie/Passport]">
    <cookie cookie="[name]" loginurl="[url]" decryptionkey="[key]">
        <credentials passwordformat="[Clear, SHA1, MD5]">
            <user name="[UserName]" password="[password]"/>
        </credentials>
    </cookie>
</authentication>

<authorization>
    <allow users="[comma separated list of users]"
           roles="[comma separated list of roles]"/>
    <deny users="[comma separated list of users]"
           roles="[comma separated list of roles]"/>
</authorization>

<identity>
    <impersonation enable="[true/false]"/>
</identity>
```

In this example, three subtags can be defined in the `Web.config` file: `<authentication>`, `<authorization>`, and `<identity>`. The first, defines the default authentication mode to be used in this ASP.NET application, and it has one attribute, called mode, that can have one of four settings: Windows, Passport, Cookie, and None. Windows authentication mode was discussed earlier in the section "Windows and IIS Security." Passport authentication is a service provided by Microsoft for centralized authentication. This authentication mode is discussed in more detail in a later section. Cookie authentication was discussed briefly in the beginning of this hour and is expanded upon below.

ASP.NET Subtags

The `<authentication>` subtag supports one subelement, called `<cookie>`. This subelement has three attributes:

- `Cookie`. Contains the name of the HTTP cookie file used for ASP.NET authentication. By default, this value is .ASPXAUTH.

- `Loginurl`. Contains the URL that users are redirected to if their cookie credentials cannot be authenticated properly. This URL is the login URL for the ASP.NET application.

- `Decryptionkey`. Contains the key used to decrypt credential information stored in the authentication cookie. This key is stored as clear text in this file.

The <cookie> subtag also can have an optional subtag called <credentials>. This subtag has one attribute, password format, that defines the encryption format used to store passwords. The encryption formats supported by ASP.NET are clear, MD5, and SHA1 (clear stands for clear-text encryption, which is no encryption, and MD5 and SHA1 are hashing algorithms used to encrypt usernames and passwords). The <credentials> subtag also supports the <user> subtag, which has two attributes, name and password, that hold username and password values.

A second subtag in the Web.config file is the <authorization> subtag. This subtag controls client access to your ASP.NET application. It supports two subtags: <allow> and <deny>. The <allow> tag enables you to explicitly identify a comma-separated list of users and roles that can access the requested resource or URL. It supports four kinds of access: users, roles, anonymous, and all. The <deny> tag specifies a comma-separated list of users and/or roles that are denied access to the requested resource. Two special identities can be used with either of these subtags. These identities are all users or roles, which are represented with an asterisk (*) instead of as a comma-separated list, as shown in the code below. The second special identity is anonymous access, which represented with a question mark (?).

When a user requests access to the URL, the <authorization> section of the Web.config file is processed from top to bottom, and the first match of the user to either <allow> or <deny> is selected. If no match for either <allow> or <deny> is found, the user is automatically denied access to the requested resource. A third type of attribute can be used with the <allow> and <deny> tags. This attribute is called *verbs*, and it specifies which users and/or roles can use the HTTP verbs, such as GET and POST.

For example, to allow Jack access to your site and deny everybody else, you would use the following syntax:

```
<authorization>
    <allow users="Jack" />
    <deny users="*" />
</authorization>
```

Alternatively, to allow Sally to use the POST method and allow everyone else to use only the GET method, you would use this syntax:

```
<authorization>
    <allow verb="GET" users="*" />
    <allow verb="POST" users="Sally" />
    <deny verb="POST" users="*"
</authorization>
```

You do not need to use the `<authorization>` section of the Web.config file if you are going to authenticate your users against a database.

The third and final subtag for the security section of the Web.config file is the `<identity>` subtag. It enables or disables impersonation authorization for the Web site. Impersonation is used by the ASP.NET application when authentication is to be performed only by IIS and Windows using user accounts and NTFS permissions on resources.

The Web.config file is discussed in more detail in Hour 22, "Configuration, Localization, and Deployment."

ASP.NET Authentication and Authorization

ASP.NET can authenticate and authorize users as well. Most traditional applications use an authentication scheme similar to this. These sites require you to go to a specific login page and enter a username and password to identify yourself to the system. As you've already seen, ASP.NET applications support the Web.config file, which contains security information for users accessing site resources. This file stores user and role information that defines which users and roles can access the site and which are denied.

This file can work in conjunction with forms-based authentication, which is another name for the cookie authentication performed by an ASP.NET application. This type of authentication is automatically performed by ASP.NET upon successful authentication to the site through the login URL. Once a user logs on to the site, the username and password are stored in the authentication cookie to be used with each subsequent resource request.

Passport Authentication

Another type of authentication not discussed in much detail yet is Passport authentication. Passport authentication is a centralized service provided by Microsoft to store user authentication information. All sites that subscribe to this service can use a one-time login system to access multiple sites and resources. To use this type of authentication, you must first purchase and download the Passport SDK from www.passport.com/business. Once you have completed that step, set the `<authentication>` subtag's mode attribute in your Web.config file to Passport. When users access your site for the first time, they will automatically be redirected to the Passport login site for authentication. If they authenticate successfully, they will be redirected back to your site along with authentication information contained in the querystring of the URL. When the URL is processed by your Web server, the authentication information in the querystring is removed and placed into a cookie for future resource requests.

Secure Connections with SSL

When using the authentication methods described in this hour, in most instances you are going through some form of data encryption, typically in the form of Secure Sockets Layer (SSL). SSL also known as https (for most web purposes) normally runs over port 443 on Web server.

Secure Sockets Layer is implemented through the use of a public-key encryption system. This type of encryption system utilizes a public key to encrypt information and a private key to decrypt it. When data is encrypted with the public key, it can be decrypted only with the private key, and vice versa.

SSL is utilized through digital certificates. A *certificate* is basically an identifier issued by a trusted third-party agency, similar to a notary public, that says you are who you say you are. Two types of certificates are used for secure communications. The first type, the server certificate, is used to identify to the client that the server is legitimate and authentic. The second type, the client certificate, acts like a digital signature to identify the client to the server.

In a secure connection using server certificates, which is the most common form of SSL connection, four major steps are performed to initiate the encrypted connection:

1. The client requests a secure connection with the server over port 443.
2. The server sends its certificate, which includes the public encryption key, to the client.
3. The client validates the server certificate, generates a session key, and encrypts it with the key sent down in the certificate from the server.
4. The server decrypts the session key with its private key and creates a secure connection.

In order to use a certificate, you must either generate one or apply for a third-party certificate from a company such as VeriSign (www.verisign.com) or Thawte (www.thawte.com). Let's begin by generating a certificate for use on a Web site.

Requesting a Certificate for SSL

Follow these instructions to get your certificate:

1. Open the Internet Services Manager under the Programs/Administrative Tools menu option.

2. View the Default Web Site Properties window by right-clicking it and selecting Properties from the menu.

3. Select the Directory Security tab and then click the Server Certificate button.

4. The welcome screen for the Web Server Certificate Wizard will appear. Click Next to continue.

5. Make sure that Create a New Certificate option is selected on this screen and then click Next.

6. Make sure the Prepare the Request Now, but Send It Later option is selected and then click Next.

7. Enter a name in the Name field on this screen. For this example, we'll use "ASP.NET in 24 Hours Test Certificate." Select 512 as the bit length for the key and click Next to continue.

8. Type your company's name or your name in the Organization field and enter the Organization Unit. You must enter values in each of these fields to continue. Click Next to continue.

9. Enter the fully qualified domain name for your site. If your site is to be located on an intranet, you can use the computer's NetBIOS name.

10. Enter your geographical information and click Next.

11. Leave the default filename and path in the Certificate Request File Name screen and click Next to continue.

12. If the summary screen looks good to you, click the Next button; otherwise, click the Back button to go back and correct any errors in the certificate request.

13. You will be notified that the certificate request has been successfully saved. You can click the Click Here link to view certificate authorities, or you can click Finish to close down the wizard. In order to complete the request, you must send or e-mail the certificate request file to a valid certificate authority.

For this book, we will use VeriSign as our certificate authority. But before we begin the process necessary to get a server certificate, let's take a look at the certificate request file generated in the previous example.

Your file should look similar to this:

```
-----BEGIN NEW CERTIFICATE REQUEST-----
MIIC1DCCAj4CAQAwgYMxIjAgBgNVBAMTGXd3dy5vc2lyaXNNpbnRlcmFjdGl2ZS5j
b20xFDASBgNVBAsTC0hvbWUgb2ZmaWN1MRswGQYDVQQKExJPU01SSVMgaW50ZXJh
Y3RpdmUxEDAOBgNVBAcTB1JhbGVpZ2gxCzAJBgNVBAgTAk5DMQswCQYDVQQGEwJV
UzBcMA0GCSqGSIb3DQEBAQUAA0sAMEgCQQDkmbwmqfPw7zUaIj/M0sQN7K1B+ygC
A661j+bNhhI4YAxXkMRuTgs+by7uBl/YqBDmdPtWvvXM0MzIv5P1Co+XAgMBAAGg
ggFTMBoGCisGAQQBgjcNAgMxDBYKNS4wLjIxOTUuMjA1BgorBgEEAYI3AgEOMScw
JTAOBgNVHQ8BAf8EBAMCBPAwEwYDVR01BAwwCgYIKwYBBQUHAwEwgf0GCisGAQQB
gjcNAgIxge4wgesCAQEeWgBNAGkAYwByAG8AcwBvAGYAdAAgAFIAUwBBACAAUwBD
AGgAYQBuAG4AZQBsACAAQwByAHkAcAB0AG8AZwByAGEAcABoAGkAYwAgAFAAcgBv
AHYAaQBkAGUAcgOBiQDSPDCWU8LC2bPGssn/b+ukYK8eurNjMBKbGvaW11U/g4mi
BAopxZDPm+TB0Q+YRjbci9qb7eNILmhnr4jni2GKd71jM0vIdnmVkrXWdqUq7903
qFvAGEF6bFSiLg2kgV93DowjGbVuaVwsXFojiO0ntQMiD6kwyIytpICjjMBoEwAA
AAAAAAAAMA0GCSqGSIb3DQEBBQUAA0EAB60NRvXtzHjt/uHF6LU7KTdABuHyinVz
iiCx+6zommkB1132f2wH/X3G+1K0BWO9X7ELLBNG1TFrM+2IpVsYDw==
-----END NEW CERTIFICATE REQUEST-----
```

This file contains various bits of information, including your public key, the name of the certificate, your geographic information, and the URL for which you want the certificate. When you create a digital certificate request, you are actually generating your public and private encryption keys. The certificate authority is used to store a copy of your public key so that when you set up an SSL connection on your Web site, your clients can compare the public key you transmit to them to the public key stored at the certificate authority's repository. This process ensures that you are a legitimate organization with a legitimate presence on the Web.

The next step in the process is to apply for a certificate from a certificate authority. In our case, we are going to use VeriSign, a well-known certificate authority that is prevalent on many secure web sites.

Obtaining a Certificate from a Certificate Authority

For the sake of expediency, we are going to obtain a trial certificate from VeriSign in this example. The normal process for obtaining a digital certificate takes days because the certificate authority must verify your identity. Here are the steps to follow:

1. Open your Web browser and go to the URL http://www.verisign.com/ products/site/index.html. On this page, you will see a list of the products VeriSign offers. Click the Try link located next to the Buy option in the Secure Site Services product listing.

2. On the next screen, enter the appropriate information and click the Submit button to continue.

3. On the next screen, you can review the requirements for obtaining a certificate. Click the Continue button to move on.

4. The next screen begins the process of obtaining the test certificate. Because we've already generated our certificate signing request in the previous example, you can click Continue to proceed to the next step.

5. On this screen, copy and paste your encrypted certificate request into the text box. Click Continue to proceed.

6. VeriSign then detects the key length that we are requesting. In our case, VeriSign is notifying us that we are requesting a 512-bit key length. Click Continue to go to the next screen.

7. This screen displays the information we entered in the previous example to request a certificate. Also on the screen is an area to include technical contact information. The person indicated here will receive the test server ID from VeriSign. Fill in the fields on the form and click the "Accept" button to accept the agreement.

8. VeriSign then processes our request and e-mails the test server ID to the recipient specified as the technical contact.

Once you receive the test certificate, you will need to install it on your Web server. Before you can install it, you must first save it from the e-mail into a text file with a .CER extension. Make sure to include the `-----BEGIN CERTIFICATE-----` and the `-----END CERTIFICATE-----` delimiters when saving this file. To install this certificate onto your Web server, follow these steps:

1. Open the Properties window for the default Web site in the Internet Services Manager Console window.

2. Select the "Directory Security" tab and then click the "Server Certificate" button to open the Certificate Wizard.

3. Click "Next" to bypass the welcome screen.

4. Select "Process the Pending Request and Install the Certificate." Then click "Next."

5. Browse to the location of the certificate file you saved from the e-mail sent by VeriSign. Click "Next" to continue.

6. The next screen displays a summary of the certificate information. Click "Next" to continue.

7. You will receive a notification that the certificate has been installed on the server. Click "Finish" to close the Certificate Wizard.

Once the certificate is installed on the server, you are ready to use SSL on your Web site. Make sure to redirect your users with the `https://` syntax instead of the regular `http://` syntax. Also, verify the SSL connection works by accessing your site through a Web browser.

10

You can also view and edit your certificate from the "Directory Security" tab of the Web site's Properties window. To view your certificate, click the "View Certificate" button on this screen. This will display a certificate window that allows you to view general and detailed certificate information.

Summary

In this hour, you learned how ASP.NET and IIS handle security in your application. When developing with ASP.NET, you can use two methods of authentication. The first is *impersonation*, in which IIS and Windows handle authentication matters and file permissions and pass an identifying token to the ASP.NET application that impersonates the client. The second method involves authentication through your ASP.NET application, using a Web.config file and its security settings.

You were also introduced to public-key encryption and utilizing Secure Sockets Layer to encrypt the data that is transmitted between your Web server and the client browser. Coupled with the security features in ASP.NET and IIS, SSL allows you to create secure solutions to quell the fears of skeptical users.

Q&A

Q. What is the best authentication method for an ASP.NET application?

A. Well, that all depends on how you design your application. Some applications require much more security than others. When you are building a secure intranet application, using Windows authentication and NTFS permissions may be the best choice. On an e-commerce site, using ASP.NET's cookie authentication with a login page may be the best solution. Weigh the pros and cons of each authentication method to help you in your decision.

Q. Based on the discussion in this hour, why would anyone use basic authentication?

A. Basic authentication is still a good method of securing Web files as long as it is used in conjunction with SSL on the server. SSL is important because username and password information is normally passed as clear text. SSL adds a layer of encryption, which prevents malicious users from gaining unauthorized access to your Web site.

Workshop

The Workshop provides quiz questions to help further your understanding of the material covered in this hour.

Quiz

1. Which authentication type uses impersonation?

2. What is a hash and what four common properties are associated with it?

3. Name the attribute in the `<authentication>` subtag and the settings for this attribute in the `Web.config` file.

Exercise

Use the two authentication methods in an application to see where they differ. Make sure to set NTFS permissions on the directories and pages when using integrated Windows, digest, or basic authentication through IIS. Use the different aspects of the `Web.config` file to gain a better understanding of how this file works in conjunction with your application.

Answers to Chapter 10

Quiz

1. Which authentication type uses impersonation?

   IIS and Windows authentication utilizes impersonation.

2. What is a hash and what four common properties are associated with it?

   A hash value, or *message digest*, contains binary data that is generated using a *hashing algorithm*. All hash values have four common properties, regardless of the type of algorithm used:

   - All hash values are between 128 and 160 bits long, even if the message being encrypted is several kilobytes, or even gigabytes, in length.

   - All messages that are hashed will create a completely different hash value, even if the messages being hashed differ by only one bit.

   - Each and every time an algorithm is applied to a message, it will always produce the same hash value.

   - All hashing algorithms are performed "one-way." It is impossible to recover the original message, even if you have a copy of the algorithm used in the hashing process.

3. Name the attribute in the `<authentication>` subtag and the settings for this attribute in the `Web.config` file.

   The attribute is called mode and can have one of the following properties: Windows, Cookie, or Passport.

10

HOUR 11

Incorporating E-mail into Your Application

With many of today's Web-based applications, the ability to send e-mail is of paramount importance. Most sites use an HTML anchor tag with the `mailto` attribute set to a receiving party. This method works most of the time, but sometimes you need to send an e-mail to a user that contains information extracted from a database. Also, not everyone has an e-mail program installed on his or her computer.

To address these needs, ASP.NET allows you to send e-mails through the built-in SMTP virtual server on Windows 2000, which we will discuss in great detail this hour. The SMTP server lets you create Web sites that offer more interactivity to your user.

In this hour, you will learn how to implement e-mail capabilities in your ASP.NET application. You will also gain a better understanding of

- Configuring the SMTP virtual server on Windows 2000
- Creating and sending e-mails using text as well as using HTML encoding
- Adding attachments to e-mails

Setting Up SMTP

SMTP, also known as the *Simple Mail Transport Protocol*, is a set of standardized procedures for sending and receiving electronic mail over a network such as the Internet. SMTP is different from the Post Office Protocol (POP3) and the Internet Message Access Protocol (IMAP) in that their function is for the receiving of e-mail only. SMTP is used only on servers for the sending and storing e-mails.

Like most everything else that uses the Internet, SMTP requires the use of DNS, the *domain name service* (or *system*), to translate the domain name of an e-mail address to the e-mail server's IP address for that domain. This method of translating names into IP addresses is called *name resolution*.

In order to use the SMTP server on Windows 2000, you must first configure it to function properly. By default, Windows 2000 installs an SMTP server during the standard installation process of installing the Internet Information Services (IIS). If, for some reason, IIS has not been installed on your operating system, you can install it now. On the Windows 2000 Server operating system use the Configure Your Server menu option under the Administrative Tools menu. When installing IIS on Windows 2000 Professional use the "Add/Remove programs" icon in the Control Panel.

To configure your SMTP server, follow these steps:

1. Open the IIS administrative console from the Administrative Tools menu.
2. Right-click the default SMTP virtual server and click the Properties menu option on the action menu.
3. On the General tab, you can change the name for your SMTP server.
4. Click the Delivery tab. On this tab, you can set delivery and routing options for your SMTP server. (The default options are appropriate for all sample code in this chapter.)

Once your SMTP server is set up properly, you can move forward with integrating e-mail capabilities into your ASP.NET application. The next section discusses this in more detail.

Sending E-mail

In an ASP.NET application, several components need to come together to enable e-mail capability. The core element to this process is the inclusion of the `System.Web.Mail` namespace. This namespace contains all the required class objects and enumerators to facilitate e-mail.

The `System.Web.Mail` Namespace

The `System.Web.Mail` namespace is the container that holds the three class objects pertaining to e-mail, along with three enumerators. These classes enable you to construct and send e-mail using the SMTP mail service build into Windows 2000. The three class objects are `SmtpMail`, `MailMessage`, and `MailAttachment`. `MailEncoding`, `MailFormat`, and `MailPriority` are the enumerators defined in this namespace. They are used to define the context of the e-mail message being sent.

In order to use the `System.Web.Mail` namespace, you will need to import it at either the top of your ASP.NET page or on your code-behind page.

The `SmtpMail` Class

The `SmtpMail` class is used in the process of sending an e-mail message. This class has one method, `Send`, which sends the e-mail to the SMTP server for transmission. There are two ways in which `Send` can be used. The first way is for you to supply all the arguments to the Send method. The `Send` method has the following arguments: `From`, `To`, `Subject`, and `MessageText`. All are of the string data type.

The syntax for using this method is as follows:

```
objectName.Send ("recipient@domain.com", "sender@domain.com",

    "Subject", "Text of the Message")
```

The second way of using the Send method is in conjunction with the MailMessage class. Specifically, you pass the `MailMessage` class to the `Send` method instead of passing the arguments directly.

The `MailMessage` Class

The `MailMessage` class is used in conjunction with the `SmtpMail` class in that you must build the object and pass that object to the `SmtpMail` class in order to send an e-mail message. The `MailMessage` class has a list of fields, or *properties*, that can be set. This list of fields is more expansive than the four parameters available on the Send method, allowing for greater control and flexibility when you're sending e-mails from ASP.NET pages. Table 11.1 lists the properties for the `MailMessage` class.

11

TABLE 11.1 MailMessage *Class Properties*

Property Name	Description
Attachments	Specifies the list of attachments to be sent with the message.
Bcc	Specifies a semicolon-separated list of addresses that will receive a private copy of the e-mail. These addresses will not be visible to the recipients of the e-mail.
Body	Specifies the body, or *message*, of the e-mail.
BodyEncoding	Specifies the encoding type—either base 64 or uuencoded—of the e-mail message.
BodyFormat	Specifies the type of e-mail message body. This can be text or HTML.
Cc	Specifies a semicolon-separated list of e-mail addresses that will receive a copy of the e-mail message
From	Specifies the e-mail address of the sender.
Headers	Specifies any custom headers that are transmitted with the message.
Priority	Specifies the priority of the e-mail message: either high, normal, or low. Normal is the default priority.
Subject	Specifies the subject line of the message.
To	Specifies the e-mail address of the recipient. This can be a semicolon-separated list of addresses.
UrlContentBase	Specifies the base of all relative URLs used in an HTML-encoded e-mail message.

The syntax for using the MailMessage class is as follows:

```
Dim objMailMessage as New MailMessage()
objMailMessage.To = "recipient"
objMailMessage.From = "sender"
objMailMessage.Subject = "subject"
objMailMessage.Body = "Message body"
...
objMailMessage = Nothing
```

The MailAttachment Class

The third and final component used in creating and sending e-mail in ASP.NET applications is the MailAttachment class. This object allows you to send attachments with your e-mails. There are two properties associated with MailAttachment. The first is Encoding, which indicates the type of encoding to use on the attachment—either base 64 or uuencoding. The second is FileName, which indicates the name of the file to attach.

You must use this class in conjunction with the `MailMessage` object. Attachments are a property of the MailMessage object.

You can make two calls when adding an attachment:

```
MailAttachment(filename as string)
```

and

```
MailAttachment(filename as string, encoding as System.Web.Mail.MailEncoding)
```

To actually add an attachment to your `MailMessage` object, you must call the `Add` method of the `Attachments` object in the MailMessage object. For example, the following code

```
objMailMessage.Attachments.Add(new MailAttachment(filename))
```

will add an attachment to your e-mail.

You can add as many attachments to an e-mail as are capable of being sent by your SMTP server. You are limited only by the amount of data your e-mail system can handle. You can adjust the data size settings through the Messages tab in the Properties window for the SMTP virtual server.

The `Attachments` property actually returns an object that implements the `IList` interface in the `System.Collections` namespace. The `IList` interface is essentially a collection of objects—in this case, *attachments*—that can be indexed. In addition to the `Add` method, the `Remove` and `IndexOf` methods allow you to remove attachments and enumerate through the attachments, respectively. The `Item` property will return the object positioned at the index you are looking at.

Given the relationship between `Ilist` and `Attachments`, one method for adding an attachment to your e-mail is the following:

```
Dim objMailAttach as MailAttachment
Dim objMailMessage as New MailMessage()
Dim objList as IList

objMailAttach = new MailAttachment(filename)
objList = objMailMessage.Attachments
objList.Add(objMailAttach)
```

This example creates the `objList` object as an `IList` interface to the `System.Collections` namespace. The `objList` object, in turn, is assigned to the `Attachments` collection associated with the `MailMessage` object. Finally, the `Add` method is called on the objList and the attachment is added to the e-mail. The only steps left are to define the properties of the e-mail and send the e-mail to its recipient.

11

The MailEncoding, MailFormat, and MailPriority Enumerators

There are three enumerators in the System.Web.Mail namespace to help you to use the "Mail" classes properly. Each is used to define a specific setting for a property of the e-mail.

- The MailEncoding enumerator specifies how your e-mail or attachment will be encoded for delivery—using either base 64 or uuencoding.

- The MailFormat enumerator specifies the values associated with sending the e-mail as either plain text or HTML.

- Finally, the MailPriority sets the priority level of your e-mail: either high, normal (default), or low.

Creating a Simple E-mail Form

Now that we've reviewed what it takes to send e-mails in ASP.NET applications, let's put that information to use.

In the following example, I want to create a Web page that allows the user to send an e-mail. To do this, I will first create an ASP.NET page containing a subroutine that sends the e-mail. This subroutine will create an object and set it to the StmpMail. Once this class is set, the Send method is called to send the e-mail using the necessary arguments to create the e-mail. Finally, the SMTP object is set to Nothing to notify the garbage collector that it is safe to destroy, freeing any resources it may have been using. Note that this would happen automatically at the end of page processing, but it is a good practice to release your object references as soon as possible.

The code to run this example is shown in Listing 11.1. This code creates a Web page in which you can enter the recipient's e-mail address, the sender's e-mail address, the subject of the e-mail, and the body of the e-mail. You can also use the check box to specify whether to send the message as plain text or as HTML. In this example, the check box is ignored; however, it will be used in subsequent e-mail examples.

LISTING 11.1 Sending E-mail Using the *SmtpMail* Object

```
 1: <%@ Page Language="vb"%>
 2: <%@ Import namespace="System.Web.Mail"%>
 3: <script language="vb" runat="server">
 4:     Public Sub btnSendEmail_Click(ByVal Sender As System.Object,
➥    ByVal e As System.EventArgs)
 5:         Dim objSmtpMail As New SmtpMail()
 6:         objSmtpMail.Send(txtTo.text, txtFrom.text, txtSubject.text,
➥    txtMessage.text)
 7:     objSmtpMail= Nothing
 8:     End Sub
 9: </script>
10: <html>
```

LISTING 11.1   continued

```
11:    <head>
12:     <meta name="GENERATOR" content="Microsoft Visual Studio.NET 7.0">
13:     <meta name="CODE_LANGUAGE" content="Visual Basic 7.0">
14:    </head>
15:    <body>
16:     <form id="WebForm1" method="post" runat="server">
17:      <table width="100%" border="0" cellpadding="3" cellspacing="1">
18:        <tr>
19:            <td>
20:                <table width="500" border="0" cellspacing="1" cellpadding=
➥"3">
21:                    <tr>
22:                        <td align="right">
23:                            <asp:label font-bold="True" font-names="tahoma"
➥    font-size="10pt" id="lblTo" runat="Server">To: </asp:label>
24:                        </td>
25:                        <td align="left">
26:                            <asp:textbox id="txtTo" runat="Server"
➥    width="100"></asp:textbox>
27:                        </td>
28:                    </tr>
29:                    <tr>
30:                        <td align="right">
31:                            <asp:label font-bold="True" font-names="tahoma"
➥    font-size="10pt" id=lblFrom runat="Server">From: </asp:label>
32:                        </td>
33:                        <td align="left">
34:                            <asp:textbox id=txtFrom runat="Server"
➥    width="100"></asp:textbox>
35:                        </td>
36:                    </tr>
37:                    <tr>
38:                        <td align="right">
39:                            <asp:label font-bold="True" font-names="tahoma"
➥    font-size="10pt" id=Label1 runat="Server">Subject: </asp:label>
40:                        </td>
41:                        <td align="left">
42:                            <asp:textbox id=txtSubject runat="Server"
➥    width="100"></asp:textbox>
43:                        </td>
44:                    </tr>
45:                    <tr>
46:                        <td align="right" valign="top">
47:                            <asp:label font-bold="True" font-names="tahoma"
➥    font-size="10pt" id=lblMessage runat="Server">Message: </asp:label>
48:                        </td>
49:                        <td align="left">
50:                            <asp:textbox id=txtMessage runat="Server"
➥    width="200" height="400"></asp:textbox>
51:                        </td>
52:                    </tr>
```

11

LISTING **11.1**   continued

```
53:                        <tr>
54:                            <td align="right">
55:                                <asp:label font-bold="True" font-names="tahoma"
➡  font-size="10pt" id=lblHTMLEncode runat="Server">HTML Encode?: 
➡  </asp:label>
56:                            </td>
57:                            <td align="left">
58:                                <asp:checkbox id="chkHTMLEncode" runat=
➡ "Server" checked="False"></asp:checkbox>
59:                            </td>
60:                        </tr>
61:                        <tr>
62:                            <td colspan="2" align="center">
63:                                <asp:button id="btnSendEmail" runat="Server"
➡  text="Send Email" onClick="btnSendEmail_Click"></asp:button>
64:                            </td>
65:                        </tr>
66:                    </table>
67:                </td>
68:            </tr>
69:        </table>
70:        </form>
71:    </body>
72: </html>
```

In order to use e-mail in your application, you must first import the System.Web.Mail namespace. Line 2 achieves this step using the <% Import %> page directive. Once this line is inserted into the page, you can use the e-mail classes in your code.

The next section of code, lines 3 through 9, creates a code block on the page that will run as VB.NET on the Web server. In this code block, I have defined a public sub that is called by a button's onClick event. In this sub, I first declare my object as a new instance of the SmtpMail class from the imported namespace. I then call its Send method in line 6, passing it the recipient's e-mail address, the sender's e-mail address, the subject, and the body of the e-mail. All these properties are collected from the text boxes that make up the form. After calling the Send method, I release the object's reference, freeing up the resources for other purposes.

The next section of code, lines 10 through 72, is the actual HTML that makes up the page. Interspersed with the HTML are Web server controls, which are identified with the <asp:> prefixes and the runat="server" properties. Line 63 defines the button that is used to send the e-mail. Its onClick event calls the btnSendEmail_Click sub in lines 3–9.

Figure 11.1 shows what this page looks like when it is run, and Figure 11.2 shows the resulting e-mail after the fields are filled in and the Send Email button is clicked. Notice that each field on the Web page corresponds to a field in the e-mail message.

FIGURE 11.1

Sending an e-mail through an ASP.NET Web page.

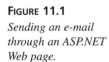

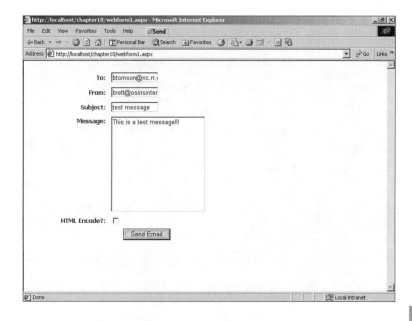

FIGURE 11.2

The resulting e-mail message.

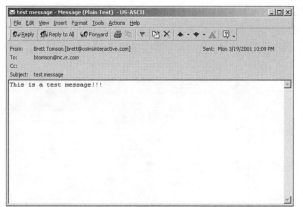

Sending an HTML E-mail

In order to send an HTML-encoded e-mail message, I need to use the MailMessage object instead of just calling the Send method of the SmtpMail object with the appropriate parameters. To do this, I need to modify the btnSendEmail_Click event to verify the value of the chkHTMLEncode check box and, if it is checked, encode the e-mail message. Here's the code:

```
1:    Public Sub btnSendEmail_Click(ByVal Sender As System.Object,
➡ ByVal e As System.EventArgs)
2:        Dim objSmtpMail As New SmtpMail()
3:        Dim objMailMessage As New MailMessage()

4:        'Set message properties
5:        objMailMessage.To = txtTo.Text
6:        objMailMessage.From = txtFrom.Text
7:        objMailMessage.Subject = txtSubject.Text

8:        'Check to see if message by is HTML
9:        If chkHTMLEncode.Checked Then
10:           objMailMessage.BodyFormat = MailFormat.Html
11:       Else
12:           objMailMessage.BodyFormat = MailFormat.Text
13:       End If

14:       'Set message body
15:       objMailMessage.Body = txtMessage.Text

16:       'Send the message
17:       objSmtpMail.Send(objMailMessage)
18:           objSmtpMail = Nothing
19:   End Sub
```

When running this example with the preceding page, I can enter the information shown in Figure 11.3, and the resulting e-mail will look like the one shown in Figure 11.4.

FIGURE 11.3

Encoding the e-mail message body as HTML.

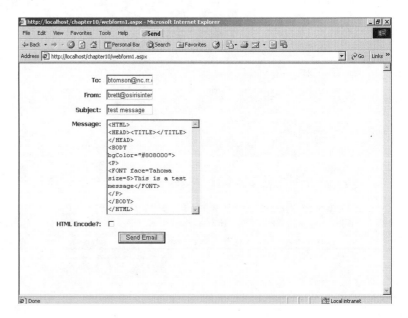

FIGURE **11.4**

The resulting HTML-encoded e-mail message.

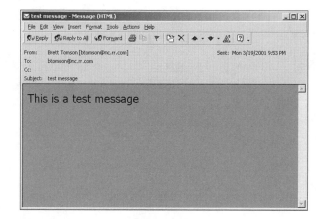

Attaching Files to an E-mail

The last e-mail feature adds and sends attachments. As described earlier in this chapter, all you need to do is call the Add method of the Attachments collection to add a file to your e-mail. To send a file called install.log that's located in c:\files, add line 16 of code to the sub created in the previous example:

```
1:    Public Sub btnSendEmail_Click(ByVal Sender As System.Object,
➥    ByVal e As System.EventArgs)
2:        Dim objSmtpMail As New SmtpMail()
3:        Dim objMailMessage As New MailMessage()

4:        'Set message properties
5:        objMailMessage.To = txtTo.Text
6:        objMailMessage.From = txtFrom.Text
7:        objMailMessage.Subject = txtSubject.Text

8:        'Check to see if message by is HTML
9:        If chkHTMLEncode.Checked Then
10:           objMailMessage.BodyFormat = MailFormat.Html
11:       Else
12:           objMailMessage.BodyFormat = MailFormat.Text
13:       End If

14:       'Set message body
15:       objMailMessage.Body = txtMessage.Text

16:       objMailMessage.Attachments.Add(New MailAttachment(
➥    "c:\files\install.log"))

17:       'Send the message
18:       objSmtpMail.Send(objMailMessage)
19:           objSmtpMail= Nothing
20:    End Sub
```

11

When this code is executed using the same values entered in the previous example, the result is the e-mail message shown in Figure 11.5.

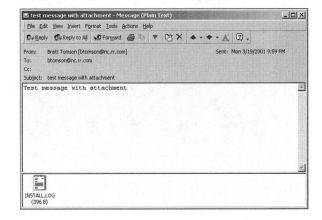

Summary

In this hour, you have been introduced to the class objects that allow you to send e-mail and attachments from your ASP.NET application. Through the use of `SmtpMail`, `MailMessage`, and `MailAttachment` objects, you can implement advanced e-mail techniques.

The next hour you will be exposed to the classes in the .Net Framework that provide file and directory access. Reading and writing to and from files is a common activity in most software applications. You can later return to this chapter and enhance your e-mail sample code to allow your sample users to navigate to a specific file(s) and add them as attachments to an e-mail.

Q&A

Q. **Can I retrieve e-mail using the `SmtpMail`, `MailMessage`, and `MailAttachment` classes?**

A. At this point in time, these classes can only be used to send e-mail from your application. A different technique will need to be used to retrieve e-mail from a mail server.

Workshop

The Workshop provides quiz questions are to help further your understanding of the material covered in this hour.

Quiz

1. How do you attach a file to an e-mail message?

2. When would you use the `SmtpMail.Send` method in conjunction with the `MailMessage` object, instead of simply utilizing the `Send` method with the appropriate string arguments?

3. True or false? You can send an e-mail with an attachment using only the `SmtpMail` class.

Exercises

1. Modify the code in the sample application we developed in this chapter to allow the user to enter in the name and path of a file to include as an attachment in the e-mail being created.

2. Modify the code in the sample application we developed in this chapter to allow the user to set a priority on the e-mail being sent.

Answers for Hour 11

Quiz

1. How do you attach a file to an e-mail message?

   ```
   objMailMessage.Attachments.Add(New MailAttachment(filename))
   ```

2. When would you use the `SmtpMail.Send` method in conjunction with the `MailMessage` object, instead of simply utilizing the `Send` method with the appropriate string arguments?

   When you want to utilize any additional properties on the `MailMessage` class, not available as a `SmtpMail.Send` argument, such as the addition of an attachment.

3. True or false? You can send an e-mail with an attachment using only the `SmtpMail` class.

   False: You need to use the `MailAttachment` in conjunction with the `MailMessage` and `SmtpMail` classes.

HOUR 12

Reading and Writing Files on the Web Server

Reading and writing to and from files is a common activity in software applications. ASP.NET applications are no exception. In this hour, you will be introduced to the .NET classes that provide file and directory access functionality. You will also develop a Web site that demonstrates these classes in an ASP.NET application.

The following topics will be discussed in this hour:

- Classes in the System.IO namespace
- Opening and creating files
- Sharing files
- Reading and writing from and to files

Classes Exposed

The .NET framework exposes, or *provides*, a large number of classes associated with file and directory access. These classes allow you to create, delete, and modify files and directories. Specific classes are provided to manipulate binary and text files as well. All the classes for dealing with files and directories are exposed in the `System.IO` namespace:

```
Imports System.IO
```

Before we get into the specifics of each class mentioned, let's go over some basics. A file refers to blocks of data that reside on a disk or other storage medium in some format, either text or binary. Text files may be viewed with a text editor such as Notepad. A binary file consists of data stored in a proprietary format and is viewable only by applications that understand the format. Word processing documents and database files are examples of binary files.

A `FileStream` object is a connection between the application and the physical file on the disk. The `FileStream` object has methods for opening, creating, modifying, and even reading from and writing to files. However, there are other objects—such as the `StreamReader` and `StreamWriter` objects for text files and the `BinaryReader` and `BinaryWriter` objects for binary files—that make the process of reading from and writing to files of different formats easier. The use of the `BinaryReader` and `BinaryWriter` classes is beyond the scope of this book, but you can learn about them in the online help system for Visual Studio.NET.

The `File` Class

The `File` class is a utility class that contains methods you can call without first having to create an instance of the `File` class. For example, the following code determines whether a given filename exists:

```
Imports System.IO
 .
 .
Dim blnExists as Boolean
blnExists = File.Exists("C:\SomePath\SomeFile.Name")
```

Static methods are the methods of an object that are available to the developer without having to first create an instance of the object that exposes them. You reference static methods by preceding the name of the method with the name of the object that exposes them. Here are the static methods available on the `File` class are:

- `AppendText`: Returns a `StreamWriter` object for adding text to a file.
- `Copy`: Creates a copy of an existing file.
- `Create`: Creates a file in the path specified.
- `CreateText`: Creates a file from the specified path and returns a `StreamWriter` object for writing text to the file.

- `Delete`: Deletes a file.
- `Exists`: Returns `True` if the file specified exists.
- `GetAttributes`: Returns a `FileAttribute` object containing the file system attributes for a file.
- `GetCreationTime`/`SetCreationTime`: Returns/sets the creation date and time for a file.
- `GetLastAccessTime`/`SetLastAccessTime`: Returns/sets the last accessed date and time for a file.
- `GetLastWriteTime`/`SetLastWriteTime`: Returns/sets the last updated date and time for a file.
- `Move`: Moves a file to a new directory and/or a new filename.
- `Open`: Returns a `FileStream` object for the file specified.
- `OpenRead`: Returns a `FileStream` object in read-only mode for the file specified.
- `OpenText`: Returns a `StreamReader` object for an existing text file.
- `OpenWrite`: Returns a `FileStream` object for an existing file with read and write access.
- `SetAttributes`: Sets the file system attributes for the file specified.

The `FileStream` Class

As you learned earlier, the `FileStream` class represents a connection to a physical file on a disk. To create a `FileStream` object, you can use the static methods discussed earlier or the constructor method.

The following code creates a file or opens a file that already exists using the static `Open` method of the `File` object:

```
Dim objFS As System.IO.FileStream
objFS = File.Open("C:\applog.txt", FileMode.OpenOrCreate)
```

To open the same file using the constructor method of the `FileStream` class, use this:

```
Dim objFS As System.IO.FileStream
objFS = new FileStream("c:\applog.txt",FileMode.OpenOrCreate)
```

The constructor method of an object is a special method that allows parameters to be passed in when the instance of the object is created. In this case, we are passing in the path to the file we want to open and the mode in which to open the file. The `FileStream` class does have methods for reading and writing data from and to a file. However, there are other classes that we'll discuss later in the `StreamReader` and `StreamWriter` sections

12

of this chapter to make this process easier. The properties and methods of the `FileStream` class most likely to be used are outlined in the following list:

- `CanRead`: Returns `True` if the current object allows data to be read from it.
- `CanSeek`: Returns `True` if the current object allows the file pointer to be moved to a different position in the file.
- `CanWrite`: Returns `True` if the current object allows data to be written to it.
- `Close`: Closes the file.
- `Flush`: Writes any buffered data to the file.
- `Length`: Returns the current length, or size, of the file.
- `Lock`: Allows part or all of a file to be locked so that any other applications that may be sharing this file will not be allowed access.
- `Name`: Returns the name of the file that this object represents.
- `Position`: Returns the current position of the file pointer and can also set the current position.
- `Read`: Allows a block of data to be read from the file and stored in an array of bytes.
- `Seek`: Allows the file pointer to be moved to a new location within the file.
- `Unlock`: Unlocks part or all of a file that had been locked.
- `Write`: Allows an array of bytes to be written to the file.

The `FileMode`, `FileAccess`, and `FileShare` Enumerations

Both of the methods described previously for opening and creating files use a constant for the second parameter that is defined in the `FileMode` enumeration.

 An *enumeration* is a group of related constants that are associated with names.

The methods also support two additional parameters that indicate what type of access to the file is needed and how the file should be shared with other processes that may need access.

FileMode

The `FileMode` enumeration defines constants that indicate whether a file should be opened, created, overwritten, or some combination of these:

- `Append`: An existing file will be opened or a new file will be created. The file pointer will be moved to the end of the file in preparation for writing.
- `Create`: An existing file will be overwritten or a new file will be created.
- `CreateNew`: A new file will be created. If a file with the same name already exists, an error occurs.
- `Open`: An existing file will be opened. If the file doesn't exist, an error occurs.
- `OpenOrCreate`: An existing file will be opened. If the file doesn't exist, a new file will be created.
- `Truncate`: An existing file will be opened. If the file doesn't exist, a new file will be created. Once the file is opened, its length will be set to zero, erasing the contents of the file.

FileAccess

The `FileAccess` enumeration defines three constants that indicate the type of access required:

- `Read`: Indicates that data will be read from the file.
- `Write`: Indicates that data will be written to the file.
- `ReadWrite`: Indicates that data will be both read from and written to the file.

FileShare

The `FileShare` enumeration defines four constants that indicate the type of access applications may have to a file:

- `None`: No other application may open this file while it is open by this application.
- `Read`: Other applications may open this file for reading while it is open by this application.
- `Write`: Other applications may open this file for writing while it is open by this application.
- `ReadWrite`: Other applications may open this file for reading and writing while it is open by this application.

The following code examples show how to use the `FileMode`, `FileAccess`, and `FileShare` enumerations when opening and creating files.

Here's how to open a file for appending, with read-only sharing access:

```
objFS = File.Open("C:\applog.txt", _
     FileMode.Append,FileAccess.Write, FileShare.Read)
objFS = new _
     FileStream ("c:\applog.txt",FileMode.Append,FileAccess.Write,
FileShare.Read)
```

12

The Append mode works only when a file is created with the `FileAccess.Write` value specified. If the file is opened with the `FileAccess.Read` value specified, an error will occur.

Here are two examples of opening an existing file for reading and writing, and with read and write sharing access:

```
objFS = File.Open("C:\applog.txt", _
        FileMode.OpenOrCreate,FileAccess.ReadWrite, FileShare.ReadWrite)
objFS = new FileStream ("c:\applog.txt", _
        FileMode.OpenOrCreate,FileAccess.ReadWrite, FileShare.ReadWrite)
```

The `StreamReader` Class

The `StreamReader` class is used to represent a `FileStream` object as a text file for reading. It has methods specifically designed for dealing with lines of characters that exist in text files. The most common way to create a `StreamReader` object is to use the constructor method of the `StreamReader` class, passing in a `FileStream` object as the single parameter:

```
Dim objSR As System.IO.StreamReader
Dim objFS As System.IO.FileStream
objFS = File.Open("C:\applog.txt", _
        FileMode.Open,FileAccess.Read, FileShare.ReadWrite)
objSR = New StreamReader(objFS)
```

Here are the most common properties and methods of the `StreamReader` class:

- `BaseStream`: Refers to the `FileStream` object that was used to create the `StreamReader` object.
- `Close`: Closes the `StreamReader` object.
- `Peek`: Lets you examine what the next character in the file is without advancing the file pointer.
- `ReadLine`: Reads a line of text from the file and returns it as a string.
- `ReadToEnd`: Reads from the current file position to the end of the file and returns the data as a string. The string will contain the embedded carriage return and line-feed characters that normally denote new lines in a text file.

The `StreamWriter` Class

The `StreamWriter` class is used to represent a `FileStream` object as a text file for writing. It has methods specifically designed for writing lines of characters to text files. The most common way to create a `StreamWriter` object is to use the constructor method of the `StreamWriter` class, passing in a `FileStream` object as the single parameter:

```
dim objSW As System.IO.StreamWriter
Dim objFS As System.IO.FileStream
objFS = File.Open("C:\applog.txt", _
       FileMode.OpenOrCreate,FileAccess.Write, FileShare.Read)
objSW = New StreamWriter(objFS)
```

Here are the most common properties and methods of the StreamWriter class:

- BaseStream: Refers to the FileStream object that was used to create the StreamWriter object.

- Close: Closes the StreamWriter object.

- WriteLine: Writes a string of text to the file and then appends the carriage return/linefeed characters to denote the end of the line.

The Directory Class

The Directory class is another utility class that provides methods and properties for dealing with directories and subdirectories on your file system. This class has many useful static methods, some of which are here:

- GetCurrentDirectory: Retrieves the current directory.

- SetCurrentDirectory: Sets the current directory.

- CreateDirectory: Creates all directories that are defined by the file-path parameter. For example, if the file-path parameter is C:\Users\JoeUser\Temp, each directory—Users, JoeUser, and Temp—will be created if it does not already exist.

- Delete: Deletes a directory from the file system. This method requires a Boolean value to indicate whether it should act recursively and delete all subdirectories as well.

- Exists: Tests whether a specific directory exists.

- GetDirectories: Returns an array of directories that exist under the current directory.

- GetFiles: Returns an array of files that exist in the current directory.

- GetLogicalDrives: Returns an array containing the logical drives that are defined on the computer or system.

- GetParent: Returns the parent directory for the file path specified.

12

The GetFiles and GetDirectories methods return arrays of objects. GetFiles returns the FileInfo class, which has the same methods as the File class discussed previously. GetDirectories returns the DirectoryInfo class, which has the same methods as the Directory class discussed previously.

Sample Application

To demonstrate the use of the topics we've covered in this hour, we are going to create
a Web application that logs site accesses with some user information and allows the user
to see directory and file contents.

The first thing we need to create is a class to encapsulate an access log containing information about who has visited our site, when they were here, and how they accessed it
(see Listing 12.1).

LISTING 12.1   LOGFILE.VB—Code Listing for the LogFile Class

```
 1:    Imports System.IO
 2:
 3:    Public Class LogFile
 4:
 5:        Private mobjSW As System.IO.StreamWriter
 6:        Private mobjSR As System.IO.StreamReader
 7:        Private mobjFS As System.IO.FileStream
 8:
 9:        Public Function ReadAll() As String
10:            'Exit if file not open/specified
11:            If mobjSR Is Nothing Then
12:                ReadAll = "File not open"
13:                Exit Function
14:            End If
15:            'Move to the beginning of the file
➥and read all of it into a string
16:            mobjSR.BaseStream.Seek(0, SeekOrigin.Begin)
17:            ReadAll = mobjSR.ReadToEnd
18:        End Function
19:
20:        Public Function ReadLast(ByVal Lines As Long) As String
21:            Dim i As Long
22:            Dim j As Long
23:            Dim strTemp As String
24:
25:            'Exit if file not open/specified
26:            If mobjSR Is Nothing Then
27:                ReadLast = "File not open"
28:                Exit Function
29:            End If
30:            'Determine the number of lines in the file
31:            mobjSR.BaseStream.Seek(0, SeekOrigin.Begin)
32:            i = 1
33:            Do
34:                mobjSR.ReadLine()
35:                If mobjSR.Peek > -1 Then i = i + 1
36:            Loop While mobjSR.Peek > -1
```

LISTING 12.1   continued

```
37:
38:                    'Now i indicates the number of lines in the input file
39:                    mobjSR.BaseStream.Seek(0, SeekOrigin.Begin)
40:                    If i <= Lines Then
41:                        ReadLast = mobjSR.ReadToEnd
42:                    Else
43:                        j = 1
44:                        Do
45:                            mobjSR.ReadLine()
46:                            j = j + 1
47:                        Loop While j <= i - Lines
48:                        ReadLast = mobjSR.ReadToEnd
49:                    End If
50:                End Function
51:
52:                Public Overloads Sub WriteLine(ByVal SessionID As String, _
53:                 ByVal FromIPAddr As String, ByVal UserID As String)
54:                    Dim dtmNow As DateTime = Date.Now
55:
56:                    'Exit if file not open/specified
57:                    If mobjSW Is Nothing Then
58:                        Exit Sub
59:                    End If
60:                    mobjSW.BaseStream.Seek(0, SeekOrigin.End)
61:                    mobjSW.WriteLine("{0}|{1}|{2}|{3}", _
62:                     dtmNow.ToLongDateString + " " + dtmNow.ToLongTimeString, _
63:                     SessionID, FromIPAddr, UserID)
64:                    mobjSW.Flush()
65:                End Sub
66:
67:                Public Overloads Sub WriteLine(ByVal SessionID As String,
⮕ ByVal Comment As String)
68:                    Dim dtmNow As DateTime = Date.Now
69:
70:                    'Exit if file not open/specified
71:                    If mobjSW Is Nothing Then
72:                        Exit Sub
73:                    End If
74:                    mobjSW.BaseStream.Seek(0, SeekOrigin.End)
75:                    mobjSW.WriteLine("{0}|{1}|{2}", _
76:                     dtmNow.ToLongDateString + " " + dtmNow.ToLongTimeString, _
77:                     SessionID, Comment)
78:                    mobjSW.Flush()
79:                End Sub
80:
81:                Protected Overrides Sub Finalize()
82:                    Me.Close()
83:                    MyBase.Finalize()
84:                End Sub
```

12

LISTING 12.1   continued

```
85:
86:         Public Sub New(ByVal FilePath As String)
87:             mobjFS = New FileStream(FilePath, _
88:             FileMode.OpenOrCreate, _
89:             FileAccess.ReadWrite, _
90:             FileShare.None.Read)
91:             mobjSW = New StreamWriter(mobjFS)
92:             mobjSR = New StreamReader(mobjFS)
93:         End Sub
94:
95:         Public Sub New()
96:             'Allow creation without specifying log file name
97:         End Sub
98:
99:         Public Sub Open(ByVal FilePath As String)
100:            If Not mobjFS Is Nothing Then
101:                Me.Close()
102:            End If
103:            mobjFS = File.Open(FilePath, FileMode.OpenOrCreate)
104:            mobjSW = New StreamWriter(mobjFS)
105:            mobjSR = New StreamReader(mobjFS)
106:        End Sub
107:
108:        Public Sub Close()
109:            'Close all files and reader/writer objects
110:            If Not mobjSW Is Nothing Then
111:                mobjSW.Close()
112:                mobjSW = Nothing
113:            End If
114:            If Not mobjSR Is Nothing Then
115:                mobjSR.Close()
116:                mobjSR = Nothing
117:            End If
118:            If Not mobjFS Is Nothing Then
119:                mobjFS.Close()
120:                mobjFS = Nothing
121:            End If
122:        End Sub
123:    End Class
```

The code that creates instances of our LogFile class and writes information to the log file is located in the Global.asax.vb file, which is the code-behind for the Global.asax file (see Listing 12.2). Here's the Global.asax code:

```
1    <%@ Application Codebehind="Global.asax.vb" Inherits="Hour12.Global" %>
```

LISTING 12.2   `GLOBAL.ASAX.VB`—Code-Behind for `Global.asax`

```
1:   Imports System.Web
2:   Imports System.Web.SessionState
3:   Imports System.ComponentModel
4:
5:   Public Class Global
6:       Inherits System.Web.HttpApplication
7:
8:   #Region " Component Designer Generated Code "
9:
10:     Public Sub New()
11:       MyBase.New()
12:
13:       'This call is required by the Component Designer.
14:       InitializeComponent()
15:
16:       'Add any initialization after the InitializeComponent() call
17:
18:     End Sub
19:
20:     'Required by the Component Designer
21:     Private components As System.ComponentModel.Container
22:
23:     'NOTE: The following procedure is required by the Component Designer
24:     'It can be modified using the Component Designer.
25:     'Do not modify it using the code editor.
26:     <System.Diagnostics.DebuggerStepThrough()> _
27:     Private Sub InitializeComponent()
28:       components = New System.ComponentModel.Container()
29:     End Sub
30:
31:   #End Region
32:
33:     Sub Application_OnStart(ByVal Sender As Object, ByVal e As EventArgs)
34:       'Set global variable indicating name of log file
35:       Application("LogFile") = Server.MapPath("/Hour12/") + "accesslog.txt"
36:     End Sub
37:
38:     Sub Session_OnStart(ByVal Sender As Object, ByVal e As EventArgs)
39:       Dim objLog As New LogFile(Application("LogFile"))
40:
41:       'Write out who's accessing this site
42:       objLog.WriteLine(Session.SessionID, _
43:        Request.ServerVariables("REMOTE_ADDR").ToString(), _
44:        Request.ServerVariables("AUTH_USER").ToString())
45:
46:       'Overloaded method to write out just a comment
47:       objLog.WriteLine(Session.SessionID, _
48:        "Browser String = " & Request.Browser.Browser())
```

12

LISTING 12.2   continued

```
49:
50:        objLog.Close()
51:        objLog = Nothing
52:
53:    End Sub
54:
55:    Sub Session_OnEnd(ByVal Sender As Object, ByVal e As EventArgs)
56:        Dim objLog As New LogFile(Application("LogFile"))
57:
58:        objLog.WriteLine(Session.SessionID, "Session Ending")
59:        objLog.Close()
60:        objLog = Nothing
61:    End Sub
62:
63: End Class
```

We put code in the Session_OnStart and Session_OnEnd event handlers to indicate when a session starts, who the user is, how the user accessed the site, and when a session ends.

On line 35, we use the MapPath method of the intrinsic Server object to get a fully qualified path for our desired log file.

Now we need a user interface so the user can specify what directory he or she wants to list the contents for. The ListContents.aspx form has a text box and a button for this purpose (see Listing 12.3). We also need to set up the table that will eventually hold the directory listing.

LISTING 12.3   LISTCONTENTS.ASPX—User Interface for Our Web Application

```
1:    <%@ Page Language="vb" AutoEventWireup="false"
2:       CodeBehind="ListContents.aspx.vb"
3:       Inherits="Hour12.WebForm1"%>
4:
5:    <HTML>
6:      <HEAD>
7:        <meta content="Microsoft Visual Studio.NET 7.0" name=GENERATOR>
8:        <meta content="Visual Basic 7.0" name=CODE_LANGUAGE>
9:        <meta content=JavaScript name=vs_defaultClientScript>
10:       <meta content="Internet Explorer 5.0" name=vs_targetSchema>
11:       <LINK href="Styles.css" type=text/css rel=stylesheet>
12:
13:   <SCRIPT language=javascript>
14:        function submitPath(Value){
15:          WebForm1.hdnPath.value=Value;
```

LISTING 12.3   continued

```
16:            WebForm1.submit();
17:         }
18:
19:      function submitRootPath(Value){
20:        WebForm1.txtPath.value=Value;
21:        WebForm1.submit();
22:      }
23:     </SCRIPT>
24: </HEAD>
25:
26: <BODY MS_POSITIONING="GridLayout">
27:
28: <form id="WebForm1"
29:   name="WebForm1"
30:   action=ListContents.aspx
31:   method=post runat="server">
32:   <input type=hidden id="hdnPath" name="hdnPath" runat=server>
33:   <asp:Table Runat=server
34:     Width="100%"
35:       HorizontalAlign=Center
36:       BorderStyle=None id=Table1>
37:       <asp:TableRow Runat="server" ID="Tablerow1">
38:       <asp:TableCell CssClass="Label"
39:          Text="Directory Path To List"
40:           Runat=server Width=25% ID="Tablecell1">
41:         </asp:TableCell>
42:         <asp:TableCell Runat=server ID="Tablecell2">
43:         <asp:TextBox ID="txtPath" Runat=server
44:           Width="75%">
45:             </asp:TextBox>
46:       </asp:TableCell>
47:     </asp:TableRow>
48:     <asp:TableRow Runat=server id=TableRow2>
49:       <asp:TableCell Runat=server
50:         ColumnSpan=2
51:         HorizontalAlign=Center
52:         ID=tablecell3>
53:         <asp:Button Text="Submit" Runat=server ID="btnSubmit">
54:         </asp:Button>
55:       </asp:TableCell>
56:     </asp:TableRow>
57:     <asp:TableRow Runat=server ID=tablerow3>
58:       <asp:TableCell Runat=server ColumnSpan="2" id=tablecell4>
59:         <asp:Table id="tblFiles"
60:           BorderStyle="Double"
61:           Runat="server"
62:           BorderColor="Maroon">
63:           <asp:TableRow Runat=server ID=tablerow4>
64:             <asp:TableCell CssClass=Label
```

12

LISTING 12.3   continued

```
65:                    Text="File Name"
66:                    Width="150px"
67:                    Runat=server ID=Tablecell5 >
68:                 </asp:TableCell>
69:                 <asp:TableCell CssClass=Label
70:                   Text="File Size"
71:                   Width="100px"
72:                   Runat=server ID=Tablecell6 >
73:                 </asp:TableCell>
74:                 <asp:TableCell CssClass=Label
75:                   Text="Attributes"
76:                   Width="100px"
77:                   Runat=server ID=Tablecell7>
78:                 </asp:TableCell>
79:                 <asp:TableCell CssClass=Label
80:                   Text="Date Created"
81:                   Width="100px"
82:                   Runat=server ID=Tablecell8>
83:                 </asp:TableCell>
84:                 <asp:TableCell CssClass=Label
85:                   Text="Date Last Accessed"
86:                   Width="100px"
87:                   Runat=server ID=Tablecell9>
88:                 </asp:TableCell>
89:                 <asp:TableCell CssClass=Label
90:                   Text="Date Last Modified"
91:                   Width="100px"
92:                   Runat=server ID=Tablecell10>
93:                 </asp:TableCell>
94:               </asp:TableRow>
95:               <asp:TableRow id=TableRow5 Runat="server">
96:                <asp:TableCell Runat=server ColumnSpan=6 ID=Tablecell11>
97:                 <hr color=Maroon width="100%">
98:                </asp:TableCell>
99:               </asp:TableRow>
100:             </asp:Table>
101:          </asp:tablecell>
102:        </asp:tablerow>
103:      </asp:Table>
104:   </form>
105:
106:  </BODY>
107:  </HTML>
```

The code-behind file for this Web form has code defined for the Load event of the page. The code in this event handler uses the value the user specified for the directory path to retrieve the contents of a directory (see Listing 12.4).

LISTING 12.4 LISTCONTENTS.ASPX.VB—Code-Behind for Our User Interface

```
 1:  Imports System.Web.UI.WebControls
 2:  Imports System.IO
 3:
 4:  Public Class WebForm1
 5:      Inherits System.Web.UI.Page
 6:
 7:      Protected WithEvents tblFiles As Table
 8:      Protected WithEvents Table1 As Table
 9:      Protected WithEvents hdnPath As HtmlInputHidden
10:      Protected WithEvents txtPath As TextBox
11:
12:  #Region " Web Form Designer Generated Code "
13:
14:      'This call is required by the Web Form Designer.
15:      <System.Diagnostics.DebuggerStepThroughAttribute()> _
16:      Private Sub InitializeComponent()
17:
18:      End Sub
19:
20:      Protected Sub Page_Init(ByVal Sender As System.Object, _
21:       ByVal e As System.EventArgs) Handles MyBase.Init
22:          'CODEGEN: This method call is required by the Web Form Designer
23:          'Do not modify it using the code editor.
24:          InitializeComponent()
25:      End Sub
26:
27:  #End Region
28:
29:      Private Sub Page_Load(ByVal sender As System.Object, _
30:       ByVal e As System.EventArgs) Handles MyBase.Load
31:          Dim objRow As TableRow
32:          Dim objCell As TableCell
33:          Dim strPath As String
34:
35:          txtPath.Text = Trim(txtPath.Text)
36:
37:          strPath = hdnPath.Value
38:          hdnPath.Value = ""
39:          If txtPath.Text = "" Then
40:             tblFiles.Visible = False
41:          Else
42:             If strPath <> "" Then
43:                If Right(txtPath.Text, 1) <> "\" Then
44:                   txtPath.Text = txtPath.Text & "\"
45:                End If
46:                txtPath.Text = txtPath.Text & strPath
47:             End If
48:
49:             'Get the contents of the path specifed
```

12

LISTING 12.4   continued

```
50:          Dim objDir As New DirectoryInfo(txtPath.Text)
51:          Dim arrSubDir As DirectoryInfo()
52:          Dim arrFiles As FileInfo()
53:          Dim objFile As FileInfo
54:          Dim objHyperlink As HyperLink
55:
56:          arrSubDir = objDir.GetDirectories()
57:        arrFiles = objDir.GetFiles()
58:
59:        With tblFiles
60:          .Visible = True
61:
62:          'Add a link for the parent directory if it exists
63:          If Not objDir.Parent() Is Nothing Then
64:            objRow = New TableRow()
65:            'Add the name of the directory
66:            objCell = New TableCell()
67:
68:            objHyperlink = New HyperLink()
69:            objHyperlink.Text = "Up One Level"
70:            objHyperlink.NavigateUrl = _
71:              "javascript:submitRootPath('" & _
72:              Replace(objDir.Parent.FullName, "\", "\\") & "')"
73:           objHyperlink.CssClass = "Label"
74:            objCell.Controls.Add(objHyperlink)
75:            objCell.ColumnSpan = 6
76:            objRow.Cells.Add(objCell).Rows.Add(objRow)
77:
78:          End If
79:
80:          'List the directories first
81:          For Each objDir In arrSubDir
82:            objRow = New TableRow()
83:            'Add the name of the directory
84:            objCell = New TableCell()
85:
86:            objHyperlink = New HyperLink()
87:            objHyperlink.Text = objDir.Name
88:            objHyperlink.NavigateUrl = _
89:              "javascript:submitPath('" & objDir.Name & "')"
90:            objHyperlink.CssClass = "Label"
91:
92:            objCell.Controls.Add(objHyperlink)
93:
94:            objCell.CssClass = "SmallText"
95:            objRow.Cells.Add(objCell)
96:            'Add the placeholder for the size
97:            objCell = New TableCell()
98:            objCell.Text = ""
```

LISTING 12.4   continued

```
 99:               objCell.CssClass = "SmallText"
100:               objRow.Cells.Add(objCell)
101:               'Add the attributes
102:               objCell = New TableCell()
103:               objCell.Text = objDir.Attributes.ToString()
104:               objCell.CssClass = "SmallText"
105:               objRow.Cells.Add(objCell)
106:               'Add the date created
107:               objCell = New TableCell()
108:               objCell.Text = objDir.CreationTime.ToString()
109:               objCell.CssClass = "SmallText"
110:               objRow.Cells.Add(objCell)
111:               'Add the date last accessed
112:               objCell = New TableCell()
113:               objCell.Text = objDir.LastAccessTime.ToString()
114:               objCell.CssClass = "SmallText"
115:               objRow.Cells.Add(objCell)
116:               'Add the date last modified
117:               objCell = New TableCell()
118:               objCell.Text = objDir.LastWriteTime.ToString()
119:               objCell.CssClass = "SmallText"
120:               objRow.Cells.Add(objCell)
121:             .Rows.Add(objRow)
122:         Next
123:
124:         'Now list the files
125:         For Each objFile In arrFiles
126:             objRow = New TableRow()
127:             'Add the name of the directory
128:             objCell = New TableCell()
129:
130:             If objFile.Extension = ".txt" Then
131:               objHyperlink = New HyperLink()
132:               objHyperlink.Text = objFile.Name
133:               objHyperlink.NavigateUrl = "ShowFile.aspx?file=" & _
134:                Replace(txtPath.Text & "\" & objFile.Name, "\\", "\")
135:               objHyperlink.Target = "_new"
136:               objHyperlink.CssClass = "SmallText"
137:               objCell.Controls.Add(objHyperlink)
138:             Else
139:                objCell.Text = objFile.Name.ToString()
140:             End If
141:
142:             objCell.CssClass = "SmallText"
143:             objRow.Cells.Add(objCell)
144:
145:             'Add the placeholder for the size
146:             objCell = New TableCell()
147:             objCell.Text = (objFile.Length() /
```

12

LISTING 12.4   continued

```
1024).ToString("#,###,###,##0.0 Kb")
148:            objCell.CssClass = "SmallText"
149:            objCell.HorizontalAlign = HorizontalAlign.Right
150:            objRow.Cells.Add(objCell)
151:            'Add the attributes
152:            objCell = New TableCell()
153:            objCell.Text = objFile.Attributes.ToString()
154:            objCell.CssClass = "SmallText"
155:            objRow.Cells.Add(objCell)
156:            'Add the date created
157:            objCell = New TableCell()
158:            objCell.Text = objFile.CreationTime.ToString()
159:            objCell.CssClass = "SmallText"
160:            objRow.Cells.Add(objCell)
161:            'Add the date last accessed
162:            objCell = New TableCell()
163:            objCell.Text = objFile.LastAccessTime.ToString()
164:            objCell.CssClass = "SmallText"
165:            objRow.Cells.Add(objCell)
166:            'Add the date last modified
167:            objCell = New TableCell()
168:            objCell.Text = objFile.LastWriteTime.ToString()
169:            objCell.CssClass = "SmallText"
170:            objRow.Cells.Add(objCell)
171:            .Rows.Add(objRow)
172:          Next
173:        End With
174:      End If
175:    End Sub
176:
177:  End Class
```

In lines 63 through 78, we create a hyperlink so the user can go up one level in the directory tree if he is not at the root already. The NavigateUrl property translates to the HREF attribute of the HTML hyperlink tag. We set the action of this control here to actually call a client-side JavaScript function that, when clicked, will assign the parent directory path to the directory path text box control and then cause the form to be submitted.

Lines 80 though 122 retrieve the subdirectories that exist in the directory specified and create new rows and cells in the existing table to display information about these directories. We create hyperlinks for the name of each subdirectory so that the user can drill down the directory tree. The hyperlink for the directory names calls another client-side JavaScript function that sets the value of a hidden text box.

In lines 37 through 47, we check to see whether the user has clicked one of the subdirectories in the table. If so, we reassign the value of the directory-path text box and retrieve the contents of the subdirectory.

Lines 124 through 172 retrieve the files in the directory specified. If the extension of any file is .txt, we create a hyperlink control that, when clicked, will open up a new window and display the contents of the text file in a text box.

The Web form to display the contents of the text file is very simple (see Listing 12.5). It consists of nothing more than a multiline text box.

LISTING 12.5 SHOWFILE.ASPX—A Web Form to Display the Contents of a Text File

```
1:    <%@ Page Language="vb"
2:        AutoEventWireup="false"
3:        Codebehind="ShowFile.aspx.vb"
4:        Inherits="Hour12.ShowFile"%>
5:
6:    <HTML>
7:      <HEAD>
8:        <title><%Response.write(request("file"))%></title>
9:          <meta name="GENERATOR" content="Microsoft Visual Studio.NET 7.0">
10:          <meta name="CODE_LANGUAGE" content="Visual Basic 7.0">
11:          <meta name=vs_defaultClientScript content="JavaScript">
12:          <meta name=vs_targetSchema content="Internet Explorer 5.0">
13:      </HEAD>
14:        <body>
15:        <form id="ShowFile" method="post" runat="server">
16:          <asp:TextBox ID="txtData"
17:              TextMode="MultiLine"
18:              Width="100%"
19:              Rows="25"
20:              Runat=server>
21:          </asp:TextBox>
22:        </form>
23:      </body>
24:    </HTML>
```

The contents of the text box are assigned by code in the Load event handler for the page (see Listing 12.6).

LISTING 12.6 SHOWFILE.ASPX.VB—Code-behind for the Web Form to Show Text File Contents

```
1:    Imports System.IO
2:
3:    Public Class ShowFile
```

12

LISTING 12.6 continued

```
4:          Inherits System.Web.UI.Page
5:          Protected WithEvents txtData As System.Web.UI.WebControls.TextBox
6:
7:    #Region " Web Form Designer Generated Code "
8:
9:        'This call is required by the Web Form Designer.
10:        <System.Diagnostics.DebuggerStepThroughAttribute()>
➡         Private Sub InitializeComponent()
11:
12:        End Sub
13:
14:        Protected Sub Page_Init(ByVal Sender As System.Object, _
15:         ByVal e As System.EventArgs) Handles MyBase.Init
16:          'CODEGEN: This method call is required by the Web Form Designer
17:          'Do not modify it using the code editor.
18:          InitializeComponent()
19:        End Sub
20:
21:    #End Region
22:
23:        Private Sub Page_Load(ByVal sender As System.Object, _
24:         ByVal e As System.EventArgs) Handles MyBase.Load
25:          Dim objSR As StreamReader
26:
27:          objSR = New StreamReader(Request("file"))
28:          txtData.Text = objSR.ReadToEnd()
29:          objSR.Close()
30:          objSR = Nothing
31:        End Sub
32:    End Class
```

When you load the ListContents.aspx file in a browser, initially all you see is the text box and the Submit button (see Figure 12.1).

Once you submit a directory path (it must be a valid path on the same machine as the Web application), you will see the listing of directories and files (see Figure 12.2).

You may click the directories and drill down the tree structure of the file system (see Figure 12.3).

If you click a text file with the .txt extension, a new browser window will open showing the contents of the file (see Figure 12.4).

The access log for this application shows the user's name and IP address. To get the name to be supplied to the Web server, we have to disable anonymous access and enable authenticated access. For this example, we used Integrated Windows Authentication so that the current Windows username and password will be sent across to the Web server without having to prompt the user for a username and password combination (see Figure 12.5).

FIGURE 12.1

ListContents.aspx *when first loaded in the browser.*

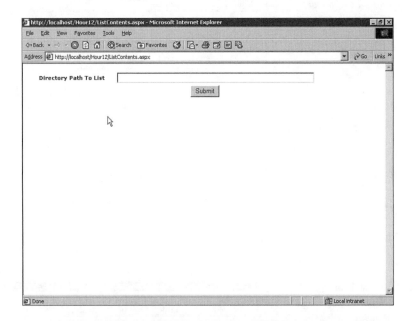

FIGURE 12.2

ListContents.aspx *after a valid directory path is submitted.*

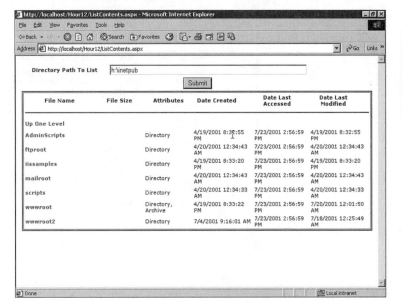

12

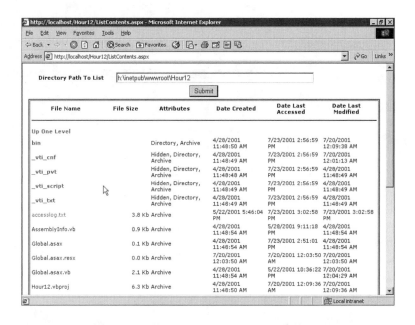

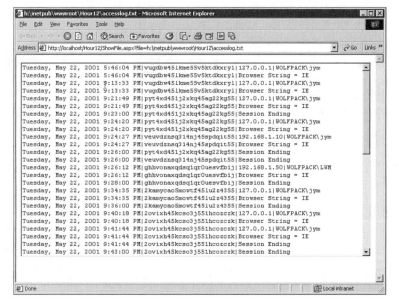

FIGURE 12.5

Enabling authenticated access for this application.

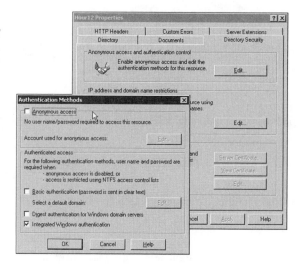

Summary

This hour introduced the classes in the .NET Framework that provide file and directory access. You learned that you must import the System.IO namespace into any files where you want to use the file- and directory-access classes. We then developed a Web application to demonstrate the use of some these classes.

Q&A

Q. How do I access binary files?

A. You can use the BinaryReader and BinaryWriter classes to access binary files. These classes work similar to the StreamReader and StreamWriter classes and have methods for reading and writing specific data types to and from binary files.

Q. How do I open a file such that other applications can also update the file and see changes that I make to the file?

A. You use the FileShare.ReadWrite constant when you initially open the file:

```
objFS = new FileStream ("c:\applog.txt", _
        FileMode.OpenOrCreate,FileAccess.ReadWrite, FileShare.ReadWrite)
```

For your application to see the changes made to this file by another application, you may need to seek to the beginning of the file, and then return to your last location.

12

Workshop

The quiz questions and exercises are provided for your further understanding of the material presented.

Quiz

1. What namespace contains the classes for file and directory access?
2. What is a static method?
3. Do you have to create a `FileStream` object before creating a `StreamReader` or `StreamWriter` object?
4. What method returns an array of `FileInfo` objects?

Exercises

1. Modify the code in the sample application we developed in this hour to allow files with other extensions to be viewed as text files.
2. Add code to specifically view the access log (`accesslog.txt`, in this case). Write this code to parse the lines of the file and remove the pipe character (|).

   Hint: You can use the `Split` command to create an array of strings from a single string. Here's an example:

   ```
   Dim arrValues() as string
   Dim strSource as string = "One|Two|Three|Four"
   arrValues = Split(strSource, "|")
   ```

   After this code executes, the `arrValues` array will contain four members, starting with index 0.

Answers for Hour 12

Quiz

1. What namespace contains the classes for file and directory access?

   `System.IO`

2. What is a static method?

   Static methods are the methods of an object that are available to the developer without having to first create an instance of the object that exposes them

3. Do you have to create a `FileStream` object before creating a `StreamReader` or `StreamWriter` object?

No. You can also use the `contructor` method of the `StreamReader` class passing in the fully qualified path to a file as the first parameter.

4. What method returns an array of `FileInfo` objects?

The `GetFiles` method of the Directory class.

12

HOUR 13

Handling Errors

No matter how well you design and plan your application, an error is bound to creep in somewhere. Still, with good planning, errors will be handled so that the application doesn't end abruptly but instead alerts the user when necessary or deals with the error condition internally. In this hour, you will be introduced to the two methods available to test for and handle error conditions in your Web applications implemented with Visual Basic:

- Unstructured exception handling
- Structured exception handling

Exception Handling Basics

The terms *exception* and *error* both refer to the same thing: an unexpected occurrence or condition that happens while a program is running. If the error is not handled by an exception handler, the .NET runtime will end the program and display some information about the error that occurred. It should be your goal to minimize the number of errors that make it all the way to the runtime without being handled.

Exception handlers should generally be used in any block of code that makes calls out to other methods or objects, even if the code belongs to you. Exceptions will bubble up the call stack until handled by an exception handler. It is important to catch the exception when it occurs—or as near to when it occurs as possible—so that you can find out why it occurred.

> A *call stack* or *stack trace* refers to the names of the methods that have been called up until the point where the exception occurred.

Unstructured exception handling is something that has been common to Visual Basic for a long time. Structured exception handling is common to C++ but is a new topic for Visual Basic. You can mix structured and unstructured exception-handling methods within an application, but not within a single procedure.

Unstructured Exception Handling

Unstructured exception handling refers to the use of the On Error statement, which you place before any block of code that may produce errors.

The On Error Statement

The On Error statement is followed by the Goto or Resume keyword, telling the runtime where to jump to when an error occurs. Here's an example:

```
'Specify line label to jump to when an error occurs
On Error Goto ErrHandler.
...
ErrHandler: 'Line Label
If Err.Number <> 0 then
    'Error handling code
End If
```

The preceding code will branch to the error-handling code when an error occurs, and if the error number is a value other than zero, the error-handling code will execute.

The On Error statement can be followed by these keywords:

- On Error Goto {Line Label or Line Number}

  Jumps to the line number or label when an error occurs.

- On Error Goto 0

  Disables the current error handler.

- On Error Resume Next

   Continues executing code, when an error occurs, starting with the line after where the error occurred. If you want to know whether an error occurred, you have to check the properties of the Err object.

The Err Object

When an error occurs, the Err object is populated with information about the error; this happens regardless of what type of exception handling is in place. The following properties and methods are available with the Err object:

- Source: Contains the source of the error, usually the name of the application.
- Number: Contains the number of the error that occurred.
- Description: Contains a string describing the error that occurred.
- Clear: Clears the current error and resets the error number to zero.
- Raise: Allows you to raise an error. You must specify a number, and you may optionally specify a source and description. Here's an example:

  ```
  Err.Raise(6, "My Source", "My Error Description")
  ```

Structured Exception Handling

Structured exception handling consists of protected blocks of code with associated exception handlers. The protected blocks of code begin with a Try statement and may be followed by Catch statements that handle specific exceptions and/or a Finally statement that contains code statements that execute whether an exception occurs or not. Here's an example:

```
Private Sub CatchException()
    Try
        MakeException()
    Catch e As Exception
        Response.Write(FormatException(e))
    Finally
        Response.Write("Finished with CatchException exception handler" & _
                "<BR>")
    End Try
End Sub

Private Sub MakeException()
    Dim x As Long
    Response.Write("MakeException...<BR>")
    x = 0
    x = 1 / x
```

13

```
        Response.Write("MakeException Finished...This Line Never Prints!<BR>")
    End Sub

    Private Function FormatException(ByVal e As Exception) As String
        Dim strTemp As String

        strTemp = "<span class='Error'>"
        strTemp = strTemp & "Message: " & e.Message & "<BR>"
        strTemp = strTemp & "Source: " & e.Source & "<BR>"
        strTemp = strTemp & "<u>Stack Trace:</u><BR>" & _
            Replace(e.StackTrace.ToString, vbCr, "<BR>") & "<BR>"
        strTemp = strTemp & "Target Site: " & e.TargetSite.ToString & "<BR>"
        strTemp = strTemp & "</span>"
        FormatException = strTemp
    End Function
```

This example demonstrates the use of structured exception handling with a single statement in the protected block, a single exception filter that, in this case, will catch all exceptions, and a Finally block that prints a notification that the exception handler executed
successfully. The call to the MakeException method generates an OverflowException
exception by dividing by zero. The Catch filter processes the exception because it is looking for any exceptions that match the filter clause of the Catch statement. A function is
then called to return a formatted string with the information from the exception.

You can have nested structured exception handlers to catch any exceptions that might
occur during your exception-handling code itself. In the preceding example, you could
change the Catch code to contain an exception handler to catch any exceptions thrown
by the FormatException function. Here's an example:

```
Private Sub CatchException()
    Try
        MakeException()
    Catch e As Exception
        Try
            Response.Write(FormatException(e))
        Catch e1 as Exception
            Response.Write("Unable to format exception!")
        Finally
            Response.Write( _
                    "Finished with nested CatchException exception handler" & _
                _"<BR>")
        End Try
    Finally
        Response.Write("Finished with CatchException exception handler" & "<BR>")
    End Try
End Sub
```

The Exception Class

All exceptions derive from the System.Exception base class. This class has four main properties that provide the information about the exception:

- Message: Describes the exception that occurred.

- StackTrace: This is an extremely useful property because it contains the trail of methods that were called leading up to when the exception occurred. If debugging information is available, the source code filename and line numbers will be supplied.

- InnerException: Contains another Exception object. This will be the case if an exception has been caught and then thrown again for a series of exception-handling blocks. This is demonstrated a little later in the hour.

- HelpLink: This is a path to a help file that might contain more information about the exception that occurred.

Debugging information can be added to a Web application by selecting Debug as the Active Solution Configuration setting in the Configuration Manager as shown in figure 13.2. Open the Configuration Manager by selecting Build, Configuration Manager from the menu inside Visual Studio (see Figure 13.1).

FIGURE 13.1

Opening the Configuration Manager.

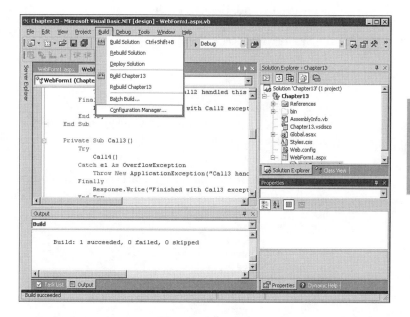

13

FIGURE **13.2**

Selecting the Debug configuration.

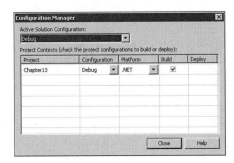

Common Exceptions

Quite a few types of exceptions are defined by the .NET runtime and associated name-spaces. Here are some of the exceptions you are most likely to encounter:

- `System.NullReferenceException`: This exception occurs when you try to access a property or call a method on an object that has not yet been initialized. Here's an example:

```
Dim obj As FileStream
Response.Write("File Length: " & obj.Length())
```

This would generate the exception `NullReferenceException` because the `FileStream` object has not yet been initialized.

- `System.OverflowException`: This exception occurs when an integer or long value is divided by zero. Here's an example:

```
1  Dim dblX As Double = 2131.1234123
2  Dim lngY As Long
3  lngY = 0
4  dblX = dblX / lngY
5  lngY = lngY / 0
```

In this example, line 5 would generate the exception `OverflowException`. Line 4 does not generate an exception even though a division by zero is occurring, because floating-point operations never generate exceptions. The result of the operation on line 4 would be positive infinity.

- `System.IndexOutOfRangeException`: This exception occurs when you try to reference an index of an array that does not exist. Here's an example:

```
Dim i As Long
Dim arr(5) As Long

For i = 0 To 10
    arr(i) = 100 / (i + 1)
Next
```

Once the counter variable reaches 6, the exception `IndexOutOfRangeException` will occur because the array has indexes from 0 to 5 only.

- `System.IO.DirectoryNotFoundException`: This exception occurs when the directory portion of a file path does not exist. Here's an example:

```
Dim objFS As FileStream
objFS = New FileStream("C:\BadPath\GoodFile.txt", FileMode.Open)
```

- `System.IO.FileNotFoundException`: This exception occurs when the file portion of a file path does not exist. Here's an example:

```
Dim objFS As FileStream
objFS = New FileStream("C:\GoodPath\BadFile.txt", FileMode.Open)
```

When you are designing your exception handlers, keep in mind that you may have multiple `Catch` blocks for each `Try` block. You need to specify the most specific exception blocks first, followed by more generic ones. If you want to make sure no exception gets through, you can use the generic `Exception` type as the filter for your last `Catch` block, as shown here:

```
Try
    MakeException()
Catch e1 as OverflowException
    'Some code
Catch e2 as FileNotFoundException
    'Some more code
Catch e3 as IndexOutOfRangeException
    'Some code
Catch e As Exception
    'This is the generic exception handler
    Response.Write(FormatException(e))
Finally
    Response.Write("Finished with CatchException exception handler" & _
              "<BR>")
End Try
```

Because all exceptions derive from the `Exception` class, this guarantees that you will catch any exception not specifically handled in the code.

Throwing Exceptions

Exceptions may be thrown as well as caught. The command to generate an exception is `Throw`. Throwing exceptions usually occurs within an exception handler, but you could technically generate one whenever you wanted to. Inside an exception handler, you would catch the initial exception and then generate a new exception, attaching the current exception with the `InnerException` property. Here's an example:

13

```
Try
    CallSomeMethod()
Catch e As Exception
    Throw New ApplicationException("This exception was caught!", e)
End Try
```

This allows you to chain exceptions together so that when they bubble up the call stack, the final exception handler would be able to see the entire exception history.

The `ApplicationException` Class

The preceding example uses the `ApplicationException` class to create a new exception. This is an exception type defined by the .NET runtime to indicate that a nonfatal, application-level exception has occurred. The following example demonstrates the three methods of creating a new instance of the `ApplicationException` class:

```
Try
    CallSomeMethod()
Catch e As Exception
    Dim obj As ApplicationException
    obj = New ApplicationException()
    obj = New ApplicationException("Some Message")
    obj = New ApplicationException("Some Message", e)
    Throw obj
End Try
```

The third form of the `New` method allows you to attach the current exception to the `InnerException` property of the new exception you want to throw.

Custom Exceptions

If the `ApplicationException` class is too generic for your application, you may create your own custom exception classes. To create your own custom exceptions in Visual Basic, you need to create a class that inherits from the `ApplicationException` class, as shown here:

```
Public Class MyException
    Inherits ApplicationException

    Public Sub New()
        MyBase.New()
    End Sub

    Public Sub New(ByVal message As String)
        MyBase.New(message)
    End Sub

    Public Sub New(ByVal message As String, ByVal innerException As Exception)
        MyBase.New(message, innerException)
```

```
    End Sub

    Protected Overrides Sub Finalize()
        MyBase.Finalize()
    End Sub
End Class
```

To create and throw an instance of your custom exception class, you do the same thing as demonstrated in the preceding section, "Throwing Exceptions":

```
Try
    CallSomeMethod()
Catch e1 As Exception
    Throw New MyException("Throwing MyException!", e1)
Finally
    Response.Write("Finished with Call2 exception handler" & "<BR>")
End Try
```

When the exception handler higher in the call stack catches this exception, the GetType property of the exception caught will return the name of your exception class—in this case MyException—and the InnerException property will contain the original exception.

Summary

In this hour, you learned about exception handling in Visual Basic Web applications. You learned about unstructured error handling using the On Error statement and how to find out information about the error that occurred by referencing the properties of the Err object. You also learned how to raise custom errors with the Raise method of the Err object.

You then learned about the preferred method of structured exception handling using the Try...Catch...Finally syntax. This method allows you to catch specific types of exceptions or simply catch any exception. You don't have to have code in the handler sections, and if you don't, the exception will be "swallowed."

You also learned how to create your own custom exception classes and how to throw new exceptions of your custom exception type.

Q&A

Q. Do I have to use structured exception handling in my Web applications?

A. No, but it is recommended that you do.

Q. Can I mix the two types of exception handling in my applications?

A. Yes, but not in the same method definition.

13

Q. What is the difference between throwing an exception and raising an error?

A. Throwing an exception is the method of propagating an error condition when you are dealing with structured exception handling (using the Try...Catch syntax). Raising an error is the method for propagating an error condition when you are dealing with unstructured error handling (using the On Error Goto/Resume syntax)

Q. What are the properties of the Err object?

A. Number, Description are the common ones. HelpFile and HelpContext provide links to external information if available.

Workshop

The quiz questions and exercises are provided for your further understanding.

Quiz

1. What types of exception handling are available to Visual Basic Web applications?

2. How do you generate exceptions using these types of exception handling?

3. What is a stack trace?

4. From what class do all exceptions derive?

Exercise

1. The Web application we developed in Hour 12, "Reading and Writing Files on the Web Server," did not have very much error handling in place. One specific cause of errors is when the user specifies a directory path that does not exist on the server. Add structured exception handling to handle this case and notify the user that he or she has specified an invalid directory path. You can determine the exception type that is thrown by deliberately submitting an invalid directory path.

Answers for Hour 13

Quiz

1. What types of exception handling are available to Visual Basic Web applications?

   Structured and unstructured

2. How do you generate exceptions using these types of exception handling?

   For unstructured exception handling, you use the Raise method of the Err object. For structured exception handling you use the Throw method.

3. What is a stack trace?

   A stack trace refers to the names of the methods that have been called up until the point where the exception occurred.

4. From what class do all exceptions derive?

   All exceptions derive from the `System.Exception` class. However, if you are creating you own exception classes, you should inherit from the `ApplicationException` class.

13

HOUR 14

Debugging Your ASP.NET Applications

Let's face it. No software application is ever perfect. A situation will always pop up that you didn't plan for.

You learned in the last hour how to use structured exception handling to catch errors during execution of code blocks. In this hour, you will learn how to use tracing to log information during the execution of your Web pages. This allows you to track what and when exceptions are occurring—even the ones you may be catching.

You will also learn how to use the debugger that is part of the .NET Framework SDK. It allows you to debug compiled Web pages and step through the source code as a page is executing. In this hour the following topics will be covered:

- The eight sections of information in trace output
- Enabling application-level tracing

- Debugging Visual Basic Web applications using the SDK debugger
- Stepping through the source code of your Web application using the ASP.NET worker process

What Is Tracing?

Tracing refers to the accumulation and display of information—either onscreen, in a client browser, or logged to a file—related to when Web pages are accessed, how long certain actions take, and what general informational messages you've included in your code. The ASP.NET Framework provides this service for you with the `Trace` object.

Enabling Page-Level Tracing

To enable tracing on a Web page, you set the page attribute `Trace` to `True`, as shown here:

```
<%@ Page Language="vb"
    AutoEventWireup="false"
    Codebehind="ShowFile.aspx.vb"
    Inherits="Hour14.ShowFile"
    Trace=True%>
```

When this page is viewed in a browser, a table of tracing information will be displayed at the bottom of the page (see Figure 14.1). For the examples in this hour, we are using the same code developed in Hour 12, "Reading and Writing Files on the Web Server," with a few modifications.

FIGURE 14.1

Web page with trace output.

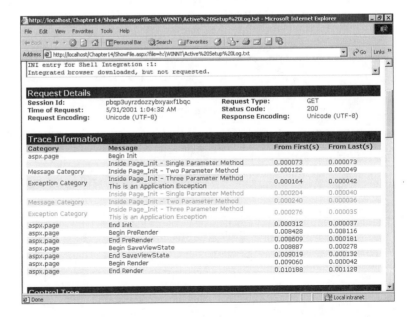

We'll go into more detail about the sections of the trace output later in this hour.

The `Trace` Object

The `Trace` object is provided as a static object available on all Web pages. It has two methods used to record information to the trace log: `Trace.Write` and `Trace.Warn`.

Both these methods have overloaded versions that accept one, two, or three parameters, as follows:

```
Dim objEx As New ApplicationException("This is an Application Exception")
'Information for trace log
Trace.Write("Inside Page_Init - Single Parameter Method")
Trace.Write("Message Category", "Inside Page_Init - Two Parameter Method")
Trace.Write("Exception Category", _
        "Inside Page_Init - Three Parameter Method", objEx)
'Warnings for trace log
Trace.Warn("Inside Page_Init - Single Parameter Method")
Trace.Warn("Message Category", "Inside Page_Init - Two Parameter Method")
Trace.Warn("Exception Category", _
"Inside Page_Init - Three Parameter Method", objEx)
```

The only difference between `Write` and `Warn` is that `Warn` messages are displayed in red when the trace output is viewed.

The versions of the methods that accept two parameters allow you to specify a string as a category that can group different types of trace messages together. The default sort order for trace information, as shown in Figure 14.2, is to display the messages in the order they are executed. You may specify the page directive `TraceMode=SortByCategory` in order to make the trace output sort by the categories you have specified. Here's an example:

```
<%@ Page Language="vb"
    AutoEventWireup="false"
    Codebehind="ShowFile.aspx.vb"
    Inherits="Hour14.ShowFile"
    Trace=true
    TraceMode=SortByCategory%>
```

The versions of the methods that accept three parameters also accept a category string as their first parameter but add an exception object as their third parameter. This method is tailored for your structured exception-handling code so that you can pass the current exception to the `Trace` object for logging.

14

FIGURE **14.2**

Trace output sorted by category.

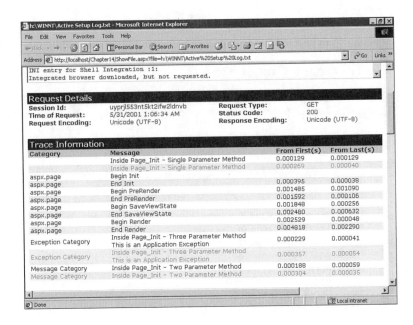

Sections of the `Trace` Output

The trace output consists up to eight sections of information:

- Request Details: Contains information related to the current session, such as the session ID, the time the request was processed, the return code for the request, and the request type (`GET`/`POST`).

- Trace Information: Contains messages from some of the lifecycle events (`Page_Init`, `Page_PreRender`, and so on) of your Web pages as well as any `Trace.Write` or `Trace.Warn` messages that have executed. The From First and From Last columns show the time since the first message was displayed and the time since the last message was displayed, respectively, in seconds.

- Control Tree: Contains a hierarchical listing of the server controls that were processed for this page. Their type and size in bytes are displayed as well as the number of bytes required to store any state information.

- Cookies Collection: Displays any cookies associated with the current session and request.

- Headers Collection: Contains the headers that were sent to the server from the client browser.

- Querystring Collection: Contains the parameters that were passed to the Web page in the query string; that is, key/value pairs in the URL after the question mark and separated by ampersands. This section may not be present in all trace output tables.

- Form Collection: Contains any values that were submitted from a form to the current Web page. This section may not be present in all trace output tables.

- Server Variables: Contains all the current server variables.

Enabling Application-Level Tracing

Tracing can be enabled for all pages in a Web application. To do this, you need to make some changes to the `Web.config` file located in the root directory of your application. The trace section of the configuration file looks like the following:

```
<trace enabled="false"
    requestLimit="10"
    pageOutput="false"
    traceMode="SortByTime"
    localOnly="true" />
```

By changing the `false` values to `true`, you enable tracing to occur on each page of your application.

> The attribute names in the configuration file must be "camel cased" (for example, `requestLimit` and not `RequestLimit`, `Requestlimit`, or `requestlimit`). The values of `"true"` and `"false"` must be lowercased. If either of these rules is broken, you will receive an error message when the configuration file is parsed as part of a client request (see Figure 14.3).

These values act as defaults for all Web pages in your application. If you specify `Trace` or `TraceMode` page directives in your Web pages themselves, those values will override the values in the configuration section.

The `Trace.axd` Application

If you remove the `Trace` and `TraceMode` page directives from your Web pages and set `pageOutput="false"` and `enabled="true"` in your configuration file, tracing is still enabled, but you won't see any output. So how do you view your tracing information? A special HTTP handler provided by ASP.NET called `Trace.axd` is used for this purpose. An *HTTP handler* is a special program that processes Web requests at a very low level, and it's a topic that's beyond the scope of this book.

14

FIGURE **14.3**

Error in the configuration file for an application.

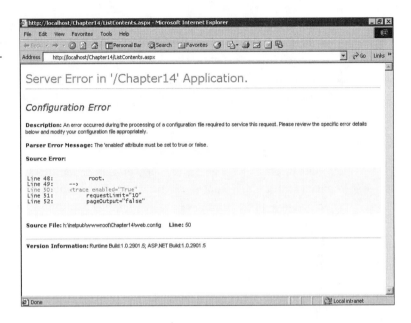

You access this application by specifying Trace.axd as the file to open in the root directory of your application (http://localhost/hour14/trace.axd). The Trace application (Trace.axd) will display a list of the last *n* requests made for Web pages in your application, where *n* is determined by the value for requestLimit in your configuration file (see Figure 14.4).

FIGURE **14.4**

Viewing Trace.axd in a browser.

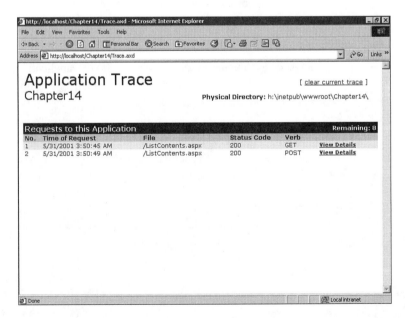

The list of requests contains a hyperlink to view the details for each request. When you click one of the hyperlinks, the trace output table—the same table that would be displayed at the bottom of a Web page, as you saw earlier—is displayed for the selected request (see Figure 14.5).

FIGURE **14.5**

Details of a selected request.

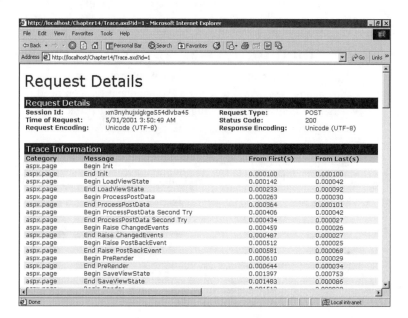

Once the number of requests reaches the requestLimit value, no new requests will be traced until you clear the current trace by clicking the Clear Current Trace hyperlink at the top right of the Trace application's main page.

You do not need to remove the trace statements from your Web pages, even when you are ready to deploy your application to a production setting. You disable the trace output by changing settings in the application's configuration file. This way, should something occur later on and you need to see the tracing information, you simply change the configuration of your Web application to reenable the tracing. No recompiling or commenting/uncommenting of code necessary!

14

Using the SDK Debugger

The .NET SDK provides a Windows application similar to the Visual Studio.NET (VS.NET) development environment for debugging any .NET-compiled applications. We are going to use it to debug Visual Basic Web applications.

Where Is the Debugger?

The debugger is installed in {*system drive*}:\Program Files\Microsoft.Net\
FrameworkSDK\GuiDebug\DbgCLR.exe. When you start the debugger, it opens with three
empty windows because you haven't specified an application or any source code to
debug.

Attaching to the ASP.NET Worker Process

All the work behind the scenes of our Web application is done by a dedicated process
called aspnet_wp.exe. To debug a Web application, you need to be on the machine
where the application is running. Then you need to attach the debugger to the
aspnet_wp.exe process. You do this by selecting Tools, Debug Processes from the menu
bar. When the Process window appears, check the Show System Processes check box
(see Figure 14.6). If aspnet_wp.exe is not in the list of processes, open a browser and
select one of the pages in the Web application you are trying to debug. Select the
aspnet_wp.exe process, click the Attach button, and then close the Processes dialog box.

FIGURE 14.6

*Attaching to the
aspnet_wp.exe process.*

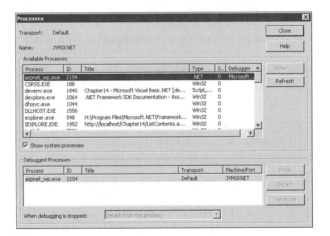

Loading Source Files

Once the debugger is attached to the worker process, you can load your source code files
(.vb and .aspx) into it by selecting File, Open on the menu bar, browsing to the location
of your Web application, and selecting all the files you want to debug. The File, Open
dialog box is multiselect capable, so you can select many files at once. At this point, you
can place breakpoints in your code files by selecting a line of code and pressing the F9
key. Now when you go back to your browser and refresh the current Web page or start
navigating through your application, the debugger will stop when it reaches one of your
breakpoints.

Depending on the options you have set for the debugger, the F10 key allows you to step through your source code one line at a time. If you are calling a method somewhere else in your code and you want the debugger to step into that code, you need to press the F11 key instead of F10. The F10 and F11 keys are the default key assignments for step over and step into. The F10 key steps over, whereas the F11 key steps into method calls (see figure 14.7). *Stepping over* means that if you are currently on a line of code that is calling a subroutine elsewhere in your application, the debugger will execute that subroutine and continue with the next line of code. *Stepping into* means that the dubugger will jump to the subroutine being called, where you can step through the lines of code for that subroutine; this process can be repeated if the subroutine you've jumped to has calls to other subroutines. Eventually, after stepping through all your subroutines, you will be returned back to the next line of code from your original calling point.

FIGURE 14.7

Stopping on a break-point and stepping through source code.

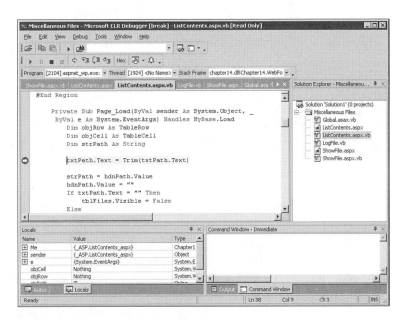

Debugger Windows

The debugger contains some valuable windows that help you step through your code. The Locals window displays the variables that exist inside the current method or code block you are stepping through. Some of the variables will have a plus sign beside them, indicating they are complex variables with methods and properties. You can click the plus sign to expand the variable and view all its methods and properties. The Output window displays various system messages related to other files, usually DLLs, that have

14

been loaded or unloaded during the execution of your application. This window also displays the text for any `Debug.Writeline` methods that may be in your code. The `Debug` object prints out information only when the application is attached to a debugger. The Command window allows you to type in Visual Basic commands to execute immediately when you press the Enter key. You have access to any of the variables that exist in the current method where the code pointer has stopped due to a breakpoint.

> If you want clients to see the descriptive information about unhandled runtime errors or exceptions that occur, you will need to make a change in your application's `Web.config` file. To do this, change
>
> `<customErrors mode="RemoteOnly" />`
>
> to
>
> `<customErrors mode="Off" />`.
>
> Otherwise, the remote clients will receive a generic page indicating that an error has occurred, but no specific information related to the error will be available.

When you are done debugging your application, you can save the current solution so that the next time you want to debug this application, you simply need to open the solution. The solution will contain all the source code files you have added, but you will still need to attach the `aspnet_wp.exe` process to it.

Summary

In this hour, you learned how to take advantage of the tracing features provided by the ASP.NET SDK, which allows you to see what is happening during the processing of your application's Web pages. You can see how long it takes to render your page as well as how many bytes each element of your page takes up. You can use tracing to log informational messages as well as information about exceptions that are caught and handled.

You also learned how to use the .NET SDK debugger to attach to the ASP.NET worker process and then step through the source code of your Web application.

Q&A

Q. Do I need to remove tracing statements that I have included in my code before I move an application into production?

A. No. You simply need to disable tracing for the application. The tracing statements will not generate any output or slow the execution of your application once disabled.

Q. Can I generate tracing output for just one page in my application as opposed to all pages?

A. Yes. To enable tracing on a Web page, you set the page attribute Trace to True, as shown here:

```
<%@ Page Language="vb"
    AutoEventWireup="false"
    Codebehind="ShowFile.aspx.vb"
    Inherits="Hour14.ShowFile"
    Trace=True%>
```

Q. How do I see more than the last 10 requests made to pages in my application using the `Trace.axd` HTTP handler?

A. You will need to modify the `requestLimit` parameter in the configuration file for your application.

Workshop

The quiz questions and exercises are provided for your further understanding.

Quiz

1. How do you enable page-level tracing output to be displayed?

2. What do you do to see tracing output for pages in your web application when page-level tracing has been suppressed?

3. What application can you use to debug your web applications that allows you to step through your code as it is executing?

4. What do you do to allow descriptive information about unhandled exceptions to be viewed by clients accessing your applications?

Exercise

Add tracing statements to the application you developed in Hour 12 to log when exceptions occur. This application will generate exceptions when you try to reference a directory or drive that does not exist on the Web server.

14

Answers for Hour 14

Quiz

1. How do you enable page-level tracing output to be displayed?

   To enable tracing on a Web page, you set the page attribute Trace to True.

2. What do you do to see tracing output for pages in your web application when page-level tracing has been suppressed?

   You use the `Trace.axd` special HTTP handler. You access this application by specifying `Trace.axd` as the file to open in the root directory of your application, (`http://localhost/hour14/trace.axd`).

3. What application can you use to debug your web applications that allows you to step through your code as it is executing?

   You can use the SDK debugger. The debugger is installed in `{system drive}:\Program Files\Microsoft.Net\FrameworkSDK\GuiDebug\DbgCLR.exe`.

4. What do you do to allow descriptive information about unhandled exceptions to be viewed by clients accessing your applications?

   You will need to modify the configuration file to your Web application by changing the following line

   from this

   ```
   <customErrors mode="RemoteOnly" />
   ```

   to this

   ```
   <customErrors mode="Off" />.
   ```

PART IV

Supplying Your Application with Data

Hour

HOUR **15**

Using Databases

Just about every application built for the business world relies on some type of data storage. Whether you're using an Excel spreadsheet, a text file, or a relational database management system (RDBMS) such as SQL Server or Oracle, storing and retrieving data is critical to the success of your application.

In this hour, you will be introduced to data access through ASP.NET and ADO.NET. You will also learn

- What defines a database
- The types of databases and when to use them
- what database-access tools are available in ASP.NET

What Is a Database?

If you are familiar with relational databases, you can skip this section and move on to the ADO.NET overview.

In the simplest terms, a *database* is a collection of information organized in such a way that one can quickly retrieve the desired information from it. It's like a filing cabinet, in which all your records are organized in some manner for easy retrieval. A database is composed of three elements: fields, records, and files. A *field* is one data element, such as a name or phone number. A *record* is a collection of fields—for example, user information such as name, street address, city, state, ZIP Code, and phone number. Finally, a *table* is a collection of records that contain similar information.

You can use two types of databases when developing your application. The first is the flat-file database. In a flat-file database, all information is stored in one table. An example of a flat-file database is an Excel spreadsheet or a comma-delimited text file. Flat-file databases are good for small applications, but if you are going to be storing vast amounts of data or performing queries relating flat files to one another, their usefulness ends. Figure 15.1 is an illustration of a flat-file database. Notice that all the data is in one table and that there are no relationships that can be made in the data.

FIGURE 15.1

A flat-file database.

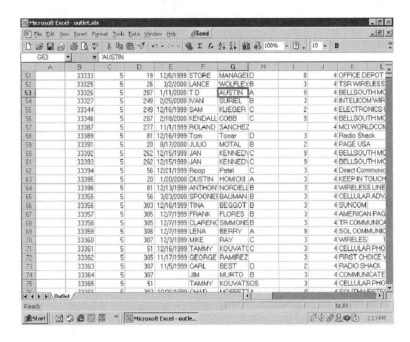

The second kind of database used in applications is the relational database. To meet the needs for more robust enterprise-class applications—whether they be client/server or Web based—the relational database management system (RDBMS) was created. It is nothing more than a collection of tables, or flat files, that can be related to one another when, for example, information in one table, usually a unique numeric identifier, is also stored in another table. This process helps the database relate the tables to one another because the same bit of information is stored in both tables. Figure 15.2 shows an

RDBMS. Notice that multiple tables make up the database and that pieces of data can be related to one another.

FIGURE 15.2

A relational database.

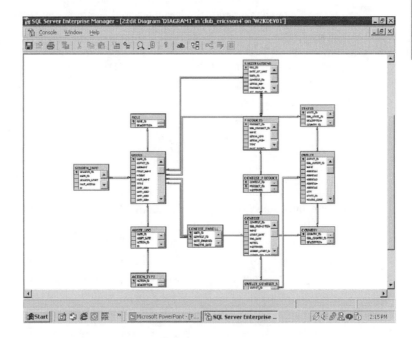

When Do I Need to Use a Relational Database?

You need to use a relational database in the following situations:

- When you need to store large quantities of disparate data
- When it is not feasible to store all the information for your application in one table
- When you need better security than that which comes with a simple text file or a program such as Microsoft Access or Microsoft Excel

Tables

The core component of a relational database is the *table*, which is a logical storage element that consists of columns and rows. The columns of a table are the same as fields in that both consist of one type of information. A *field* is the smallest unit of information in a table, such as a first name, a telephone number, or a social security number. A field is defined by the type and size of the data it collects. Data types include strings, numbers, dates, timestamps, and even binary data. As mentioned earlier, a collection of fields is called a *record*. Each row in a table is a record.

There are many relational databases available. Some work on all platforms; some work only on Windows. The following list is just a sampling of the relational databases available and does not in any way reflect all the relational databases on the market:

- Microsoft SQL Server
- Microsoft Data Engine (MSDE)
- Oracle
- Informix
- Sybase
- MySQL

Normally, one column in a table acts as an identifier for the record. This column contains data that is unique in every row. This identifier is called a *primary key*, and it allows one to easily extract information about a record in a table. This field is also indexed by the database to help it retrieve records quickly and efficiently. Figure 15.3 shows a table of user information that has a primary key. In most instances, a primary key is a numeric counter that is incremented by one with each new record to the table.

FIGURE 15.3

A table of user data with a primary key.

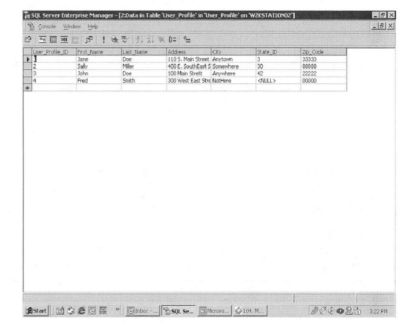

In a relational database, we relate tables to one another by adding a field to the relating table that will store the same data as the primary key of the table that we want to relate from. This new field is called a *foreign key*, because it relates back to the primary key of the original table. For example, our User_Profile table contains a State field that normally holds the state's abbreviation. In database design, we would *normalize* our tables, which means that we pull out repeating data fields and store them in their own table. Because the State field would have repeating state abbreviations, we can create a State table that has all 50 U.S. states in it and relate it back to the User_Profile table using a foreign key on the User_Profile table. Figure 15.4 illustrates the foreign key relationship between the User_Profile table from Figure 15.3 and a new State table.

FIGURE 15.4

The User_Profile *table with foreign key relationship to the State table.*

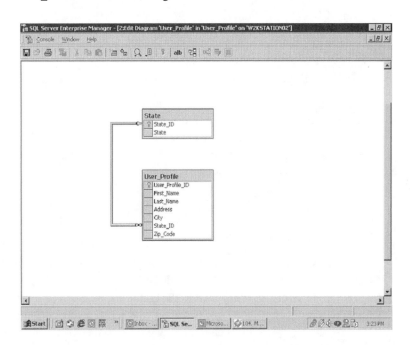

Now we can easily relate records in the User_Profile table to the State table through the foreign key relationship on the State field. We save excess keystrokes by using this relationship, and we can also ensure that the same state abbreviation is going to be used every time a particular state is selected.

Structured Query Language

When working with a relational database, and even when working with Microsoft Access, you need to have a solid understanding of Structured Query Language (SQL).

SQL is a standardized query language for extracting and manipulating data stored in a database. First created by an IBM research center in the mid 1970s, SQL was introduced commercially by Oracle in 1979. From there, it spread from mainframes and minicomputers to desktop PCs.

Although a full discussion of the features of SQL is beyond the scope of this book, it is essential that you at least understand the basics of data manipulation with SQL. When working with SQL, you will generally execute four actions: selecting records from a table (SELECT), inserting records into a table (INSERT), updating records in a table (UPDATE), and deleting records in a table (DELETE).

SELECT

The SELECT statement is used to retrieve data from a database table. In its simplest form, the SQL statement necessary to extract data is as follows:

```
SELECT * FROM tablename
```

This statement will extract every field and every row from a table. The asterisk (*) is a wildcard character, meaning that the query will return all the fields in a table. If you want to retrieve only a certain set of fields from the table, you would list the column names separated by commas instead of using the asterisk (*) character. For example, to select John Doe's name and address from the User_Profile table, you would use the following syntax:

```
SELECT First_Name, Last_Name, Address, City, State, Zip_Code FROM User_Profile
➥WHERE User_Profile_ID = 3
```

The main difference between this query and the first query is that the fields are explicitly referenced, as opposed to all the fields being retrieved, which was done in the first query. Also, a WHERE clause is attached to the end of the SELECT statement. The WHERE clause filters out records from the table based on whether they meet the condition it specifies. In this example, the WHERE clause is looking to see which record has a 3 in its User_Profile_Id field; once it finds that record, it returns the data stored in the appropriate fields.

All this is great for retrieving data in one table, but what is required to extract data from multiple tables? This is a relational database, isn't it? Well, to get data from multiple tables, we need to find some way to connect these tables to each other. In SQL, you can do this using a JOIN clause in your SELECT statement.

In SQL, there are three types of joins. The first is the *inner join*. This type of join connects only those records in the originating table to those records that match them in the joining table. These records are typically joined through the primary/foreign key relationships defined when the table was created. For example, to get the name of the state that

John Doe lives in, we would need to join the `User_Profile` table to the State table. The syntax for such a join depends on the database. For Microsoft SQL Server, MSDE, Microsoft Access, Sybase and others, you would use the following syntax:

```
SELECT First_Name, Last_Name, Address, City, State_Name, Zip_Code
    FROM User_Profile u
    INNER JOIN STATE s ON u.State = s.State
    WHERE User_Profile_ID = 3
```

For Oracle databases, the syntax would be this:

```
SELECT First_Name, Last_Name, Address, City, State_Name, Zip_Code
    FROM User_Profile u, State s
    WHERE u.State = s.State AND
    User_Profile_ID = 3
```

Notice the difference between the two statements. The first statement uses the `JOIN` clause, and the `INNER` keyword is added in front of the `JOIN` keyword. The clause then specifies which table is going to be joined to the `User_Profile` table. In our example, that table is the State table. The lowercase u after the `User_Profile` table and the lowercase s after the State table are aliases for the tables. Aliases allow us to refer to tables through a form of shorthand. Instead of typing `User_Profile.State`, we can refer to the State field in the `User_Profile` table by typing **u.State**. The State table name is then followed by a join criterion, which specifies on which fields the tables are to be joined. The second SQL statement says basically the same thing—except instead of using a `JOIN` clause, it lists all the tables in the `FROM` clause, along with their corresponding aliases. From there, the `WHERE` clause is added to specify which fields will be joined together. The second SQL statement will work with all the databases mentioned previously.

The second type of join is the *outer join*. There are two types of outer joins: left joins and right joins. When you use a left join, you are specifying that you want all the records from the original table and only those records from the joined table that match the join criterion. The right join reverses this outcome. In a right join, only those records that match the join criterion are returned from the original table, and all the records in the joined table are returned. The syntax for writing an outer join `SELECT` statement also depends on the database being used. For Microsoft SQL Server, MSDE, Microsoft Access, Sybase, and others, you would use the following syntax for a left join:

```
SELECT First_Name, Last_Name, Address, City, State_Name, Zip_Code
    FROM User_Profile u
    LEFT JOIN STATE s ON u.State = s.State
```

For Oracle databases, the left join syntax is as follows:

```
SELECT First_Name, Last_Name, Address, City, State_Name, Zip_Code
    FROM User_Profile u, State s
    WHERE u.State *= s.State
```

When either of these statements are executed, you get all the rows in the User_Profile table and only those matching fields in the State table. On records that do not match, the database returns a null value, which means that no value was found in the database.

For Microsoft SQL Server, MSDE, Microsoft Access, Sybase, and others, you would use the following syntax for a right join:

```
SELECT First_Name, Last_Name, Address, City, State_Name, Zip_Code
    FROM User_Profile u
    RIGHT JOIN STATE s ON u.State = s.State
```

For Oracle databases, the right join syntax would be this:

```
SELECT First_Name, Last_Name, Address, City, State_Name, Zip_Code
    FROM User_Profile u, State s
    WHERE u.State =* s.State
```

When either of the preceding RIGHT JOIN statements are executed, the database will return all the values in the State table and only those records in the User_Profile table that meet the join criterion. Again, any records in the User_Profile table that do not meet the criterion will be returned as null values.

The third and final type of join is called a *union*. In SQL, the UNION operator returns all the records from all the tables that are joined together. The only stipulation is that all the fields being returned *must* be the same data type in all the tables joined together. Here's the syntax for using a UNION operator:

```
SELECT field1, field2, [fieldN] FROM table1
UNION
SELECT field1, field2, [fieldN] FROM table2
[UNION
SELECT field1, field2, [fieldN] FROM tableN]
```

The resulting records would contain values from table1, table2, all the way through tableN, as one contiguous group of records.

INSERT

The INSERT statement is used to add records to a table. The syntax for using the INSERT statement is as follows:

```
INSERT INTO table (column1, column2, [columnN]) VALUES (value1, value2,
{valueN})
```

For example, suppose you have a table in your database called USER_PROFILE that's used to store user-specific information for your application. A table like this would probably have the following columns: FIRST_NAME, LAST_NAME, ADDRESS, CITY, STATE, and ZIP_CODE. For this example, let's say we want to add the following user data to the table:

John Doe, 100 Main St., Anywhere, NC, 27999. The following statement illustrates the proper SQL statement needed to add the user's information to the database.

```
INSERT INTO USER_PROFILE (FIRST_NAME, LAST_NAME, ADDRESS, CITY, STATE, ZIP_CODE)
➥ VALUES ('John', 'Doe', '100 Main St.', 'Anywhere', 'NC', '27999')
```

One thing to keep in mind when using this statement is that the values you want to insert into the database must be in the same order as the column list in the first set of parentheses. Also, when working with strings, which are groups of characters and numbers, you must use single quotes (' ') around each string element in order for the database to save the data as a string. Numeric data does not take single quotes. In fact, if you use single quotes around numeric values, the database will automatically convert the number to a string. Any calculations performed on this string will generate an error unless the string is converted back to a number.

Also notice that no value is inserted into the primary key of this record. In this and most instances, the primary key is automatically inserted into the record by the database. Therefore, if we were to look at this data in the table, the row would look something like the one shown in Figure 15.5.

FIGURE 15.5

The John Doe record in User_Profile *table.*

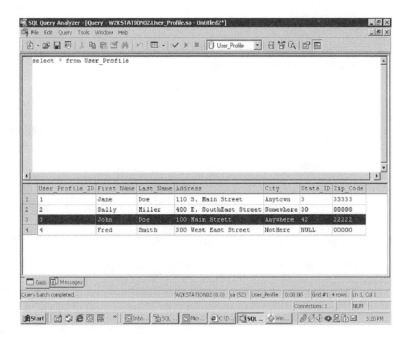

Notice that the User_Profile_ID column has a value in it, 3, even though we didn't explicitly insert a value into the column.

DELETE

The DELETE command is used to delete records stored in a table. The syntax for using DELETE is as follows:

```
DELETE FROM tablename [WHERE field1 = value1 [AND | OR] field2 = value2 [[AND |
OR] fieldN = valueN]]
```

Be careful with this command, because if you do not specify a WHERE clause condition, it will delete all the rows in your table. If you specify a WHERE clause, it will remove only those records that successfully meet the criteria.

To remove the John Doe record in our User_Profile table, you would use the following code:

```
DELETE FROM User_Profile WHERE User_Profile_ID = 3
```

Once this command is executed, the John Doe record is deleted from the User_Profile table. Any reference to the User_Profile_ID value of 3 will be broken if it is used as a foreign key in another table. Due to this breakdown, it is important that you first remove any foreign-key–related records before removing the original record.

UPDATE

The UPDATE statement is used in SQL to modify a record in a database table. Here's the syntax for the UPDATE statement:

```
UPDATE table SET column1 = value1, column2 = value2, [columnN = valueN] [WHERE
id_column = value]
```

In this syntax, columns and their new values are paired together with an equals sign (=). A new element added to this syntax is the optional WHERE clause, appended to the end of the SQL statement. This clause allows the user to modify a specific set of information. If this clause is omitted, the SQL statement would modify all the records in the table.

Take our last example using the John Doe record. Suppose Mr. Doe has moved across town to 600 Broad St. and needs to change his address. The SQL statement to modify this record would be as follows:

```
UPDATE USER_PROFILE SET ADDRESS = '600 Broad St.' WHERE USER_PROFILE_ID = 3
```

When this command is executed, the database searches for the record that has the matching value in its User_Profile_ID field. Once it locates that record, it updates the Address field with the new information and saves the record.

Now that you know how to insert and update records in a relational database, let's now take a look at retrieving records from a database table.

The four commands introduced in this hour are a brief sampling of the many commands you can use with a relational database. There just isn't enough room in this book to describe all of the features of SQL. If you want to get more information on SQL, or any of the databases mentioned, there are plenty of books dedicated to these subjects at brick-and-mortar and online bookstores.

Server-Side Data Access

In Web application development, database access is typically performed from the Web server itself. There are special circumstances in which another server will perform the database connection, but overall, no database connectivity occurs on the user's computer.

ASP.NET and other Web-development languages have a set of tools you use to access a database. These tools allow you to connect to a database and manipulate the data in that database using SQL or another tool that can interface with the data. In ASP.NET, ADO.NET is the medium through which you can access and manipulate data in a database.

ADO.NET Overview

The *ADO* in ADO.NET stands for *ActiveX Data Objects*. This is Microsoft's latest iteration of its successful universal data-access technology, which allows developers to interact with just about any database on the market.

In ADO.NET, there are several namespaces that developers can use when working with data and databases. Two important ones are the `Dataset` object and the Managed Provider. The `Dataset` object is the core component to manipulating data in the database. It represents a complete set of data from a database, including tables, constraints, and relationships between the tables. Unlike previous versions of ADO, ADO.NET `Dataset` objects can store multiple sets of records, those records can be manipulated within the confines of the `Dataset` object itself. Hour 16, "Reading from Database Tables," will delve into ADO.NET in much more detail.

The second part to ADO.NET is the Managed Provider. It describes the type of connection and mediates communication between your application, your `Dataset` object, and the database. There are currently two types of Managed Providers: the SQL Server Managed Provider and the OleDB Managed Provider. The SQL Server Managed Provider provides all the tools necessary to communicate effectively between your application and a Microsoft SQL Server database. The OleDB Managed Provider provides all the tools necessary to communicate effectively between your application and any data source that supports OleDB.

Table 15.1 shows the providers with which ADO.NET has been tested and the drivers used with them.

TABLE 15.1   ADO.NET Drivers and Providers

Driver	Provider
SQLOLEDB	SQL Server OLE DB provider
MSDAORA	Oracle OLE DB Provider
JOLT	Jet (Access) OLE DB Provider
MSDASQL/SQLServer ODBC	SQL Server ODBC Driver via OLE DB for ODBC Provider
MSDASQL/Jet ODBC	Jet ODBC Driver via OLE DB Provider for ODBC Provider

Defining Database Access Using ADO.NET

`System.Data`, `System.Data.SQLClient`, and `System.Data.oledb` are the namespaces that define database access using ADO.NET. You will need to import these namespaces into your application in order to use ADO.NET to access a database. Each of these namespaces will be discussed in more detail in the next hour. For now, here are some points to keep in mind:

- `System.Data` is the general namespace that stores all of the classes that make up the core ADO.NET architecture.
- `System.Data.OleDB` is the namespace for the ADO.NET managed provider for OleDB-supported data sources.
- `System.Data.SQLClient` is the namespace for the SQL Server Managed Provider. This namespace was written specifically for Microsoft SQL Server and has increased performance benefits from previous versions of SQL Server.

Summary

In this hour, you were introduced to databases and were given a general overview of ADO.NET. If you are new to databases, you should understand the general structure of a relational database and have a basic comprehension of the SQL commands necessary to manipulate data in a database. You were also introduced to the world of universal data access through ADO.NET, Microsoft's latest iteration of data-access technology. The next four hours will focus on working with databases and other data sources using ADO.NET in an ASP.NET application.

Q&A

Q. What are the four basic data-manipulation commands in SQL?

A. The four basic data-manipulation commands in SQL are SELECT, UPDATE, INSERT, and DELETE.

Q. Where can I get more information on ADO.NET?

A. You can get more information on ADO.NET on Microsoft's Web site or from one of the many books published on the subject. You can also get information from many of the ASP.NET-dedicated Web sites available online.

Workshop

The quiz questions and exercises are provided for your further understanding.

Quiz

1. What does this SQL statement do when executed?

   ```
   UPDATE User_Profile SET First_Name = "Joe"
   ```

2. What are the two Managed Providers that come with ADO.NET?

3. What type of information does a Dataset object hold?

Exercises

If you don't have access to a copy of SQL Server 7 or later, take the time to download MSDE from Microsoft's Web site. It is a free download, and you can use Microsoft Access to connect to the data engine.

Take some time to familiarize yourself with the SQL syntax presented in this hour. You will find it especially helpful to know SQL inside and out when the time comes to develop your first application. Re-create the User_Profile table used in this hour. Insert records into it, update records in it, and delete records from it. Create some other tables and use some of the JOIN syntax to extract data from multiple tables as one group of records.

Once you have gained a solid familiarity to working with a database, you will be well on your way to becoming a competent developer.

Answers for Hour 15

Quiz

1. What does this SQL statement do when executed?

   `UPDATE User_Profile SET First_Name = "Joe"`

   This SQL statement will update every record in the `User_Profile` table and set the `First_Name` field to `"Joe"`.

2. What are the two Managed Providers that come with ADO.NET?

   The two Managed Providers for ADO.NET are the ADO Managed Provider and the SQL Server Managed Provider.

3. What type of information does a `Dataset` object hold?

   A data set contains all the records stored in one or more tables, their field constraints, and any foreign key relationships between the tables stored in the data set.

HOUR **16**

Reading from Database Tables

In the previous hour, you were introduced to databases and Microsoft's latest data access technology, ADO.NET. Now that you have a foundation to build upon, let's take a look at connecting to a database and extracting data from it.

In this hour, you will be introduced to data access through ASP.NET and ADO.NET. You will also learn the following:

- How to connect to an OLE DB–compliant database, such as Microsoft SQL Server or Oracle
- The properties and methods of the `SQLConnection` and the `OleDbConnection` objects
- The properties and methods of the `SQLCommand` object
- How to execute SQL statements and display the results on an ASP.NET page

Connecting to a Database

When building your ASP.NET application, you will need to connect to a database to extract or manipulate data. Using ADO.NET, you can easily access a database and manipulate data using a variety of means. ADO.NET offers ASP pages a rich, powerful suite of data-handling facilities.

The first step in working with any database is to make a connection to it. A connection to a database is like the hose used at the gas station to fuel up your car. Think of the gasoline as being the data that your application needs to run properly. When your car is low on gas, you connect it to the gas pump using the hose, and the fuel is added to your car through that hose. An application works in a similar way: When it needs to access data (its fuel), it makes a connection to the database, and the data is fed to the application through that connection, much like the fuel is fed to the car through the gas pump hose.

Microsoft SQL Server Databases

With ADO.NET, there are two ways to connect to a database, and which one you use depends on which kind of database you are connecting to. If you are connecting to a Microsoft SQL Server database, you use the `SQLConnection` object; if you are connecting to another kind of database, such as an Oracle database, you use the `OleDbConnection` object. The following sections discuss these objects in more detail.

SQLConnection

When you wish to connect to a Microsoft SQL Server database from your application, you use the `SQLConnection` object. In order to use this object, you must first import the `System.Data.SqlClient` namespace into your application using the `Import` keyword. The syntax for adding this namespace to your ASP.NET page is the following:

```
<%@ Import Namespace="System.Data.SqlClient"%>
```

Once this namespace has been added to you page, you will have access to the `SQLConnection` class object.

The `SQLConnection` object has a variety of properties and methods you can use when constructing your application. Tables 16.1 and 16.2 list the available properties and methods, respectively, of the `SQLConnection` object, including a brief description of the functionality of each.

TABLE 16.1   *SQLConnection* Properties

Property	Description
ConnectionString	Gets or sets the string used to open a connection to a Microsoft SQL Server database
ConnectionTimeout	Specifies the time to wait for making a connection to the database before terminating the attempt and generating an error
Database	Gets the name of the current database
DataSource	Gets the name of the instance of SQL Server
ServerVersion	Gets a string containing the version of the instance of SQL Server to which you are connected to
State	Gets the current state of the database connection. SQLConnection supports only the Open and Closed connection state values

TABLE 16.2   *SQLConnection* Methods

Method	Description
BeginTransaction	Begins a database transaction
ChangeDatabase	Changes the current database for an open SQL connection
Close	Closes the connection to the database
Dispose	Disposes of the SQLConnection object, releasing component resources
Open	Opens a database connection with the property settings specified by the ConnectionString

A database transaction allows the application to perform a data manipulation operation in an all-or-nothing fashion. If an error occurs or the operation fails to do something, all the data modified by the operation can be restored (or *rolled back*) to its original state. If the operation succeeds, the transaction can be committed to the database. Once a transaction is committed to the database, there is no programmatic way to restore that data to its premodified state.

When making a connection to a SQL Server database, you can define your connection using the SQLConnection class:

Alternatively, you can use the ConnectionString property:

```
Dim oConn as New SQLConnection

oConn.ConnectionString = "server=localhost;user id=sa;password=;database=pubs"
```

You can also use a shortcut for the ConnectionString property by assigning the connection string value when declaring the SQLConnection object. To do this, use the following syntax:

```
Dim oConn as New SQLConnection("server=localhost;user
id=sa;password=;database=pubs")
```

SQLCommand

Now that you have your connection to your database set up, you need some mechanism for executing SQL queries. In ADO.NET, you'll use the SQLCommand object to meet this need.

The SQLCommand object acts as the data carrier over the connection made by the SQLConnection object to your database. It is composed of several properties and methods that aid you, the developer, in data manipulation. Tables 16.3 and 16.4 summarize the properties and methods, respectively, associated with SQLCommand.

TABLE 16.3 *SQLCommand* Properties

Property	Description
CommandText	Specifies the SQL query to be executed.
CommandTimeout	Specifies the timeout value to wait before terminating the query execution and returning an error.
CommandType	Specifies the type of command to execute in the CommandText property. The value can be one of the following:
	StoredProcedure: The CommandText property specifies the name of a stored procedure.
	TableDirect: The CommandText property specifies the table name whose columns are all returned.
	Text: The CommandText property is the actual SQL query to execute.
Connection	Specifies the SQLConnection object to use.
Parameters	Specifies the SQLParameters collection for this SQLCommand object. The SQLParameters collection can be used to define parameters for a stored procedure or to filter data stored in a DataSet object.
Transaction	Gets or sets the transaction in which the SQL command executes.
UpdatedRowSource	Gets or sets how command results are applied to the data row when used by the Update method of the DbDataAdapter.

TABLE 16.4 *SQLCommand* Methods

Method	Description
Cancel	Cancels the execution of a SQL command.
ExecuteNonQuery	Executes a SQL statement that does not return any data from the database.
ExecuteReader	Sends the CommandText to the Connection and builds a SQLDataReader.
ExecuteScalar	Executes the query and returns the first column of the first row in the resultset returned by the query. Extra columns or rows are ignored.
ExecuteXmlReader	Sends the CommandText to the Connection and builds an XmlReader object.
Prepare	Creates a prepared version of the command on an instance of SQL Server.
ResetCommandTimeOut	Resets the CommandTimeout property to its default value.

To instantiate the SQLCommand object, you would use the following syntax:

```
Dim myCommand As SQLCommand = New SQLCommand(SQLQuery, mySQLConnection)
```

SQLQuery is the SQL statement you want to execute, and *mySQLConnection* is the name of the SQLConnection object you want to use as the database connection. For example, to retrieve all of the rows in the Customers table in the Northwind database that's included on Microsoft SQL Server, you would use the following code:

```
Dim myConnection As SQLConnection = New
SQLConnection("server=localhost;uid=sa;pwd=;database=Northwind")
Dim myCommand As SQLCommand = New SQLCommand("select * from Customers",
myConnection)

...
```

The first line creates the connection to the Northwind database using the SQLConnection object. The second statement creates the SQLCommand object, initializes the object to the query "SELECT * FROM CUSTOMERS", and attaches it to the SQLConnection object, myConnection, created in the first statement.

If you want to execute a SQL statement that does not return any rows of data (for example, an UPDATE query, an INSERT statement, or a DELETE statement), you would use the ExecuteNonQuery method of the SQLCommand object. If you want to update the phone field of a specific record in the Customers table, for example, you would use the following syntax.

```
Dim myConnection As New
SQLConnection("server=localhost;uid=sa;pwd=;database=Northwind")
Dim mycommand As New SQLCommand( _
```

```
                        "UPDATE Customers SET phone='(800) 555-1212' WHERE CustomerID
= 'ALFKI'",  _
                        myConnection)

myCommand. Connection.Open()
myCommand.ExecuteNonQuery()
myCommand. Connection.Close()
```

The preceding code snippet connects to the Northwind database located on the same server that's executing the code. The second statement creates a new SQLCommand object and sets its query to update the Phone field in the row with the ALFKI customer ID to '(800) 555-1212'. Notice that you *must* explicitly open the connection when using the SQLCommand object to call the ExecuteNonQuery method. This is also true if you are calling a query to return records from a data source.

> Keep in mind that you must explicitly close your connection to the data source after every call to the database. Although any open connections to a database will be cleaned up eventually, you run the risk of exceeding the number of connections you can have to your data source. If this occurs, your application will fail due to its inability to operate with the database.

If instead of updating you want to *retrieve* records from a database, you will need a third object to store that data. Normally, you would use a DataSet object to store this data. The DataSet object stores a disconnected set of data and keeps it available until it is discarded by the application. In standard client/server applications, the DataSet object works well. However, in the Web world, you typically work with a series of requests to a data source instead of working with one DataSet object and modifying as you see fit. In order to accommodate the disconnected nature of Web applications, you'll use an object called SQLDataReader.

SQLDataReader

The SQLDataReader object is used to provide you with a forward-only, read-only group of records. The forward-only part of the description means that you can loop through the records in only one direction: from beginning to end. The read-only part of the description means that the data cannot be updated through the SQLDataReader object. When you're building Web applications, this is the exact type of data container you need to work with. In most instances, you are going to display data only on the page, and this object provides the best performance in retrieving information from a data source.

SQLDataReader has a multitude of properties and methods you can invoke. These properties and methods are illustrated in Tables 16.5 and 16.6, respectively.

TABLE 16.5 *SQLDataReader* Properties

Property	Description
Depth	Gets a value indicating the depth of nesting for the current row
FieldCount	Specifies the number of fields in the current record
IsClosed	Specifies whether the SQLDataReader object is closed
Item	Gets the value of the column referenced
RowsAffected	Gets the number of rows changed, inserted, or deleted by the execution of the Transact-SQL statement

TABLE 16.6 *SQLDataReader* Methods

Method	Description
Close	Closes the SQLDataReader object
GetBoolean	Returns the value of the specified field as a Boolean
GetByte	Returns the value of the specified field as a Byte
GetBytes	Returns the value of the specified field as a Byte array
GetChar	Returns the value of the specified field as a Character
GetChars	Returns the value of the specified field as a Character array
GetDataTypeName	Returns the name of the data type
GetDateTime	Returns the value of the specified field as a DateTime
GetDecimal	Returns the value of the specified field as a Decimal
GetDouble	Returns the value of the specified field as a Double
GetFieldType	Returns the data type of the object
GetFloat	Returns the value of the specified field as a Float
GetInt16, GetInt32, GetInt64	Returns the value of the specified field as an Int16, an Int32, or an Int64
GetName	Returns the name of the column
GetOrdinal	Returns the ordinal value of the column and the column name
GetSchemaTable	Returns a data table that describes the column metadata of the SQLDataReader object
GetSQLBinary	Returns the value of the specified field as a SQL Server Binary data type
GetSQLByte	Returns the value of the specified field as a SQL Server Binary data type
GetSQLDateTime	Returns the value of the specified field as a SQL Server DateTime data type

16

TABLE 16.6 continued

Method	Description
GetSQLDecimal	Gets the value of the specified column as a SQL Server Decimal data type
GetSQLDouble	Returns the value of the specified field as a SQL Server Double data type
GetSQLGuid	Returns the value of the specified field as a SQL Server GUID data type
GetSQLInt16, GetSQLInt32, GetSQLInt64	Returns the value of the specified field as a SQL Server Int16, Int32, or Int64 data type
GetSQLMoney	Returns the value of the specified field as a SQL Server Money data type
GetSQLSingle	Returns the value of the specified field as a SQL Server Single data type
GetSQLString	Returns the value of the specified field as a SQL Server String data type
GetSQLValues	Returns all the attribute fields in the collection for the current column
GetValue	Returns the value of the specified column
GetValues	Returns all the attribute fields in the collection for the current record
IsDBNull	Specifies whether a field contains a nonexistent value
NextResult	Advances the SQLDataReader object to the next result when processing batch SQL statements
Read	Advances the SQLDataReader object to the next record

Here's the syntax for using SQLDataReader:

```
Dim dr As SQLDataReader = cmd.ExecuteReader()
```

This creates a new instance of the SQLDataReader object. This is done by using the Dim statement, which sets the dr variable to the SQLDataReader object. In order for data to be added to the SQLDataReader object, the cmd.ExecuteReader is executed. Once the ExecuteReader method is invoked without any errors, the SQLDataReader object will contain the data specified in the SQLCommand object's CommandText property.

Now, let's examine the three objects necessary for retrieving data from a data source other than Microsoft SQL Server.

Other Data Sources

The OleDbConnection object is used when you wish to connect to a data source other than a Microsoft SQL Server database. In this instance, you must define another property when making your database connection. This new property is called the provider. The provider specifies the type of data source you are going to connect to. In this instance, that data source could be an Oracle database, an Access database, a spreadsheet, or even a text file.

OleDbConnection

Tables 16.7 and 16.8 list the properties and methods, respectively, of the OleDbConnection object.

TABLE 16.7 *OleDbConnection* Properties

Property	Description
ConnectionString	Specifies the string used to open a connection to a database.
ConnectionTimeout	Specifies the time to wait for making a connection to the database before terminating the attempt and generating an error.
Database	Gets the name of the database.
DataSource	Gets the location and filename of the data source.
Provider	Gets the name of the OLE DB provider.
State	Gets the current state of the database connection. OleDbConnection supports only the Open and Closed connection state values.

TABLE 16.8 *OleDbConnection* Methods

Method	Description
BeginTransaction	Begins a database transaction
ChangeDatabase	Changes the current database for an open OleDbConnection object
Close	Closes the connection to the database
CreateCommand	Creates and returns an OleDbCommand object associated with the OleDbConnection object
GetOleDbSchemaTable	Returns the schema table and associated restriction columns of the specified schema
Open	Opens the connection to the database

When making a connection to a database or other data source, you can define your connection using one of two methods.

First, here's how you would set the connection string for a SQL Server connection:

```
Dim oConn as New OleDbConnection
oConn.ConnectionString = "Provider=SQLOLEDB;Initial Catalog = pubs;Data Source =
myDataServer;User ID = sa;password=;"
```

Second, you can use a shortcut for the connection string method by assigning the connection string value when declaring the SQLConnection object. To do this, use the following syntax:

```
Dim oConn As New OleDbConnection("Provider=SQLOLEDB;Initial Catalog = pubs;Data
Source = myDataServer;User ID = sa;password=;")
```

OleDbCommand

The OleDbCommand object is very similar to its SQLCommand object counterpart. Like the SQLCommand object, OleDbCommand is used to set the SQL statement to execute or specify the stored procedure to execute.

The OleDbCommand object has the properties and methods shown in Tables 16.9 and 16.10, respectively.

TABLE 16.9   *OleDbCommand* Properties

Property	Description
CommandText	Specifies the SQL query or the provider-specific syntax to execute against the data source.
CommandTimeout	Specifies the time to wait when executing the command before terminating the attempt and returning an error.
CommandType	Specifies how the CommandText property is to be interpreted. The values are the same as the SQLCommand object: StoredProcedure, TableDirect, and Text.
Connection	Specifies the OleDbConnection object that will be used.
Parameters	Specifies the collection of ADO parameters for this command object.
Transaction	Gets or sets the transaction in which the OLE DB command executes.
UpdatedRowSource	Gets or sets how command results are applied to the data row when used by the Update method of the DbDataAdapter.

TABLE 16.10   *OleDbCommand* Methods

Method	Description
Cancel	Cancels the execution of the command.
CreateParameter	Creates a new instance of an OleDbParameter object.

TABLE 16.10 continued

Method	Description
ExecuteNonQuery	Executes a query with no return value. This is typically an UPDATE, INSERT, or DELETE statement.
ExecuteReader	Sends the CommandText to the Connection and builds an OleDbDataReader.
ExecuteScalar	Executes the query and returns the first column of the first row in the resultset returned by the query. Extra columns or rows are ignored.
Prepare	Creates a prepared version of the command on the data source.
ResetCommandTimeout	Resets the CommandTimeout property to its default value.

16

Here's the syntax for creating an OleDbCommand object:

```
1: Dim myConnection As OleDbConnection = New
OledbConnection("provider=sqloledb.1;data source=localhost;uid=sa;pwd=;initial
catalog=Northwind")
2: Dim myCommand As OleDbCommand = New OleDbCommand("select * from Customers",
myConnection)
```

Note that you must use the OleDbCommand object with an OleDbConnection object. This syntax creates a new OleDbConnection object in the first line of the code snippet. The second line of the code snippet creates a new instance of an OleDbCommand object. It also specifies the query that is to be executed and which OleDbConnection object to use when executing that query.

Like the SQLCommand object, the OleDbCommand object needs some type of container in which to hold the data retrieved from the data source. In this case, the data container is the OleDbDataReader object.

OleDbDataReader

The OleDbDataReader object is the data container for the OleDbCommand object.

When created, OleDbDataReader has the properties and methods shown in Tables 16.11 and 16.12, respectively.

TABLE 16.11 *OleDbDataReader* Properties

Property	Description
Depth	Gets a value indicating the depth of nesting for the current row
FieldCount	Specifies the number of fields in the current record
IsClosed	Specifies whether the OleDbDataReader object is closed

TABLE 16.11 continued

Property	Description
Item	Gets the value of a column in its native format
RecordsAffected	Gets the number of rows changed, inserted, or deleted by the execution of the SQL statement

TABLE 16.12 *OleDbDataReader* Methods

Method	Description
Close	Closes the SQLDataReader object.
GetBoolean	Returns the value of the specified field as a Boolean.
GetByte	Returns the value of the specified field as a Byte.
GetBytes	Returns the value of the specified field as a Byte array.
GetChar	Returns the value of the specified field as a Character.
GetChars	Returns the value of the specified field as a Character array.
GetDataTypeName	Returns the name of the data type.
GetDateTime	Returns the value of the specified field as a DateTime.
GetDecimal	Returns the value of the specified field as a Decimal.
GetDouble	Returns the value of the specified field as a Double.
GetFieldType	Returns the data type of the object.
GetFloat	Returns the value of the specified field as a Float.
GetGuid	Returns the value of the specified field as a GUID.
GetInt16, GetInt32, GetInt64	Returns the value of the specified field as an Int16, an Int32, or an Int64.
GetName	Returns the name of the column.
GetOrdinal	Returns the ordinal value of the column and the column name.
GetSchemaTable	Returns a data table that describes the column metadata of the OleDbDataReader object.
GetString	Returns the value of a column as a String.
GetTimeSpan	Returns the value of a column as a TimeSpan object.
GetUInt16, GetUInt32, GetUInt64	Returns the value of a column as an unsigned Int16, Int32, or Int64 data type.
GetValue	Returns the value of the specified column.

TABLE 16.12 continued

Method	Description
GetValues	Returns all the attribute fields in the collection for the current record.
IsDBNull	Specifies whether a field contains a nonexistent value.
NextResult	Advances the SQLDataReader object to the next result when processing batch SQL statements.
Read	Advances the SQLDataReader object to the next record.

16

The syntax for using the OleDbDataReader object is very similar to the syntax for using the SQLDataReader object. The first step is to create a new instance of the OleDbDataReader object. This is done by using the Dim statement, which sets the dr variable to the OleDbDataReader object. In order for data to be added to the OleDbDataReader object, the OleDbCommand.ExecuteReader is executed. The code to do this is as follows:

```
Dim dr As OleDbDataReader = cmd.ExecuteReader()
```

```
var myConnection:SQLConnection = new
SQLConnection("server=localhost;uid=sa;pwd=;database=pubs");
var myCommand:SQLCommand = new SQLCommand("select * from Authors",
myConnection);

myConnection.Open();

var dr:SQLDataReader;
myCommand.Execute(&dr);

...

myConnection.Close();
```

After the cmd.ExecuteReader method is processed, the OleDbDataReader object, dr, will contain the data retrieved from the data source.

Now let's take a look at these objects in action.

Executing SQL to Retrieve Data

When developing a Web-based application, you'll use most instances of database access to display data on a page or in a drop-down list. In this example, we will look at extracting customer data from the Northwind database. To access this data, we will need to use the SQL Server–specific objects described earlier. The Northwind database is also available in Microsoft Access; however, you will need to use the OLE DB–specific objects instead of the SQL Server–specific objects.

The first step in extracting data is to import the namespaces necessary for database connectivity and manipulation. The namespaces necessary for Microsoft SQL Server connectivity are System.Data and System.Data.SQLClient. Remember that the System.Data.SQLClient namespace is SQL Server specific and cannot be used on other types of data sources.

Once the namespaces have been added, we can create the code necessary to retrieve data from the database. Listing 16.1 shows the Page_Load event that is called when our ASP.NET loads.

LISTING 16.1   The *Page_Load* Event for Northwind Customer Data Retrieval

```
 1: Sub Page_Load(Src As Object, E As EventArgs)
 2:
 3:     Dim MyConnection As SQLConnection
 4:     Dim MyCommand As SQLCommand
 5:
 6:     MyConnection = New
SQLConnection("server=localhost;uid=sa;pwd=;database=Northwind")
 7:
 8:     MyCommand = New SQLCommand("select * from customers", MyConnection)
 9:
10:     MyConnection.Open()
11:
12:     Dim DS As SQLDataReader= MyCommand.ExecuteReader()
13:
14
15:     MyConnection.Close()
16: End Sub
```

In this code listing, line 3 declares the MyConnection object as an instance of the SQLConnection object. Line 4 declares the MyCommand object as an instance of the SQLCommand object. Line 6 initializes the MyConnection object and specifies the parameters necessary to connect to the database server. Line 8 sets the SQL query "select * from customers" and specifies the connection to use when executing the query. Line 10 opens the active connection, which must be done in order to for us to use the SQLDataReader object, which is created and executed in line 12. Finally, line 15 closes up the active connection, which in turn frees up system resources.

All we need to do now is insert this code into our ASP.NET page and add some code to display the results on the page.

Displaying the Results with Data Binding

We can display our data in one of two ways. The first method is to scroll through our SQLDataReader object and write out each field on the page. This method is very flexible in that we have a lot of control over how the data is displayed. However, it can be very time consuming to implement.

ASP.NET provides an alternative to manually writing out each field in our data set. This alternative is called *data binding*, and it applies to the Web form server controls in our ASP.NET pages. The Web form page framework provides an easy-to-use, flexible means of binding controls to information in a data class (in our example, the SQLDataReader object). Data binding–type controls do all the work necessary to iterate through the data objects, load the data into the control properties, and display the data retrieved. This functionality frees us from writing the code to scroll through the data object load control properties and/or writing out each field on the page.

Two Web form server controls—the DataGrid control and the DataList control—are specifically designed to be bound to data returned from a database. The DataGrid control is a multicolumn, data-bound grid that has many additional features for laying out its contents, along with features for sorting, editing, selecting, and paging through data. The DataList control is similar to the DataGrid control, although it lacks the more sophisticated functionality found in the DataGrid control.

In this example, we will use the DataGrid control. There are two steps necessary to bind a DataGrid control to a data set returned in a SQLDataReader object. The first step is to assign the SQLDataReader object to the DataSource property of the DataGrid control. The second step is to call the DataBind method of the DataGrid control. This step actually binds the data in the SQLDataReader object to the DataGrid control. Listing 16.2 illustrates the code needed to build this page.

LISTING 16.2 The Northwind Customers ASP.NET Page

```
1: <%@ Page Language="vb"%>
2: <%@ Import Namespace="System.Data" %>
3: <%@ Import Namespace="System.Data.SQLClient" %>
4: <html>
5: <script language="VB" runat="server">
6:
7:    Sub Page_Load(Src As Object, E As EventArgs)
```

LISTING **16.2**   continued

```
8:
9:    Dim MyConnection As SQLConnection
10:    Dim MyCommand As SQLCommand
11:
12:       MyConnection = New
          ➥SQLConnection("server=localhost;uid=sa;pwd=;database=Northwind")
13:       MyCommand = New SQLCommand("select * from customers", MyConnection)
14:
15:       MyConnection.Open()
16:
17:       Dim DS As SQLDataReader = MyCommand.ExecuteReader()
18:
19:
20:     MyDataGrid.DataSource = DS
21:      MyDataGrid.DataBind()
22:
23:      MyConnection.Close()
24:   End Sub
25:
26:  </script>
27:
28:  <body>
29:
30:  <h3><font face="Verdana">Northwind Customers</font></h3>
32:
33:  <ASP:DataGrid id="MyDataGrid" runat="server"
34:     Width="700"
35:      BackColor="#FFFFFF"
36:      BorderColor="black"
37:      ShowFooter="false"
38:      CellPadding=3
39:      CellSpacing="0"
40:      Font-Name="Verdana"
41:     Font-Size="8pt"
42:      HeaderStyle-BackColor="#cfcfcf"
43:      EnableViewState ="false"
44:    />
45:
46:  </body>
47:  </html>
```

Lines 2 and 3 import the System.Data and System.Data.SQLClient namespaces, which are necessary to perform any database operations in this page. Lines 7–24 create the Page_Load event. The two lines necessary to bind the data returned to the DataGrid control are on lines 20 and 21. Line 20 sets the SQLDataReader object, DS, to the DataSource property of the DataGrid control, MyDataGrid. Line 21 then executes the

DataBind method of the DataGrid control, MyDataGrid, to actually bind the data to the control. The DataGrid control is defined on lines 33–44. Each line sets one of the numerous attributes of the DataGrid control. Figure 16.1 shows what the page looks like when the code in Listing 16.2 is executed.

FIGURE 16.1

Northwind customer list.

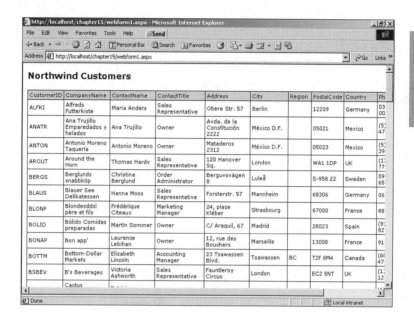

16

Now that we've successfully accessed data from a database, let's wrap things up so that we can move on to the fun stuff—modifying data in a database.

Summary

In this hour, you were introduced to database access in ASP.NET pages and to Microsoft's latest iteration of its data access technology, ADO.NET. ADO.NET provides the means to access any OLE DB–compliant data source available. It also provides a specific set of functionality for use with Microsoft SQL Server. Using a DataGrid control, you learned how to display a data listing on an ASP.NET page. In later hours, you will be introduced to data manipulation and some other important database objects that will be of great use to you when creating more advanced ASP.NET pages.

Q&A

Q. Is it possible to work with a DB2 database within the .NET framework?

A. Yes, the `System.Data.OleDb` namespace provides objects necessary to connect to any OLE DB–compliant data source. In addition to DB2, OLE DB provider databases include but are not limited to Access, Paradox, dBASE, Oracle.

Q. Is it possible to use any binding controls when reading data from a non–SQL Server database?

A. Yes, the `System.Data.OleDb` namespace provides comparative objects to the `System.Data.SQLClient` namespace. For example, you can bind an `OleDbDataReader` class to the same type of DataGrid control presented earlier in the hour.

Workshop

The quiz questions and exercises are provided for your further understanding.

Quiz

1. What is the difference between the `System.Data.OleDb` and `System.Data.SQLClient` namespaces.

2. True or false? You do not need to explicitly open and close the active connection when using the `SQLDataReader` object.

3. What method binds a set of data to the DataGrid server control?

Exercises

1. Expand on your knowledge of SQL queries by adding some JOIN statements to the SQL query defined in the `SQLCommand` object.

2. Modify the properties of the DataGrid control and examine the results of your modifications. There are plenty of other properties that were not used on the DataGrid control in Listing 16.2.

3. Add the DataList control to your ASP.NET page and compare the differences between the DataList control and the DataGrid control.

Answers for Hour 16

Quiz

1. What is the difference between the System.Data.OleDb and
   System.Data.SQLClient namespaces.

   The System.Data.OleDb namespace provides objects necessary to connect to any
   OLE DB–compliant data source. The System.Data.SQLClient namespace provides objects necessary to connect to Microsoft SQL Server only.

2. True or false? You do not need to explicitly open and close the active connection
   when using the SQLDataReader object.

   False. You *must* explicitly open and close the active connection; otherwise, you will
   generate an error.

3. What method binds a set of data to the DataGrid server control?

   The DataBind() method.

16

HOUR 17

Inserting, Updating, and Deleting Database Records

In the previous hour, you learned how to connect to a database and retrieve records using `SQLCommand` objects. You also learned the basics of using the `SQLDataReader` object to display retrieved data information to the screen.

This hour will introduce the concept of parameterized SQL statements and then apply this concept to the four major SQL statement types (`SELECT`, `INSERT`, `UPDATE`, and `DELETE`). In this hour, you will learn how to implement parameterized SQL statements to dynamically manipulate your database based on input from the user. Additionally, this hour will reinforce your understanding of data binding as it relates to generating parameterized queries, as discussed in Hour 16, "Reading from Database Tables."

In this hour you will learn

- What a parameterized SQL statement looks like
- What the benefits of parameterizing your SQL are
- How to use the `Parameters` collection of the `SQLCommand` object for `SELECT`, `INSERT`, `UPDATE`, and `DELETE` statements

Using Parameterized SQL Statements

If you have experience using older ASP versions, you will be all too familiar with the following structure. This example builds a SQL statement on-the-fly using criteria obtained from a form submission:

```
MySQL = "SELECT CustomerID, CompanyName, ContactName, City, Country, Phone " & _
    "FROM CUSTOMERS " & _
    "WHERE " & _
        "Country IN (" & _
            "'" & request("Country1") & "', " & _
            "'" & request("Country2") & "')" & _
        "CompanyName >='" & request("StartRange") "' " & _
    "ORDER BY CompanyName"
```

You also might realize that you need to do additional work on the format of the data in order to ensure success of your SQL execution (such as replacing single quotes with double quotes, validating data types, and so on).

ASP.NET cleans up this process significantly, by introducing parameterized SQL statements. You have already seen how to execute a simple SQL statement that retrieves data, so let's take that idea a step further using the `Parameters` collection property of the `SQLCommand` class, which was introduced in the previous hour.

The parameterization of the `SQLCommand` class provides several benefits. It aids in data validation, enhances code readability, brings the increased flexibility that comes from object-oriented design, and, most importantly, provides explicit data type declaration. Because the data type information is compiled in the ASP.NET code, the data typing is not done at runtime by the SQL server, which enhances the execution speed.

Let's dive right into the details of the `SQLParameters` and `SQLParameter` classes.

The `SQLParameters` Class

The `SQLParameters` class has the methods shown in Table 17.1 and the following properties:

- `Count`: This property gets the number of parameters in the collection.
- `Item`: This property gets the `SQLParameter` object with a specified attributed.

TABLE 17.1 Methods of the *SQLParameters* class

Methods	Description
Add	Adds a SQLParameter object to SQLParameterCollection.
Clear	Removes *all* items from the collection.
Contains	Indicates whether a parameter is in a collection.
CopyTo	Copies SQLParameter objects from SQLParameterCollection to the specified array.
Equals	Determines whether two object instances are equal.
GetHashCode	Serves as a hash function for a particular type. This method is suitable for use in hashing algorithms and data structures such as a hash table.
GetType	Gets the type of the object.
IndexOf	Returns the location of the SQLParameter object within the collection.
Insert	Inserts a SQLParameter object in the collection at the specified index.
Remove	Removes the specified SQLParameter object from the collection.
RemoveAt	Overloaded. Removes the specified SQLParameter object from the collection.
ToString	Returns a string that represents the current object.

The SQLParameter Class

The SQLParameter class has the properties and methods shown in Tables 17.2 and 17.3, respectively.

TABLE 17.2 Properties of the *SQLParameter* Class

Property	Description
DbType	Gets or sets the Dbtype of the parameter
Direction	Gets or sets whether the parameter is input only, output only, bidirectional, or a return value parameter
IsNullable	Gets or sets whether the parameter accepts null values
Offset	Gets or sets the offset to the Value property
ParameterName	Gets or sets the name of the SQLParameter object
Precision	Gets or sets the maximum number of digits used to represent the value
Scale	Gets or sets the number of decimal places to which the value is resolved
Size	Gets or sets the maximum size, in bytes, of the data within the field

TABLE 17.2   continued

Property	Description
SourceColumn	Gets or sets the name of the source column mapped to the dataset and used for loading or returning the value
SourceVersion	Gets or sets the data row version to use when loading Value
SqlDbType	Gets or sets the SqlDbType of the parameter
Value	Gets or sets the value of the parameter

TABLE 17.3   Methods of the *SQLParameter* Class

Method	Description
Equals	Determines whether two object instances are equal.
GetHashCode	Serves as a hash function for a particular type. This method is suitable for use in hashing algorithms and data structures such as hash tables.
GetType	Gets the type of the current instance.
ToString	Returns a string containing the parameter name.

 Additional details on each of these methods and properties can be found in the .NET reference section of Microsoft's MSDN Web site.

It's time to apply these classes to our original ad-hoc SQL example given at the beginning of this hour. We will select customers in two specified countries and with a company name in a certain alphabetic range.

Remember to import the necessary namespaces, as discussed in the previous hour. We will use SQL Server as our data source, so we must import the .SQLClient namespace rather than the .OleDb namespace:

```
<%@ Import Namespace="System.Data" %>
<%@ Import Namespace="System.Data.SQLClient" %>
```

Now we must initialize the variables:

```
Dim MyConnection As SQLConnection
Dim MyCommand As SQLCommand
Dim MySQL As String
```

To construct the SQL command, we simply insert variable identifiers, which are denoted with the @ sign, in the appropriate locations. (Once again, it is worth mentioning that a firm grasp of SQL is essential to efficiently build data-driven Web applications.) In a moment, we will specify values for these identifiers using the methods and properties described previously:

```
MyConnection = New SQLConnection("server=localhost; uid=sa;pwd=;dsn=Northwind")
MySQL = "SELECT CustomerID, CompanyName, ContactName, City, Country, Phone " & _
    "FROM CUSTOMERS " & _
    "WHERE " & _
        "Country IN (@Country1,@Country2) AND " & _
        "CompanyName >= @StartRange " & _
    "ORDER BY Country, CompanyName"
```

Create the SQLCommand using the connection and SQL string.

```
MyCommand = New SQLCommand(MySQL, MyConnection)
```

At this point, we will add SQL parameters to the Parameters collection of the SQLCommand object we have instantiated:

```
' // Specify the name, type and size of the parameter to add to the collection
MyCommand.Parameters.Add(New SQLParameter("@Country1", SQLDataType.VarChar, 50))
MyCommand.Parameters.Add(New SQLParameter("@Country2", SQLDataType.VarChar, 50))
MyCommand.Parameters.Add(New SQLParameter("@StartRange", SQLDataType.VarChar,
1))

' // Assign values to these parameters… in many situations this would be
requested from the form object
' // and would not actually be hard coded as we do in this example.
MyCommand.Parameters("@Country1").Value = "Germany"
MyCommand.Parameters("@Country2").Value = "UK"
MyCommand.Parameters("@StartRange").Value = "D"
```

> Note that the OleDb namespace has a slightly different property name for the data type specification: OleDBType.

Here is an alternate syntax for doing exactly the same thing as before—namely, adding three parameters to our SQLCommand object. The difference between the two is simply readability and developer preference, so take your pick!

```
Dim pCountry1 As New SQLParameter("@Country1", SQLDbType.VarChar,50)
Dim pCountry2 As New SQLParameter("@Country2", SQLDbType.VarChar,50)
Dim pStartRange As New SQLParameter("@StartRange", SQLDbType.VarChar,50)

MyCommand.Parameters.Add(pCountry1)
MyCommand.Parameters.Add(pCountry2)
MyCommand.Parameters.Add(pStartRange)
```

```
pCountry1.Value = "Germany"
pCountry2.Value = "UK"
pStartRange.Value = "D"
```

Note that with Visual Basic, you can streamline some of the repetitive coding by using the With command, as demonstrated here. The following code would replace the three lines beginning with MyCommand.Parameters in the preceding example:

```
With MyCommand.Parameters
    .Add(pCountry1)
    .Add(pCountry2)
    .Add(pStartRange)
End With
```

To demonstrate how some of the additional properties work, we will write some information to the screen about the specified collection of parameters (in practical terms, you would use this to set variables for process flow logic rather than screen display):

```
Response.Write ("Test Output…<br>")
Response.Write ("There are " & MyCommand.Parameters.Count & "
SQLParameters.<BR>")
```

We can get information about a specific named parameter,

```
Response.Write ("@Country2: " & MyCommand.Parameters("@Country2").Value &
"<Br>")
```

or we can loop through the entire collection, retrieving information about each parameter in it:

```
For Each Parameter In MyCommand.Parameters
Response.Write (Parameter.ParameterName & ": " & Parameter.Value & "<BR>")
Next
```

To see the results of the parameterized SQL statement, use the SQLDataReader object and the DataGrid control to display the results to the screen, as discussed in the previous hour:

```
MyConnection.Open()
Dim myDR as SQLDataReader =  MyCommand.ExecuteReader()
MyDataGrid.DataSource = myDR
MyDataGrid.DataBind()
MyConnection.Close()
```

Figure 17.1 shows the output of generated by the previous code examples.

FIGURE 17.1

Output generated by the previous code examples.

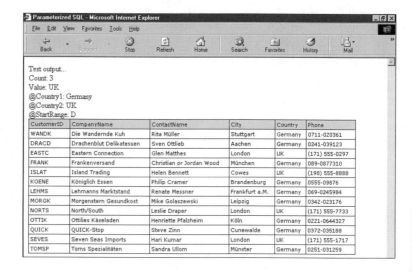

> You don't need to specify the delimiting character in your parameterized SQL command because you are specifying the data type for the parameter when you add the parameter to the collection.

17

Inserting Records

Now that you have an understanding of how parameterized SQL commands work to retrieve data, let's examine how we would insert a new record into a database. This can be done using a simple SQL string (as touched on in the previous hour) or using parameterized SQL. The latter is the approach we will use for this discussion.

The difference between SQL statements that insert, update, and delete records and those that select records is that the first three do not return record sets for data binding, but rather simply execute an action against the database. They return no records. As shown in Hour 16, there are two distinct ways to execute the two types of SQL commands: using `.ExecuteReader`, which is reserved for SQL commands that return records, and `.ExecuteNonQuery`.

Let's insert a record into our Customers table using a parameterized query (remember to import the appropriate namespaces):

```
<%@ Import Namespace="System.Data" %>
<%@ Import Namespace="System.Data.SQLClient" %>
```

Define the variables we will use.

```
Dim myConnection as SQLConnection
Dim myCommand as SQLCommand
Dim mySQL as String
```

Create the `SQLConnection` and the `SQLCommand` objects using a parameterized `INSERT` statement:

```
MyConnection = New SQLConnection("uid=sa;pwd=;dsn=pub")
MySQL = "INSERT INTO CUSTOMERS (CustomerID,CompanyName, ContactName, Country) "
& _
"VALUES (@CustID, @CompName, @ContName, @Country)"
MyCommand = New SQLCommand(MySQL, MyConnection)
```

Add the appropriate SQL parameters to the `Parameters` collection for this `SQLCommand` object:

```
Dim pCustID As New SQLParameter("@CustID", SQLDbType.VarChar,50)
Dim pCompName As New SQLParameter("@CompName", SQLDbType.VarChar,50)
Dim pContName As New SQLParameter("@ContName", SQLDbType.VarChar,50)
Dim pCountry As New SQLParameter("@Country", SQLDbType.VarChar,50)

With MyCommand.Parameters
    .Add(pCustID)
    .Add(pCompName)
    .Add(pContName)
    .Add(pCountry)
End With

' // Assign values to these parameters… in many
' // situations this would be requested from the form object
' // and would not actually be hard coded as we do in this example.
pCustID.Value = "ZTEST"
pCompName.Value = "Z Ltd."
pContName.Value = "Example Name"
pCountry.Value = "Germany"
```

Now all that is left to do is to open the connection, execute the query (notice that we use `.ExecuteNonQuery` because it will not return any resulting records), and then close the connection:

```
MyCommand. Connection.Open()
MyCommand.ExecuteNonQuery()
MyCommand. Connection.Close()
```

That's it! Now let's dig deeper into the `SQLCommand` object and examine `ResetParameters`. This example will show you how to insert multiple records into the table using a simple loop and the `ResetParameters` method.

For the purposes of this example, we are simply looping and inserting something meaningless, but you will have many opportunities to apply this in the practical world of Web development. For example, you might use it to read from a text file and insert records into the database based on that information, or you might place values in an array to update the database.

Assume the `Connection` and `Command` objects are set and that the name, type, and size of each parameter has already been specified, as done previously. Open the connection:

```
MyCommand. Connection.Open()
```

Now loop, setting parameter values, executing the query, and then resetting those parameters each time through the loop, as shown here:

```
For i = 0 to 4
 pCustID.Value = "ZZZ" & i
 pCompName.Value = "Z" & i & " Ltd."
 pContName.Value = "Example Nbr " & I
 p@Country.Value = "Germany"
 MyCommand.ExecuteNonQuery()
Next
```

Finally, don't forget to close the connection:

```
MyCommand. Connection.Close()
```

Figure 17.2 shows what the recordset looks like after the preceding code is executed. Note the five additional records that have a CustomerID value beginning with ZZZ.

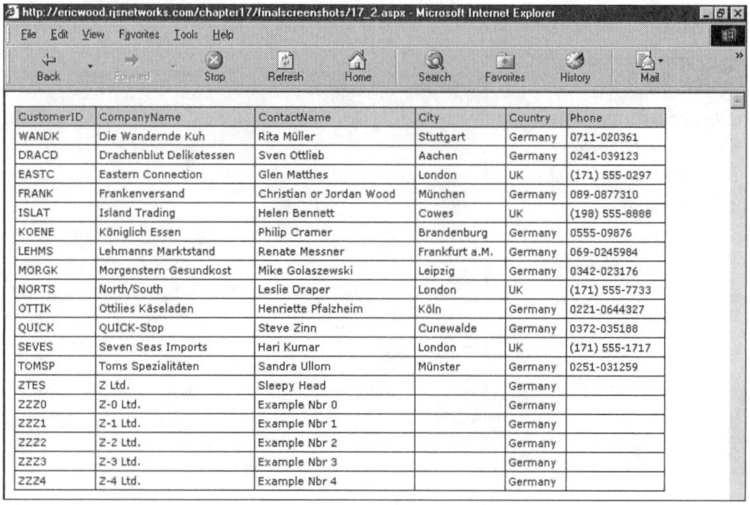

FIGURE 17.2

Additional records in the recordset.

CustomerID	CompanyName	ContactName	City	Country	Phone
WANDK	Die Wandernde Kuh	Rita Müller	Stuttgart	Germany	0711-020361
DRACD	Drachenblut Delikatessen	Sven Ottlieb	Aachen	Germany	0241-039123
EASTC	Eastern Connection	Glen Matthes	London	UK	(171) 555-0297
FRANK	Frankenversand	Christian or Jordan Wood	München	Germany	089-0877310
ISLAT	Island Trading	Helen Bennett	Cowes	UK	(198) 555-8888
KOENE	Königlich Essen	Philip Cramer	Brandenburg	Germany	0555-09876
LEHMS	Lehmanns Marktstand	Renate Messner	Frankfurt a.M.	Germany	069-0245984
MORGK	Morgenstern Gesundkost	Mike Golaszewski	Leipzig	Germany	0342-023176
NORTS	North/South	Leslie Draper	London	UK	(171) 555-7733
OTTIK	Ottilies Käseladen	Henriette Pfalzheim	Köln	Germany	0221-0644327
QUICK	QUICK-Stop	Steve Zinn	Cunewalde	Germany	0372-035188
SEVES	Seven Seas Imports	Hari Kumar	London	UK	(171) 555-1717
TOMSP	Toms Spezialitäten	Sandra Ullom	Münster	Germany	0251-031259
ZTES	Z Ltd.	Sleepy Head		Germany	
ZZZ0	Z-0 Ltd.	Example Nbr 0		Germany	
ZZZ1	Z-1 Ltd.	Example Nbr 1		Germany	
ZZZ2	Z-2 Ltd.	Example Nbr 2		Germany	
ZZZ3	Z-3 Ltd.	Example Nbr 3		Germany	
ZZZ4	Z-4 Ltd.	Example Nbr 4		Germany	

Deleting Records

Deleting records is very similar to inserting them in terms of how ASP.NET and ADO.NET are constructed. The only differences are in the SQL. Let's delete all records with a CustomerID value beginning with the letter Z to get rid of the records we inserted to the database in the previous section.

We're going to assume that the namespaces have been imported, all the declarations are done, and the SQLConnection object has been created. Here, we create the parameterized SQL statement and instantiate a SQLCommand object:

```
MySQL = "DELETE FROM CUSTOMERS WHERE LEFT(CustomerID,1)=@CustID"
MyCommand = New SQLCommand(MySQL, MyConnection)
```

Once again, we add the appropriate parameter and set its value:

```
MyCommand.Parameters.Add(New SQLParameter("@CustID", SQLDbType.Char, 1))
MyCommand.Parameters("@CustID").Value = "Z"
```

Next, we open the connection, execute the query without returning any rows, and close the connection:

```
MyCommand. Connection.Open()
MyCommand.ExecuteNonQuery()
MyCommand. Connection.Close()
```

Figure 17.3 shows what the recordset looks like after the preceding code is executed (note the CustomerID values beginning with Z are no longer present).

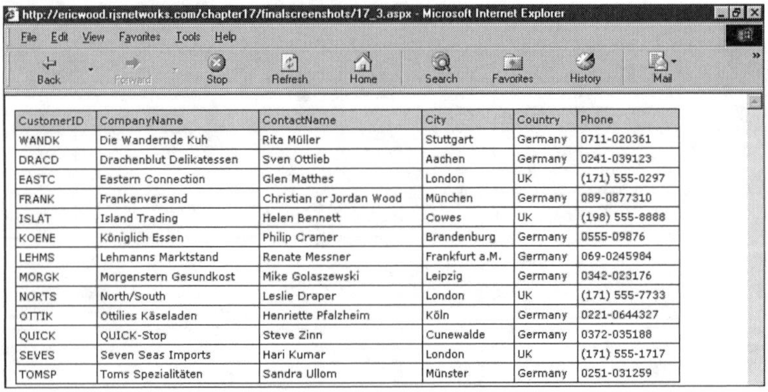

FIGURE 17.3

The recordset after the CustomerID values beginning with Z have been deleted.

CustomerID	CompanyName	ContactName	City	Country	Phone
WANDK	Die Wandernde Kuh	Rita Müller	Stuttgart	Germany	0711-020361
DRACD	Drachenblut Delikatessen	Sven Ottlieb	Aachen	Germany	0241-039123
EASTC	Eastern Connection	Glen Matthes	London	UK	(171) 555-0297
FRANK	Frankenversand	Christian or Jordan Wood	München	Germany	089-0877310
ISLAT	Island Trading	Helen Bennett	Cowes	UK	(198) 555-8888
KOENE	Königlich Essen	Philip Cramer	Brandenburg	Germany	0555-09876
LEHMS	Lehmanns Marktstand	Renate Messner	Frankfurt a.M.	Germany	069-0245984
MORGK	Morgenstern Gesundkost	Mike Golaszewski	Leipzig	Germany	0342-023176
NORTS	North/South	Leslie Draper	London	UK	(171) 555-7733
OTTIK	Ottilies Käseladen	Henriette Pfalzheim	Köln	Germany	0221-0644327
QUICK	QUICK-Stop	Steve Zinn	Cunewalde	Germany	0372-035188
SEVES	Seven Seas Imports	Hari Kumar	London	UK	(171) 555-1717
TOMSP	Toms Spezialitäten	Sandra Ullom	Münster	Germany	0251-031259

Updating Records

Updating records works very much like inserting and deleting records, syntactically, in that no records are returned. Here is how you would update the database using a parameterized command:

```
01: <%@ Import Namespace="System.Data" %>
02: <%@ Import Namespace="System.Data.SQLClient" %>
03:
04: <html>
05: <head>
06: </head>
07: <body>
08:
09: <script language="VB" runat="server">
10:
11: Sub Page_Load(Source As Object, E As EventArgs)
12:
13:     Dim myConnection as SQLConnection
14:     Dim myCommand as SQLCommand
15:     Dim mySQL as String
16:
17:     MyConnection = New SQLConnection("uid=sa;pwd=;dsn=Northwind")
18:     MySQL = "UPDATE CUSTOMERS " & _
19:         "SET ContactName=@ContactName " & _
20:         "WHERE CustomerID=@CustID"
21:     MyCommand = New SQLCommand(MySQL, MyConnection)
22:
23:     MyCommand.Parameters.Add(New SQLParameter("@ContactName",
➡SQLDbType.Char, 50))
24:     MyCommand.Parameters.Add(New SQLParameter("@CustID", SQLDbType.Char, 5))
25:
26:     MyCommand.Parameters("@ContactName").Value = "Matthew Brunton"
27:     MyCommand.Parameters("@CustID").Value = "QUICK"
28:
29:     MyCommand. Connection.Open()
30:     MyCommand.ExecuteNonQuery()
31:     MyCommand. Connection.Close()
32:
33: End Sub
34:
35: </script>
36: Execution Complete.
37: </body>
38: </html>
```

Lines 1 and 2 import the necessary namespaces. Line 11 is where the subroutine begins that executes on Page_Load. On lines 13–15, we initialize the variables we will use. Line 17 opens the connection to the Northwind database. Lines 18–20 build our parameterized SQL statement, and the SQLCommand object is created in line 21. In lines 23–27, we define the data types, name the parameters, and assign them values. Lines 29–31 open the connection, execute the SQLCommand object, and close the connection. In line 36, we simply use HTML to write a line to the screen so that we know when execution has completed successfully.

That's it! We just updated the Customers table and changed the contact name on the record with the CustomerID value "QUICK". Figure 17.4 shows what the recordset looks like after this is done.

FIGURE **17.4**

The recordset after the CustomerID value has been updated to "QUICK".

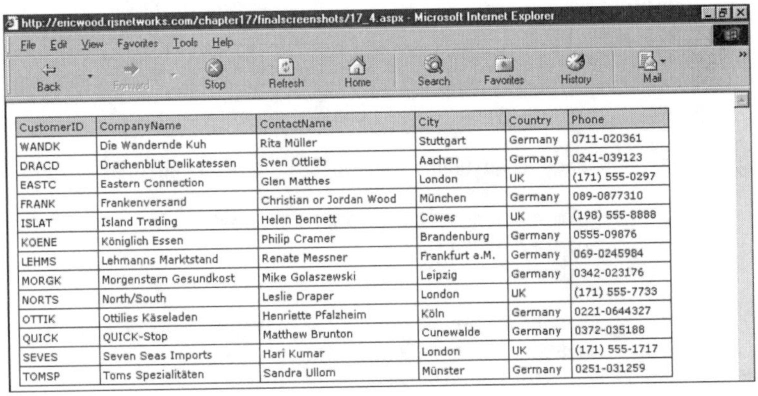

CustomerID	CompanyName	ContactName	City	Country	Phone
WANDK	Die Wandernde Kuh	Rita Müller	Stuttgart	Germany	0711-020361
DRACD	Drachenblut Delikatessen	Sven Ottlieb	Aachen	Germany	0241-039123
EASTC	Eastern Connection	Glen Matthes	London	UK	(171) 555-0297
FRANK	Frankenversand	Christian or Jordan Wood	München	Germany	089-0877310
ISLAT	Island Trading	Helen Bennett	Cowes	UK	(198) 555-8888
KOENE	Königlich Essen	Philip Cramer	Brandenburg	Germany	0555-09876
LEHMS	Lehmanns Marktstand	Renate Messner	Frankfurt a.M.	Germany	069-0245984
MORGK	Morgenstern Gesundkost	Mike Golaszewski	Leipzig	Germany	0342-023176
NORTS	North/South	Leslie Draper	London	UK	(171) 555-7733
OTTIK	Ottilies Käseladen	Henriette Pfalzheim	Köln	Germany	0221-0644327
QUICK	QUICK-Stop	Matthew Brunton	Cunewalde	Germany	0372-035188
SEVES	Seven Seas Imports	Hari Kumar	London	UK	(171) 555-1717
TOMSP	Toms Spezialitäten	Sandra Ullom	Münster	Germany	0251-031259

Summary

In this hour, you were introduced to the SQLParameter and SQLParameters classes and took a detailed look at parameterized SQL statements. You also implemented parameters in all four primary types of SQL commands (SELECT, INSERT, DELETE, and UPDATE). We demonstrated that parameterizing SQL statements can make them more flexible and readable This also enhances execution speed by doing the data typing in the compiled code rather than the database engine doing it at runtime.

We again used the DataGrid control to display data from our parameterized SELECT statement. We read the data, inserted new records, deleted those records, and then updated an existing record.

In Hour 19, "Stored Procedures and Functions," we will look at streamlining what you have learned here by implementing functions and stored procedures using SQL Server. Before we do that, however, we must take a look at datasets, which we will do in Hour 18, "Examining the ADO.NET Dataset."

Q&A

Q. What are the primary benefits of parameterized SQL statements?

A. They are more flexible, they are object-oriented, and they execute faster.

Q. What is different about how I execute a SELECT statement versus how I execute any of the other three types of SQL statements that do not return data?

A. The SELECT statement uses the SQLDataReader object, and you call the SQL command's ExecuteReader method. For the other types of SQL statements, which do not return data, you will execute the statements using ExecuteNonQuery.

Workshop

The quiz questions and exercises are provided for your further understanding.

Quiz

1. What character must all variable identifiers in a parameterized SQL statement begin with?

2. How do you remove all items from the Parameters collection?

Exercises

1. Provide the user with an input box asking for the name of a country. Then return all customers from the Northwind database for that country when the user submits the form.

2. Provide the user with an input form for adding an entirely new customer to the database. Then create a new record for that customer.

3. Show the user a drop-down list of all the company names with a button labeled "Delete". Remove all records with that company name from the Customers table.

4. Experiment with passing values into other types of parameterized queries from forms submitted by the user. This is the most common way of receiving user input, and you will want to fully understand how to implement parameterized SQL in this scenario.

Answers for Hour 17

Quiz

1. What character must all variable identifiers in a parameterized SQL statement begin with?

   The @ symbol.

2. How do you remove all items from the `Parameters` collection?

   Use the `.Clear` method of the `SQLParameters` class.

HOUR 18

Examining the ADO.NET Dataset

Over the course of the past three hours, you have become very familiar with working with data in ASP.NET applications. You've updated, inserted, and deleted records using the appropriate `Command` and `Connection` objects, and you've used the `Bind` method to attach data from a `DataReader` object to a grid. Now, it's time to examine one of the crucial elements of the ADO.NET architecture: the dataset.

In this hour, you will be introduced to the `DataSet` object and its properties, methods, and events. You will also learn the following:

- How to create and populate a dataset

- How the `DataTable` and `DataRelations` objects interact with the `DataSet` object

- How to modify and update a database using the `DataSet` object

Data Reading Objects in ADO.NET

The DataSet Object

The central data manipulation object in ADO.NET is the data set. The DataSet object can be defined as an in-memory cache of data similar in construction to a database. It is very much like a database because it is comprised of DataTable objects, which can in turn be related to one another by using DataRelation objects. DataTable objects are very similar in size and structure to traditional database tables, and DataRelation objects are very similar to foreign key relationships.

Unlike in previous versions of ADO, the DataSet object in ADO.NET stores data only as XML and only in a stateless environment. The main benefit of providing stateless data is that developers using other XML-enabled programming languages, such as Java, can use your XML dataset in their applications.

In order to use the DataSet object, you must include its namespace—System.Data—in your application. To do this, use the following syntax:

```
<% import system.data %>
```

Once you've included this statement in your Web form, you will have access to the DataSet object and all of its corresponding properties, methods, and events. The System.Data namespace also provides access to the specific objects used to generate a dataset. These objects are DataTable, DataAdapter, DataRow, DataColumn, and DataRelation. Each of these objects is discussed in more detail later in this hour.

Properties

The properties shown in Table 18.1 can be found in the DataSet object.

 The properties and methods listed in the tables throughout this hour were chosen because they are unique to the class being discussed. If you're interested in learning about inherited properties not listed in these tables, consult msdn.microsoft.com/net/.

TABLE 18.1 The Properties of the *DataSet* Object

Property Name	Description
CaseSensitive	Specifies whether the string comparisons within DataTable objects are case sensitive.
DataSetName	Specifies the name of the DataSet object.

TABLE 18.1   continued

Property Name	Description
DefaultViewManager	Returns a custom view of the data contained by the DataSet object. The custom view may allow filtering, searching, or navigating through the custom DataViewManager.
EnforceConstraints	Specifies whether constraint rules are followed when updating data.
ExtendedProperties	Returns the collection of custom user information.
HasErrors	Returns a value indicating whether there are errors in any of the rows in any of the tables of this DataSet object.
Locale	Specifies the locale information used to compare strings within the table.
Namespace	Specifies the namespace of the DataSet object.
Prefix	Specifies the XML prefix that aliases the namespace of the DataSet object.
Relations	Returns the collection of relations that link tables and allow navigation from parent tables to child tables.
Tables	Returns the collection of tables contained in the DataSet object.

Methods

The methods shown in Table 18.2 are defined for the DataSet object. This table, like all those in this Hour, focuses only on properties that are unique to the class, and does not list inherited properties.

TABLE 18.2   The Methods of the *DataSet* Object

AcceptChanges	Commits all the changes made to this DataSet object since it was loaded or the last time AcceptChanges was called.
BeginInit	Begins the initialization of a DataSet object that is used on a form or used by another component. The initialization occurs at runtime.
Clear	Clears the DataSet object of any data by removing all rows in all tables.
Clone	Clones the structure of the DataSet object, including all DataTable schemas, relations, and constraints.
Copy	Copies both the structure and data for this DataSet object.
Dispose	Disposes of the resources used by the component.
EndInit	Ends the initialization of a DataSet object that is used on a form or used by another component. The initialization occurs at runtime.

18

TABLE 18.2 continued

GetChanges	Returns a copy of the DataSet object containing all changes made to it since it was last loaded or since AcceptChanges was called.
GetXml	Returns the XML representation of the data stored in the DataSet object.
GetXmlSchema	Returns the XSD schema for the XML representation of the data stored in the DataSet object.
HasChanges	Returns a value indicating whether the DataSet object has changes, including new, deleted, or modified rows.
InferXmlSchema	Infers the XML schema from the specified TextReader or file into the DataSet object.
Merge	Merges this DataSet object with a specified DataSet object.
ReadXml	Reads XML schema and data into the DataSet object.
ReadXmlSchema	Reads an XML schema into the DataSet object.
RejectChanges	Rolls back all the changes made to the DataSet object since it was created or since the last time DataSet.AcceptChanges was called.
Reset	Resets the DataSet object to its original state. Subclasses should override Reset to restore a DataSet object to its original state.
ResetRelations	Resets the Relations property to its default state.
ResetTables	Resets the Tables property to its default state.
WriteXml	Writes XML schema and data from the DataSet object.
WriteXmlSchema	Writes the DataSet object's structure as an XML schema.
HasSchemaChanged	Gets a value indicating whether the schema has changed.
OnPropertyChanging	Raises the OnPropertyChanging event.
OnRemoveRelation	Occurs when a TableRelation object is removed. This method can be overridden by subclasses to restrict tables being removed.
OnRemoveTable	Occurs when a DataTable object is being removed.
ShouldSerializeRelations	Returns a value indicating whether the Relations property should be persisted.
ShouldSerializeTables	Returns a value indicating whether the Tables property should be persisted.

Events

The DataSet object can fire the event MergFailed, which occurs when target and source DataRow objects have the same primary key value and EnforceConstraints is set to True.

Using the `DataSet` Object

The following example demonstrates the syntax necessary to create a DataSet object:

```
<%@ Imports System.Data%>

<script language="vb" runat="server">
Dim dsDataSet as new System.Data.DataSet

dsDataSet = New System.Data.DataSet()
```

Once the `DataSet` object has been created, you will need to add `DataTable` objects to it and fill them with data.

> If you are going to populate your `DataSet` object from a database or update a database with a dataset, you must use `SQLDataAdapter` or `OleDBDataAdapter`, included in the Framework, to facilitate in the translation of data from dataset to database, and vice versa.

> The `DataSet` object's data types are based on the .NET Framework data types. In the .NET Framework, the Decimal data type only supports up to 28 characters, whereas the Decimal data type in SQL Server supports values up to 38 digits. When used in a `DataSet` object, these values throw an exception error and terminate the fill operation.

18

The `DataTable` Object

The `DataTable` object represents a table of information in the dataset. It is comprised of a collection of columns, called `DataColumnCollection`, derived from the `DataColumn` object and a collection of rows, called `DataRowCollection`, derived from the `DataRow` object. `DataColumnCollection` defines the schema, or structure, for this table. `DataRowCollection` contains the data in the table and maintains the state of the data in the table by tracking any and all changes. It also maintains a complete copy of the data in its original state in case data changes are discarded.

Properties

The `DataTable` object has the properties shown in Table 18.3.

TABLE 18.3   The Properties of the *DataTable* Object

Property Name	Description
CaseSensitive	Specifies whether string comparisons within the table are case sensitive
ChildRelations	Returns the collection of child relations for this DataTable object
Columns	Returns the collection of columns that belong to this table
Constraints	Returns the collection of constraints maintained by this table
DataSet	Returns the DataSet object to which this table belongs
DefaultView	Returns a customized view of the table, which may include a filtered view or a cursor position
ExtendedProperties	Returns the collection of customized user information
HasErrors	Returns a value indicating whether there are errors in any of the rows in any of the tables of the DataSet object to which the table belongs
Locale	Specifies the locale information used to compare strings within the table
MinimumCapacity	Specifies the initial starting size for this table
Namespace	Specifies the namespace for the XML representation of the data stored in the DataTable object
ParentRelations	Returns the collection of parent relations for this DataTable object
Prefix	Specifies the namespace for the XML representation of the data stored in the DataTable object
PrimaryKey	Specifies an array of columns that function as primary keys for the data table
Rows	Returns the collection of rows that belong to this table
TableName	Specifies the name of the DataTable object

Methods

The DataTable object has the methods shown in Table 18.4.

TABLE 18.4   The Methods of the *DataTable* Object

AcceptChanges	Commits all the changes made to this table since the last time AcceptChanges was called.
BeginInit	Begins the initialization of a DataTable object that is used on a form or used by another component. The initialization occurs at runtime.
Clear	Clears the DataTable object of all data.
Clone	Clones the structure of the DataTable object, including all schemas, relations, and constraints.

TABLE 18.4 continued

Compute	Computes the given expression on the current rows that pass the filter criteria.
Copy	Copies the structure and data for this DataTable object.
EndInit	Ends the initialization of a DataTable object that is used on a form or used by another component. The initialization occurs at runtime.
GetChanges	Returns a copy of the DataTable object containing all changes made to it since it was last loaded or since AcceptChanges was called.
GetErrors	Gets an array of DataRow object objects that contain errors.
ImportRow	Copies a DataRow object, including original and current values, DataRowState values, and errors into a DataTable object.
LoadDataRow	Finds and updates a specific row. If no matching row is found, a new row is created using the given values.
NewRow	Creates a new DataRow object with the same schema as the table.
RejectChanges	Rolls back all changes that have been made to the table since it was loaded or since the last time AcceptChanges was called.
Select	Returns an array of DataRow objects.
GetRowType	Returns the row type.
HasSchemaChanged	Returns a value indicating whether the column count has changed.
OnColumnChanged	Raises the ColumnChanged event.
OnColumnChanging	Raises the ColumnChanging event.
OnPropertyChanging	Raises the OnPropertyChanging event.
OnRemoveColumn	Notifies the DataTable object that a data column is being removed.
OnRowChanged	Raises the RowChanged event.
OnRowChanging	Raises the RowChanging event.
OnRowDeleted	Raises the OnRowDeleted event.
OnRowDeleting	Raises the OnRowDeleting event.

Events

The DataTable object has the events shown in Table 18.5.

TABLE 18.5 The Events of the *DataTable* Object

Event Name	Description
ColumnChanged	Occurs after a value has been changed for the specified data column in a DataRow object.
ColumnChanging	Occurs when a value is being changed for the specified data column in a DataRow object.

TABLE 18.5   continued

Event Name	Description
RowChanged	Occurs after a DataRow object has been changed successfully.
RowChanging	Occurs when a DataRow object is changing.
RowDeleted	Occurs after a row in the table has been deleted.
RowDeleting	Occurs before a row in the table is about to be deleted.

Using the DataTable Object

Once you have your DataSet object created and initialized, you need to add tables to it in order to hold your data. The following syntax will add a DataTable object to your dataset:

```
Dim dtUserProfile As DataTable = new DataTable("UserProfile")
```

This code snippet will create a new instance of the DataTable object with the name UserProfile.

To add a column to the DataTable object, you must first create the column you want to add and define its properties:

```
Dim dcID As DataColumn

' Create new DataColumn, set DataType, ColumnName and add to DataTable.
dcID = New DataColumn()
dcID.DataType = System.Type.GetType("System.Int32")
dcID.ColumnName = "id"
dcID.ReadOnly = True
dcID.Unique = True
```

This code snippet creates a new DataColumn object called dcID and instantiates it as an integer column with the name "id." Furthermore, it is set to be a read-only column as well as a unique column. Once the DataColumn object is created, you would use the following syntax to add it to the data table:

```
' Add the Column to the DataColumnCollection.
dtUserProfile.Columns.Add(dcID)
```

Finally, it is added to the DataSet object dsDataSet as a table. To add a data table to a dataset, you can use the following syntax:

```
dsDataSet.Tables.Add(dtUserProfile)
```

Now that you know how to create a `DataTable` object and add it to your dataset, let's examine the `DataColumn` and `DataRow` objects so you can learn how to create a proper `DataTable` object and add data to it.

The `DataColumn` Object

The `DataColumn` object is a key element in defining your table's schema. The schema for a table defines its structure and also what type of data can be stored in each column.

Properties

The `DataColumn` object has the properties shown in Table 18.6.

TABLE 18.6   The Properties of the *DataColumn* Object

AllowDBNull	Specifies whether a column can contain null values.
AutoIncrement	Specifies whether a column's value will automatically increment when a new row is added to the table. This column is typically used as an ID column for each row in the table, and it's also set to be the primary key for the table.
AutoIncrementSeed	If the `AutoIncrement` property is set to `True`, this property specifies the initial value.
AutoIncrementStep	If the `AutoIncrement` property is set to `True`, this property specifies the increment amount.
Caption	Specifies the caption heading for this column.
ColumnMapping	Specifies the `MappingType` value of the column. The `MappingType` values are `Attribute`, which maps the column to an XML attribute, `Element`, which maps the column to an XML element, `Hidden`, which maps the column to an internal structure, and `SimpleContent`, which maps the column to the text.
ColumnName	Specifies the name of the column within `DataColumnCollection`.
DataType	Specifies the type of data stored in the column.
DefaultValue	Specifies the default value for the column.
Expression	Returns the expression used to filter rows, calculate the column's value, or create an aggregate column.
ExtendedProperties	Returns the collection of custom user information.
Namespace	Specifies the namespace of the `DataColumn` object.
Ordinal	Returns the position of the column in the `DataColumnCollection` collection.
Prefix	Specifies an XML prefix that aliases the namespace of the `DataTable` object.

18

TABLE 18.6   continued

ReadOnly	Specifies a value indicating whether the column allows changes once a row has been added to the table.
Table	Returns the DataTable object to which the column belongs.
Unique	Specifies a value indicating whether the values in each row of the column must be unique.

Methods

The DataColumn object has the methods OnPropertyChanging, which raises the OnPropertyChanging event, and VerifyUnique, which returns a value verifying whether a column value is unique.

Using the DataColumn Object

To add a column to the DataTable object created previously, you would use the following syntax:

```
Dim dcAge As DataColumn = New DataColumn
  dcAge.DataType = System.Type.GetType("System.Int32")
  dcAge.AllowDBNull = False
  dcAge.Caption = "Age"
  dcAge.ColumnName = "Age"
  dcAge.DefaultValue = 18
  ' Add the column to the table.
  dtUserProfile.Columns.Add(dcAge)
```

The DataColumn object is instantiated with the New keyword. Once it is created, several properties are defined and initialized to hold Age values for each row in the DataTable object. The DataColumn object is then added to the DataTable object by using the Add method of the DataColumnsCollection object in the data table.

Once all the data columns are added to the data table, you need to populate your data columns with data rows.

The DataRow Object

The DataRow collection of the DataTable object contains the data stored in the data table. This object works in conjunction with the DataColumn object, which defines the schema for this data stored in the DataRow object.

Properties

The DataRow object has the properties shown in Table 18.7.

TABLE 18.7 The Properties of the *DataRow* Object

Property Name	Description
HasErrors	Returns a value indicating whether there are errors in a columns collection
Item	Specifies the data stored in a specified column
ItemArray	Specifies all the values for this row through an array
RowError	Specifies the custom error description for a row
RowState	Returns the current state of the row in regard to its relationship to DataRowCollection
Table	Returns the DataTable object for which this row has a schema

Methods

The DataRow object has the methods shown in Table 18.8.

TABLE 18.8 The Methods of the *DataRow* Object

Method Name	Description
AcceptChanges	Commits all the changes made to this row since the last time AcceptChanges was called.
BeginEdit	Begins an edit operation on a DataRow object.
CancelEdit	Cancels the current edit on the row.
ClearErrors	Clears the errors for the row, including RowError and errors set with SetColumnError.
Delete	Deletes the row.
EndEdit	Ends the edit occurring on the row.
GetChildRows	Returns the child rows of a DataRow object.
GetColumnError	Returns the error description for a column.
GetColumnsInError	Returns an array of columns that have errors.
GetParentRow	Returns the parent row of a DataRow object.
GetParentRows	Returns the parent rows of a DataRow object.
HasVersion	Returns a value indicating whether a specified version exists.
IsNull	Returns a value indicating whether the specified column contains a null value.
IsUnspecified	Returns a value indicating whether the row has no value.
RejectChanges	Rejects all changes made to the row since AcceptChanges was last called.
SetColumnError	Specifies the error description for a column.
SetParentRow	Specifies the parent row of a DataRow object.

18

TABLE 18.8   continued

Method Name	Description
SetUnspecified	Sets the value of a row to Unspecified.
SetNull	Sets the value of the specified DataColumn object to a null value.

Using the DataRow Object

To create a new DataRow object, use the following syntax:

```
Dim drUserProfileRow As DataRow
drUserProfileRow = dtUserProfile.NewRow()
```

Alternatively, you can use this:

```
Dim drUserProfileRow As DataRow
drUserProfileRow = New DataRow
```

To specify the data for a data row and add it to the data table, use the following syntax:

```
drUserProfile("First_Name") = "John"
drUserProfile("Last_Name") = "Smith"
dtUserProfile.Rows.Add(myRow)
```

Once all your data is added to your data tables and all your data tables have been added to your dataset, you can then add data relations to help you navigate the data between tables. To set up relationships between DataTable objects, you will need use the DataRelation object.

The DataRelation Object

The DataRelation object is used to relate two DataTable objects to each other. This relationship is set up on one DataColumn object in each of the DataTable objects that has the exact same data type. Once it is established, the DataRelation object will validate all data inserts to make sure they conform to the constraints defined by the relationship. If an invalid data type is inserted into a row, the DataRelation object will catch the error, invalidate the insert, and raise an exception error.

Properties

The DataRelations object has the properties shown in Table 18.9.

TABLE 18.9   The Properties of the DataRelations Object

Property Name	Description
ChildColumns	Returns the child columns of this relation
ChildKeyConstraint	Returns the foreign key constraint for the relation

TABLE 18.9 continued

Property Name	Description
ChildTable	Returns the child table of this relation
DataSet	Returns the DataSet object to which the relation's collection belongs
ExtendedProperties	Returns the collection of custom user information
Nested	Specifies a value indicating whether relations are nested
ParentColumns	Returns the parent columns of this relation
ParentKeyConstraint	Returns the constraint that ensures values in a column are unique
ParentTable	Returns the parent table of this relation
RelationName	Specifies the name used to look up this relation in the parent dataset's collection DataRelationCollection

Methods

The DataRelation object has the method CheckStateForProperty, which checks to ensure the data relation is a valid object, even if it doesn't belong to a dataset.

Listing 18.1 creates two DataTable objects, relates them to one another, and adds them to a dataset:

LISTING 18.1 Creating and Relating DataTable Objects with a DataSet Object

```
1: private myDataSet As DataSet

2: ' Create a new DataTable.
3: Dim myDataTable As DataTable = new DataTable("ParentTable")
4: ' Declare variables for DataColumn and DataRow objects.
5: Dim myDataColumn As DataColumn
6: Dim myDataRow As DataRow

7: ' Create new DataColumn, set DataType, ColumnName and add to DataTable.
8: myDataColumn = New DataColumn()
9: myDataColumn.DataType = System.Type.GetType("System.Int32")
10: myDataColumn.ColumnName = "id"
11: myDataColumn.ReadOnly = True
12: myDataColumn.Unique = True
13: ' Add the Column to the DataColumnCollection.
14: myDataTable.Columns.Add(myDataColumn)

15: ' Create second column.
16: myDataColumn = New DataColumn()
17: myDataColumn.DataType = System.Type.GetType("System.String")
18: myDataColumn.ColumnName = "ParentItem"
19: myDataColumn.AutoIncrement = False
```

18

LISTING 18.1 continued

```
20: myDataColumn.Caption = "ParentItem"
21: myDataColumn.ReadOnly = False
22: myDataColumn.Unique = False
23: ' Add the column to the table.
24: myDataTable.Columns.Add(myDataColumn)

25: ' Make the ID column the primary key column.
26: Dim PrimaryKeyColumns(0) As DataColumn
27: PrimaryKeyColumns(0)= myDataTable.Columns("id")
28: myDataTable.PrimaryKey = PrimaryKeyColumns

29: ' Instantiate the DataSet variable.
30: myDataSet = New DataSet()
31: ' Add the new DataTable to the DataSet.
32: myDataSet.Tables.Add(myDataTable)

33: ' Create three new DataRow objects and add them to the DataTable
34: Dim i As Integer
35: For i = 0 to 2
36:    myDataRow = myDataTable.NewRow()
37:    myDataRow("id") = i
38:    myDataRow("ParentItem") = "ParentItem " + i.ToString()
39:    myDataTable.Rows.Add(myDataRow)
40: Next i

41: ' Create a new DataTable.
***42: Dim myChildDataTable As DataTable = New DataTable("childTable")
43: Dim myChildDataColumn As DataColumn
44: Dim myChildDataRow As DataRow ***

45: ' Create first column and add to the DataTable.
46: myChildDataColumn = New DataColumn()
47: myChildDataColumn.DataType= System.Type.GetType("System.Int32")
48: myChildDataColumn.ColumnName = "ChildID"
49: myChildDataColumn.AutoIncrement = True
50: myChildDataColumn.Caption = "ID"
51: myChildDataColumn.ReadOnly = True
52: myChildDataColumn.Unique = True
53: ' Add the column to the DataColumnCollection.
54: myChildDataTable.Columns.Add(myChildDataColumn)

55: ' Create second column.
56: myChildDataColumn = New DataColumn()
57: myChildDataColumn.DataType= System.Type.GetType("System.String")
58: myChildDataColumn.ColumnName = "ChildItem"
59: myChildDataColumn.AutoIncrement = False
60: myChildDataColumn.Caption = "ChildItem"
61: myChildDataColumn.ReadOnly = False
```

LISTING 18.1 continued

```
62: myChildDataColumn.Unique = False
63: myChildDataTable.Columns.Add(myChildDataColumn)

64: ' Create third column.
65: myChildDataColumn = New DataColumn()
66: myChildDataColumn.DataType= System.Type.GetType("System.Int32")
67: myChildDataColumn.ColumnName = "ParentID"
68: myChildDataColumn.AutoIncrement = False
69: myChildDataColumn.Caption = "ParentID"
70: myChildDataColumn.ReadOnly = False
71: myChildDataColumn.Unique = False
72: myChildDataTable.Columns.Add(myChildDataColumn)

73: myDataSet.Tables.Add(myChildDataTable)
74: ' Create three sets of DataRow objects, five rows each, and add to DataTable.
75: Dim i As Integer
76: For i = 0 to 4
77:    myChildDataRow = myChildDataTable.NewRow()
78:    myChildDataRow("childID") = i
79:    myChildDataRow("ChildItem") = "Item " + i.ToString()
80:    myChildDataRow("ParentID") = 0
81:    myChildDataTable.Rows.Add(myChildDataRow)
82: Next i
83: For i = 0 to 4
84:    myChildDataRow = myChildDataTable.NewRow()
85:    myChildDataRow("childID") = i + 5
86:    myChildDataRow("ChildItem") = "Item " + i.ToString()
87:    myChildDataRow("ParentID") = 1
88:    myChildDataTable.Rows.Add(myChildDataRow)
89: Next i
90: For i = 0 to 4
91:    myChildDataRow = myChildDataTable.NewRow()
92:    myChildDataRow("childID") = i + 10
93:    myChildDataRow("ChildItem") = "Item " + i.ToString()
94:    myChildDataRow("ParentID") = 2
95:    myChildDataTable.Rows.Add(myChildDataRow)
96: Next i

97: ' DataRelation requires two DataColumn (parent and child) and a name.
98: Dim myDataRelation As DataRelation
99: Dim parentColumn As DataColumn
100: Dim childColumn As DataColumn
101: parentColumn = myDataSet.Tables("ParentTable").Columns("id")
102: childColumn = myDataSet.Tables("ChildTable").Columns("ParentID")
103: myDataRelation = new DataRelation("parent2Child", parentColumn, childColumn)
104: myDataSet.Tables("ChildTable").ParentRelations.Add(myDataRelation)
```

18

When executed, this code creates two tables. The first is called ParentTable. It contains two columns: ID and ParentItem. Once created and added to the ParentTable table, the ID column is set to be the primary key for the table. Then some records are added to the ParentTable table using the `DataRow` object. This code can be found from line 1 through line 40.

The next section of this code listing, lines 41 through 96, creates the ChildTable data table. This table contains three columns: ChildID, which is also the primary key for the table, ChildItem, which contains string data, and ParentID, which is our foreign key to the table ParentTable. Then some data is added to ChildTable with values added to the ParentID column that match values already in the ParentTable table.

Finally, ParentTable and ChildTable are related to one another by setting a relationship between the ID column in the ParentTable table to the ParentID column in ChildTable (lines 97 through 103). This `Relationship` object is then added to ChildTable to create the `foreign-key` relationship (line 104).

Summary

In this hour, you have been introduced to one of the main building blocks of ADO.NET —the `DataSet` object—and its corresponding objects—the `DataTable` object, the `DataColumn` object, the `DataRow` object, and the `DataRelation` object—each of which plays a vital role in the creation and manipulation of the `DataSet` object.

Q&A

Q. What is the difference between `DataColumnCollection` and `DataRowCollection`?

A. `DataColumnCollection` defines the schema and data types for each column in the `DataTable` object. `DataRowCollection` stores that actual data for the `DataTable` object.

Q. Which namespace contains the class objects for the dataset, data table, data column, data row, and data relation?

A. The `System.Data` namespace.

Workshop

The quiz questions and exercises are provided for your further understanding.

Quiz

1. What object is needed to populate a dataset with data extracted from a data source such as a database or an XML document?

2. True or false? You must always use a `DataSet` object when working with data in your ASP.NET application.

3. True or false? When a change is made to a `DataRow` object in a data table, that change is automatically implemented into the `DataTable` object and cannot be revoked.

Exercise

Using the Northwind database found in Access or SQL Server, select two tables that are related to one another—for example, the Products table and the Suppliers table. Re-create the column structure in using the `DataColumn` object and add them to each of the `DataTable` objects. Then create the relationship between the two tables using the `DataRelation` object. Finally, add some sample data to the dataset from the Northwind database to test your dataset.

Answers for Hour 18

Quiz

1. What object is needed to populate a dataset with data extracted from a data source such as a database or an XML document?

   A `DataAdapter` object is necessary to extract data from a data source into a dataset. The type of `DataAdapter` object—`SQLDataAdapter` or `OleDbDataAdapter`—depends on the data source you wish to extract data from.

2. True or false? You must always use a `DataSet` object when working with data in your ASP.NET application.

   False. The `DataSet` object is just one means of working with data. You have already worked with the `DataReader` object and the `Command` objects, which aid in reading and manipulating data from a database or some other data source.

3. True or false? When a change is made to a `DataRow` object in a data table, that change is automatically implemented into the `DataTable` object and cannot be revoked.

   False. You must call the `AcceptChanges` method of the `DataTable` object to make all changes permanent in your `DataTable` object.

18

HOUR 19

Stored Procedures and Functions

In the last several hours, you learned how to interact with database tables using SQL. You now have an understanding of how to display database-driven results to the user's browser through data binding using `SQLDataReader` and `SQLDataSet`.

In this hour, we will look at two tools SQL Server provides that greatly streamline your code—not only in terms of development time but also in terms of readability and speed of execution. These two powerful tools are stored procedures and functions. Both are essentially precompiled collections of SQL statements stored under a single name and processed as a single logical unit.

There are two primary functional differences between functions and stored procedures:

- Functions return a single scalar value or table in place of their names, whereas stored procedures can output multiple parameters or generate a recordset.

- Functions can be used directly in expressions (including SQL statements); stored procedures cannot.

In this hour you will learn

- About the benefits of stored procedures and functions
- How to create a stored procedure
- How to execute a stored procedure with ASP.NET
- What types of functions can be created
- How to create the different types of functions
- How to execute and use the different types of functions with ASP.NET

Benefits of Stored Procedures and Functions

At first, you may wonder why we would even build stored procedures and functions, given the ability to directly code logic into ASP.NET pages themselves. There are four answers to this question, the importance of which will vary depending on your specific application:

- Modular programming
- Faster execution
- Reduced network traffic
- Enhanced application security

These topics are detailed in the following subsections.

Modular Programming

You may be familiar with the idea of modular programming if you have experience in other development languages or platforms. Modular programming allows you to encapsulate reusable logic or actions so that they can be easily called by your code. For example, if you know you are going to need to find the age of a specified customer based on his or her birth date in several places within your application, it would make sense to create a stored procedure or function that provides you with this value simply by calling the procedure or function and passing it a customer-identification parameter.

This modularity also allows for much more flexible distributed application development and easier program maintenance. Stored procedures and functions can be created by a programmer specializing in databases, and they can be referenced by the ASP.NET developer. In this way, not only is the development distributed, but when those inevitable changes to the logic come in the future, the stored procedures and functions can be changed without having to modify the ASP.NET code at all. This is commonly known as "isolating business rules."

Faster Execution

Because these two types of procedures are compiled and optimized at the time they are created on the SQL Server, executing them is faster than executing SQL commands directly from your code. Note that even though the ASP.NET code itself is precompiled, the SQL Server compiler still needs to compile the Transact-SQL commands that are sent from ASP.NET if the SQL is coded into your page.

Reduced Network Traffic

Because many applications have the ASP.NET code residing on a physical server (or servers) separate from the physical database server that contains SQL Server, network traffic management becomes important. In cases where operations require many lines of SQL transactions to be performed, a stored procedure or function is called with one simple command to the database server, which will then execute all those transactions without requiring that they all be sent across the network with every execution. Depending on the application, this consolidation can greatly reduce traffic on the network.

Enhanced Application Security

There may be a situation in which a user does not have the security credentials to execute the individual statements within a procedure directly, but he or she can be granted security credentials to execute the stored procedure or function as a whole. In this way, you can protect your database through validation code in your procedures while still giving users the power they need to perform certain actions.

Stored Procedures

A *stored procedure* is a precompiled collection of Transact-SQL statements stored under one name and processed as a unit.

Stored procedures in the context of SQL Server are very much like procedures in any other programming language in that they have three primary characteristics:

- They accept input parameters from the code that called them, and their execution is based on those parameters.

- They can contain logical-flow programming statements, execute Transact-SQL, and even call other stored procedures.

- They can return multiple values to the calling code (often based on the input parameters).

Designing Stored Procedures

Creating a stored procedure consists of two steps. The first step is to design the procedure by declaring (or *naming*) it and defining each parameter. The second step is to write the code that makes up the actual body of the procedure.

Stored procedures are created using the CREATE PROCEDURE command, which we will look at in a moment. Once created, stored procedures can be altered using ALTER PROCEDURE and removed from the database using DROP PROCEDURE. Note that the primary advantage of using ALTER rather than a succession of DROP and CREATE statements is that with ALTER, all permissions and dependencies are maintained.

The key to a stored procedure is its parameters. Similar in concept to the ASP.NET Parameters collection we examined in Hour 17, "Inserting, Updating, and Deleting Database Records," but different in implementation, these parameters are values passed to the stored procedure that tell it how to act.

A stored procedure can have up to 2,100 parameters. Each parameter in a stored procedure contains four properties: Name, Parameter Direction, Default Value, and Data Type.

Parameter Name

Like SQL variables used for parameterized SQL, every parameter in a stored procedure must have a unique name that begins with the "at" symbol (@).

Parameter Direction

Stored procedure parameters can be input only, output only, or bidirectional (often referred to as *passed-by-reference*). By default, a parameter is an input parameter. To specify it as an output parameter, the OUTPUT attribute must be explicitly specified. An output parameter becomes bidirectional if it is assigned a value prior to execution by the calling procedure.

Default Value

A parameter does not need to have a default value, but there are many situations in which you will want to use one to prevent the procedure from crashing ungracefully if the user leaves a parameter empty. This would typically be a null, a zero, a wildcard, or whatever default value would be appropriate in your particular application.

Data Type

A parameter can be defined as any valid SQL Server data type or as any user-defined data type. The data type of a parameter will determine what type of data the parameter can hold.

Valid data types for SQL Server are shown in Table 19.1.

TABLE 19.1 SQL Server Data Types

Data Type	Description
bigint	Integer data from -2^{63} through $2^{63} - 1$.
int	Integer data from -2^{31} through $2^{31} - 1$.
smallint	Integer data from -2^{15} through $2^{15} - 1$.
tinyint	Integer data from 0 through 255.
bit	Integer data with a value of either 1 or 0.
decimal	Fixed precision and scale numeric data from $-10^{38} + 1$ through $10^{38} - 1$.
numeric	Functionally equivalent to decimal.
money	Monetary data values from -2^{63} through $2^{63} - 1$, with accuracy to one ten-thousandth of a monetary unit.
smallmoney	Monetary data values from $-214,748.3648$ through $+214,748.3647$, with accuracy to one ten-thousandth of a monetary unit.
float	Floating precision number data from $-1.79E + 308$ through $1.79E + 308$.
real	Floating precision number data from $-3.40E + 38$ through $3.40E + 38$.
datetime	Date and time data from January 1, 1753 through December 31, 9999, with an accuracy of three-hundredths of a second (or 3.33 milliseconds).
smalldatetime	Date and time data from January 1, 1900 through June 6, 2079, with an accuracy of one minute. (Note the limitation of the year 2079.)
char	Fixed-length non-Unicode character data with a maximum length of 8,000 characters.
varchar	Variable-length non-Unicode data with a maximum of 8,000 characters.
text	Variable-length non-Unicode data with a maximum length of $2^{31} - 1$ characters.
nchar	Fixed-length Unicode data with a maximum length of 4,000 characters.
nvarchar	Variable-length Unicode data with a maximum length of 4,000 characters.
ntext	Variable-length Unicode data with a maximum length of $2^{30} - 1$ characters.
binary	Fixed-length binary data with a maximum length of 8,000 bytes.
varbinary	Variable-length binary data with a maximum length of 8,000 bytes.
image	Variable-length binary data with a maximum length of $2^{31} - 1$ bytes.

19

Now that we have looked at the concepts of the four properties of a stored procedure's parameters, you are almost ready to learn how to implement them. First, though, a brief discussion of the basic structure of a stored procedure is in order.

The syntax for the CREATE PROCEDURE command is as follows:

```
CREATE PROC [ EDURE ] procedure_name [ ; number ]
  [ { @parameter data_type }
    [ VARYING ] [ = default ] [ OUTPUT ]
  ] [ ,...n ]

[ WITH
  { RECOMPILE | ENCRYPTION | RECOMPILE , ENCRYPTION } ]

[ FOR REPLICATION ]

AS sql_statement [ ...n ]
```

The most basic header for creating a procedure simply contains the name. Here's an example:

```
CREATE PROCEDURE getContactInfo
AS
     ... procedure body
```

If we wanted to designate two parameters for this procedure to accept, this is how it would be done:

```
CREATE PROCEDURE getContactInfo
    @companyname varchar(50),
    @country varchar(50)
AS
    … procedure body
```

Here's the syntax to add a default value to these parameters, such as a null value:

```
??: There is a strange break in the preceding paragraph after "Here's the
syntax" - Eric Wood
CREATE PROCEDURE getContactInfo
    @companyname varchar(50)= NULL,
    @country varchar(50) = "USA"
AS
     ... procedure body
```

If we wanted to return the contact name and phone number based on the record found from the parameters specified, we could set the parameters up like this (using the OUTPUT specification):

```
CREATE PROCEDURE getContactInfo
    @companyname varchar(50) = NULL,
    @country varchar(50) = "USA",
    @contactname varchar(100) OUTPUT,
    @phone varchar(50) OUTPUT
AS
     ... procedure body
```

That is all we need to do to build the header of a stored procedure that will accept a company name (default to "NULL" if not specified) and a country (default to "USA" if not specified) and that has the capability of returning the contact name and phone number for that company. We will use the Customers table of the Northwind database for this example.

Now we will build the body of the stored procedure:

```
CREATE PROCEDURE getContactInfo
    @companyname varchar(50)= NULL,
    @country varchar(50) = "USA",
    @contactname varchar(100) OUTPUT,
    @phone varchar(50) OUTPUT
AS
    IF (SELECT COUNT(*) FROM CUSTOMERS WHERE
        CompanyName = @companyname AND
        Country = @country) > 0
    BEGIN
        SELECT @contactname = ContactName, @phone = Phone WHERE
        CompanyName = @companyname AND
        Country = @country
    END
```

This code counts the number of customers matching the specified criteria, and if any exist, it will return the resulting values in the output parameters.

One more thing needs to be added to this stored procedure to perform some basic error handling. By default, all stored procedures return a value of zero if no return value is specified and the procedure executes successfully. However, you can override the default return values with customized error numbers. Let's rewrite the body of this procedure one more time, returning an error of 101 if there are no records found matching the specified criteria:

```
... Header
AS
    IF (SELECT COUNT(*) FROM CUSTOMERS WHERE
        CompanyName = @companyname AND
        Country = @country) > 0
    BEGIN
        SELECT @contactname = ContactName, @phone = Phone WHERE
            CompanyName = @companyname AND
            Country = @country
    END
    ELSE
    BEGIN
        SELECT @contactname = null
        SELECT @phone = null
        RETURN 101
    END
RETURN 0
```

Once the RETURN statement is processed, the procedure is immediately terminated and nothing after that is executed. In this case, if the ELSE command block is executed and

19

RETURN 101 is triggered, the execution of the procedure immediately ceases and control returns to the calling code.

To actually create the procedure, we simply execute the preceding string as a SQL statement against the database using ExecuteNonQuery, as shown in Listing 19.1. Remember to import the appropriate namespaces and enclose the code in a script block.

LISTING 19.1   Creating a Stored Procedure

```
01: Dim myConnection as SQLConnection
02: Dim CreateProcCommand as SQLCommand
03: Dim mySQL as string
04:
05: myConnection = New SQLConnection & _
➥("server=localhost;uid=sa;pwd=;database=Northwind")
06:
08:
09: mySQL = "CREATE PROCEDURE getContactInfo " & _
10:     "@companyname varchar(50)= NULL, " & _
11:     "@country varchar(50) = 'USA', " & _
12:     "@contactname varchar(100) OUTPUT, " & _
13:     "@phone varchar(50) OUTPUT " & _
14:     "AS " & _
15:     "IF (SELECT COUNT(*) FROM CUSTOMERS WHERE " & _
16:         "CompanyName = @companyname AND " & _
17:         "Country = @country) > 0 " & _
18:     "BEGIN " & _
19:         "SELECT @contactname = ContactName, " & _
20:         "@phone = Phone " & _
21:         "FROM CUSTOMERS WHERE " & _
22:             "CompanyName = @companyname AND " & _
23:             "Country = @country " & _
24:     "END"
25:
26: CreateProcCommand = New SQLCommand (mySQL, MyConnection)
27: MyConnection.Open()
28: CreateProcCommand.ExecuteNonQuery()
29: MyConnection.Close()
```

By now, the preceding process is probably becoming familiar to you, but to reiterate, here is what we just did: Lines 1–3 create the variables we need to execute this page. Line 5 creates the SQL connection to our database. Lines 9–24 build the CREATE PROCEDURE SQL statement. Line 26 creates a SQL command; line 27 opens it, and line 28 executes the query (remember that the use of ExecuteNonQuery is for SQL commands that do not return recordsets). Finally, line 29 closes the connection.

There is now a stored procedure in our copy of the Northwind database called `getContactInfo` that we can access from our ASP.NET page. The next section explains how to execute this stored procedure and access the output variables.

Executing Stored Procedures

Stored procedure execution using ADO.NET is very much like executing a SQL statement, as we just did to create the stored procedure in the preceding section. There are some significant differences that are worth noting, however, as we go through the code.

First, we must import the appropriate namespaces:

```
<%@ Import Namespace="System.Data" %>
<%@ Import Namespace="System.Data.SQLClient" %>
```

Next, we initialize the variables we'll use on this page:

```
Dim myConnection as SQLConnection
Dim myCommand as SQLCommand
```

Finally, we open the connection to our Northwind database:

```
myConnection = New
SQLConnection("server=localhost;uid=sa;pwd=;database=Northwind")
```

So far, there are no differences between this code and the code in previous sections. This is where we begin to see that stored procedures are handled differently. The first difference is that when we create the `SQLCommand` object, we reference the name of the stored procedure rather than entering a SQL statement. The second difference is that once we create the `SQLCommand` object, we must set its `CommandType` property to `StoredProcedure`, as shown here:

```
myCommand = new SQLCommand("getContactInfo", myConnection)
myCommand.CommandType = CommandType.StoredProcedure
```

Next, we will create all of our SQL parameters, name them to correspond to their names in the stored procedure, and then define their data types (this is the same syntax we used for the parameterized SQL statements in Hour 17):

```
dim pCompanyName as New SQLParameter("@CompanyName", SQLBBTypeVarChar, 50)
dim pCountry as New SQLParameter("@Country", SQLDBType. VarChar, 50)
dim pContactName as New SQLParameter("@ContactName", SQLDBType. VarChar, 100)
dim pPhone as New SQLParameter("@Phone", SQLDBType. VarChar, 50)
```

The next four lines set the parameter direction for each of the parameters by setting the `Direction` property to `ParameterDirection.Input` or `ParameterDirection.Output`.

```
pCompanyName.Direction = ParameterDirection.Input
pCountry.Direction = ParameterDirection.Input
```

19

```
pContactName.Direction = ParameterDirection.Output
pPhone.Direction = ParameterDirection.Output
```

Next we add the four SQL parameters to the `Parameters` collection of this `SQLCommand` object:

```
myCommand.Parameters.Add(pCompanyName)
myCommand.Parameters.Add(pCountry)
myCommand.Parameters.Add(pContactName)
myCommand.Parameters.Add(pPhone)
```

Now let's set a value for the company name and country parameters so that we can query the stored procedure and try to get the contact information (note once again that in practice, you would rarely "hard-code" these values into your page but rather would allow them to be driven by user information):

```
pCompanyName.Value = "Blauer See Delikatessen"
pCountry.Value = "Germany"
```

Now we open the connection and execute the `SQLCommand` object (containing our stored procedure name as its `CommandText` value), which does not return any records using `ExecuteNonQuery`:

```
myConnection.Open
myCommand.ExecuteNonQuery()
```

The following code will demonstrate that the output parameters now contain values, as set by the stored procedure we just executed (here, we are just writing the values of the relevant parameters to the screen for display to the user):

```
with myCommand
    response.write ("<b>Results of first execution of getContactInfo:</b><br>")
    response.write ("Contact: " & .Parameters("@ContactName").Value.ToString())
    response.write ("<br>")
    response.write ("Phone: " & .Parameters("@Phone").Value.ToString())
    response.write ("<br><br>")
end with
```

To further demonstrate that our stored procedure is working correctly, it is time to test the defaults. Recall that in the previous section, where we created `getContactInfo`, we set the default value for the `@Country` parameter to be "USA" if none was specified by the user. Here, we set a new value for the company name parameter and remove the country parameter from the collection entirely to demonstrate that the default value for the country parameter is working correctly:

```
pCompanyName.Value = "Rattlesnake Canyon Grocery"
myCommand.Parameters.Remove(pCountry)

myCommand.ExecuteNonQuery()
```

```
with myCommand
    response.write ("<b>Results of second execution of getContactInfo:</b><Br>")
    response.write ("Contact: " & .Parameters("@ContactName").Value.ToString())
    response.write ("<br>")
    response.write ("Phone: " & .Parameters("@Phone").Value.ToString())
    response.write ("<br><Br>")
end with
```

Finally, we close the connection:

```
myConnection.Close()
```

Figure 19.1 shows the output of these two sections. Notice that rather than generating an error about a missing parameter value, the second pass-through assumes that the country is USA and executes the stored procedure correctly.

FIGURE 19.1

Demonstrating the output of the preceding stored procedures.

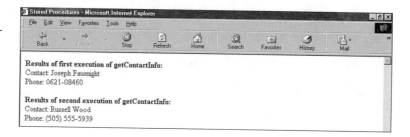

Note also that stored procedures can return records from the database. As an example, we will create a stored procedure called `getCustomers` that returns all customers in a specified country, defaulting to USA if the country is not specified:

```
Dim myConnection as SQLConnection
Dim CreateProcCommand as SQLCommand
Dim mySQL as string

MyConnection = New
SQLConnection("server=localhost;uid=sa;pwd=;database=Northwind")

mySQL = "CREATE PROCEDURE getCustomers " & _
    "@Country Varchar(50) = 'USA' " & _
    "AS " & _
    "SELECT CustomerID, CompanyName, ContactName, City, Region, Country " & _
    "FROM CUSTOMERS WHERE COUNTRY=@Country ORDER BY COMPANYNAME"

CreateProcCommand = New SQLCommand(mySQL, MyConnection)
MyConnection.Open()
CreateProcCommand.ExecuteNonQuery()
MyConnection.Close()
```

Now, let's execute this stored procedure and display the results in a `DataGrid` control.

19

Listing 19.2 displays the results (to the screen) of executing this stored procedure without any parameters being specified. The output of this page is shown in Figure 19.2.

LISTING 19.2　Displaying the Results of the Stored Procedure in a Data Grid

```
01: <%@ Import Namespace="System.Data" %>
02: <%@ Import Namespace="System.Data.SQLClient" %>
03:
04: <html><head><title>Stored Procedures</title></head>
05: <body>
06:
07: <script language="VB" runat="server">
08:
09: sub Page_Load(Src as object, E as EventArgs)
10:
11: Dim myConnection as SQLConnection
12: MyConnection = New
➡SQLConnection("server=localhost;uid=sa;pwd=;database=Northwind")
13:
14: Dim myCommand as SQLCommand
15: myCommand = new SQLCommand("getCustomers", myConnection)
16: myCommand.CommandType = CommandType.StoredProcedure
17:
18: MyConnection.Open()
19
20: Dim myDR as SQLDataReader
21: MyCommand.ExecuteReader(myDR)
22:
23: MyDataGrid.DataSource = myDR
24: MyDataGrid.DataBind()
25
26: MyConnection.Close
27
28: end sub
29:
30: </script>
31: <ASP:DataGrid id="MyDataGrid" runat="server"
32:     Width="700"
33:     BackColor="#FFFFFF"
34:     BorderColor="black"
35:     ShowFooter="false"
36:     CellPadding=3
37:     CellSpacing="0"
38:     Font-Name="Verdana"
39:     Font-Size="8pt"
40:     HeaderStyle-BackColor="#cfcfcf"
41:     MaintainState="false"
42:     />
43: </body>
44: </html>
```

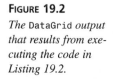

FIGURE 19.2

The DataGrid *output that results from executing the code in Listing 19.2.*

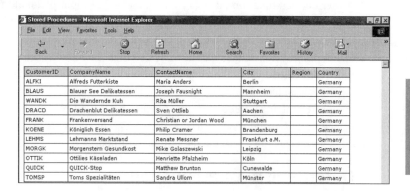

The exact same code, with the following three lines inserted between lines 17 and 18, will display all customers in Germany, as shown in Figure 19.3.

```
Dim pCountry as New SQLParameter("@Country", SQLDataType.Varchar, 50)
pCountry.Direction = ParameterDirection.Input
myCommand.Parameters.Add(pCountry)
pCountry.Value = "Germany"
```

FIGURE 19.3

Creating an input parameter.

19

In this section, you have seen how stored procedures can simplify actions and logic that will be executed repeatedly. You have also seen how they can be used to separate the business logic from the page code for maintainability. We have returned entire records and bound them to a data grid and have also examined how to retrieve individual variables from stored procedures.

Now that you have an understanding of stored procedures, let's examine SQL Server functions.

Functions

A *function* is a subroutine made up of one or more Transact-SQL statements that can be used to encapsulate code for reuse. It operates as a single logical unit.

Functions are, in many ways, similar to stored procedures. They are single logical units that execute one or more SQL statements or perform some programmatic function. There are, however, significant differences between the two tools, as mentioned at the beginning of this hour. Let's look at the different types of functions and then create a user-defined function.

Types of Functions

There are three types of functions, as distinguished by the structure of the function and the type of data it returns:

- Scalar functions
- Inline table-valued (or *tabular*) functions
- Multistatement table-valued (tabular) functions

A user-defined function takes between 0 and 1,024 input parameters and returns either a scalar value or a table. The scalar function returns a single value of the type defined in the RETURNS clause of the function. All scalar data types are supported, but user-defined data types and nonscalar types such as datetime, table, and cursor, are not. Table-valued functions return a table. There are two types of table-valued functions. The first is the inline table-valued function, which returns a table that results from a single SELECT statement and contains no BEGIN...END block. The second type is the multistatement table-valued function, and it contains a BEGIN...END block made up of SQL statements that build and insert rows into the table to be returned.

Determinism of a Function

Every function is classified as either a deterministic or a nondeterministic function. A deterministic function always returns the same result any time it is called with a specific set of input parameters. A nondeterministic function may return different results.

That may sound confusing at first, but an example should clear it up quickly. Let's compare two built-in functions: GETDATE and DATEADD. GETDATE will always return the current date, which of course changes depending on when GETDATE is called, even though it is not passed any different parameters. DATEADD, however, always returns the same value given a specific set of input for its three parameters. GETDATE is nondeterministic, and DATEADD is deterministic.

Several things make it important to understand the difference. First, in SQL Server 2000, you cannot create indexes on columns that are calculated based on nondeterministic functions. You also cannot create a clustered index on a view if that view references any nondeterministic functions.

A user-defined function is deterministic if

- It is schema bound.
- All functions called by it are deterministic.
- Its body references no database objects outside the scope of the function.
- It does not call any extended stored procedures.

 Built-in nondeterministic functions (such as GETDATE) are not allowed in the body of user-defined functions. You can find a full listing of all deterministic and nondeterministic functions for SQL Server in the documentation on Microsoft's MSDN Web site.

Designing Functions

One significant difference to keep in mind when determining whether to use a stored procedure or a function is that the actions inside of the BEGIN...END block of the function cannot have any "side effects" outside the scope of the function itself. This means that, for example, a function cannot modify information in a database or make modifications to cursors that are not local to the function.

Scalar Functions

Here's the syntax for creating a scalar function:

```
CREATE FUNCTION [ owner_name. ] function_name
  ( [ { @parameter_name [AS] scalar_parameter_data_type [ = default ] } [ ,...n
] ] )
RETURNS scalar_return_data_type
[ WITH < function_option> [ [,] ...n] ]
[ AS ]
BEGIN
  function_body
  RETURN scalar_expression
END
```

As an example of a scalar function, we will create a function that determines the total cost of an order, given the quantity, the price per unit, and the discount on the order:

19

```
CREATE FUNCTION fnOrderCost (@qty int, @price money, @discount decimal (4,3))
RETURNS money
AS
BEGIN
    RETURN (@qty * @price * (1-@discount))
END
```

This function could be referenced anywhere a value with a data type of money can be referenced with SQL. We will look at an example of how to access this function in the next section, where we discuss the execution of functions.

Inline Table-Valued Functions

Here's the syntax for creating an inline table-valued function:

```
CREATE FUNCTION [ owner_name. ] function_name
  ( [ { @parameter_name [AS] scalar_parameter_data_type [ = default ] } [ ,...n
] ] )
RETURNS TABLE
[ WITH < function_option > [ [,] ...n ] ]
[ AS ]
RETURN [ ( ] select-stmt [ ) ]
```

To demonstrate an inline table-valued function, let's create a function that is nearly identical to the getCustomers stored procedure we created earlier in this hour:

```
CREATE FUNCTION fnCustomers (@Country varchar(50))
RETURNS TABLE
AS
RETURN (SELECT CustomerID, CompanyName, ContactName, City, Region, Country
    FROM Customers
    WHERE Country = @Country)
```

You may be wondering why we would want a function when we can do this with a stored procedure. The answer is crucial to understanding why functions exist. Unlike a stored procedure, a function can be referenced anywhere in a SQL statement that permits a value of the data type returned by that function. What this means is that once this function is created, we can access it from *within* a SQL statement directly. It acts very much like a view in this respect.

Multistatement Table-valued Functions

Here's the syntax for creating a multistatement table-valued function:

```
CREATE FUNCTION [ owner_name. ] function_name
  ( [ { @parameter_name [AS] scalar_parameter_data_type [ = default ] } [ ,...n
] ] )
RETURNS @return_variable TABLE < table_type_definition >
[ WITH < function_option > [ [,] ...n ] ]
[ AS ]
BEGIN
```

```
    function_body
    RETURN
END
< function_option > ::=
    { ENCRYPTION | SCHEMABINDING }
< table_type_definition > :: =
    ( { column_definition | table_constraint } [ ,...n ] )
```

Now consider the following example, which creates a multistatement table-valued function on the Customers table in the Northwind database. This will return a table as defined in the RETURNS section of the function. Although the results of the function in this example are really no different from the results of our inline example, the implementation is different—it allows for greater flexibility in case more complex logic is needed. Here's the code:

```
CREATE FUNCTION fnCustomers2 (@Country varchar(50))
RETURNS @CustTab TABLE
    (CustomerID varchar(6),
    CompanyName varchar(50),
    ContactName varchar(100),
    City varchar(50),
    Region varchar(50),
    Country varchar(50))
AS
BEGIN
    INSERT @CustTab
        SELECT CustomerID, CompanyName, ContactName, City, Region, Country
        FROM Customers
        WHERE Country=@Country
    RETURN
END
```

Multistatement table-valued functions are a great alternative to views when the processing to build the resulting table requires more logic than can be incorporated into a view.

Executing Functions

Functions are executed from within SQL statements or from within other functions. We will look at how to execute both scalar and table-valued functions using ADO.NET from ASP.NET in this section.

One unique thing about functions is that when referencing them, you need to include the owner name. The syntax for reference is *owner_name.function_name*, as shown in the examples in this section.

Scalar Functions

User-defined scalar functions can be accessed just like any built-in scalar functions (such as computational or type-conversion functions). You could add a column to the

19

[Order Details] table in Northwind with a computational column using the fnOrderCost function we built previously, like so:

```
ALTER TABLE [Order Details]
ADD TotalOrderCost AS
dbo.fnOrderCost (Quantity, UnitPrice, Discount)
```

Alternatively, you could use it in a SQL statement to calculate the total order cost on-the-fly, based on three specified values (note that brackets are required around the name of the table because there is a space in the table name):

```
SELECT
    Quantity,
    UnitPrice,
    Discount,
    dbo.fnOrderCost(Quantity, UnitPrice, Discount) TotalOrderCost
FROM [Order Details]
```

You would then execute this SQL and display it to the screen using data binding, just as you would any other SELECT statement we have looked at so far.

Table-Valued Functions

Inline and multistatement table-valued functions are accessed the same way, because both return a table. They are referenced from within SQL statements just as a table or view would be referenced.

Let's select just the CustomerID and the ContactName fields from the table that is returned from fnGetCustomers or fnGetCustomers2 (which, in the following example, contains only customers in Germany). This is a very simple usage of a table-valued function, but it demonstrates that you can use this function anywhere you can reference a table using SQL. Lines 15 and 16 in Listing 19.3 show this in action.

LISTING 19.3   Populating a Data Grid with the Results from a SQL Statement

```
01: <%@ Import Namespace="System.Data" %>
02: <%@ Import Namespace="System.Data.SQLClient" %>
03:
04: <html><head><title>Stored Procedures</title></head>
05: <body>
06:
07: <script language="VB" runat="server">
08:
09: sub Page_Load(Src as object, E as EventArgs)
10:
11: Dim myConnection as SQLConnection
12: MyConnection = New
➥SQLConnection("server=localhost;uid=sa;pwd=;database=Northwind")
```

LISTING 19.3 continued

```
13: Dim myCommand as SQLCommand
14: Dim mySQL as String
15: mySQL = "SELECT CustomerID, ContactName FROM " & _
16:         "dbo.fnCustomers ('Germany') ORDER BY COMPANYNAME"
17: myCommand = new SQLCommand(mySQL, myConnection)
18:
19: MyConnection.Open()
20
21: Dim myDR as SQLDataReader
22: MyCommand.ExecuteReader(myDR)
23: MyDataGrid.DataSource = myDR
24: MyDataGrid.DataBind()
25
26: MyConnection.Close
27
28: end sub
29:
30: </script>
31: <ASP:DataGrid id="MyDataGrid" runat="server"
32:     Width="700"
33:     BackColor="#FFFFFF"
34:     BorderColor="black"
35:     ShowFooter="false"
36:     CellPadding=3
37:     CellSpacing="0"
38:     Font-Name="Verdana"
39:     Font-Size="8pt"
40:     HeaderStyle-BackColor="#cfcfcf"
41:     MaintainState="false"
42:     />
43: </body>
```

The resulting output from this example can be seen in Figure 19.4.

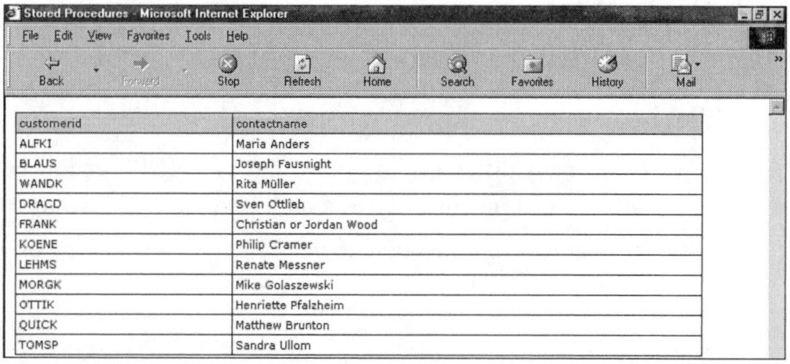

FIGURE 19.4

Output from Listing 19.3 demonstrating the results of a SQL statement displayed in a DataGrid.

19

Summary

In this hour, you learned what stored procedures and functions are in SQL Server 2000. We also discussed why it is often more advantageous to use functions or procedures than to construct SQL command processing in the ASP.NET code directly. Stored procedures enhance modularity of code, thus easing code maintenance as business logic changes. They also increase execution speed due to the precompilation of the SQL statements.

You also learned how to build and execute both stored procedures and functions from within ASP.NET code. We've barely scratched the surface of the power of stored procedures and functions; entire books are devoted to these topics. The goal of this hour was simply to introduce the concepts and give you the tools you need to build simple procedures and execute them from ASP.NET.

Q&A

Q. What are the basic differences between a stored procedure and a function?

A. Like a function, a stored procedure can return a recordset or a value, but it cannot be referenced from within other SQL statements. Functions provide an enormous amount of flexibility in that they can be referenced just as any built-in function (scalar functions) or as a table or view (table-valued functions).

Q. What is the difference between a deterministic and a nondeterministic function?

A. A deterministic function returns the same results every time it is called given a certain set of parameters (such as DATEDIFF or a mathematical calculation), whereas a nondeterministic function (such as a GETDATE or a function based on contents of a database) will not.

Workshop

The quiz questions and exercises are provided for your further understanding.

Quiz

1. Is there any difference in syntax in the ASP.NET code when accessing an inline table-valued function versus a multistatement table-valued function?

2. In what part of a function do you specify the data type of what the function will return?

3. Which of the following are deterministic functions?

    a. DATEADD

    b. ISNULL

    c. HOST_NAME

    d. SUM

    e. GETDATE

4. With what character must all parameter names begin for both stored procedures and functions?

Exercises

1. Create a stored procedure that returns all orders from the [Order Details] table of the Northwind database that have a quantity larger than the specified value. (Hint: Pass the value in via a parameter.)

2. Create a stored procedure that will give you the customer ID of the customer who ordered the largest quantity of any item in a specified date range. (Hint: Pass the start and end date as parameters and return the customer ID as an output parameter.)

3. Create a function that will calculate the total amount of all orders by a given customer based on the customer ID. This should accept CustomerID as a parameter and return the sum of all that customer's order totals (Hint: Quantity * UnitPrice * (1-Discount)).

4. **Challenge Exercise:** Create a function that uses the previous function to return a table containing the total for each customer in the database.

Answers for Hour 19

Quiz

1. Is there any difference in syntax in the ASP.NET code when accessing an inline table-valued function versus a multistatement table-valued function?

    No. They both return tables that are internal to the function and either explicitly defined or created based on a SELECT statement. They are called in exactly the same manner from ASP.NET.

2. In what part of a function do you specify the data type of what the function will return?

    In the RETURN clause.

19

3. Which of the following are deterministic functions?

    a. `DATEADD`

    b. `ISNULL`

    c. `HOST_NAME`

    d. `SUM`

    e. `GETDATE`

`DATEADD`, `ISNULL`, and `SUM` are deterministic because they do not change based on when or where they are called, as long as they are passed the same set of parameters. `HOST_NAME`, on the other hand, does change, depending on the application's server, and `GETDATE` changes depending on the date when it is called.

4. With what character must all parameter names begin for both stored procedures and functions?

The "at" symbol (@).

Hour **20**

Using Advanced Database Techniques

By now, you've probably heard something about XML and its relationship to the future of Web and application development. Here's your chance to work with it.

In this hour, you will be introduced to XML, and you will learn

- How XML is implemented in the .NET Framework
- How XML interoperates with ADO.NET
- How XML can work with ASP.NET

What Is XML?

XML, also known as *extensible markup language*, is a markup language similar in structure to HTML, the markup language used to design and develop Web pages. Like HTML, XML uses sets of opening and closing tags, which in turn have attributes that can be set. However, unlike HTML, which is limited to a specific number of tags, XML can be extended to support any number of tags. It is this extensibility that makes XML a wonderful mechanism for transferring data between disparate systems.

Because the tags used in XML can be called anything, you can easily transmit hierarchical data wrapped in `<column name>` tags, for example, each again wrapped in tags that define and describe the table. Figure 20.1 shows an XML document that describes the data it contains. This data describes movie-listing information for some local theaters.

FIGURE 20.1

XML Document Viewed in Internet Explorer

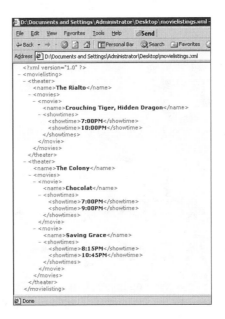

In the XML document shown in Figure 20.1, several things stand out. For starters, the first line of the document specifies that it contains XML. The next thing you notice is that there are many sets of tags that contain text along with other sets of tags. Tags in XML are words that are surrounded by angle brackets; opening tags contain a word only, whereas closing tags contain a word preceded by a forward slash. For example, the first tag in the document is `<movielisting>`; its closing tag, at the end of the document is `</movielisting>`.

The actual data is found between the opening and closing XML tags. The purpose of the tag is to describe and define the particular piece of data it surrounds.

For example, within the `<movielisting>` tags is the tag set for each theater in the area. These theaters are enclosed in `<theater>` tags. Within the `<theater>` tag is a `<name>` tag, which holds the name of the theater. Also within the `<name>` tag is a tag called `<movies>`.

The <movies> tag contains a tag set for each movie that is playing at the theater. This tag set is defined by an opening and closing <movie> tag, which in turn contains other tag sets that describe the movie that is playing at the theater. The tags that describe the movie are the <name> tag and the <showtimes> tag, which contains showtime information for the movie.

You can also have an XML tag without a separate closing tag. This contains the forward slash at the end of the opening tag: <tagname/>. Because these tags hold no information, they are mainly used to launch some type of action for the parser. This is very much like the HTML <hr> tag, which also has no closing tag and tells the HTML parser to put a horizontal line across the screen.

Well-Formed and Valid

An XML document must achieve two things to be effective. It must be well-formed and valid. *Well-formed* means that the entire document must follow the syntax rules of XML. The following list outlines some of the requirements for a document to be well-formed.

- It must obey XML syntax rules. (Rules and other information on XML can be found at http://www.w3.org/XML/.)

- All tags must have an opening and closing tag, <tagname></tagname>, or close themselves off, like <tagname/>.

- Tags must be properly nested. For example, the following tags are not well-formed: <tagname1><tagname2></tagname1></tagname2>. They are not in the correct order. You cannot close the first tag before closing the second tag.

When a document is considered well-formed, you should check it to make sure that the XML document is valid and well-formed. This can be done using a third-party XML utility, or by simply opening the XML document in Internet Explorer. After you have determined that the document contains a valid structure, you can use it as XML.

Benefits of XML

XML is one of the building blocks of Web and application development. It can be used for a multitude of purposes including, but not limited to, the following tasks:

- Passing data between disparate systems. XML documents are transmitted through HTTP with SSL (Secure Sockets Layer), which means they can easily pass through corporate firewalls and still maintain a secure connection. This means that companies can share information with their business partners much more easily than ever before.

20

- Cross-browser, cross-platform delivery of content. XML documents coupled with XSL stylesheets can provide your content to any system on any platform. Whether you are running Netscape Navigator, Internet Explorer, a Mac, a PC, or a handheld device, the XSL stylesheet can tell which system is being used and deliver the appropriate content without needing to code differently for each system.

- XML documents provide a great way to store data on handheld devices. Because the data is stored as text, it has a low overhead on system resources, which will increase the performance of your handheld application. When running on a wireless network, XML documents can be transmitted back and forth to a central server for data transformation and updates.

- Web Services are touted as the next big thing on the Internet. Based on XML, these services allow you to create an application that performs a specific task, such as gathering stock information, and that can be called from anywhere in the world over the Internet. Again, because XML is transmitted over HTTP (port 80), this service can be carried out through a firewall. Web Services play a major part of Microsoft's .NET initiative and will be discussed in more detail in Hour 21.

To get the most out of XML, many major database vendors have released databases data as XML documents. SQL Server 7 and SQL Server 2000 are two databases that are XML-enabled.

Microsoft's new .NET initiative incorporates a lot of XML into its structure. In fact, if you look closely you can see that the ASP.NET server controls look very much like XML, especially because your ASP.NET page will work in Netscape and Internet Explorer without any additional coding, such as XSL stylesheets. You might also notice that the web.config file is a well-formed XML file.

XML is also an integral data component to building ASP.NET applications with ADO.NET. The next section discusses using XML components in ADO.NET to work with XML in your ASP.NET application.

ADO.NET and XML

In ADO.NET, many classes have been developed to provide you with the most robust set of API tools for programming with XML. Table 20.1 lists a subset of defined classes. A complete list can be found in the MSDN (Microsoft Developer Network).

TABLE 20.1   ADO.NET Components Necessary for XML

Class	Description
XMLDataDocument	Represents an implementation of XMLDocument that can be associated with an ADO.NET DataSet object. You can simultaneously view and manipulate structured XML through the relational representation of the DataSet or the Document Object Model (DOM) representation of XMLDataDocument.
XMLReader	Represents a reader that provides fast, noncached, forward-only stream access to XML data. This reader can read a stream or an XML document.
XMLWriter	Provides fast, noncached, forward-only generation of well-formed XML streams. This writer can write to a stream or a document.
XMLNameTable	A table of string objects that provides an efficient way for the XML parser to use the same string object for all repeated element and attribute names in an XML document.
XMLNodeReader	Represents a reader that provides fast, noncached, forward-only stream access to XML data in an XMLDocument or a specific XMLNode within an XMLDocument.
XslTransform	Transforms XML data using an XSLT stylesheet.
XMLException	Returns detailed information about the last parse error, including the error number, line number, character position, and a text description.

Several classes are considered core components that are used when building your application to work with XML. These components—DataSet, XMLDocument, and XMLDataDocument—are discussed in more detail in Table 20.2.

TABLE 20.2   ADO.NET Core Components for XML

Component	Description
DataSet	The DataSet class is used to represent the data in an XML document as relational data. This class is found in the System.Data namespace. The DataSet object was discussed in Hour 18; please refer to that hour for more information on how to use it.
XMLDocument	The XMLDocument class represents the XML DOM. The DOM is an in-memory tree representation of an XML document. The XMLDocument class is found in the System.XML namespace.
XMLDataDocument	The XMLDataDocument is a subclass of the XMLDocument class. It represents relational data stored in an XML document. This class is also located in the System.XML namespace.

20

The DataSet Class

Although the DataSet class was discussed in detail in Hour 18, it's important to examine two methods of the DataSet class, the ReadXML and WriteXML methods.

ReadXML

The ReadXML method is an overloaded method call, which means that it can accept several different sets of parameters. Table 20.3 shows all of the ways you can call the ReadXML method.

TABLE 20.3 ReadXML Method (Overloaded)

Parameter	Description
ReadXML(Stream)	Reads XML Schema and Data into the DataSet using the specified Stream object.
ReadXML(String)	Reads XML Schema and Data into the DataSet using the specified file.
ReadXML(TextReader)	Reads XML Schema and Data into the DataSet using the specified TextReader object.
ReadXML(XMLReader)	Reads XML Schema and Data into the DataSet using the specified XMLReader object.
ReadXML(Stream, XMLReadMode)	Reads the XML Schema and Data into the DataSet using the specified Stream object and XMLReadMode setting.
ReadXML(String, XMLReadMode)	Reads the XML Schema and Data into the DataSet using the specified file path and XMLReadMode setting.
ReadXML(TextReader, XMLReadMode)	Reads the XML Schema and Data into the DataSet using the specified TextReader object and XMLReadMode setting.
ReadXML(XMLReader, XMLReadMode)	Reads the XML Schema and Data into the DataSet using the specified XMLReader object and XMLReadMode setting.

Two important arguments are Schema and XMLReadMode. An XML Schema is used to define the structure, content, and semantics of an XML document. The XMLReadMode argument specifies to the ReadXML method call how it should determine the schema of the XML document. The XMLReadMode argument has the following values:

- DiffGram: Reads a DiffGram, applying any changes from the DiffGram to the DataSet. This is very similar to the Merge method of the DataSet, and will be discussed later in this hour. DiffGrams are typically used with SQL Server calls.

- `Fragment`: Reads XML documents containing inline XDR schema fragments.

- `IgnoreSchema`: Ignores any inline schema and reads data into an existing `DataSet` schema. Data not matching the existing schema is discarded.

- `InferSchema`: Ignores any inline schema, inferring the schema from the data being loaded, and loads the data into the `DataSet`.

- `ReadSchema`: Reads any inline schema and loads the data into the `DataSet`.

- `Auto`: Default setting. Performs the most appropriate action from this list.

WriteXML

The `WriteXML` method is also overloaded. Its acceptable parameters are listed in Table 20.4.

TABLE 20.4   `WriteXML` Method (Overloaded)

Parameter	Description
WriteXML(Stream)	Writes the current schema and data using the specified `Stream` object.
WriteXML(String)	Writes the current schema and data using the specified file path.
WriteXML(TextWriter)	Writes the current schema and data using the specified `TextWriter` object.
WriteXML(XMLWriter)	Writes the current schema and data using the specified `XMLWriter` object.
WriteXML(Stream,	Writes the current schema and `XMLWriteMode`)data using the specified `Stream` object and `XMLWriteMode` value.
WriteXML(String,	Writes the current schema and `XMLWriteMode`)data using the specified file path and `XMLWriteMode` value.
WriteXML(TextWriter,	Writes the current schema and `XMLWriteMode`)data using the specified `TextWriter` object and `XMLWriteMode` value.
WriteXML(XMLWriter,	Writes the current schema and `XMLWriteMode`) data using the specified `XMLWriter` object and `XMLWriteMode` value.

The `XMLWriteMode` method has the following values:

- `DiffGram`: Writes the entire `DataSet` as a `DiffGram`, including the original and current values. Again, `DiffGrams` are typically used with SQL Server calls.

- `IgnoreSchema`: Writes the current contents of the `DataSet` as XML data without a schema.

- `WriteSchema`: Default setting. Writes the current contents of the `DataSet` as XML data with an inline schema.

20

The XMLDocument Class

The XMLDocument class provides programmatic access to the XML Document Object Model (DOM). Tables 20.5 and 20.6 list a subset of the properties and methods found in the XMLDocument class. A complete list, additional information, and samples can be found in the MSDN documentation.

TABLE 20.5 XMLDocument Class Properties

Class	Description
DocumentElement	Retrieves the root XMLElement for the document.
DocumentType	Retrieves the node for the DOCTYPE declaration.
InnerXML	Gets or sets the markup representing the children of this node.
IsReadOnly	Gets a value indicating whether the node is read-only.
LocalName	Gets the name of the current node without the namespace prefix.
Name	Gets the name of the node.
NameTable	Gets the XMLNameTable associated with this implementation.
NodeType	Gets the type of the current node.
PreserveWhitespace	Gets or sets a value indicating whether to preserve whitespace.

TABLE 20.6 XMLDocument Class Methods

Method	Description
CloneNode	Creates a duplicate of this node.
CreateAttribute	Creates an XMLAttribute with the specified name.
CreateCDataSection	Creates an XMLCDataSection containing the specified data.
CreateComment	Creates an XMLComment containing the specified data.
CreateDocumentFragment	Creates an XMLDocumentFragment.
CreateDocumentType	Returns a new XMLDocumentType object.
CreateElement	Creates an XMLElement.
CreateEntityReference	Creates an XMLEntityReference with the specified name.
CreateNode	Creates an XMLNode.
CreateProcessingInstruction	Creates an XMLProcessingInstruction with the specified name and data strings.
CreateSignificantWhitespace	Creates an XMLSignificantWhitespace node.
CreateTextNode	Creates an XMLText with the specified text.
CreateWhitespace	Creates an XMLWhitespace node.

TABLE 20.6 continued

Method	Description
CreateXMLDeclaration	Creates an XMLDeclaration node with the specified values.
GetElementById	Returns the XMLElement with the specified ID.
GetElementsByTagName	Returns an XMLNodeList containing a list of all descendant elements that match the specified name.
ImportNode	Imports a node from another document to this document.
Load	Loads the specified XML data. By default, the Load method preserves SignificantWhitespace.
LoadXML	Loads the XML document from the specified string.
ReadNode	Creates an XMLNode object based on the information in the XMLReader. The reader must be positioned on a node or attribute.
Save	Saves the XML document to the specified location.
WriteContentTo	Saves all the children of the node to the specified XMLWriter.
WriteTo	Saves the node to the specified XMLWriter.

The XMLDataDocument Class

The XMLDataDocument class is used to generate an XML document from a DataSet. This class has one property, called DataSet, which provides a relational representation of the data in this XMLDataDocument. Table 20.7 contains a subset of methods found in the XMLDataDocument Class. As previously mentioned, a complete list and additional information can be found in the MSDN documentation.

TABLE 20.7 XMLDataDocument Class Methods

Method	Description
CreateElement	Creates an XMLElement.
GetElementFromRow	Retrieves an XMLElement object for the currently selected row.
GetRowFromElement	Retrieves a row from the XMLElement.
Load	Loads the specified XML data.
LoadDataSetMapping	Builds a relational view according to the specified schema.
Save	Saves the XML document to the specified location.
SaveDataSetMapping	Saves the relational view according to the specified schema.
WriteTo	Saves the current node to the specified XMLWriter.

20

Using ADO.NET and XML

The following examples illustrate how to perform some common tasks using ADO.NET, ASP.NET, and XML. These examples include how to retrieve data from a database and save it as an XML file and how to retrieve data from an XML file and display it on your page.

Retrieving Data and Saving As XML

Nowthat you've been inundated with XML-related class objects and their properties and methods, it's time to take a look at how to use them in your application. For starters, we are going to examine how to load data from an XML document and display it on your ASP.NET Web form.

The first example shows how to retrieve data from a database, specifically the Northwind database that comes with SQL Server and Microsoft Access, and save that information as an XML document.

Listing 20.1 demonstrates how to create an XML document from data stored in a database. It also displays the data retrieved from the database using a `DataGrid` control so that you can compare it to the XML document created.

LISTING 20.1   Retrieving Data from a Database and Saving It as an XML Document

```
1: <%@ Page Language="vb" AutoEventWireup="false" Codebehind="WebForm1.aspx.vb"
➥Inherits="Chapter20.WebForm1"%>
2: <%@ import namespace="System.Data.SQLClient" %>
3: <%@ import namespace="System.Data" %>
4: <%@ import namespace="System.XML" %>
5: <%
6:
7: Dim dsNorthwind as DataSet = new DataSet()
8:
9: 'Create the connection string.
10: Dim sConnect as String
11: sConnect="Data Source=localhost;Integrated Security=SSPI;
➥Initial Catalog=Northwind"
12:
13: 'Create a connection object to connect to the northwind db.
14: Dim nwconnect as SqlConnection
15: nwconnect = new SqlConnection(sConnect)
16:
17: 'Create a command string to select all the customers in the database.
18: Dim sCommand as String = "Select * from Customers where Country = 'USA'"
19:
20: 'Create an Adapter to load the DataSet.
```

LISTING 20.1 continued

```
21: Dim myDataAdapter as SqlDataAdapter
22: myDataAdapter = new SqlDataAdapter(sCommand, nwconnect)
23:
24: 'Fill the DataSet with the selected records.
25: myDataAdapter.Fill(dsNorthwind, "Customers")
26:
27: 'Load the document with the DataSet.
28: Dim doc as XMLDataDocument = new XMLDataDocument(dsNorthwind)
29:
30: 'Write the data to a file.
31: Dim writer as XMLTextWriter = new XMLTextWriter
 ➥ ("D:\inetpub\wwwroot\chapter20\myCust.XML", nothing)
32: writer.Formatting = Formatting.Indented
33: doc.Save(writer)
34:
35: dgXML.DataSource = dsNorthwind
36: dgXML.DataBind()
37:
38: writer.Close()
39: myDataAdapter.Dispose()
40:
41: dsNorthwind = Nothing
42: myDataAdapter = Nothing
43: writer = Nothing
44: doc = Nothing
45: %>
46: <HTML>
47:   <HEAD>
48:    <meta name="GENERATOR" content="Microsoft Visual Studio.NET 7.0">
49:    <meta name="CODE_LANGUAGE" content="Visual Basic 7.0">
50:    <meta name=vs_defaultClientScript content="JavaScript">
51:    <meta name=vs_targetSchema content="Internet Explorer 5.0">
52:   </HEAD>
53:   <body MS_POSITIONING="GridLayout">
54:        <asp:DataGrid Runat="server" ID="dgXML">
55:        </asp:DataGrid>
56:   </body>
57: </HTML>
```

20

The first section of this page includes the page directives and import statements that are necessary to execute the code in the page. For this page to function properly, the System.Data.SQLClient, System.Data, and System.XML namespaces were imported.

The next section of this page includes the code to build our DataSet and eventually our XML document. Line 7 creates our empty DataSet. We then connect to our data source—in this instance, Microsoft SQL Server 2000—in line 25 and populate our

`SQLDataAdapter` object with all of the customers located in the United States from the Customers table in the Northwind database.

After our `SQLDataAdapter` object has the data loaded into it from the database, we create our XML document shell in lines 28 and 31. Notice that line 31 specifies where to save this document and what to name it. In this case, it's being saved in the same Chapter20 directory under the `wwwroot` directory and named `myCust.XML`.

After our document has been created, we call the `Save` method of the `XMLDataDocument` object and pass it the `XMLTextWriter` reference to the XML document we want to create.

Next, we bind the `SQLDataAdapter` to our `DataGrid` server control so that we can see the data that was saved to the XML file.

Finally, we clean up after all the objects and the browser receives the HTML document that was generated.

Figure 20.2 illustrates the final result of the page.

FIGURE 20.2

The recordset bound to the `DataGrid` *control.*

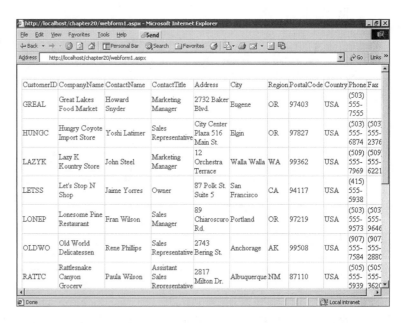

The `myCust.XML` is shown in Figure 20.3.

Now that you've seen how to create XML documents with ASP.NET and ADO.NET, let's examine how to retrieve our data from an XML document and display it on our page.

FIGURE 20.3

The myCust.XML *document generated by Listing 20.1.*

Retrieving Data in an XML Document

The next example borrows a bit from the first example. In this example, we are going to look at how to retrieve data from an XML document—the myCust.XML document generated in the first example—and display that information on our page.

Listing 20.2 shows the code that does this.

LISTING 20.2   Retrieving Data from an XML Document for Display

```
1: <%@    Page Language="vb" AutoEventWireup="false"
➥Codebehind="WebForm2.aspx.vb" Inherits="Chapter20.WebForm2"%>
2: <%@    import namespace="System.Data" %>
3: <%
4: Dim    dsCustomers as DataSet = new DataSet()
5:
6: dsCustomers.ReadXML("d:\inetpub\wwwroot\chapter20\myCust.XML",
➥XMLReadMode.Auto)
7:
8: dgXML.DataSource = dsCustomers
9: dgXML.DataBind()
10:
11: dsCustomers = Nothing
12: %>
13: <HTML>
14:   <HEAD>
```

20

LISTING 20.2 continued

```
15:    <meta name="GENERATOR" content="Microsoft Visual Studio.NET    7.0">
16:    <meta name="CODE_LANGUAGE" content="Visual Basic 7.0">
17:    <meta name=vs_defaultClientScript content="JavaScript">
18:    <meta name=vs_targetSchema content="Internet Explorer 5.0">
19:  </HEAD>
20:  <body MS_POSITIONING="GridLayout">
21:       <asp:DataGrid Runat="server" ID="dgXML" Font-Name="Verdana"
➡AlternatingItemStyle-BackColor="#00ffff" Font-Size="10px"
➡HeaderStyle-Font-Bold="True" HeaderStyle-Font-Size="13px" BorderWidth="0"
➡cellpadding="0" cellspacing="0">
22:       </asp:DataGrid>
23:  </body>
24:  </HTML>
```

Again, the first section of this page declares any necessary page directives and imports the required namespace for using this page. In fact, you only need to import the System.Data namespace. Though it's counterintuitive, the System.XML namespace is not needed to display data in an XML document on the screen.

By far the easiest way to get data from an XML document and display it on the page is to use the ReadXML method of the DataSet class. After you've loaded the XML document into the DataSet object, you need only bind it to the DataGrid server control through the DataSource property and the DataBind method.

Figure 20.4 shows the data retrieved from the myCust.XML file.

Now that we can get data from our XML document, let's look at how we can modify our document.

Retrieving Data from XML, Modifying It, and Saving It as XML

This next example illustrates how to load an XML document into your page, edit it via a delete call, and save it back to our XML document.

Listing 20.3 shows how to create a page that loads an XML document and how to delete records from that document.

FIGURE 20.4

The myCust.XML *document data.*

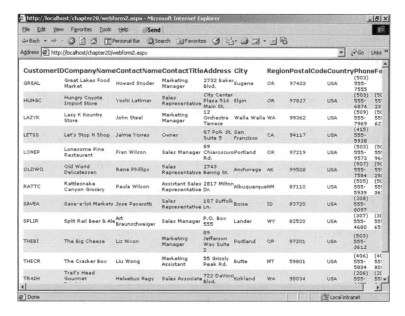

LISTING 20.3 Retrieving, Modifying, and Saving Data to and from an XML Document

```vb
1: <%@ Page Language="vb" AutoEventWireup="false" Codebehind="WebForm3.aspx.vb"
➥Inherits="Chapter20.WebForm3"%>
2: <%@    import namespace="System.Data" %>
3: <%
4: Dim dsCustomers As DataSet = New DataSet()
5: Dim CompanyID As String = Request.QueryString("CompanyID")
6:
7: '-- Read the data in our XML document
8: dsCustomers.ReadXML("d:\inetpub\wwwroot\chapter20\myCust.XML",
➥XMLReadMode.Auto)
9:
10: '-- If a CompanyID was passed over, delete it.
11: If CompanyID <> "" Then
12:    Dim t As DataTable
13:    Dim r As DataRow
14:
15:    '-- Loop through all of the tables in the DataSet object
16:    For Each t In dsCustomers.Tables
17:        '-- Loop through all of the rows in the DataTable object
18:        For Each r In t.Rows
19:            '-- If the CustomerID field matches the CompanyID passed over
20:            '-- in the querystring, then mark the record as deleted
21:            If r.Item("CustomerID").ToString = CompanyID Then
22:                r.Delete()
```

LISTING 20.3 continued

```
23:                    Exit For
24:                End If
25:            Next r
26:        Next t
27:
28:        Dim dsCustomerEdit As DataSet
29:
30:        '-- GetChanges() will generate another DataSet with the modified row
31:        dsCustomerEdit = dsCustomers.GetChanges()
32:        '-- Merge() will merge the new DataSet, dsCustomerEdit, into the
➥original DataSet
33:        dsCustomers.Merge(dsCustomerEdit)
34:        '-- WriteXML() will rewrite the XML document from the DataSet
35:        dsCustomers.WriteXML("d:\inetpub\wwwroot\chapter20\mycust.XML",
➥XMLWriteMode.WriteSchema)
36:
37:    '-- Clean up
38:    dsCustomerEdit.Dispose()
39:    dsCustomerEdit = Nothing
40: End If
41:
42: '-- Bind the DataSet to the DataGrid
43: dgXML.DataSource = dsCustomers
44: dgXML.DataBind()
45:
46: '-- Clean Up
47: dsCustomers.Dispose()
48: dsCustomers = Nothing
49: %>
50: <HTML>
51: <HEAD>
52:  <meta name="GENERATOR" content="Microsoft Visual Studio.NET  7.0">
53:  <meta name="CODE_LANGUAGE" content="Visual Basic 7.0">
54:  <meta name=vs_defaultClientScript content="JavaScript">
55:  <meta name=vs_targetSchema content="Internet Explorer 5.0">
56:  </HEAD>
57:  <body  MS_POSITIONING="GridLayout">
58:     <asp:DataGrid Runat="server" ID="dgXML"
59:        Font-Name="Verdana"
60:        AlternatingItemStyle-BackColor="#00ffff"
61:        Font-Size="10px"
62:        HeaderStyle-Font-Bold="True"
63:        HeaderStyle-Font-Size="13px"
64:        BorderWidth="0"
65:        cellpadding="0"
66:        cellspacing="0">
67:      <Columns>
68:        <asp:HyperLinkColumn Text="Delete"
➥DataNavigateUrlField="CustomerID"
```

LISTING 20.3 continued

```
➥DataNavigateUrlFormatString="webform3.aspx?CompanyID={0}"/>
69:          <asp:BoundColumn HeaderText="Customer ID"
➥DataField="CustomerID" ItemStyle-Width="200px">
70:          </asp:BoundColumn>
71:          <asp:BoundColumn HeaderText="Name" DataField="CompanyName"
➥ItemStyle-Width="200px">
72:          </asp:BoundColumn>
73:          <asp:BoundColumn HeaderText="Contact Name"
➥DataField="ContactName" ItemStyle-Width="200px">
74:          </asp:BoundColumn>
75:       </Columns>
76:     </asp:DataGrid>
77:  </body>
78: </HTML>
```

Two important sections of this code listing are new to you. The first is line 5 and lines 11–40. Line 5 is the container variable for the CompanyID that will be passed back to the page when a row is deleted. Line 11 checks this variable to see if any changes need to be made. If so, it launches into a looping structure that loops through all of the DataTable objects in the DataSet and through all of the DataRow objects in the DataTable object. If a row is found that has a CompanyID field matching the CompanyID variable passed in to the page, that row is marked for deletion by calling the Delete() method of the row selected.

After a row has been selected for deletion, the For loop is exited and we need to create a copy of our dataset, which consists only of the record that has been marked for deletion. This is accomplished in lines 28 and 31 by creating another DataSet object and calling the GetChanges() method of the original DataSet object, dsCustomers. After the changes have been pulled from the original DataSet, we call the Merge() method of that DataSet and pass it the new DataSet generated from the GetChanges() method call. This updates the original DataSet by removing the record originally selected for deletion.

After the row has been deleted from the DataSet, we re-create the XML document by calling the WriteXML method of the DataSet object and passing it the location of our XML document.

Finally, we clean everything up and bind our revised DataSet to the DataGrid.

Another thing to notice is in the HTML portion of the document. Here, I have defined a couple of columns for the DataGrid. The most important line is 68. Here I create a new column called "Delete" that contains a link to reload this page and pass it the CompanyID in the querystring. The {0} located at the end of the DataNavigateUrlFormatString value tells the DataSet to place the first column, the CompanyID column, in this place on the page.

20

Summary

In this hour, we looked at how you can use XML as a data store in your application. Through several techniques and examples you learned how to build an XML document from a DataSet, how to modify data in that XML document, and how to save it back out to a file.

So far, we've only reached the tip of the iceberg with what you can do with XML, ADO.NET, and ASP.NET. In upcoming hours, you will become familiar with Web Services and other uses for XML.

Q&A

Q. I've gone goo-goo for XML. Where can I drown myself in technical information?

A. Head on over to http://www.w3.org. There you can find the original RFCs (Request For Comments) regarding XML, XSLT, and everything in between.

Q. What else is XML used for?

A. XML has a wide variety of uses including but not limited to mobile solutions, e-commerce, graphics sharing, business data sharing, Web Services, and many other tools. Visit www.XML.org and www.XML.com to get more information on what XML can do for you.

Q. Are XML tags case sensitive?

XML tags are case sensitive. When you write opening and closing tags, they must use the same case (that is, <Movie> is different from the tag <movie>).

Workshop

The quiz questions and answers are provided for your further understanding.

Quiz

1. What two conditions must be met before a document can be considered XML?

2. What three classes are core to using XML in ADO.NET?

3. What does the GetChanges() method do in the DataSet class?

The following two figures illustrate the page in action. Figure 20.5 shows the original page and Figure 20.6 shows the page after clicking on the first item.

FIGURE 20.5

The original page derived from myCust.XML.

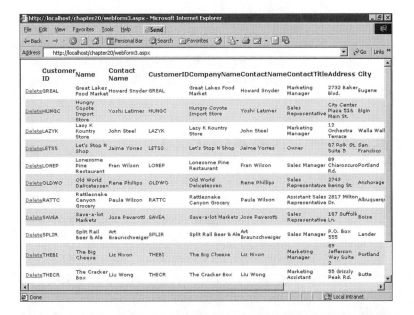

FIGURE 20.6

The same page after clicking the Delete link next to the first entry.

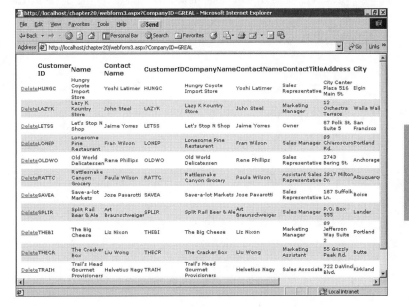

20

Exercise

Build your own XML file on the fly from the Northwind database. Use any of the tables in the database. After the file has been created, locate it and open it in Internet Explorer. Notice the format of the document and how the XML tags are named. Close the document and build another page that retrieves the XML data from the file you've just created and displays it on your page. Write a routine to modify a record in the page and save the data back to your XML file. View the XML file again and notice how the data has been manipulated.

Answers for Hour 20

Quiz

1. What two conditions must be met before a document can be considered XML?

   To be considered an XML document, a document must be well-formed and it must be valid.

2. What three classes are core to using XML in ADO.NET?

   The three classes that are core to using XML in ADO.NET are `DataSet`, `XMLDocument`, and `XMLDataDocument`.

3. What does the `GetChanges()` method do in the `DataSet` class?

   The `GetChanges()` method in the `DataSet` class sets a copy of the current `DataSet` with only the changes made to it since the last `Merge()` method was called.

Part V

Extending ASP.NET

Hour

HOUR 21

Web Services

In this hour, you will learn about Web Services, a programmable component that can be used by a range of applications from desktop to Web. The following topics will be covered in this hour:

- Web Services
- Web methods
- How to access Web Services
- Data types available from Web Services
- How to access data using Web Services
- How to use session and application objects in Web Services

What Are Web Services?

Web Services are a .NET technology used to create programmable components. What is so different about that? Many applications use distributed component technologies, such as Distributed Component Object Model (DCOM) and Remote Procedure Calls (RPCs). A problem common to these technologies is platform dependency. Web Services use standard Internet technologies such as HTTP and XML. What does this buy the developer? A lot. Platform independence opens up the opportunity for heterogeneous systems to access these applications.

Users no longer need to know what language the application or service is developed in. All that the users need to know is what features are provided and how to use them in their own applications.

Web Services have great potential for use in the wide variety of applications running on the Internet, including weather services, stock tickers, newsfeed services, package tracking services, and associate services. For instance, an online bookseller such as Amazon.com could incorporate package-tracking capability by using a Web Service provided by a delivery company such as UPS. An online news provider could provide a Web Service to all the Web sites publishing the news.

Web Services use standard Internet technologies such as HTTP and XML to communicate between the provider and consumer. In this case, a provider is the one who develops the Web Service and deploys it in the server for the consumers to use in their application.

The consumers should be aware of the existence of the Web Service, the functionality provided by the Web Service, the arguments to be provided to the Web Service to utilize the functionality, and a standard way of communicating with the Web Service.

Web Services use a new lightweight protocol called SOAP (Simple Object Access Protocol). Why another protocol? Many of the distributed component technologies available now are tied to the operating system, forcing us to rewrite objects for various clients. The problem gets bigger when distributing objects across the Internet because of security concerns: Most corporate Web applications have firewalls. With SOAP, which uses HTTP as a carrier, there is no need to open new ports in the firewall. The communication between the Web Service provider and the consumer will be a SOAP message in an XML format.

For consumers to use a Web Service in their applications, the Web Service developer should provide information such as the methods exposed by the Web Service, the parameters expected, and the values returned by the methods. Web Service Description Language (WSDL) accomplishes this by providing information about the Web Service in an XML format. WSDL is generated by ASP.NET.

To view the WSDL contract, type the URL to call the .asmx file with a suffix of ?WSDL. For instance, if you create myWebService.asmx file under http://localhost/, you can use http://localhost/myWebService.asmx?WSDL to view the WSDL contract.

Now, we know that the WSDL contract provides information about the Web Service. But the consumers should know about the existence of the Web Service before using the detailed information provided by the WSDL contract. Discovery of Web Services, or DISCO, is the mechanism that is used to locate a Web Service. An XML file with a .disco extension is created when building the Web Service using VS.NET.

All Web Services take the file extension .asmx. Writing a Web Service could take anywhere from a few minutes to days depending on the functionality exposed by the Web Service. Note that ASP.NET takes care of building the WSDL contract and SOAP message for communication.

What Are Web Methods?

Web Services typically contain one or more public or private functions within itself. WebMethod is a custom attribute applied to the public functions to allow access to the function from remote Web clients. As the name suggests, private functions cannot be called from remote Web clients. Public functions within a Web Service that does not have the WebMethod attribute cannot be called from remote Web clients.

The following code defines a method called TestMethod, which takes a String as input and returns a String value as output.

```
Public Function <WebMethod()> TestMethod(strInput as String) as_ String
     'implementation code goes here
End Function
```

When adding the WebMethod() attribute to the public function, you can also set properties to control ***buffering, session state, and caching*** among others. The following are the properties that you can specify when adding the WebMethod() attribute:

- BufferResponse: Sets whether the response is buffered in memory before sending it to the client. Setting this property to true buffers the response; setting it to false sends the response back to the client when the response is generated. The default is true.

- CacheDuration: Sets, in seconds, the duration during which the response should be stored in the cache. The default value is 0, so the response is not cached. If you set the value greater than 0, the response will be stored in cache for the duration specified. A subsequent request within the cache duration will get the response from the cache.

- Description: Provides a descriptive statement about WebMethod for the consumers of the service. This statement is displayed next to the WebMethod in the Service Description or in the Service Help page, as shown in Figure 21.1.

21

FIGURE 21.1

Value of the
Description *property*
shown in the Service
Help page.

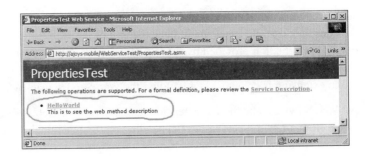

- EnableSession: Sets whether session state is enabled for the Web Service. Setting the value to true enables the session state; setting it to false disables the session state. By default the session state is disabled.

- MessageName: The name used for the Web Service method in the data passed to and returned from a Web Service method. This is useful when there are two or more methods with the same name.

- TransactionOptions: Indicates the transaction support of the Web method.

> There can be multiple Web methods in a Web Service. When you access the .asmx file from your browser, you see all the Web methods exposed by the Web Service.

Creating a Web Service

Now is the time to create our first Web Service. We'll start with a simple Web Service to get a good understanding of how to build a Web Service and expose the methods to ASP.NET applications.

We will be using Notepad to create a Web Service that exposes a method to get the price of some of the .Net books being published by SAMS, as shown in Listing 21.1.

LISTING 21.1   BookPriceList.asmx **Source Code**

```
1: <%@ WebService Language="vb" class="BookPriceList"%>
2: Imports System
3: Imports System.Web.Services
4:   Public Class BookPriceList: Inherits WebService
5:     <WebMethod(Description:="Provides price information")>Public Function _
  GetBookInfo(strBookId As String) As String
6:       Select Case strBookId
```

LISTING 21.1 continued

```
 7:                Case "0672320886"
 8:                return "49.99"
 9:                Case "0672321262"
10:                    return "39.99"
11:                 Case "0672321068"
12:                   return "39.99"
13:           Case "0672320894"
14:                    return "39.99"
15:               Case Else
16:                   return "Book Not Found"
17:         End Select
18:     End Function
19:   End Class
```

Line 1 tells ASP.NET that this page contains a Web Service. The language="vb" directive specifies that the page will be written in Visual Basic.NET. The class="BookPriceList" attribute tells ASP.NET that this page contains the class BookPriceList. Lines 2 and 3 import the namespaces required for building a Web Service.

Line 4 declares the class for the Web Service. It is defined as a public class and inherits WebService. Line 5 defines the method GetBookInfo as a public method. Notice the <WebMethod()> attribute included in the method definition. The description property of the WebMethod() attribute is set in Line 5. The BookPriceList method takes a string argument "strBookId" and returns a String as output. Lines 6–17 contain a Select Case block that returns the price of the book identified by the BookId.

That's it. We have developed our first Web Service.

▼ To Do

1. Create a folder called WebServiceTest.

2. Create a virtual directory using the IIS Management Console and map this to the WebServiceTest folder. Refer to the "Creating Your First Web Site" section in Hour 2 for more information on creating a virtual directory.

3. Save this file as BookList.asmx.

4. Now let's access this Web Service using a browser. Launch your browser and call the .asmx file using http://yourservername/WebServiceTest/BookList.asmx. Replace *yourservername* with the name of your server

▲

You will see a page like the one shown in Figure 21.2. It is a formatted page that contains information about the Web Service, the methods it exposes, the parameters it expects, and the response type.

FIGURE 21.2

BookPriceList.asmx *accessed using a browser.*

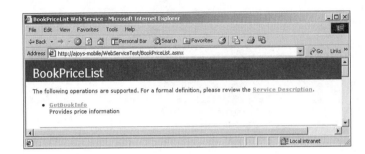

Did we build this page? No. ASP.NET built the page for us when it detected the call to the Web Service. In this case, this page identified the BookPriceList Web Service, with one method, GetBookInfo, exposed by the Web Service. Note that GetBookInfo is a hyperlink. Clicking on the GetBookInfo link takes us to the screen shown in Figure 21.3.

FIGURE 21.3

GetBookInfo *method test screen.*

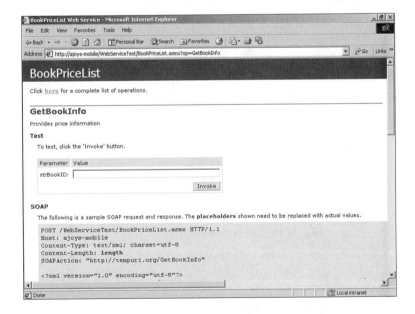

We can test this method by supplying a value for the BookId parameter. Enter **0672321262** in the BookIdParameter text box and click the Invoke button. This page will now call the WebMethod and return the results in a new window, as shown in Figure 21.4.

As mentioned earlier, ASP.NET builds the WSDL contract. To see the WSDL contract for this Web Service, either click on the Service Description link shown in Figure 21.2 or browse the .asmx file with a ?WSDL suffix to the URL. Figure 21.5 shows the portion of WSDL for our BookPriceList.asmx Web Service.

FIGURE 21.4

Result from the
`GetBookInfo` *method.*

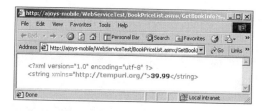

FIGURE 21.5

Service Description for the
`BookPriceList.asmx` *file.*

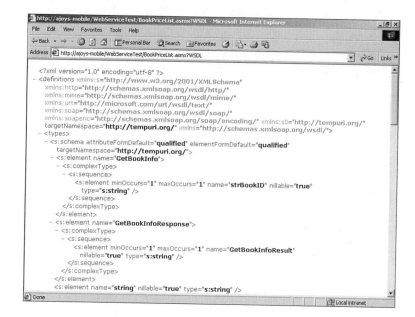

Accessing a Web Service

Now let us build a client to access the `BookPriceList` Web Service. Creating a client is as simple as creating a Web Service. So far we have accessed the Web Service using the browser by calling the `.asmx` file. But in real-world implementation, the Web Service will be accessed either from a client, such as a Web form, or from another Web Service. To access the Web Service from a client, we need to create a proxy class for the Web Service using the wsdl.exe utility described in the next section.

Using `wsdl.exe` to Generate a Web Service Proxy Class

To create the proxy class for the Web Service, we will be using the `wsdl.exe` utility. This utility will be run from the command line with parameters to create the proxy class as following:

```
wsdl.exe <parameters>
```

21

For a list of all the parameters that can be passed with `wsdl.exe`, search the .NET Framework SDK document for `wsdl.exe` and the result will show you the list of parameters.

There are two steps to access the Web Service from a client. First, use the `wsdl.exe` utility to generate a proxy class for the Web Service.

The `wsdl.exe` utility will generate a proxy class in the language that is specified using the language parameter. For instance, if the language used is VB.NET, `wsdl.exe` will generate a .vb file, whereas if the language used is C#, `wsdl.exe` will generate a .cs file.

The second step is to use a compiler to create a DLL. We will use `VBC.exe` if the language used is VB.NET or `CSC.exe` if the language used is C#.

Let's create a proxy class and the DLL for our `BookPriceList` Web Service.

Launch a command window and execute the following two lines one after another:

```
wsdl /language:VB  /protocol:SOAP /namespace:nsbpl /
➥out:bookpricelist.vb
➥ http://localhost/WebServiceTest/
➥BookPriceList.asmx?WSDL
VBC /out: BookPriceList.dll /t:library /r:system.web.services.dll /
➥r:system.xml. dll
➥ /r:System.dll bookpricelist.vb
```

The command screen is shown in Figure 21.6.

FIGURE 21.6

Using Wsdl.exe *and* VBC.exe.

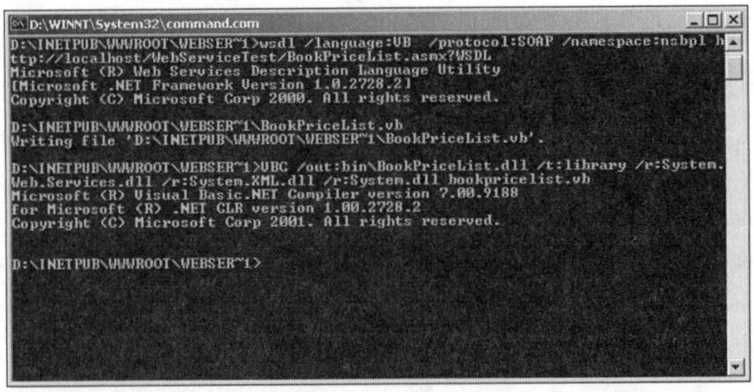

Either provide the full path for all the files or change the directory to the folder in which the files should be created before calling the `wsdl.exe` and the compiler.

Using the Web Service in a Client Application

In this section we will build an ASP.NET page to use the `BookPriceList` Web Service. Create a `.aspx` file and import the DLL we created for the `BookPriceList` Web Service proxy class as shown in Listing 21.2.

LISTING 21.2   `BookPriceListConsumer.aspx` Source Code

```
 1: <%@ Import Namespace="nsbpl" %>
 2: <HTML>
 3: <HEAD>
 4: <script language=vb runat="server">
 5:     sub GetBookInfo(Src as Object,E as EventArgs)
 6:        dim wsBookPriceList as new BookPriceList
 7:        dim bookPrice = wsBookPriceList.GetBookInfo(bookID.text)
 8:        lblBookPrice.InnerText = bookPrice
 9:     end sub
10: </script>
11: </HEAD>
12: <body>
13:    <form id="WebForm1" method="post" runat="server">
14:       <asp:Label id=Label1 runat="server">Enter Book ID:</asp:Label>
15:       <asp:TextBox id="bookID" runat="server"></asp:TextBox>
16:       <asp:Button id="Button1" runat="server" Text="Get Book Info"
➥ onClick="GetBookInfo"></asp:Button><br>
17:       Price for the Book is:<h4 id="lblBookPrice" runat="server"></h4>
18:    </form>
19: </body>
20: </HTML>
```

Line 1 imports the DLL for the Web Service proxy. The rest of the `.aspx` page should be familiar to you by now. We are using a text box to enter the `BookId` that will be passed to the `GetBookInfo` method of our Web Service. The result from the Web Service, which is the price of the book, will be displayed in the `lblBookPrice`.

The call to the `WebMethod` happens in lines 5–9. This is the function that is called when you click the `GetBookPrice` button. Line 6 defines a variable `wsBookPriceList` as `BookPriceList`, which is our Web Service. In Line 7, we invoke the `GetBookInfo` method and store the results to a string variable, `bookPrice`. Save this file as `BookPriceListconsumer.aspx`, and then open it using a browser. Figure 21.7 shows the price for the `bookId` supplied in the text box.

21

FIGURE 21.7

BookPriceListConsumer
.aspx *in a browser.*

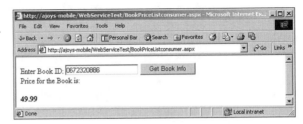

Data Access Using Web Services

In this section we are going to build a Web Service that will access a database and provide results. We will use the Pubs database, which is the SQL demo database that is installed when installing MSDE (Microsoft SQL Server Desktop Engine). For more information on installing MSDE and the database, please check the Microsoft .NET Framework SDK QuickStart Configuration Details page after installing SDK.

This Web Service will accept one parameter, a `title_id`. It will query the Titles table in the Pubs database for records with this `title_id` and will return the following three fields:

- Title
- Price
- Notes

We used Notepad to build our first, simple Web Service, `BookPriceList.asmx`. Now we are going to use VS.NET to build a Web Service and a Web application to use the Web Service. Let us start with building the Web service.

> Refer to Hour 15 for more information on database accessing techniques and how to use the ADO.NET objects. Refer to Hour 1 for more information on downloading and installing VS.NET and system requirements for using it.

1. Open Visual Studio.NET and click the Create New Project link in the Start Page or the New Project icon on the toolbar.

2. When the New Project dialog box appears, click on Visual Basic Projects under Project Types and then on ASP.NET Web Service under Templates. Enter **BookDetails** in the Name text box. Your screen should look like the one shown in Figure 21.8. Click OK to continue.

FIGURE 21.8

The New Project dialog box.

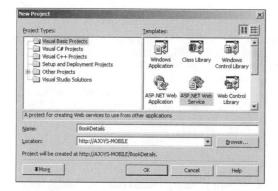

3. Visual Studio.NET will create a Web Service project. This process can take a few moments.

   When project creation is completed, you will see a blank Web Service file called `Service1.asmx`. Rename this file to `BookDbList.asmx`.

   Now, you will see a design screen for `BookDbList.asmx`. Right-click on the `BookDbList.asmx` file and then click View Code. You will see the code for the new Web Service. Rename the public class `Service1` to `BookDbList`. Now we are ready to add methods to our Web Service.

As you can see, VS.NET adds an `Imports` statement to import the `System.Web.Services` namespace and also create a public class.

Now we can add a new Web method as shown in Line 12 below:

```
1: Imports System.Web.Services
2: Imports System.Data
3: Imports System.Data.SqlClient
4: Public Class BookDbList Inherits System.Web.Services.WebService
5: 'Web Services Designer Generated Code
6:    ' WEB SERVICE EXAMPLE
7:    ' The HelloWorld() example service returns the string Hello World.
8:    ' To build, uncomment the following lines then save and build the project.
9:    ' To test this Web Service, ensure that the .asmx file is the start page
10:   ' and press F5.
11:   '
12:   <WebMethod(Description:="Provides information from PUBS Database",
➥ EnableSession:=False)>_
Public Function GetBookPrice(ByVal strTitleID As String) As DataSet
13:       Dim MyConnection As SqlConnection
14:       Dim MyCommand As SqlDataAdapter
```

21

```
15:        Dim DS As New DataSet()
16:        Dim strSQL As String
17:        strSQL = "select title_id,title,price,notes from titles
➥ where title_id='" & strTitleID & "'"
18:        MyConnection = New SqlConnection("server=localhost;
➥ uid=sa;pwd=;database=pubs")
19:        MyCommand = New SqlDataAdapter(strSQL, MyConnection)
20:        MyCommand.Fill(DS, "BookListInfo")
21:        Return DS
22:        MyConnection.Close()
23:    End Function
24: End Class
```

Lines 1–3 import three namespaces. Please refer to Hour 4 for more information about namespaces. VS.NET imports the `System.Web.Services` namespace when creating a `.asmx` file. The next two namespaces provide data-access capabilities. The following namespaces are imported:

- `System.Web.Services`: Provides access to classes and interfaces for building and using Web Services.
- `System.Data`: Provides access to the classes and interfaces that make up the ADO.NET architecture for universal data access.
- `System.Data.SqlClient`: Provides classes such as `SqlConnection` and `SqlCommand` for accessing a data source such as a database.

Line 5 contains Web Service designer-generated code. Within this region, there are calls and procedures that are required by the Web Service designer. To see the code under this section, expand this line in VS.NET.

Line 6 to 11 are commented code generated by VS.NET when it created the `.asmx` file.

Line 12 defines the method `GetBookPrice`. Notice the `WebMethod()` keyword placed before the method name. We also have a description specified for this method and the session state is set to `false`.

This method expects one argument, `strTitleID`, as a string, and returns a `DataSet`.

Line 13, 14, and 15 declare variables for storing instances of `SqlConnection`, `SqlDataAdapter`, and `DataSet` classes. Line 16 declares a string variable `strSQL` to store the SQL query statement.

In Line 17, we have created the SQL query which is, in this case, a `select` statement to fetch the title, price, and notes fields from the titles table in the Pubs database based on the `title_id` supplied by the consumer of this Web Service.

In Line 18 , we create the connection using the `SqlConnection` class by supplying `localhost` as the value for Server, `sa` as the user id, `blank` for password, and `pubs` for database.

In line 19, we are creating `SqlDataAdapter` by supplying the SQL string and connection, which is then used in line 20 to load the dataset using the `Fill` method of the `SqlDataAdapter` class. `SqlDataAdapter` represents data commands and database connections that are then used to fill the dataset.

In line 21, the `DataSet` is returned. In line 22 the `SqlConnection` is closed because we no longer need it. Lines 23 and 24 close the function and class respectively.

> Refer to Hour 16 for a detailed discussion on accessing database and relevant classes such as `SqlConnection` and `SqlCommand`.

With that, we have completed developing our Web Service. To view the Web Service in a browser, you can

- Right-click the filename `BookDbList.asmx` and then click View in Browser.
- Right-click `BookDbList.asmx` and then click Set as Start Page. Then click the Start icon from the toolbar.

Figure 21.9 shows the result of viewing this page using a browser.

FIGURE 21.9

`BookDbList.asmx` *file viewed in a browser.*

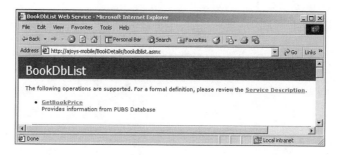

Click the `GetBookPrice` link to get to the next screen. From this screen, shown in Figure 21.10, we will test this Web Service by providing a `title_id` in the parameter text box.

FIGURE 21.10

WebMethod *test screen.*

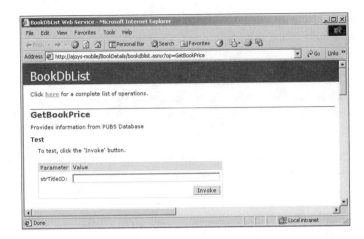

Enter **BU2075** in the `strTitleID` text box and click the Invoke button. You will see a screen that looks like the one shown in Figure 21.11.

FIGURE 21.11

The result screen.

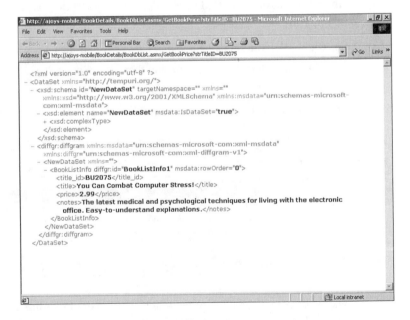

Now we have created and tested our Web Service. The next step is to create the proxy class for other applications to use the Web Service. We created the proxy class using `wsdl.exe` and the language compiler for the `BookPriceList.asmx` Web Service. In this example, we will be using VS.NET to create a proxy class.

1. Click Build from the toolbar in VS.NET and then click the Build menu option. This will build the DLL for the Web Service. When the build process is completed, which you can see in the output window in VS.NET, a DLL is created in the Bin folder.

After the Build is completed, you should see the BookDetails.dll file in the Bin folder in the `BookDetails` folder.

Developing a Web Service Consumer

Now we are going to build an ASP.NET application to use the Web Service we just created. We will be using VS.NET to create the ASP.NET application.

1. After Visual Studio.NET opens, click the Create New Project link or the New Project icon on the toolbar.

2. When the New Project dialog box appears, click on Visual Basic Projects under Project Types and then click ASP.NET Web Application under Templates. Then enter **BookDetailsConsumer** in the Name text box. Your screen should look like the one shown in Figure 21.12. Click OK to continue.

FIGURE 21.12

New Project dialog box.

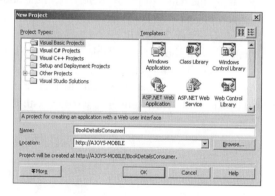

3. Visual Studio.NET will create your Web application project. This process can take a few moments.

   When project creation is completed, you will see a blank Web form called `WebForm1.asmx`. Rename this file by right-clicking on this filename in the Solution Explorer to `BookDetailsConsumer.aspx`.

4. Now is the time to import the Web Service we just created. Remember, we manually imported the Web Service last time when we created a `.aspx` page using Notepad. In VS.NET you will use the Project Reference option to do this. Click on Project, then Add Web Reference. Figure 21.13 shows the Add Web Reference window.

21

FIGURE 21.13

The Add Web Reference window.

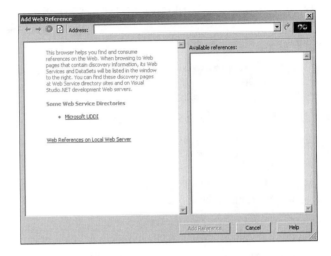

5. What we are referencing here is the SOAP Discovery file for the Web Service. You can either supply the name of the Web Service in the address box or click on the Web References on Local Web Server link to find all the Web Services available on the local Web server. This will give a list of available disco files. Select `BookDetails` and this will show the available Web Services, in this case, the `BookDbList.asmx` along with links to the Service Description and Service Help page. Select the Web Service, `BookDbList`, and then click the Add Reference button. Figure 21.14 shows the Add Web Reference window with the Web Service listed.

FIGURE 21.14

The Add Web Reference window.

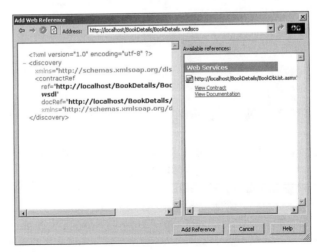

▼
▲

6. A new Web reference section named `localhost` will be added under the Web References folder in the Solution Explorer. Rename `localhost` to `BookDbList`. We are ready to use this Web Service in our ASP.NET applications.

Now we'll develop our .aspx page to use the Web Service.

```
1: <%@ Page Language="vb" AutoEventWireup="false"
➥Codebehind=" BookDetailsConsumer.aspx.vb"
➥Inherits="BookDetailsConsumer.WebForm1"%>
2: <%@ import namespace="System.Data"%>
3: <HTML>
4: <HEAD>
5: <meta content="Microsoft Visual Studio.NET 7.0" name=GENERATOR>
6: <meta content="Visual Basic 7.0" name=CODE_LANGUAGE>
7: <meta content=JavaScript name=vs_defaultClientScript>
8: <meta content="Internet Explorer 5.0" name=vs_targetSchema>
9: <script language=vb runat="server">
10:        public sub GetBookDetails(Src as Object,E as EventArgs)
11:          dim myBookDbList as new BookDbList.BookDbList()
12:          dim myDS as DataSet = myBookDbList.GetBookPrice(titleID.text)
13:          MyDataGrid.DataSource = myDS.Tables("BookListInfo").DefaultView
14:           MyDataGrid.DataBind()
15:        end sub
16: </script>
17: </HEAD>
18: <body MS_POSITIONING="GridLayout">
19:    <form id="WebForm1" method="post" runat="server">
20:      <asp:Label id=Label1 runat="server">Enter Book ID:</asp:Label>
21:      <asp:TextBox id="titleID" runat="server"></asp:TextBox>
22:      <asp:Button id="Button1" runat="server"
➥Text="Get Book Details" OnClick="GetBookDetails"></asp:Button>
23:      <asp:DataGrid id="MyDataGrid" runat="server"></asp:DataGrid>
24:    </form>
25: </body>
26: </HTML>
```

Line 1 is the page directive with the `Codebehind` and `Inherits` classes. Please refer to Hour 5 for more information on code-behind and page directives. In Line 2, we import the `System.Data` namespace for using `DataSet` later in the page.

Lines 3–8 contain HTML tags added by VS.NET when creating the Web form, along with the <HTML> and <HEAD> tags.

In Lines 20–23, we add a label; a text box for entering the titleID, which will be passed to the Web Service method; a button that will call the function `GetBookDetails`; and a `DataGrid`, to display the returned `DataSet` from the Web Service.

21

Lines 10–15 define a function, `GetBookDetails`, which creates an instance of the `BookDbList` Web Service in Line 11 and calls the Web Service method `GetBookPrice` in Line 12. The text entered in the `titleId` text box is passed to this method. The result of this method is stored in a `DataSet`. In Line 13, the `DataGrid`'s `DataSource` property is set to the `DataSet` returned in the previous line. In Line 14, we use the `DataBind()` method of the `DataGrid` control to bind the control to the `DataSet`.

Now we are ready to view this page. Save the file and view it in the browser. Your screen should look like the one shown in Figure 21.15.

FIGURE 21.15

The `BookDetailsConsumer.` `aspx` *file in a browser.*

Enter a titleID and click the Get Book Details button. You will see the results displayed in a grid, as shown in Figure 21.16.

FIGURE 21.16

`BookDetailsConsumer.` `aspx` *result in a* *browser.*

Using Session and Application Objects in Web Services

Session and application objects can be used in a Web Service the same way you use them in ASP.NET applications, to maintain state. The `System.Web.Services` class has session and application properties that get the application and session object for the current request. This is the class we inherit when creating a Web Service.

The application object stores information for all sessions, whereas the session object stores information specific to a session. To maintain state using these two objects, the `EnableSession` property should be set to `true`.

Let us build a Web Service to display the time the application and the session was started. Listing 21.3 shows the details of the code.

LISTING 21.3 The `StateTest.asmx` File

```
 1: Imports System.Web.Services
 2: Public Class StateTest Inherits System.Web.Services.WebService
 3: Web Services Designer Generated Code
 4:     ' WEB SERVICE EXAMPLE
 5:     ' The HelloWorld() example service returns the string
➥ Hello World.
 6:     ' To build, uncomment the following lines then save and
➥ build the project.
 7:     ' To test this Web Service, ensure that the .asmx file is
➥ the start page
 8:     ' and press F5.
 9:     '
10:     '<WebMethod()> Public Function HelloWorld() As String
11:     '    HelloWorld = "Hello World"
12:     ' End Function
13:     <WebMethod(enableSession:=True)> Public Function StartTime()
➥ As String
14:         If Application("AppStart") = Nothing Then
15:             Application("AppStart") = Date.Now.ToLongTimeString
16:         End If
17:         If Session("SesStart") = Nothing Then
18:             Session("SesStart") = Date.Now.ToLongTimeString
19:         End If
20:         Return "This application was started at:"
➥ + Convert.ToString(Application("AppStart")) +_
21:     "; This Session was started at:" + Convert.ToString(Session("SesStart"))
22:     End Function
23: End Class
```

Lines 13–22 are what we need to look at. In line 13 we define a Web method `StartTime()` with the session state enabled. Between lines 14 and 19, the start time of the application and the session are stored to an application and a session variable respectively if the variables do not already contain the time.

In line 20, the information we stored in the variables is returned.

Call this Web Service using a browser and invoke the Web method. You will see the time the application and the session was started as shown in Figure 21.17. Notice that the first time you view this page, the application and session start time are the same.

21

FIGURE **21.17**

Result window.

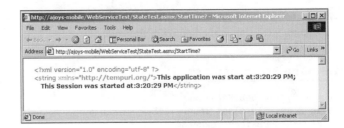

Summary

In this hour, you have been introduced to Web Services, a .NET technology that allows you to create programmable components that can be used by a wide range of applications including desktop applications, Web applications, and even another Web service. First, we talked about various pieces necessary to create and make the Web Service work. Next, we created a simple Web Service using Notepad. We accessed this Web Service from an .aspx page after creating a proxy and DLL from the Web Service .asmx file.

Later, we created another Web Service, this time using VS.NET, accessed the Pubs database, and returned a DataSet. We also saw how to use this Web Service from a .aspx file.

Finally, we saw how to use session and application objects in Web Services to maintain the state information of the user accessing the Web Service from an ASP.NET Application.

Q&A

Q. How do you import a Web Service using VS.NET?

A. Click Project and then click Add Web Reference. In the Add Web Reference window, either type the name of the Web Service file or click Web Reference on Local Web Server. Then select the Web Service and click Add Reference.

Q. Which property is used to enable the session state of a Web Service?

A. The EnableSession property of the WebMethod() attribute is used to enable the session state.

Workshop

The quiz questions are provided for your further understanding of the material.

Quiz

1. What keyword is necessary to expose a public function as a method of a Web Service?

2. What are the three different protocols used to access Web Service?

3. What class does a Web Service inherit?

4. What utility is used to compile the Web Service Proxy Class?

5. How do you view the WSDL contract for a Web Service using a browser?

Exercise

Spend some time understanding the different parameters for `wsdl.exe`. Create a Web Service that will accept information from the user in a text box, validate the information against a table in a database, and return the result of the validation.

Answers for Hour 21

Quiz

1. What keyword is necessary to expose a public function as a method of a Web Service?

   `WebMethod()`

2. What are the three different protocols used to access Web Service?

   SOAP, HTTP-GET, HTTP-POST

3. What class does a Web Service inherit?

   `System.Web.Services`

4. What utility is used to compile the Web Service Proxy Class?

   A compiler is used. For instance, if VB.NET is used to develop the Web Service, `VBC.exe` is used.

5. How do you view the WSDL contract for a Web Service using a browser?

   Using ?WSDL suffix in the URL. For instance, if the URL is `http://servername/applicationame/webservice1.asmx` then use `http://servername/applicationame/webservice1.asmx?WSDL` to get the contract.

21

HOUR 22

Configuration, Localization, and Deployment

In the last 20 hours or so, you learned how to build ASP.NET applications, how to access data using ADO.NET, and how to build and consume Web services. In this hour, you will learn about ASP.NET application configuration, localization, and deployment. The following topics will be covered in this hour:

- What a configuration file is
- Retrieving a configuration
- Setting culture and encoding
- Localizing ASP.NET applications
- Deploying ASP.NET applications

Configuration

There are lots of devices we use on a daily basis that need to be configured to our requirements—from the washer and dryer, which we configure the settings such as wash time, water temperature, and so on, to the universal remote, which we configure to work with the TV, VCR, and cable or satellite system. Similarly, there are plenty of computer systems and applications that require configuration to produce the results we expect. You could think of the configuring process as a customization technique to tune the system or server to meet the needs of your applications. This is true with Web applications—all the more so because we run plenty of applications from the same server that require different setups.

Those of us who worked in previous versions of ASP have made frequent trips to our servers to change settings such as Session Timeout, Script Timeout, and so on using the IIS Management Console. Although this provided a visual interface to the settings, there was a need for direct access to the server and the IIS MMC.

Then came the option of programmatically accessing these configurations, which are stored in the metabase, using ADSI (Active Directory Services Interface). However, this was kind of difficult to work with.

With ASP.NET, the need for a flexible configuration system is fulfilled. Applications can now be easily configured using a hierarchical configuration system.

ASP.NET uses a file-based configuration system. The configuration information is stored in XML format. This provides easy access to the configuration information with just a text editor such as Notepad to view the settings.

Because the information is stored in a file, it can be saved along with the application files. This simplifies the deployment and installation of ASP.NET applications.

What Is a Configuration File?

ASP.NET configuration files are text files that contain information in XML format. This information is stored in files named `machine.config` and `Web.config`. There can be any number of `Web.config` files stored under various directories in an ASP.NET application server. Each `Web.config` file applies settings to the resources in the directory it is located in and its child directories. The `Web.config` file in a child directory can either override or inherit settings from the `Web.config` file in its parent directory.

There is a root configuration file that provides configuration settings for the entire machine. Remember the settings in the `Web.config` file override the settings in the `machine.config` file.

The root configuration file (`machine.config`) is located at

`c:\winnt\Microsoft.net\framework\version\config\`

If you are using the .NET Framework Beta 2, the `machine.config` file is located at

`c:\winnt\Microsoft.Net\framework\v1.0.2914\config\`

Figure 22.1 shows a portion of the `machine.config` file viewed using Visual Studio.NET (VS.NET).

FIGURE 22.1

The `machine.config` file viewed using VS.NET.

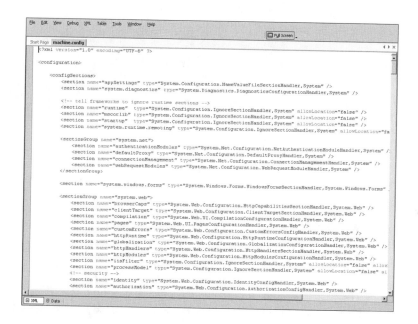

As mentioned earlier, there can be many `Web.config` files in various directories. Figure 22.2 shows a sample `Web.config` file viewed using VS.NET

ASP.NET uses a hierarchical configuration system. Here's what this means: Suppose you have a directory named `myapps` with two child directories: `app1` and `app2`. You also have a `Web.config` file in the `myapps` directory that allows access to all the users to view the resources under this directory.

Likewise, you have another `Web.config` file under the `app2` directory that allows access to only those users given permission to view the resources under this folder.

Therefore, if a user visited the `myapps` directory, that user would have access to all of the resources in that directory, excluding sub-directories. Resources in this case would be

.aspx files, .asmx files, etc. Furthermore, the user would have access to all of the resources under the app1 directory because the Web.config file was set up to allow access to all users. However, if the user was not explicitly given permission in the Web.config file under the app2 directory, they will not have access to any resources located in this directory.

FIGURE 22.2

The Web.config *file viewed using VS.NET.*

The changes to the configuration file are detected by ASP.NET and are applied to the resources affected by the changes. There is no need for restarting the service or server, as was the case in the past.

ASP.NET also caches the configuration settings for a resource when the resource is accessed for the first time. These settings are applied for the subsequent calls to the same resource.

Although the configuration file remains in the application folder, along with other resources, ASP.NET prevents access to these files from browser. If you try to access a configuration file, you will receive HTTP access error 403, with the message "This type of page is not served."

Now with an overview of the ASP.NET configuration system and configuration files, let's get into the details. As mentioned earlier, Web.config is a text file with configuration settings defined using XML tags.

The configuration file must be a well-formed XML file; therefore, the tags and attributes are case sensitive.

The Web.config file contains a root element called <configuration>. The following is an example:

```
<configuration>
    <!--Configuration settings goes here -- >
</configuration>
```

All configuration settings are defined within this XML tag and are placed into two groups. The first is the declaration group, which contains information between <configSections> and </configSections> XML tags. The second is the settings group, which contains information for every section defined in the declaration.

The machine.config file declares sections and settings that are applied for all the applications on the machine. Once a declaration is specified in the machine.config file, we do not have to make the same declaration again in the Web.config file. For instance, if the machine.config file contains a declaration for the <customErrors> section, the Web.config file could be used to provide detailed settings for this section, without the need for declaring this section again.

Let's take a closer look at the each of these two groups.

Declaration

The declaration section appears at the top of the Web.config file. Each declaration is defined using the <section> tag along with attributes to specify the name of a section that supplies the configuration data and the name of the corresponding .NET class that handles the configuration data.

The following example shows two section handlers defined within <configSections>:

```
<configSections>
<section name="authorization"
➥type="System.Web.Configuration.AuthorizationConfigHandler" />
    <section name="webServices"
➥type="System.Web.Services.Configuration.WebServicesConfigurationSectionHandler"
>
</configSections>
```

The first section handler, authorization, is being handled by System.Web. Configuration.AuthorizationConfigHandler, and the second section handler, webServices, is handled by System.Web.Services.Configuration. WebServicesConfigurationSectionHandler.

Different sections could be grouped together as a section group using the <sectionGroup> tag. The following is an example of a section group:

```
<sectionGroup name="groupExample">
    <section name="firstSection"
➥type="System.Configuration.NameValueSectionHandler">
    <section name="secondSection"
➥type="System.Configuration.NameValueSectionHandler">
</sectionGroup>
```

The following is an example of providing settings information for the section defined in the preceding section group:

```
<groupExample>
    <firstSection>
        <add key="firstKey" value="firstValue" />
    </firstSection>
    <secondSection>
        <add key="secondKey" value="secondValue" />
    </secondSection>
</groupExample>
```

Back in Figure 22.1, you will see a section group with the name system.net containing four sections.

A list of various configuration section handlers provided by ASP.NET can be found under the .NET Framework SDK documentation.

There is also a section to supply application-specific configuration settings:

```
<appSettings>:
```

This section is used to add application-specific configurations such as data source name, file paths, and any other key/value pairs.

The following is an example of the appSettings section:

```
    <appSettings>
        <add key="MyKey" value="SomeValue" />
    </appSettings>
```

The configuration settings you provide with the Web.config file applies to the directory in which the file is located and its child directories. However, by using the <location> tag within the Web.config file, you can specify settings for specific folders.

For example, here we have an application root folder called myapps with two folders underneath it—app1 and app2—and a configuration file:

22

```
web.config: <configuration>
  <system.web>
    <customErrors mode="remoteOnly" defaultRedirect="myErrorPage.aspx" />
  </system.web>
 <location path="app1">
  <system.web>
    <customErrors mode="remoteOnly" defaultRedirect="app1ErrorPage.aspx" />
  </system.web>
 </location>
 <location path="app2">
<system.web>
    <customErrors mode="remoteOnly" defaultRedirect="app2ErrorPage.aspx" />
</system.web>
 </location>
</configuration>
```

In this configuration file, we have specified three different <customErrors> sections within the same Web.config file.

In general, the <customErrors> section is used to provide a custom error page that the user will be redirected to when an error occurs in the application. As shown in the preceding code, the URL for the custom error page is specified using the defaultRedirect attribute.

The first <customErrors> section, with a URL of myErrorPage.aspx, is applied to the resources and directories under the myapps folder.

The second <customErrors> section, with a URL of app1ErrorPage.aspx, is applied to the resources and directories under app1. This is made possible by using the location tag, which allows us to specify a subfolder path. The settings defined within this location tag will only apply to the resources under that path. Similarly, the third <customErrors> section, with a URL of app2ErrorPage.aspx, applies only to resources and directories under the app2 folder.

Settings

Each of the section handlers defined in <configSections> will be supplied with settings. The settings can be provided either at the machine level, using the machine.config file, or at the application level, using the Web.config file. The following example shows the <authorization> section supplied with settings:

```
<authorization>
    <allow users="*" /> <!--Allow all users -- >
</authorization>
```

Within the <authorization> section, we have defined an <allow> tag with one attribute, users, and a value of *. The <authorization> module checks the values in the <allow> tag before allowing access to the resource required by the user. Similarly, there is a

<deny> tag that we can define within this section to provide the names of the users we want to deny access to.

Note that for every section defined in the settings group, there is a need for a declaration. Also, you can declare the sections in the machine.config file and then supply the settings in the Web.config files. You do not have to declare the sections again in the Web.config files if this has already been done in the machine.config file.

Retrieving a Configuration

Now that you know how to store settings in the configuration file Web.config, it is time to talk about retrieving the settings from the configuration files.

To retrieve the configuration information, we will be using the ConfigurationSetting class under the System.Configuration namespace. As mentioned earlier, the AppSettings section is used to add application configurations. Let's look at how to retrieve the configuration stored in this section to use it in our application. Here are the steps to follow:

1. Create a new project from VS.NET and name it ConfigApplication.

2. Add the following AppSettings section between the <configuration> and </configuration> tags, as shown here:

```
<configuration>
  <appSettings>
    <add key="MyKey1" value="MyValue1" />
    <add key="MyKey2" value="MyValue2" />
  </appSettings>
</configuration>
```

3. Rename the webForm1.aspx as RetrieveConfig.aspx.

Now let's build an ASPX page to retrieve the values of the keys from the AppSettings section:

```
1: <%@ Page Language="vb" AutoEventWireup="false"
➥Codebehind="retrieveconfigRetrieveConfig.aspx.vb"
➥Inherits="ConfigApplication.WebForm1"%>
3: <HTML>
4:   <HEAD>
5:     <meta name="GENERATOR" content="Microsoft Visual Studio.NET 7.0">
6:     <meta name="CODE_LANGUAGE" content="Visual Basic 7.0">
7:     <meta name=vs_defaultClientScript content="JavaScript">
8:     <meta name=vs_targetSchema content="Internet Explorer 5.0">
9:     <script language="vb" runat="server">
10:        sub retrieveConfig(Src as Object, E as EventArgs)
11:            dim firstkey as string =
➥ConfigurationSettings.AppSettings("MyKey1")
12:            dim secondkey as string =
```

```
➥configurationSettings.AppSettings("MyKey2")
13:            Key1.InnerText = firstkey
14:            Key2.InnerText = secondkey
18:        end sub
19:    </script>
20: </HEAD>
21: <body MS_POSITIONING="GridLayout">
22:    <form id="WebForm1" method="post" runat="server">
23:      <asp:Button id=Button1 runat="server" Text="Retrieve"
➥OnClick="retrieveConfig"></asp:Button><br />
24:      <asp:Label id=Label1 runat="server">Key1</asp:Label>
25:      <h5 id="Key1" runat="server"></h5><br />
26:      <asp:Label id="Label3" runat="server">Key2</asp:Label>
27:      <h5 id="Key2" runat="server"></h5><br />
28:    </form>
29: </body>
30:</HTML>
```

In the preceding code, lines 10–18 and lines 22–28 are of interest to us. Between lines 10–18, we define a function that is called when the button defined in line 23 is clicked. In lines 11 and 12, we define two variables to store the values retrieved from the configuration file. These two variables are set to the values defined in the AppSettings section using the AppSettings method of the ConfigurationSettings class. The key name is passed to this method as the argument to get the value for the key specified in the Web.config file.

In lines 13 and 14, we display these two variables using the InnerText property of the <h5> elements defined in lines 25 and 27.

Figure 22.3 shows what this ASPX file looks like when viewed in a browser.

FIGURE 22.3

RetrieveConfig.aspx *viewed in browser.*

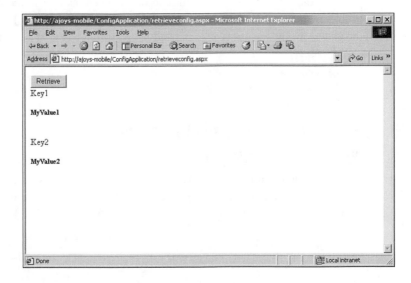

To retrieve the settings from other sections of the configuration file, you can use the GetConfig method of the ConfigurationSetting class, as shown here:

```
ConfigurationSettings.GetConfig(sectionname)
```

Working in Other Languages

Localization is the process of making your application work with languages other than the language it was developed in originally. There are two parts to building applications that work in different languages. The first part is to internationalize the application for use in different languages, and the second part is to localize the globalized application for use in a particular language. In this section, you will learn about the internationalization and localization processes.

Internationalization Overview

Internationalization is the process of making your application work in multiple locales.

New Term   A *locale* provides preference information about language, environment, and cultural conventions. The values to these preferences are used by the operating system to identify the input language, the keyboard layout, and the format of numbers, dates, and time. Windows 2000 supports 126 locales, and the users from the countries whose locales are supported can select the appropriate locale for the correct display of characters, time, dates, and numbers.

The process of internationalization starts with identifying the languages you want to support for your application. The configuration file contains a section for settings pertaining to internationalization under the <globalization> section. The following example shows the values for the requestEncoding and responseEncoding attributes set to "utf-8":

```
<globalization
    requestEncoding="utf-8"
    responseEncoding="utf-8"
/>
```

Setting Culture and Encoding

Just what is requestEncoding and responseEncoding?

In order to answer this question, it is necessary to discuss how strings are handled in ASP.NET applications. In an ASP.NET application, all strings are handled as Unicode values.

NEW TERM   *Unicode* is a fixed-width, 16-bit, worldwide character encoding that represents the characters used in text interchange across the world. It was developed by the Unicode Consortium—a nonprofit computer-industry organization.

Unicode allows for characters found outside of the normal 26-letter alphabet in English and also includes Kanji characters and Arabic characters among others. In order for the appropriate characters to be displayed on the page, it is necessary to encode all strings for the appropriate culture or language. That way, when the string is rendered, it will appear in the appropriate character set specified in the `requestEncoding` and `responseEncoding` fields.

ASP.NET encodes the response data and the request data, based on the values specified for `responseEncoding` and `requestEncoding`, respectively. The values for these attributes are set in either the `Web.config` file or the `machine.config` file.

The `<globalization>` section in the configuration file can be used to set the culture information, as shown here:

```
<globalization culture="en-us"/>
```

Note that settings for `responseEncoding`, `requestEncoding`, and `CultureInfo` can also be set in the page directive, in which case the settings will only apply to the specific page. For instance, the following page directive sets the culture to English, United Kingdom (en-GB) and the response and request encoding to "utf-8":

```
<%@Page Culture="en-GB" ResponseEncoding="utf-8" RequestEncoding="utf-8"%>
```

The `System.Globalization` namespace contains classes such as `Calendar`, `CultureInfo`, `DateTimeFormatInfo` for representing information about the language for a specific culture and the format for displaying the date, time, and so on. The `CultureInfo` class can be used to retrieve or specify the culture settings.

Localizing ASP.NET Applications

Localization is the process of using a global application in a particular locale. This is achieved by supplying the culture information to the application. Specifying a value for the culture either in the configuration file or the page directive will localize either the whole application or the specific page.

Working with Resource Files

A *resource* is data, such as a welcome message or an error message that is used by the application. This resource can be stored separate from your application in what is called a resource file. A resource file is a repository for locale or culture-specific messages that can be used in your application. By using resource files, you can isolate information and messages specific to a particular locale or culture and display that locale-specific information to a client that has the locale settings that match your resource file. For example, an error message can be stored in a resource file in multiple languages and based on the user's locale setting, the application will display the error message in the appropriate language.

The .NET Framework provides classes such as `ResourceManager`, `ResourceWriter`, and `ResourceReader` to work with resources in an application.

A resource file can be created using a text editor such as Notepad. ASP.NET provides a resource file generator (`Resgen.exe`) that can be used to convert a file created using a text editor into a `.resource` file.

Deploying ASP.NET Applications

Deploying ASP.NET applications is as simple as copying files over to local or remote services using XCOPY or FTP. ASP.NET applications running in IIS will be stored in a physical directory located in a local or remote server.

The deployment of ASP.NET applications does not require Registry entries because ASP.NET looks for components in the `bin` directory under the application root directory. As you saw in the previous hour, when you're building a Web service, the DLL file for the Web service is created in the `bin` folder.

ASP.NET uses shadow copies of the assemblies, so there's no need to stop an application before copying the new version.

Summary

In this hour, you learned about configuring ASP.NET applications using `machine.config` and `Web.config` files. This hour introduced you to the various sections of the configuration file and how to use these sections to configure your application.

You were also introduced to the localization and internationalization of ASP.NET applications using the `<globalization>` section and the `System.Globalization` namespace.

Finally, this hour covered deploying ASP.NET applications and how the .NET Framework simplifies the deployment process.

Q&A

Q. How do I apply settings for a specific folder in the configuration file?

A. Use the `<location>` tag to specify the folder name to which the settings will be applied.

Q. Which class do I use to retrieve culture settings?

A. Use the `CultureInfo` class provided by the `System.Globalization` namespace.

Workshop

The quiz questions and exercises are provided for your further understanding of the material.

Quiz

1. What are the two files that contain configuration information for ASP.NET applications?

2. What is the root element of a configuration file?

3. How do you specify application-specific settings in the configuration file?

4. Which namespace provides classes pertaining to internationalization?

Exercise

1. Review the various configuration section handlers provided by ASP.NET. Create an application and modify the settings in different sections, such as `<sessionState>`, `<customErrors>`, and `<authentication>`, in the `Web.config` file for this application. Call an ASPX page from this application to see how your changes work.

Answers for Hour 22

Quiz

1. What are the two files that contain configuration information for ASP.NET applications?

   The two files that contain configuration information are `machine.config` and `Web.config`.

2. What is the root element of a configuration file?

   The root element is called `<configuration>`.

3. How do you specify application-specific settings in the configuration file?

   In the `<appSettings>` section of the configuration file.

4. Which namespace provides classes pertaining to internationalization?

   `System.Globalization`

Hour 23

Optimizing and Profiling ASP.NET Applications

Now that you're an ASP.NET expert, it's time to discuss some of the optimization features built in to the .NET Framework, as well as a few techniques you can use to evaluate and analyze the performance of your ASP.NET application. However, this hour is optional because of the advanced level of the topic itself and the fact that you, the reader, are expected to have a certain level of experience with ASP programming as well as broad application development. If you feel uncomfortable with the technical level of the content in this hour, feel free to skip this hour and move on to Hour 24, "Web Workshop." In this hour, we will cover the following topics:

- Garbage collection and other optimization features of the .NET Framework
- Important considerations for high-performance ASP.NET applications
- Using the Performance Counter component
- Using Performance Monitor and various performance counters to profile ASP.NET applications

Optimizing ASP.NET Applications

Already plagued by slow connections, the last thing today's Web applications need is further performance degrades caused by bad code in the applications themselves. Furthermore, the dynamic nature of ASP.NET applications can easily cause performance issues that can go undetected. Therefore, it is extremely important for developers to design and develop their applications with performance and scalability in mind. We'll start by taking a closer look at some of the features built in to the .NET Framework that enable well-designed and implemented ASP.NET applications to perform in an efficient and robust manner.

Optimization Features of the .NET Framework

Taking advantage of the .NET Framework, ASP.NET enjoys many enhancements and optimizations under the hood. Some of these require no extra effort on the programmer's part to implement, whereas others require the developer to have a little more understanding of the concepts. In the next few paragraphs, we will discuss some of the highlights of the .NET Framework's built-in optimization features.

Enhanced Code Execution

With the advent of the .NET Framework and the Common Language Runtime (CLR), source code is compiled into Intermediate Language (IL) and then into native code the first time the application is executed. Native code is also known as *binary code* and is specific to a hardware platform, such as the *x*86 family of processors found in most PCs. When source code becomes native code, it is cached and ready for execution for subsequent requests, resulting in fast, efficient execution. This alone improves the overall performance of ASP.NET pages when compared to the way regular ASP pages are executed. ASP pages are interpreted by the ASP runtime (asp.dll), a process in which little code optimization occurs.

Garbage Collection

Garbage collection is another shining feature of the .NET Framework. Simply stated, garbage collection relinquishes memory space previously allocated for use by objects that are no longer active. The best part about garbage collection is that it is almost completely automatic and requires next to no intervention from the programmer. The CLR keeps track of the memory allocated to objects, such as variables defined in an application. Upon determining that an object has no references pointing to it by the application, the CLR will go ahead and clear the memory reserved by that object. This relieves you from having to write code to take care of so-called housekeeping chores. You can also invoke the garbage collector manually by calling the GC.Collect method.

High-Performance ASP.NET Applications

As mentioned earlier, you cannot rely on ASP.NET and the .NET Framework alone for performance enhancements and optimizations. Although the .NET Framework does offer significant advantages over the ASP, it is ultimately up to you to write code intended to leverage the new features. After all, it is the programmer who writes the application and therefore is responsible for ensuring its performance integrity. In this section, we'll take a more in-depth look at some important considerations to keep in mind as well as useful tips and techniques for developing high-performance ASP.NET applications.

Caching in ASP.NET

The true beauty of today's Web applications lies in their flexibility and dynamic nature, in that the output of a page can be determined at runtime. Long gone are the days when most Web applications consisted of plain, stagnant HTML pages. Nevertheless, there is a small price to pay for this great feature—the performance of the Web application, another all too critical factor. Even though ASP.NET pages are compiled, many operations in the pages can consume a good chunk of server resources. Fortunately, ASP.NET has a caching feature. Caching ASP.NET pages alleviates some of the load on the Web server and allows the cached files to be served more efficiently. In this section, we are going to examine various caching features of ASP.NET and possible situations in which their use would be appropriate.

Output Caching

ASP.NET has essentially two types of caching: output caching (also known as *page caching*), which debuted in ASP.NET, and the more classical caching method, called *application caching* or *data caching*. We'll start by examining output caching.

As implied by its name, output caching allows dynamic ASP.NET pages to be stored (or *cached*) in a special location on the server and served directly to the client using very few resources. Output caching keeps the targeted page in cache and enables you to specify the duration desired for a page to remain cached as a specific time, such as 10:00 A.M., or as a relative time, such as 15 minutes since the last page request. This is ideal for situations in which the data on the page is not going to be subject to much change within a specified time range. For example, suppose that breaking news has just occurred and people rush to an Internet news site that is running on ASP.NET. This sudden surge in traffic is further complicated by users continually refreshing the page for up-to-the-minute information. The news site's performance can be significantly improved by via caching. For example, the main news page can be cached for a number of minutes, in which case the server would be able to handle more users because cached pages consume much less resources, just as if the pages were HTML.

It only takes one line at the top of an ASPX page to specify the time for a page to be cached. For instance, if you wanted to cache a particular ASPX page for 10 minutes, you would use the @OutputCache directive, as shown here:

```
<%@OutputCache Duration="600" VaryByParam = "none"%>
```

 Note that the actual time is specified in seconds, not minutes.

You can also set the absolute expiration on a page at runtime by using Response.Expires. The correct syntax for using the OutputCache directive is as follows:

```
<%@outputCache Duration="#ofseconds" Location="Any| Client | Downstream |
Server |None VaryByControl="controlname" VaryByCustom="browser | customstring"
VaryByHeader="headers" VaryByParam="parametername" %>
```

As you can see, Duration is just one of several attributes of the OutputCache directive. Table 23.1 lists all its attributes.

TABLE 23.1 Attributes of the OutputCache Directive

Attribute	Description
Duration	Number of seconds the page or user control is cached. Setting this attribute on a page or user control sets an expiration policy for the object and caches the page or user control for output. This is a required attribute.
Location	Defines the physical location of the cached data.
VaryByCustom	Defines custom output caching requirements.
VaryByHeader	Varies the output cache by the specified HTTP header(s).
VaryByParam	Varies the output cache by the specified string, which by default is the value(s) of a query string or the result of a form POST. This is a required parameter and carries the default value "none".
VaryByControl	Varies the output cache based on a property of a specific user control.

Application/Data Caching

Caching can also be used in ASP.NET to share objects and/or data among several pages by storing key/value pairs in much the same manner as the Session and Application objects, as discussed earlier in this book. However, data caching using the Cache object in ASP.NET has more to offer. It adds functionality such as automatic expiration and support for dependencies and callbacks. Although discussing these added features in any depth would quickly go beyond the scope of this hour, we will try to at least give you a basic understanding of them. A dependency is stored along with a cached object or piece of data. When the dependency data undergoes any change, the cached data will then be removed completely from memory. The dependency is typically a file, a cached key, or a specific point in time. Automatic expiration simply removes the cached object from memory if the object has no dependencies. Finally, all cached data will be reset when the application is restarted.

Now that you have an overview of data caching in ASP.NET, let's look at a few small examples and code snippets to better illustrate the correct use of the Cache object.

Let's say you want to store a connection string for database access. You can assign the connection string to the Cache object, as shown here:

```
Cache("ConnectionString") =
"server=localhost;uid=sa;pwd=;database=pubs"
```

However, to take advantage of the expiration, scavenging, and dependency support offered by the Cache object, you must use either Cache.Add or Cache.Insert. These methods are almost identical, except that Add returns an object representing the actual cached item. For instance, to save a database connection string in the Cache object using the Add method, you can make a slight change to the previous line of code to read as follows:

```
Cache.Add ("ConnectionString") =
"server=localhost;uid=sa;pwd=;database=pubs"
```

The Insert method allows you to define values for expiration and dependencies for the cached data.

If you decide to remove the connection string from the Cache object, you can simply call the Remove method of the Cache object, as shown here:

```
Cache.Remove("ConnectionString")
```

ASP.NET caching is indeed powerful; however, discussing it in its entirety would quickly go beyond the scope of this hour. For further information regarding ASP.NET caching, refer to the MSDN documentation.

Tips and Techniques for High-Performance ASP.NET Applications

A Web application is only as efficient as it is designed to be. ASP.NET does offer many new and exciting features, but appropriate use of these features is indispensable to overall performance. In this section, we will discuss recommended practices as well as more specific tips and techniques for getting the most out of your ASP.NET applications.

Judicious Use of ASP.NET Server-Side Controls

Without a doubt, the use of ASP.NET Web forms is one of the greatest features of ASP.NET. Without validation controls, for instance, the tedious task of state management and validation is much more time consuming. Just make sure you have a good reason for using the ASP.NET server-side controls and understand their benefits and shortcomings. Keep in mind that although server controls have a clear advantage over their HTML counterparts when it comes to features and programmer productivity, they require more resources and are not quite as fast as client-side HTML controls. Don't completely replace HTML controls with ASP.NET controls for the sake of full conversion to ASP.NET. It is perfectly legitimate to have HTML controls if, for example, you are simply displaying some data on the screen.

Session State

First, ask yourself whether the ASP.NET page you are developing needs to use session states. If the page is relatively simple and does not need to keep state across several pages, disable session state for that page. Despite its convenience, session state consumes extra server resources and is best turned off when it is not being used. You can use the `SessionState` attribute of the page directive to disable session state, as shown here:

```
<%@ Page EnableSessionState="false" %>
```

The preceding code applies only to the page itself and not to the rest of the ASP.NET Web application, which can consist of numerous pages. If session state is not going to be used anywhere in the application, disable it at the application scope level by setting the mode of the `<sessionstate>` tag to `"off"` in the `Web.config` file, as shown in the following line:

```
<sessionstate mode="off" />
```

If a single ASP.NET page requires access to session variables defined in other pages and will not create or modify any of the session variables, set the `EnableSessionState` attribute of the page directive to `ReadOnly`.

Finally, `Session` and `Application` objects can have performance drawbacks when large pieces of data are stored in them. Try to keep the size of the data in those objects to a bare minimum and remember that using databases, `Session` objects, and `Application` objects are not the only methods for keeping state information. Four other prominent methods can be used for state management, as listed in Table 23.2 (along with ideal situations for their use). These methods rely on saving the state information on the client side. Refer to the MSDN documentation for a more in-depth look at each of the listed methods.

TABLE 23.2   State Management Methods

Method	Ideal Use
Cookies	When you need to store small bits of data on the client and security is not an issue.
Hidden fields	When you need to store small amounts of information for a page that will post back to itself or another page. Keep in mind that a page would have to be submitted for a hidden field to be accessible.
Query string	When you need to pass small bits of information from one page to another and security is not much of an issue. This is often used when linking to another page.
ViewState	When a page will post back to itself. This Boolean field can be altered by changing the maintainState attribute of the target control.

Early Binding

Another great feature of ASP.NET is support for type-safe code written in programming languages such as VB.NET and C#. This offers significant performance advantages when compared to the typeless code produced by VBScript in ASP, where all variables are 32-bit variants. For instance, you can just define a variable without specifying the type of the variable, as follows:

```
Dim x
x = "Hello World"
x = 4
```

As you can see, the variable x has not been defined with a specific type, and it can accept anything from an integer to a string. Late binding requires more overhead time and is more resource intensive than early binding, which occurs when variables are defined with a specific type, as in the following variable declaration:

```
Dim x as String
```

It is strongly recommended that you always specify a type for your variables. However, for compatibility purposes, ASP.NET still supports typeless code for VB and JScript.NET. If your application does not contain migrated code from ASP and all variables in your code are of a particular type, it is a good idea to disable support for the typeless code by including the Strict compiler directive at the top of your ASP.NET page, as shown here:

```
<%@ Page Language="VB" Strict="true" %>
```

Data Access

As you are aware by now, ADO.NET has introduced a number of new classes and methods packed with new functionality and performance enhancements. You must know how to evaluate the scenario and choose the data-access method best suited to use for that scenario. For example, there is no need to instantiate a `DataSet` class and populate it with data if all you need to do with the data is display it on a Web page. In that case, you can use the `SqlDataReader` class, which offers fast performance and is ideal for situations where you need only fast forward access to the SQL Server data to display in a table.

Finally, as a general rule, use SQL stored procedures residing on the database server for operations that contain complex queries. Stored procedures generally perform better than ad-hoc queries, especially when the queries are larger and more complex because they are compiled and ready for execution on the server. Furthermore, stored procedures allow data manipulation logic to be encapsulated and shared by all client applications.

Value Types

There are basically two kinds of types in the CLR: reference types and value types. *Reference types* simply hold the location of the actual data, whereas *value types* contain the very bits of the data itself in memory. For small and primitive data, such as integers, it is recommended that you use value types because they reside on the stack and offer better performance. Another point to keep in mind is that value types, by default, are always initiated to zero and derived from the .NET Framework namespace `System.ValueType`, by means of which you can define your own value types. Finally, declare variable types appropriately. For instance, do not declare a variable of type Double if all you need is for the variable to be able to hold integer values. The larger variable types, such as Double, consume more system resources.

Monitoring and Profiling ASP.NET Applications

No application can be considered complete without thorough testing. It is not unusual to catch memory leaks or other sources of bottlenecks that hinder performance when the application is subject to strenuous testing. Many of these problems could go undetected without application profiling. In Hour 14, "Debugging Your ASP.NET Applications," you learned about debugging and tracing your ASP.NET application. In this section, you will learn the basics of profiling and monitoring your ASP.NET applications.

ASP.NET Runtime Profiling

Profiling is essentially the process of collecting information pertaining to your target application's performance. For the purposes of this hour, we are going to talk primarily about using .NET performance counters and Windows NT/2000 System Monitor to profile our ASP.NET applications, because the two go hand in hand.

Performance Counters

The metric for the collection of performance data is known as the *performance counter* and is made to allow for real-time examination of a target application. Numerous counters are available depending on the number of applications and/or services installed on the machine. Each counter is specific to an area of system functionality and is stored in the Windows Registry. There is a set of counters—for such things as memory usage, processor's busy time, and the number of processes currently being handled by the operating system—that is standard on all Windows NT/2000 machines. These counters are not application specific.

As you might have guessed, the ASP.NET and the .NET Framework have their share of counters. Not only does the .NET Framework have many new performance counters, but it also allows you to construct your own performance counters to address specific areas of your target application.

ASP.NET supports two classes of performance counters: application and system. The application counters can be seen in Windows NT/2000 System Monitor as ASP.NET Applications, whereas the system counters are seen as ASP.NET System. We'll take a quick look at the Windows NT/2000 System Monitor later in this hour. First, let's have a look at some of the ASP.NET application performance counters. These counters are intended to be used to monitor the performance of a single ASP.NET application. If there are no ASP.NET applications running on your machine at the time you use these counters, all the counters with "Total" in the middle of their titles would show 0, indicating that no ASP.NET applications are currently active.

ASP.NET Application Performance Counters

ASP.NET performance counters are dependent on an instance of an application. Therefore, different ASP.NET applications can have their own instances of the performance counters. Table 23.3 lists some of the ASP.NET application counters (there are too many to display in this hour). Refer to the Microsoft MSDN documentation for a complete list of all the performance counters.

23

TABLE 23.3 ASP.NET Application Performance Counters

Performance Counter	Description
Anonymous Requests	Number of requests with anonymous authentication.
Cache Total Hits	Total number of hits from the cache. This counter includes both internal use of the cache by the ASP.NET Framework and external use of the cache through exposed APIs.
Errors Total/Sec	Total number of errors per second that occurred during the execution of requests.
Output Cache Hits	The total number of requests serviced from the output cache.
Requests Executing	Number of requests currently executing.
Requests Failed	Total number of failed requests for any reason.
Requests Not Found	Number of requests that failed because the requested resource was not found.
Requests Succeeded	Number of requests executed successfully.
Requests Total	Total number of requests since Internet Information Services (IIS) was last started.
Requests/Sec	Number of requests executed per second.
Sessions Active	Number of sessions currently active.
Transactions Aborted	Number of transactions aborted.
Transactions Committed	Number of transactions committed.
Transactions/Sec	Number of transactions started per second.

ASP.NET System Performance Counters

Table 23.4 lists all the performance counters in the ASP.NET System group.

TABLE 23.4 Performance Counters in the ASP.NET System Group

Performance Counter	Description
Application Restarts	Total number of times an ASP.NET application has been restarted during the Web server's lifetime since the last time Internet Information Services (IIS) has been restarted.
Application Running	Total number of ASP.NET applications currently running on the server.
Requests Disconnected	Number of disconnected or failed requests due to a communication failure.
Requests Queued	Number of requests waiting to receive service from the queue.

TABLE 23.4   continued

Performance Counter	Description
Request Wait Time	Amount of time, in milliseconds, spent waiting by the most recent request to receive service.
State Server Sessions Abandoned	Number of sessions that have been explicitly abandoned and are no longer active. These are typically sessions ended by specific user actions, such as closing the browser or navigating to another site.
State Server Sessions Active	Total number of currently active user sessions.
State Server Sessions Timed Out	Total number of user sessions that have become inactive due to user inactivity after a specific amount of time.
State Server Sessions Total	Total number of sessions created during the lifecycle of the ASP.NET application, including State Server Sessions Active, State Server Sessions Abandoned, and State Server Sessions Timed Out.
Worker Process Restarts	Total number of times a worker process has been restarted on the server.
Worker Process Running	Total number of worker processes running on the server.

Using Windows NT/2000 System Monitor

System Monitor can measure the performance of the machine it is running on by collecting and reporting detailed performance data in real time. Think of it as measuring the heartbeat of your target application to monitor its health. As mentioned earlier, performance counters are used as metrics of information collection. Windows 2000 System Monitor is the successor of the Performance Monitor in Windows NT. System Monitor does have some added functionality, but for the most part the two share the same set of functions when it comes to displaying a graphical representation of the performance counters. Also, System Monitor allows you to configure logs to record performance data and set system alerts to notify you when a specified counter's value is above or below a defined threshold.

System Monitor is located in Administrative Tools under Performance. You can also access it by typing **perfmon.msc** at the command prompt. After it's started, simply click the icon with the plus sign to add a performance counter. A new dialog box will pop up asking you to specify a performance counter. Select ASP.NET Application as the performance object. Also select the particular instance of the application you want to inspect or click the All Instances radio button if you decide to inspect all instances of your application. Finally, add the following performance counters, as shown in Figure 23.1:

- Sessions Total
- Sessions Active
- Requests/Sec
- Requests Executing

FIGURE 23.1

Performance counter types.

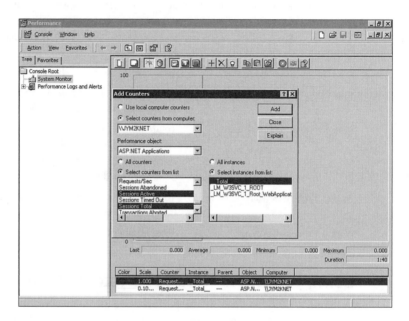

System Monitor will build a graph representing the selected performance counters in real time. You can add as many performance counters as you want. As shown in Figure 23.2, looking at the graph in real time reveals a great deal about the health of the application. Bottlenecks are quite evident if you look at the right performance counters. For extra detail, you can use the reports from tracing in conjunction with the graphs generated by System Monitor. Several other more advanced tools are available from Microsoft and third-party vendors. These tools—such as the Web Application Stress (WAS) tool, available for free at http://homer.rte.microsoft.com, and Microsoft Application Center 2000—are designed to help monitor the performance of your Web application.

FIGURE 23.2

The graph created by System Monitor.

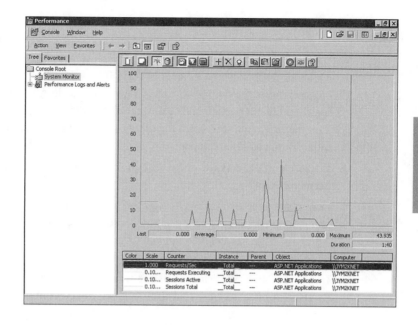

23

Summary

We certainly covered quite a bit of material in this hour. We started by discussing some of the performance-enhancing features already built in to the .NET Framework, such as the CLR and some of the services it offers. We then moved on to talk about more low-level and ASP.NET-specific tips and techniques for developing high-performance ASP.NET applications. We talked about ASP.NET caching and briefly discussed good practices for session management and data access. This alone is a huge topic all by itself, and a more in-depth discussion of it would take several chapters, if not an entire book. We then shifted gears and talked about performance counters in ASP.NET and how you can measure the pulse of your application with the help of the performance counters and Windows System Monitor.

Q&A

Q. What are the benefits of compiled ASP.NET pages?

A. An under-the-hood enhancement of ASP.NET is the fact that pages are compiled as opposed to interpreted in real time, as was the case in ASP. This makes possible some significant performance gains because native code generated by the CLR after the first request is saved for use by subsequent calls until the ASP.NET application is unloaded or stopped.

Q. What are the two types of caching in ASP.NET and what is the difference between them?

A. Output caching, also known as *page caching*, and data caching, also known as *application caching*. Output caching is used to cache the output of a dynamic ASP.NET page for a certain amount of time, whereas data caching is used to hold bits of data, much like the Session object.

Q. If my ASP.NET application spans several servers, can I use one instance of the System Monitor to view real-time performance counter information from all servers?

A. Absolutely. In System Monitor, you can select various performance counters and view the data generated by them for virtually all the servers in your network.

Workshop

The quiz questions are provided for your further understanding of the material.

Quiz

1. What method do you have to use in order to manually invoke the garbage collector?

2. Which performance counter would you have to monitor in order to view the total number of active sessions?

3. True or false? You should always disable session state in a page if you know the page is not going to be using any data from Session objects.

Exercise

Create a new ASP.NET page that, among other things, displays some data from the Pubs database via a DataGrid control. Enable output caching in that page for 10 minutes (600 seconds). Change the value of a few elements of the queried data in the Pubs database and reload the page. (Note that the content of the page remains unchanged even though the underlying data in the database has been changed.)

Answers for Hour 23

Quiz

1. What method do you have to use in order to manually invoke the garbage collector?

   To manually invoke the garbage collector, use the `GC.Collect` method.

2. Which performance counter would you have to monitor in order to view the total number of active sessions?

   To view the total number of active sessions, use the "Sessions Active" performance counter found in the ASP.NET Application group.

3. True or false? You should always disable session state in a page if you know the page is not going to be using any data from `Session` objects.

   True. You should always disable session state in a page if you know the page is not going to be using any data from `Session` objects because disabling session state does yield better overall performance.

Hour **24**

Web Workshop

We've spent the past 23 hours going over the basics of ASP.NET Web application development. In this hour (or more), we'll create a Web application that incorporates many of the topics that were covered earlier. The application we're going to develop covers the following topics:

- HTML server controls
- ASP server controls
- Tracing
- Database programming with OleDB
- User server controls
- Data binding
- Structured exception handling

The Idea

We are going to create a simple Web contest site. The name of our site will be TakeAChance.com. Because of the length of the application's code, the source code included in this chapter has been abbreviated; you can find the full source code for the application on the book's Web site at www.samspublishing.com.

Let's outline the features of our application:

The home page (see Figure 24.1) will be a login page, with a navigation menu on the left. The navigation menu will have a few extra options if the current user is an administrator—we'll cover this a little later.

FIGURE 24.1

Home page for TakeAChance.com showing all available menu options.

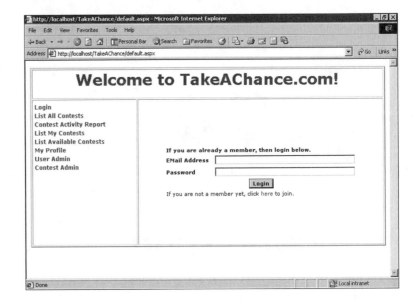

The login page will have a field for the user's e-mail address and password, and a button to submit the information for validation. There will be a hyperlink for new users to create an account in the system as well. The user's e-mail address will serve as the unique ID for each user in our database.

The navigation menu will appear only on the home page; any other pages will have a hyperlink to return them to the home page. The basic options in the navigation menu are available to all users even if they have not yet logged in:

- Login displays the home page with the login fields.
- List All Contests shows a form that lists all contests that are currently in the system.
- Contest Activity Report displays a form that summarizes each contest with the number of users who have joined it, the dates that the contest is active, and the winner of the contest if one has been chosen.

The standard menu options are available to users who have registered in the system:

- List My Contests displays a form listing the contests that the current user has joined.
- List Available Contests displays a form listing the contests that the current user has not yet joined. This form will have a hyperlink to each contest that will allow the current user to join that contest.
- My Profile shows the user-profile information for the current user.

The administrative options are available to those users who are designated as administrators in the system. This setting will be available on the user information form, which we will get to later.

- User Admin displays a form that has a list of users on the left, and user profile information on the right. The fields for the user information will be populated when the administrator selects a user from the list on the left.
- Contest Admin displays a form that has a list of contests on the left and contest information on the right. The fields for the contest information will be populated when the user selects a contest from the list on the left.

Table 24.1 describes the Web form pages and user controls for this application.

TABLE 24.1 Web Form Pages and Code-Behind Files for the Contest Application

Form/Control File	CodeBehind File	Description
listcontests.aspx	listcontests.aspx.vb	Lists all contests in the database
contestactivity.aspx	contestactivity.aspx.vb	List contests with number of users registered, contest prize, and winner if available
listmycontests.aspx	listmycontests.aspx.vb	List contests that currently logged-in user has registered for
listavailablecontests.aspx	listavailablecontests.aspx.vb	List contests that currently logged-in user has not registered for yet
join.aspx	join.aspx.vb	Gather user profile information and register user as a new user in the database
myuserprofile.aspx	myuserprofile.aspx	Display user profile information for the currently logged-in user

24

TABLE 24.1 continued

Form/Control File	CodeBehind File	Description
useradmin.aspx	useradmin.aspx.vb	Allow administrators to view and modify user profile information for users in the database
contestadmin.aspx	contestadmin.aspx.vb	Allow administrators to create, view, and modify contest information
userinfo.ascx	userinfo.ascx.vb	User server control to display and update user profile information
contestinfo.ascx	contestinfo.ascx.vb	User server control to display and modify contest information
contestlist.ascx	contestlist.ascx.vb	User server control to display a list of contests

This Web site is as plain (and maybe slightly boring!) as they get, but our goal for this hour is to demonstrate the architecture of a Web application. User interface design is a totally separate area.

The Home Page

The default.aspx home page uses a set of compound HTML tables to implement the menu and the login form.

ASP.NET LinkButton controls are used for the menu. The administrative and standard menu options are managed by setting the Visible property of the LinkButton controls appropriately based on the current user. This is done in the code-behind for the page, default.aspx.vb.

The code-behind for this page, default.aspx.vb, uses Server.Transfer several times to efficiently route the user's request to the appropriate Web page when he or she clicks on one of the LinkButtons in the menu.

```
Private Sub showContests_Click(ByVal sender As System.Object, _
    ByVal e As System.EventArgs) Handles showContests.Click
    Server.Transfer("listcontests.aspx")
End Sub
```

In the btnLogin_Click event handler, there is a reference to a class called ContestData.

```
Private Sub btnLogin_Click(ByVal sender As System.Object, _
    ByVal e As System.EventArgs) Handles btnLogin.Click
    'Validate the user's login credentials against the database
Dim objData As New ContestData()
    Dim strUserID As String
    If objData.ValidateUser(userid.Text, password.Text, strUserID) Then
        Dim objDR As OleDb.OleDbDataReader
        objDR = objData.GetUsers(strUserID)
        objDR.Read()
        Session.Item("userid") = strUserID
        Session.Item("administrator") = objDR.Item("administrator")
        Session.Item("username") = objDR.Item("username")
    End If
    SetAdminControls()
End Sub
```

What is this reference to ContestData? We put all database-related functionality in its
own class and its own file, contestdata.vb. This makes it easier to maintain and modify, and keeps your other code modules cleaner.

The Database

Before we go into detail about the data class, let's look at the SQL needed to generate the
three tables that our Web application will use. The SQL code for the takeachance.sql
file shown in Listing 24.1 creates three tables that are used by this Web application. The
tables need to be created in a database named TakeAChance for the connection string used
below in the New method declared in the contestdata class to work.

LISTING 24.1   TAKEACHANCE.SQL—SQL Script for the TakeAChance Database

```
1:    CREATE TABLE [User] (
2:        [UserID] uniqueidentifier ROWGUIDCOL
3:           NOT NULL CONSTRAINT [DF_User_UserID] DEFAULT (newid()),
4:        [UserName] [varchar] (50)
5:           COLLATE SQL_Latin1_General_CP1_CI_AS NOT NULL ,
6:        [EMailAddress] [varchar] (50)
7:           COLLATE SQL_Latin1_General_CP1_CI_AS NOT NULL ,
8:        [Password] [varchar] (50)
9:           COLLATE SQL_Latin1_General_CP1_CI_AS NOT NULL ,
10:       [Address] [varchar] (50)
11:          COLLATE SQL_Latin1_General_CP1_CI_AS NULL ,
12:       [CityProvince] [varchar] (50)
13:          COLLATE SQL_Latin1_General_CP1_CI_AS NULL ,
14:       [State] [varchar] (50)
15:          COLLATE SQL_Latin1_General_CP1_CI_AS NULL ,
16:       [Country] [varchar] (50)
17:          COLLATE SQL_Latin1_General_CP1_CI_AS NULL ,
18:       [PostalCode] [varchar] (15)
```

24

LISTING 24.1   continued

```
19:            COLLATE SQL_Latin1_General_CP1_CI_AS NULL ,
20:        [Administrator] [bit]
21:            NOT NULL CONSTRAINT [DF_User_Administrator] DEFAULT (0),
22:        CONSTRAINT [PK_User] PRIMARY KEY CLUSTERED
23:        (
24:            [UserID]
25:        ) ON [PRIMARY] ,
26:        CONSTRAINT [IX_User] UNIQUE NONCLUSTERED
27:        (
28:            [EMailAddress]
29:        ) ON [PRIMARY] ,
30:        CONSTRAINT [IX_User_1] UNIQUE NONCLUSTERED
31:        (
32:            [UserName]
33:        ) ON [PRIMARY]
34:    ) ON [PRIMARY]
35:    GO
36:
37:    CREATE TABLE [Contest] (
38:        [ContestID] uniqueidentifier ROWGUIDCOL
39:            NOT NULL CONSTRAINT [DF_Contest_ContestID] DEFAULT (newid()),
40:        [ContestName] [varchar] (50)
41:            COLLATE SQL_Latin1_General_CP1_CI_AS NOT NULL ,
42:        [StartDate] [smalldatetime] NULL ,
43:        [EndDate] [smalldatetime] NULL ,
44:        [PrizeDescription] [varchar] (50) COLLATE
➥SQL_Latin1_General_CP1_CI_AS NULL ,
45:        [PrizeValue] [money] NULL ,
46:        CONSTRAINT [PK_Contest] PRIMARY KEY CLUSTERED
45:        (
46:            [ContestID]
47:        ) ON [PRIMARY]
48:    ) ON [PRIMARY]
49:    GO
50:
51:    CREATE TABLE [ContestUser] (
52:        [ContestID] [uniqueidentifier]
53:            NOT NULL CONSTRAINT [DF_ContestUser_ContestID] DEFAULT (newid()),
54:        [UserID] uniqueidentifier
55:            ROWGUIDCOL NOT NULL CONSTRAINT [DF_ContestUser_UserID]
56:            DEFAULT (newid()),
57:        [DateAdded] [datetime] NOT NULL
58:            CONSTRAINT [DF_ContestUser_DateAdded] DEFAULT (getdate()),
59:        [Winner] [bit] NULL ,
60:        CONSTRAINT [PK_ContestUser] PRIMARY KEY CLUSTERED
61:        (
62:            [ContestID],
63:            [UserID]
64:        ) ON [PRIMARY] ,
```

LISTING 24.1 continued

```
65:         CONSTRAINT [FK_ContestUser_Contest] FOREIGN KEY
66:         (
67:             [ContestID]
68:         ) REFERENCES [Contest] (
69:             [ContestID]
70:         ),
71:         CONSTRAINT [FK_ContestUser_User] FOREIGN KEY
72:         (
73:             [UserID]
74:         ) REFERENCES [User] (
75:             [UserID]
76:         )
77:     ) ON [PRIMARY]
78:     GO
```

24

The `ContestData` Class

As we mentioned in the preceding section, the data access methods for this application have been isolated to their own class. The `ContestData` class (see `contestdata.vb`) consists of two sections: transactional and nontransactional methods. The transactional methods use the `OleDbTransaction` class to implement transactions when updating the database. This provides integrity of the data in the database if an error occurs during the execution of the code in each function or method. Only if the code executes successfully will the changes be committed, or made permanently, to the database.

```
Public Function AddUser(ByVal UserName As String, _
    ByVal EMailAddress As String, _
    ByVal Password As String, _
    ByVal Address As String, _
    ByVal CityProvince As String, _
    ByVal State As String, _
    ByVal Country As String, _
    ByVal PostalCode As String, _
    ByVal Administrator As Boolean) As Integer
    Dim strSQL As String
    Dim objTransaction As OleDbTransaction
    Dim objCommand As OleDbCommand
    mobjLastException = Nothing
    Try
        'Build our insert statement with tokens
        strSQL = "INSERT INTO [User] (username, emailaddress, password, " & _
        "address, cityprovince, state, country, postalcode, administrator) " & _
        "VALUES($@1,$@2,$@3,$@4,$@5,$@6,$@7,$@8,$@9)"
        'Replace tokens with parameter values
        strSQL = strSQL.Replace("$@1", "'" & Replace(UserName,"'","''") & "'")
        strSQL = strSQL.Replace("$@2", "'" & _
                    Replace(EMailAddress,"'","''") & "'")
strSQL = strSQL.Replace("$@3", "'" & Replace(Password,"'","''") & "'")
```

```
            strSQL = strSQL.Replace("$@4", "'" & Replace(Address,"'","''") & "'")
            strSQL = strSQL.Replace("$@5", "'" & _
                        Replace(CityProvince,"'","''") & "'")
    strSQL = strSQL.Replace("$@6", "'" & Replace(State,"'","''") & "'")
            strSQL = strSQL.Replace("$@7", "'" & Replace(Country,"'","''") & "'")
            strSQL = strSQL.Replace("$@8", "'" & Replace(PostalCode,"'","''") & "'")
            strSQL = strSQL.Replace("$@9", IIf(Administrator, 1, 0))
            objTransaction = mobjConnection.BeginTransaction()
            objCommand = New OleDbCommand(strSQL, mobjConnection, objTransaction)
            AddUser = objCommand.ExecuteNonQuery()
            objTransaction.Commit()
        Catch e As Exception
            AddUser = 0
            mobjLastException = __
                            New ApplicationException("AddUser - Exception caught", e)
If Not objTransaction Is Nothing Then
                objTransaction.Rollback()
            End If
        Finally
            objTransaction = Nothing
            objCommand = Nothing
        End Try
End Function
```

These methods use structured exception handling to catch any exceptions that occur and save them so that the developers using our class can evaluate what exceptions occurred and determine how to deal with them.

The Join Page

The `join.aspx` page is referenced by a hyperlink on the `default.aspx` home page. This page seems quite small in code, and the reason is that the user information code is contained in a user server control, `userinfo.ascx`. User server controls are explained in the next section. Figure 24.2 shows the join page.

The code-behind for the `join.aspx` page, `join.aspx.vb`, has even less code in it. The only real line of code is the `Server.Redirect` line inside the `btnHome_Click` event handler.

User Server Controls

User controls are similar to Web forms in that you can use the same controls and programming logic to develop them.

A user control is a special file that contains Web server controls, HTML controls, script blocks, and anything else you need to define a user interface. However, the user control file cannot contain <html>, <body>, or <form> tags. User controls are intended to be instantiated from within a server form control. The user control file needs to end with an

.ascot extension. If you use Visual Studio to create your user control file, it will append the proper extension and create a code-behind file for you with the same name but with an additional .vb extension added. The code-behind for the user control works exactly like the Web forms we've been developing.

FIGURE 24.2

The join.aspx *page.*

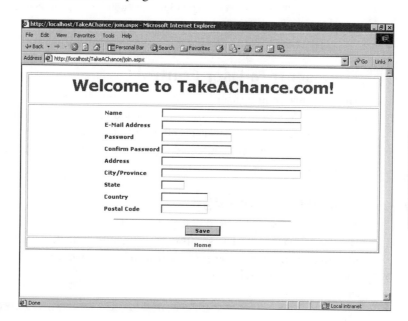

24

One additional feature of user controls is that they can raise events that can be handled by the parent control or form. Examples of creating and raising events can be seen in the user controls for this application.

The @ Page directive is not allowed in user control files. Instead you use the @ Control directive.

Using a User Control on a Web Form

To use a user control on a Web form or within another user control, you need to do a couple of things:

- Add an @ Register directive to the top of your page or control file.
  ```
  <%@ Register TagPrefix="myUI" TagName="User" Src="controls/userinfo.ascx"%>
  ```

  The TagName, TagPrefix, and Src are required. The TagName and TagPrefix can be any strings you want. The Src attribute specifies the user control file.

- Declare an instance of the control somewhere between the <form> and </form> tags of your Web forms page.

```
<td>
    <myUI:User UserID="" AdminMode="True"
        runat=server id="User1"></myUI:User>
</td>
```

The myUI and User correspond to the TagName and TagPrefix defined in the @Register directive. The AdminMode attribute is actually a property defined on the user control. We can assign this property a value when we declare the control.

The UserInfo User Control

The userinfo control (userinfo.ascx and userinfo.ascx.vb) is very helpful. It allows you to put all of the user-specific data validation and ContestData method calls inside the user control. This encapsulates all of the data access functionality for users in our database, so we have very little to do to use the control, as we saw in the source code of the join.aspx page.

The UserAdmin Page

The userinfo control is used in the useradmin.aspx page, and it makes this page a lot simpler. When we select a user from the list on the left, all we have to do is set the UserID property of the userinfo control and all the work is done for us. Figure 24.3 shows the User Admin form.

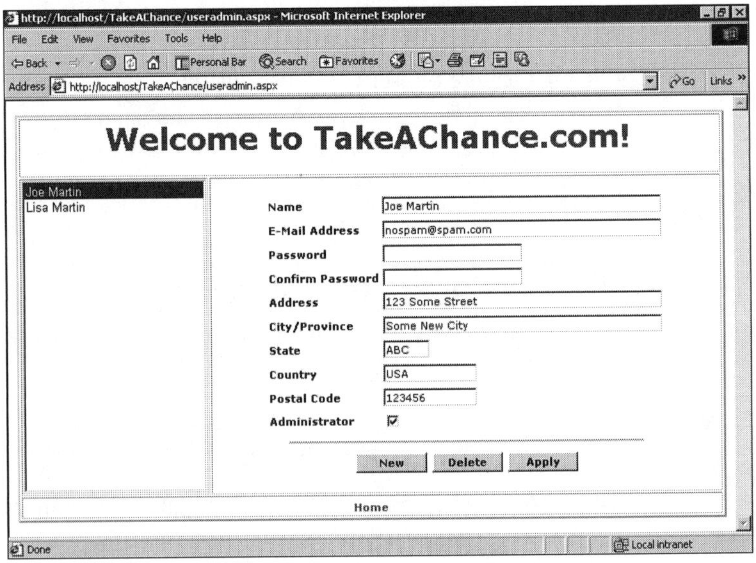

FIGURE 24.3

The User Admin form.

My User Profile Page

The userinfo control is also used in the myuserprofile.aspx page. This page is much simpler than the useradmin.aspx page, because it only has the userinfo control as its user interface. Figure 24.4 shows the My User Profile page.

FIGURE 24.4

The My User Profile page.

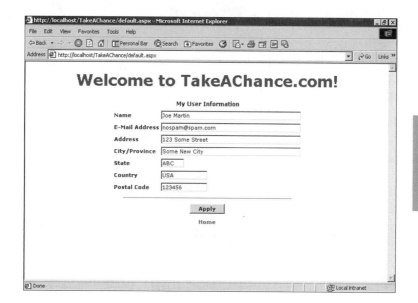

The Contestinfo User Control

The contestinfo control is similar to the userinfo control we examined earlier. It encapsulates all of the validation and ContestData method calls, so again, we have to do very little to use this control.

The Contest Admin Page

The contestadmin.aspx page uses the contestinfo control to display, update, and delete contests. This page is almost identical to the User Admin page in both design and function, but with the additional function of creating a new contest. Figure 24.5 shows the Contest Admin page.

The Contest Activity Page

The Contest Activity page is a summary of all of the contests currently in the system, how many users have joined each contest, the prize of the contest, and the winner of the contest if one has been chosen. Figure 24.6 shows the Contest Activity page.

FIGURE 24.5

The Contest Admin page.

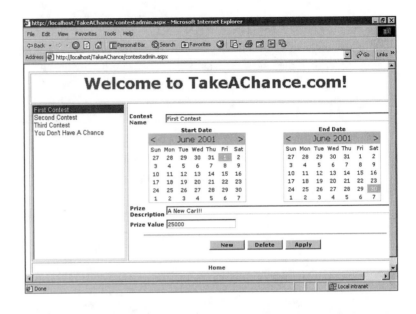

FIGURE 24.6

The Contest Activity page.

The ContestList User Control

The ContestList control (see contestlist.ascx and contestlist.ascx.vb) is implemented using the ASP.NET Repeater control to create a table for the results of an SQL
query. When each row of the SQL result set is evaluated, a new HTML row is generated

in the table. A `LinkButton` is used to allow the user to click on each contest. The `CommandArgument` and `CommandName` attributes are assigned values to supply enough information to be able to raise an event to our parent control indicating the contest ID of the contest that was selected.

```
User Control File
          <td class="smalltext">
        <asp:LinkButton ID="Contest"
           CommandName=Contest_Clicked
           CommandArgument=
                          <%# DataBinder.Eval(Container.DataItem,
"contestid")%>
Runat="server" cssclass="smalltext">
            <%# DataBinder.Eval(Container.DataItem, "contestname")%>
        </asp:LinkButton></td>
      <td align=center class="smalltext">

CodeBehind File
Public Event Contest_Clicked(ByVal ContestID As String)
Private Sub repContest_ItemCommand(ByVal source As Object, _
    ByVal e As System.Web.UI.WebControls.RepeaterCommandEventArgs) _
    Handles repContest.ItemCommand
    RaiseEvent Contest_Clicked(e.CommandArgument)
    End Sub
```

List Contests Page

The `listcontest.aspx` page uses the `contestlist` control to display a list of all contests. Because all of our user interface and database code is encapsulated in the `contestlist` user control, the code for this page, and for its code-behind, is very simple. Figure 24.7 shows the List Contests page.

List My Contests Page

The `listmycontests.aspx` page uses the `contestlist` control to display a list of contests that the current user has already joined. Again, these files contain very little code because we can use the `contestlist` user control. If you set the `UserID` property of the `contestlist` user control to a valid user ID, the control filters the contest list for that user ID. Figure 24.8 shows the List My Contests page.

```
Codebehind File
Private Sub Page_Load(ByVal sender As System.Object, _
        ByVal e As System.EventArgs) Handles MyBase.Load
        'Put user code to initialize the page here
        Contest1.UserID = Session.Item("userid")
    End Sub
```

24

FIGURE 24.7

The List Contests page.

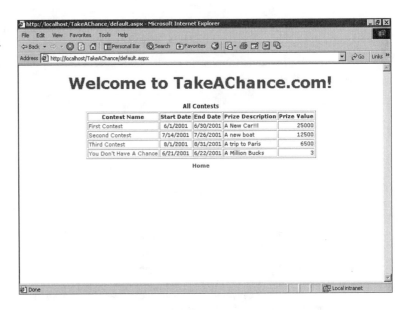

FIGURE 24.8

The List My Contests page.

List Available Contests Page

The listavailablecontests.aspx page uses the contestlist user control to display a list of contests that the current user has not already joined. If you also set the AvailableContests property of the contestlist user control to True, the control filters out contests that the current user has already joined. Figure 24.9 shows the List Available Contests page.

```
Web Form File
32:          <td>
33:              <myUI:Contest id=Contest1
34:                  runat="server"
35:                  AvailableContests=True>
36:              </myui:Contest>
37:          </td>
```

FIGURE 24.9

The List Available Contests page.

24

Summary

In this hour, we went assembled several code files to demonstrate how to develop a Web application using ASP.NET and Microsoft Visual Studio.NET. This application is quite small, and it seems like a lot of code only because of the way we separated our GUI design code from our application logic and rules and database access.

One very useful technique introduced in the chapter is user controls. This feature allows you to easily reuse blocks of user interface code and encapsulate related functionality to make your development process more efficient and your user interface more consistent.

Exercise

Create a method such that an administrator can select a random winner for a contest from the list of users currently registered for the contest. Then create a method to send the newly selected winner of the contest an e-mail indicating that he or she has won.

INDEX

X-Z

Other Related Titles

STY VB.NET in 24 Hours
James Foxall
0-672-32080-0
$34.99 US/$50.95 CAN

Sams Teach Yourself C# Web Programming in 21 Days
Phil Syme, Peter Aitken
0-672-32235-8
$39.99 US/$59.95 CAN

Commerce Server 2000: Building eBusiness Solutions
Gopal Sreeraman
0-672-32220-X
$54.99 US/$79.95 CAN

ASP.NET for Developers
Mike Amundsen
0-672-32038-X
$39.99 US/$59.95 CAN

Deploying Microsoft .NET Web Farms
Barry Bloom
0-672-320576-6
$54.99 US/$79.95

Programming Data-Driven Web Applications with ASP.NET
Doug Seven, Donny Mack
0-672-32106-8
$39.99 US/$59.95 CAN

XML for ASP.NET Developers
Dan Wahlin
0-672-32039-8
$39.99 US/$59.95 CAN

Pure Active Server Pages.NET
Robert Lair
0-672-32069-X
$39.99 US/$59.95 CAN

ASP.NET: Tips, Tutorials and Code
Scott Mitchell, et al
0-672-32143-2
$39.99 US/$59.95 CAN

SAMS

www.samspublishing.com

All prices are subject to change.

Hey, you've got enough worries.

Don't let IT training be one of them.

Get on the fast track to IT training at InformIT,
your total Information Technology training network.

 | www.informit.com | SAMS

- Hundreds of timely articles on dozens of topics ■ Discounts on IT books from all our publishing partners, including Sams Publishing ■ Free, unabridged books from the InformIT Free Library ■ "Expert Q&A"—our live, online chat with IT experts ■ Faster, easier certification and training from our Web- or classroom-based training programs ■ Current IT news ■ Software downloads
- Career-enhancing resources